REVISION GUIDE

Cambridge International AS and A Level

Physics

Robert Hutchings

CAMBRIDGE
UNIVERSITY PRESS

CAMBRIDGE
UNIVERSITY PRESS

University Printing House, Cambridge CB2 8BS, United Kingdom

Cambridge University Press is part of the University of Cambridge.

It furthers the University's mission by disseminating knowledge in the pursuit of education, learning and research at the highest international levels of excellence.

Information on this title: education.cambridge.org

© Cambridge University Press 2015

First published 2015
Reprinted 2016

Printed in the United Kingdom by Latimer Trend

A catalogue record for this publication is available from the British Library

ISBN 978-1-107-61684-4 Paperback

Additional resources for this publication at www.cambridge.org/delange

Contents

iv Contents

Contents   v

vi Contents

How to use this Book

Introduction

Explains the layout of each chapter, helps with navigation through the book and gives a reminder of what is important about each topic.

Introduction

The application of a pair of squeezing or stretching forces to a solid will cause a change in the shape of a solid. This chapter will deal only with solids, because for liquids and gases, changes in shape are dependent on the container holding them.

Teacher's tips

Quick suggestions to remind you about key facts and highlight important points.

Teacher's Tip

Be careful when subtracting temperatures. A temperature change from 6 °C to 80 °C is obviously 74 °C. This could have been written 353 K − 279 K = 74 K. The temperature interval between two temperatures must be the same whether the Celsius scale or the Kelvin scale are used. You must not add on 273 when considering temperature intervals.

Example 2

On a linear air track, a mass of 120 g is travelling to the right with a velocity of 83 cm s⁻¹. It collides elastically with a mass of 200 g travelling with velocity 47 cm s⁻¹ in the opposite direction, as shown in Figure 4.9.

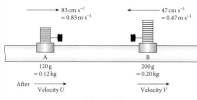

Figure 4.9

With what velocity do the masses travel after the collision?

Answer Before collision total momentum to right
= $(0.12 \times 0.83) - (0.20 \times 0.47)$

After the collision total momentum to right = $(0.12 \times U) + (0.20 \times V)$

These two terms are equal by the principle of conservation of energy, so

$(0.0996 - 0.0940) = 0.0056 = 0.12U + 0.20V$

Sometimes it is worthwhile multiplying both sides of an equation by a large number to get rid of all the zeroes. Multiplying through by 100 gives

$(9.96 - 9.40) = 0.56 = 12U + 20V$

Neither U nor V can be obtained from this equation but using the fact that the velocity of approach equals the velocity of separation gives

$(0.83 + 0.47) = V - U$

By substituting into the first equation we get

$12U + 20(1.30 + U) = 0.56$
$12U + 26 + 20U = 0.56$ so $32U = -25.44$ and
$U = -0.795 \, \text{m s}^{-1} = -80 \, \text{cm s}^{-1}$ to 2 sig figs. and
$V = 0.505 \, \text{m s}^{-1} = 51 \, \text{cm s}^{-1}$ to 2 sig figs.

Examples

A step by step approach to answering questions, guiding you through from start to finish.

How to use this Book

Progress Check

3.1 A car travels a distance of 720 km in moving 480 km south and 370 km west as shown in Figure 3.11. What is the displacement of the car from its starting point after completing the journey?

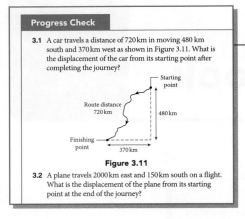

Figure 3.11

3.2 A plane travels 2000 km east and 150 km south on a flight. What is the displacement of the plane from its starting point at the end of the journey?

Progress check questions

Check your own knowledge and see how well you are getting on by answering regular questions. Sample answers for these are provided at the back of the book.

Examination questions

Help prepare for examination by completing the questions taken from Cambridge past-examination papers.

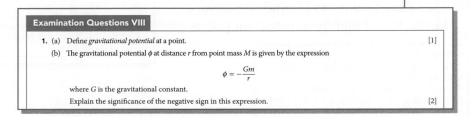

Examination Questions VIII

1. (a) Define *gravitational potential* at a point. [1]

(b) The gravitational potential ϕ at distance r from point mass M is given by the expression

$$\phi = -\frac{Gm}{r}$$

where G is the gravitational constant.

Explain the significance of the negative sign in this expression. [2]

Chapter summary

At the end of each chapter so you can check off the topics as you revise them.

Chapter Summary

- ✓ Newton's first law. Every object continues in its state of rest or state of uniform motion in a straight line unless acted upon by a resultant external force.
- ✓ Newton's second law. The rate of change of momentum of a body is proportional to the resultant force acting on it.
- ✓ Newton's third law. If body A exerts a force on body B then body B exerts an equal and opposite force on body A.
- ✓ Mass is a measure of how difficult it is to accelerate a body. It is measured in kilograms.

- ✓ Weight is the force of gravitational attraction acting on a body. It is measured in newtons.
- ✓ Momentum is the product of an object's mass and velocity. It is measured in N s. To determine the time t an object takes to stop when a force F is applied, use its momentum in the equation $mv = Ft$.
- ✓ The principle of conservation of momentum states that in all collisions the total momentum is constant provided that there is no resultant external force acting.

Physical Quantities and Units

1

You are already familiar with much of this chapter but it does contain a large amount of detail that you must use accurately. Using units and quantities correctly and showing your workings are very important skills to practice so that you avoid making errors, particularly when writing up practical work or when writing answers to tests.

Physical quantities

All measurements of physical quantities require both a numerical value and a unit in which the measurement is made. For example, your height might be 1.73 metres. The number and the unit in which it is measured need to be kept together because it is meaningless to write 'height = 1.73'. The numerical value is called the **magnitude of the quantity** and the magnitude has meaning only when the unit is attached. In this particular case it would be correct to write 'height = 173 centimetres', since there are 100 centimetres in a metre. You can help avoid making mistakes when converting units by using this method.

Write the conversion as an equation.

$$1.73\,\text{m} = 1.73\,\text{m} \times 100\,\frac{\text{cm}}{\text{m}} = 173\,\text{cm}$$

The m on the top cancels with an m on the bottom so you are certain the conversion is the right way round. Many students make the mistake of not reviewing what they have written in an equation to make sure it makes sense.

Teacher's Tip

Look out for incorrect statements. Check you write numbers and units correctly and do not write, for example, 1.73 cm = 173 m.

Other conversions are not necessarily so obvious.

Another matter of convention with units concerns the way they are written on graph axes and in tables of values. You might often use or see a statement such as 'energy/joule' or in an abbreviated form 'E/J'. This means the quantity energy divided by its SI unit, the joule. For example

$$\frac{\text{energy}}{\text{joule}} = \frac{780\ \text{joule}}{\text{joule}} = 780$$

The figure 780 is now just a number with no unit. That is what will appear in a table of values or on a graph so there is no need to add the unit to every value in tables or graphs, provided the unit is shown on the heading or axis.

In order to answer the questions given, you will need to use the prefixes on multiples and sub-multiples of units. Table 1.1 shows the meaning of each term you might have to use.

Table 1.1

Prefix	Abbreviation	Multiplying factor
tera	T	10^{12}
giga	G	10^{9}
mega	M	10^{6}
kilo	k	10^{3}
deci	d	10^{-1}
centi	c	10^{-2}
milli	m	10^{-3}
micro	µ	10^{-6}
nano	n	10^{-9}
pico	p	10^{-12}

So, for example, light of wavelength 456 nm is a wavelength of 456×10^{-9} m. This will equate to 4.56×10^{-7} m or 0.000 000 456 m. Always be careful with any of these prefixes and double check to see that you are not using them the wrong way round. It is amazing how often some students will, for example, find the speed of a car as an unrealistic 0.0052 m s^{-1} when it ought to be 52 m s^{-1}. The reason for the difference is that at some stage in the calculation the student has divided by 100 when he or she should have multiplied.

SI units (Système International d'unités)

All the units you use during your AS course are called the SI units. They are derived from five base units. These are, together with the abbreviation used for each, as follows:

- the kilogram (kg) as the unit of mass,
- the metre (m) as the unit of length,
- the second (s) as the unit of time,
- the ampere (A) as the unit of electric current and
- the kelvin (K) as the unit of absolute temperature.

The definition of these five units is amazingly complicated and you are not required to know the definitions. Each definition is very precise and enables national laboratories to measure physical quantities with a high degree of accuracy.

Although you do not need to know these definitions, you will need to know how many other definitions of SI units are derived from the base units. All the definitions and their corresponding units are given in this book, when required in appropriate chapters. Knowledge of units is essential since every numerical question you might have to answer will be dependent upon using units.

To find the expression of a unit in base units it is necessary to use the definition of the quantity. For example, **the newton (N), as the unit of force, is defined by using the equation**

$$\textbf{force} = \textbf{mass} \times \textbf{acceleration.}$$

So, $1\,\text{N} = 1\,\text{kg} \times 1\,\text{m s}^{-2}$ or $1\,\text{N} = 1\,\text{kg m s}^{-2}$.

Estimating physical quantities

In making estimates of physical quantities it is essential that you do not just guess a value and write it down. It is important to include the method you use, not just the numerical values. Answers you write might have numerical values stretching from 10^{-30} to 10^{40}. You need to remember some important values, to one significant figure, in SI units. The following list is by no means complete but is a starting point.

Do not forget that various atomic sizes and masses may be given in the exam paper data.

mass of an adult	70 kg
mass of a car	1000 kg
height of a tall man	2 m
height of a mountain	5000 m
speed of car on a high-speed road	30 m s^{-1}
speed of a plane	300 m s^{-1}
speed of sound in air at sea level	300 m s^{-1}
weight of an adult	700 N
energy requirement for a person for one day	10 000 000 J
power of a car	60 kW
power of a person running	200 W
pressure of the atmosphere	100 000 Pa
density of water	1000 kg m^{-3}
A few astronomical values are useful too.	
distance from the Earth to the Moon	400 000 km
distance from the Earth to the Sun	150 000 000 km
radius of the Earth	6000 km
mass of the Earth	6×10^{24} kg

Once you have some basic data you can use it to find an approximate value for many quantities. As a general rule, always get your values into SI units, even though you may well remember some values in non-SI units. Never use non-SI units such as miles, yards, pounds, etc.

For example, a question might ask you to estimate a value for the kinetic energy of a cruise liner. 'Estimate' means the values you choose do not have to be precise, but they should be sensible. A suitable answer to this question might look like this:

Mass of cruise liner estimated as 20 000 tonnes

$$1 \text{ tonne} = 1000 \text{ kg}$$

so mass of cruise liner $= 20\,000 \times 1000 = 2 \times 10^7 \text{ kg}$

Speed of cruise liner $= 15 \text{ m s}^{-1}$ (half the speed of a car)

$$\text{Kinetic energy} = \frac{1}{2}mv^2$$
$$= 0.5 \times 2 \times 10^7 \times 15^2$$
$$= 2 \times 10^9 \text{ J (to 1 significant figure).}$$

Table 1.2

Scalars	Vectors
mass	displacement
length	velocity
time	acceleration
area	force
volume	momentum
density	
speed	
pressure	
work	
energy	
power	

Scientific equations

You also need to be able to check the *homogeneity* of any equation. This means that both sides of any equation must have the same units.

For example, consider the equation for kinetic energy $E_k = \frac{1}{2}mv^2$.

The unit of energy (the joule) is the unit of force $\times$ distance, i.e. the unit of mass $\times$ acceleration $\times$ distance. So the unit of E_k is kg $\times$ m s^{-2} $\times$ m, which simplifies to kg m^2 s^{-2}.

Looking at the right-hand side of the equation for kinetic energy, the unit of $\frac{1}{2}mv^2$ is kg $\times$ m^2 $\times$ s^{-2}, which is the same as the unit of E_k (the $\frac{1}{2}$ has no unit).

This means that the equation for kinetic energy is homogeneous.

If you ever find that the units on both sides of an equation are not the same, then either the equation is incorrect or you have made a mistake somewhere.

Vectors and scalars

A vector is a quantity that has direction as well as magnitude; a scalar is a quantity with magnitude only.

Table 1.2 lists quantities in their correct category.

Combining vectors

Adding or subtracting scalars is just like adding or subtracting numbers, as long as you always remember to include the unit. Adding vectors can be difficult; subtracting vectors can be even more difficult. Forces are vector quantities. When adding two forces together the total force is called the resultant force. The resultant force is not an actual force at all. It is just the sum of all the forces acting on an object. The forces that we add might be caused by different things, for example one force could be a gravitational force and the other could be an electrical force. It might seem impossible for a force of 8 N to be added to a force of 6 N and get an answer 2 N, but it could be correct if the two forces acted in opposite directions on an object. In fact, for these two forces a resultant force can have any magnitude between a maximum of 14 N and a minimum of 2 N, depending on the angle that the forces have with one another. In order to find the resultant of these two forces, a triangle of forces is used, as shown in Figure 1.1. The two vectors are drawn to scale, with 1 cm representing 2 N.

The mathematics of finding the resultant can be difficult but if there is a right angle in the triangle things can be much more straightforward.

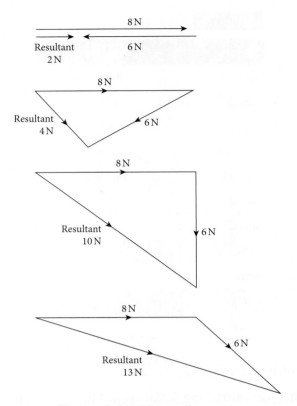

Figure 1.1 Addition of vectors

Subtracting vectors also makes use of a vector triangle. Note that you can always do subtraction by addition. If you want to know how much money you can spend if you want to keep $20 out of a starting sum of $37, then instead of $37 − $20 = $17 you can think 'what needs to be added to 20 to get 37'.

To subtract vector B from vector A, a triangle of vectors is used in which −(vector B) is added to vector A. This is shown in Figure 1.2. Note that A + (−B) is the same as A − B.

Resolution of vectors

Not only is it possible for you to add vectors, it is often useful to be able to split a single vector into two. This process is called **resolution** of a vector and almost always resolution means to split one vector into two components at right angles to one another. This is illustrated in Figure 1.3.

In Figure 1.3(a) an object has velocity v at an angle θ to the horizontal. The velocity can be considered equivalent to the two other velocities shown. $v \sin \theta$ is its vertical component and $v \cos \theta$ is its horizontal component. In Figure 1.3(b), force F is the force the sloping ground exerts on a stationary object resting on it. (This force will be equal and opposite to the weight of the object.) F can be resolved into two components. $F \sin \phi$ is the force along the slope and is the frictional force that prevents the object sliding down the slope. $F \cos \phi$ is the component at right angles to the slope.

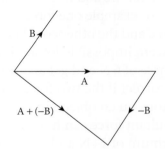

Figure 1.2 Subtraction of vectors

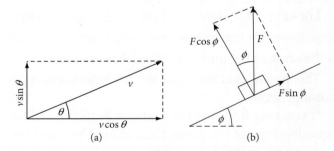

Figure 1.3 Resolution of a vector

Chapter Summary	
✓ Almost all physical quantities require a numerical value and a unit.	✓ Some physical quantities have direction. These are called vectors and can be added using a vector triangle.
✓ The units used throughout the book are SI units.	✓ Quantities without direction are called scalars. These are added arithmetically.

Progress Check

1.1 Convert
  (a) 2.86 kilograms into grams,
  (b) 0.0543 kilograms into grams,
  (c) 48 grams into kilograms,
  (d) 3.8 hours into seconds,
  (e) 6 500 000 seconds into days.

1.2 Convert
  (a) 1.00 square metres into square centimetres,
  (b) 7.38 cubic metres into cubic centimetres,
  (c) 6.58 cubic centimetres into cubic metres,
  (d) a density of 3.45 grams per cubic centimetre into kilograms per cubic metre,
  (e) a speed of 110 kilometres per hour into metres per second.

1.3 Derive the base units for
  (a) the joule, the unit of energy
  (b) the pascal, the unit of pressure
  (c) the watt, the unit of power.

1.4 Use base units to show whether or not these equations balance in terms of units. (Note: this does not mean that the equations are correct.)
  (a) $E = mc^2$
  (b) $E = mgh$
  (c) power = force × velocity
  (d) $p = \rho gh$

1.5 Estimate the following quantities.
  (a) The energy required for you to go upstairs to bed.
  (b) The average speed of a winner of a marathon.
  (c) The power requirement of a bird in a migration flight.
  (d) The vertical velocity of take-off for a good high jumper.
  (e) The acceleration of a sports car.
  (f) The density of the human body.
  (g) The pressure on a submarine at a depth of 1000 m.

1.6 Explain why these suggested estimates are incorrect.
  (a) The power of a hot plate on a cooker is 2 W.
  (b) The speed of a sub-atomic particle is $4 \times 10^8 \, \text{m s}^{-1}$.
  (c) The hot water in a domestic radiator is at a temperature of 28 °C.
  (d) The pressure of the air in a balloon is 15 000 Pa.
  (e) The maximum possible acceleration of a racing car is $9.81 \, \text{m s}^{-2}$.

1.7 Using a copy of Figure 1.2, determine the value of vector B – vector A.

1.8 A car changes speed from $30 \, \text{m s}^{-1}$ to $20 \, \text{m s}^{-1}$ while turning a corner and changing direction by 90°. What is the change in velocity of the car? State the angle of the resultant velocity of the car relative to the initial velocity.

1.9 The Moon moves around the Earth in a circular orbit of radius $3.84 \times 10^8 \, \text{m}$. Its speed is $1020 \, \text{m s}^{-1}$. Deduce
  (a) the time taken for a complete orbit of the Earth,
  (b) the angle the Moon moves through in 1.00 s,
  (c) the change in velocity of the Moon in 1.00 s.

1.10 An athlete, just after the start of a race, has a force of 780 N exerted on her by the ground and acting at an angle of 35° to the vertical. What is the weight of the athlete and what is the force causing her horizontal acceleration?

1.11 A kite of weight 4.8 N, shown in Figure 1.4, is being pulled by a force in the string of 6.3 N acting in a direction of 27° to the vertical.

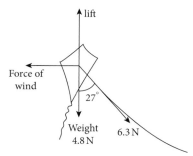

Figure 1.4

  (a) Resolve the force in the string into horizontal and vertical components.
  (b) Assuming that the kite is flying steadily, deduce the upward lift on the kite and the horizontal force the wind exerts on the kite.

Measurement Techniques

Introduction

Throughout this book reference will be made to many experiments that you could carry out yourself. It will also describe some of the experiments done in the past that have had a great influence on our understanding of the physical world. In all of these experiments, there are certain basic techniques that need to be used and in this chapter some of the principles of experimenting will be explained. Much of the importance of all experiments depends on their reliability. An experiment will always be unreliable if the experimenter changes results to try to make the results fit what is expected. This does not mean that all measured data must be exact, as this is impossible. The data itself must be found honestly and an estimate made of its uncertainty. This chapter will explain the way uncertainties can be evaluated, but first it will explain methods for recording readings, for evaluating results from graphs and with problems associated with obtaining information from a mixture of both analogue and digital equipment.

Record taking

What should be a golden rule about recording the results of any experiment is that readings must be written in the form they are taken. In other words, do not do any arithmetic on readings before writing them down. A simple example is when measuring the period of oscillation of a simple pendulum. If you are able to time 50 oscillations then the heading of the first column of your table should read 'length of pendulum' and the second 'number of oscillations' with 50 as the first entry. The third column should be headed 'total time/s' and the time might be e.g. 86.5 s. Only at the fourth column should you include the heading 'period *T*/s'. A complete table might look like Table 2.1, after

applying the relationship between the period T of a simple pendulum, its length l and the acceleration g due to gravity.

$$T = 2\pi\sqrt{\frac{l}{g}}$$

Table 2.1

Length of pendulum / m	Number of oscillations	Total time / s	Period T/s	g / m s^{-2}
0.980	50	99.3	1.986	9.81
0.885	50	94.4	1.888	9.80
0.790	50	89.2	1.784	9.80
0.745	40	69.2	1.730	9.83
0.665	40	65.4	1.635	9.82
0.545	30	44.3	1.477	9.86
0.460	30	40.8	1.360	9.82
0.335	30	34.8	1.160	9.83
0.245	30	29.8	0.993	9.81

A few points of detail should be noted.

- The average value of g is 9.82 m s^{-2} with an uncertainty explained later in this chapter.
- Keep the number of **significant figures** constant in any column unless a figure is lost or gained naturally, as with 0.993 in the fourth column.
- Four significant figures are given in most of the fourth column in order not to reduce the accuracy given in the third column. 0.993 is given to about one part in a thousand. If T were quoted only to three significant figures, the first of the period readings, for example, would only be given as 1.99 and be known only to one part in 200.

- Do not drop off final zeroes. In the first column, all the lengths are given to the nearest 5 mm. If the first figure was quoted as 0.98, it would imply less accuracy than the second figure 0.885.
- One important part of this experiment is to start and stop a stopwatch after a complete number of cycles. The amplitude of swing has made it necessary in this experiment to reduce the number of swings when the length is reduced.
- Whenever swings are being counted, avoid counting 'one' in your head at the start of the first swing; ensure you count 'zero'. If you start at 'one' then all the periods will be too short.
- It is preferable for you to time for a larger number of swings in one count rather than to make several repeats of a small number of swings. Repeating introduces starting and stopping errors; a larger number of swings reduce these errors.

Graphical work

Very frequently the best way of analysing results is to make use of a graph. Often an equation can be rearranged into a form that enables a straight line graph to be drawn. Graphs can be drawn very accurately. It is important for you to use a sensible scale and to mark the points on the graph accurately. This does mean using the whole range the graph paper allows. Do use fractional parts of a small square when putting data on to the graph or when taking readings from the graph.

The general equation of a straight line graph is

$$y = mx + c$$

where x is the independent variable, y the dependent variable, m the gradient of the graph and c is the intercept on the y-axis.

How this graphical technique can be used will be illustrated by using it for the pendulum experiment mentioned earlier. Since

$T = 2\pi\sqrt{\dfrac{l}{g}}$, by squaring both sides we get $T^2 = \dfrac{4\pi^2}{g} l$.

This will give a straight line graph provided T^2 is plotted against l. The gradient of this graph will be

$4\pi^2/g$ and since c is zero the graph will pass through the origin.

The graph is plotted in Figure 2.1.

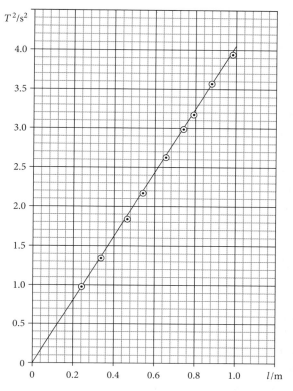

Figure 2.1 Graph of T^2 against l

When taking the gradient of a straight line graph, choose two values on major lines as far apart as possible. In this case, the obvious values of length to choose are 0 and 1.

The gradient of the graph is given by

$$\text{gradient} = \frac{4\pi^2}{g} = \frac{4.06 - 0}{1.00 - 0} = 4.06$$

$$\text{Hence } g = \frac{4\pi^2}{4.06} = 9.72\,\text{m s}^{-2}$$

Analogue scales and digital displays

A simple metre rule gives an analogue reading while a digital watch gives a digital reading. Do not assume that a digital reading is more accurate than an analogue reading. Most digital readings come from analogue readings. A digital thermometer, for example, will probably be using a thermistor as its source of information. The potential difference (p.d.) across the thermistor will be measured; this will be combined with a calibration curve available from the manufacturer, that gives its resistance at different temperatures. The value of the p.d. will then be digitised and finally displayed.

It may seem to you that a reading from a digital balance of, say, 486 grams, means that the mass is exactly 486 grams. This is not the case for three reasons. The first is that the original calibration might not have been done correctly, the second is that the calibration might have changed as a result of wear and tear or misuse and the third that any mass between 485.5 and 486.4 would result in the instrument reading 486 grams, if the instrument reads to just three significant figures.

Experimental uncertainty

Experimental **uncertainty** used to be called experimental **error**. However, the change was made because 'error' seems to imply that a mistake has been made and that is not the issue. All readings have uncertainties. A ruler might measure to the nearest millimetre, a clock to the nearest second, a thermometer to the nearest degree; so one person using a metre ruler might record the length as 86.0 cm and another person measuring the same length might record it as 86.1 cm. This type of variation is called a **random uncertainty**. It might come about through the limitations of the scale on an instrument or through the way the instrument is used. Checking measurements will show up the random nature of readings and taking an average of readings will minimise the overall uncertainty.

If the instrument itself is faulty or if it is being used incorrectly, there will be **systematic uncertainty**. This might be an error in the instrument. For example, its zero reading might be incorrect. Systematic uncertainties or errors are often much more difficult to detect. There is no easy way to account for systematic errors or uncertainties, though one check that can be made with electrical instruments would be to use

a different meter and if it gives the same reading there is unlikely to be a serious systematic error.

Precision and accuracy

Any readings taken to high precision have low random uncertainty. Any readings taken to high accuracy have low systematic uncertainty.

This is illustrated in Figure 2.2 where an archery target is marked with the position of arrows fired at it.

- Figure 2.2(a) shows that the archer is very skilled, so there is little random uncertainty but that his equipment has a systematic error in it.
- Figure 2.2(b) shows that the archer is unskilled, so there is considerable random uncertainty but that his equipment has no systematic error in it. The average position of his arrows is in the centre of the target.
- Figure 2.2(c) shows that the archer is unskilled, so there is considerable random uncertainty, and that his equipment has a systematic error in it.
- Figure 2.2(d) shows that an archer has high precision equipment and great accuracy, so there is minimal random uncertainty and no systematic error.

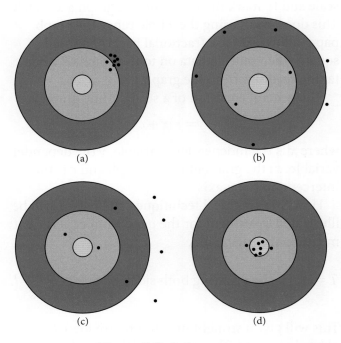

Figure 2.2 Archery target

Choice of measuring instrument

To say that there is an uncertainty of 1 mm in measuring a length is not very helpful by itself. The length being measured also needs to be given. For example, an uncertainty of 1 mm in a distance of 2 km is of very high accuracy, the uncertainty is 1 part in 2 000 000, a fractional uncertainty of only 0.000 000 5 or 0.000 05%, the same uncertainty of 1 mm in a metre is a fraction of 0.001 or 0.1%. 1 mm in 20 mm is a fraction of 0.05 or 5%.

A reading that is uncertain to 1 mm when measuring a wire's diameter of 0.2 mm is useless. This shows that a choice of different instruments will be necessary for measuring different lengths. Figure 2.3 shows an instrument called a **Vernier calliper**. This instrument is useful in measuring the internal or external diameter of tubes, for example. It will give a reading to the nearest 0.1 mm or better.

When the two jaws of the calliper are closed, the zeroes on both the scales coincide. The jaws are then opened and the object to be measured is placed between them as shown. From the diagram it is clear that the object has a diameter of between 1.9 cm and 2.0 cm. However, the size of the scale divisions on the sliding or moveable jaw is not quite the same size as those on the fixed jaw. They differ, for this calliper, by a tenth of a millimetre. By looking along the Vernier scale you will see that at 5 divisions along the sliding scale both the main scale and the Vernier scale coincide. The distance arrowed, therefore, is 0.5 mm and the diameter of the object is, therefore, 1.95 cm.

A Vernier calliper, however, would not be suitable for measuring the diameter of a wire. For measurements such as this a micrometer is needed. This is illustrated in Figure 2.4.

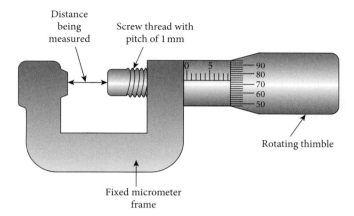

Figure 2.4 A micrometer screw gauge

A micrometer uses a screw thread and, at its simplest, divides up one rotation of the screw into 100 divisions. If the pitch of the screw is 1 mm then each division represents one hundredth of a millimetre. (The pitch of a screw thread is the distance the screw moves forward each rotation.) The reading on the micrometer in Figure 2.4 is 9.74 mm.

Figure 2.5 shows the enlarged reading on a micrometer in which the pitch is only 0.5 mm. This pitch is very common on micrometers but it does need careful use. The rotating scale only goes up to 50 but the main scale shows half millimetres, so you need to know whether the reading is under or over half a millimetre.

The reading on this micrometer is 2.5 mm on the main scale and 28 divisions on the rotating micrometer scale. The full reading is, therefore, 2.5 mm + 0.28 mm = 2.78 mm.

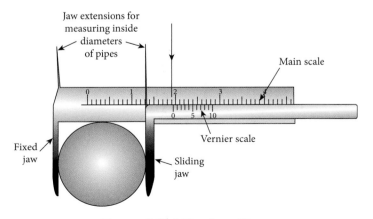

Figure 2.3 A Vernier calliper

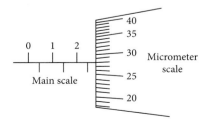

Figure 2.5 Reading on a micrometer

Calibration curves

Many measuring devices are checked by the manufacturer against international standards of length, temperature, electric current. Details are produced of how any particular instrument's accuracy is dependent on external factors, such as temperature. These details are available from the manufacturer on request. The information will often be in the form of a calibration curve in which the reading obtained under particular conditions, is plotted against a corrected value under standard conditions. The shapes of two particular calibration curves are shown in Figure 25.1 (the resistance of a light-dependent resistor at different levels of illumination) and Figure 25.4 (the resistance of a thermistor at different temperatures).

Estimating uncertainties

If finding the value of a physical quantity is difficult, finding the uncertainty in that quantity is even more difficult. There is almost never any sense in quoting a result as, for example, $density = (7.805 \pm 0.076) \times 10^3\,\mathrm{kg\,m^{-3}}$. This shows that the uncertainty is much greater than the final decimal place of the result and that $density = (7.80 \pm 0.08) \times 10^3\,\mathrm{kg\,m^{-3}}$ would be more sensible. The third significant figure is very doubtful and $density = (7.8 \pm 0.1) \times 10^3\,\mathrm{kg\,m^{-3}}$ can be stated with greater confidence.

Any reading has uncertainty. As explained above, if a measurement of length is made using a ruler, the length obtained will usually be measured to the nearest millimetre. If you measure a length as 249 mm with an uncertainty of 1 mm at the zero and another 1 mm at the other end then the reading, together with its uncertainty is (249 ± 2) mm.

This gives the actual uncertainty as 2 mm, the fractional uncertainty as 2/249 or 0.0080 and the percentage uncertainty as 0.8%.

In performing any experiment it is usual to make measurements of several quantities. In order to find the overall uncertainty of an experiment it is necessary to know the uncertainty of each quantity separately. If these uncertainties are estimated as percentages then they can be added together to determine the overall uncertainty of the experiment. Percentage uncertainties also make it easy to see

which of the measurements causes the greatest uncertainty. The final result of this procedure should be expressed in numerical rather than percentage uncertainties, for example as (4.73 ± 0.03) N for a force measurement, rather than $(4.73 \pm 6\%)$ N.

The question that needs answering is "How do you find the uncertainty of an experimental result?" The answer to the question comes in two stages.

Stage 1 Estimate the uncertainty in each of the readings you take. The most straightforward way of doing this is to use the smallest division available on the instrument you are using. On a clock this will probably be a second, on a stop-watch it might well be 0.01 s. Unfortunately, this method does tend to underestimate uncertainty for the following reasons.

- All systematic uncertainties will not be accounted for.
- It might underestimate some uncertainties badly. A stop-watch might give a reading to a hundredth of a second but you might have pressed the stop button at the wrong moment.
- Poor technique might make readings far less reliable than the instrument might otherwise have given. e.g. If you hold a ruler in your hand without a firm support, it will not give reliable readings.
- An instrument viewed from the wrong angle will give a *parallax* error. Keep your eye vertically above a needle on an ammeter so that the scale reading is the one directly beneath the needle.
- Any mistaken reading from a scale will certainly increase uncertainty. The reading on the scale in Figure 2.6 is NOT 2.4 but 2.8.

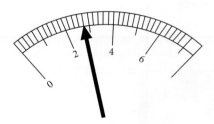

Figure 2.6

Stage 2 Combine these individual uncertainties to find the overall uncertainty.

Here, examples can show you how to proceed.

Example 1

(Uncertainty in addition of values.)
An object with momentum $(85 \pm 2)\,\text{N s}$ catches up with, and sticks to another object with momentum $(77 \pm 3)\,\text{N s}$. Find the total momentum of the two objects and its uncertainty after the collision.

Answer $(162 \pm 5)\,\text{N s}$ is a straightforward calculation. The maximum value is $87 + 80 = 167\,\text{N s}$ and the minimum is $83 + 74 = 157\,\text{N s}$. In percentage terms, the uncertainties of the initial values are 2.3% and 3.9%, respectively. The percentage uncertainty in the answer is 3.1% so you must not add percentage uncertainties. Here you just add values and uncertainties.

Example 2

(Uncertainty in subtraction of values.)
A reading on a balance of the mass of an empty beaker is $(105 \pm 1)\,\text{g}$. After some liquid is poured into the beaker, the reading becomes $(112 \pm 1)\,\text{g}$. Deduce the mass of liquid added and its uncertainty.

Answer $(7 \pm 2)\,\text{g}$. $113 - 104 = 9$ is the maximum and $111 - 106 = 5$ is the minimum.

This is not straightforward. It shows that subtracting two nearly equal numbers increases the uncertainty appreciably. You must subtract the values but **add** the uncertainties. Two readings with percentage uncertainties about 1% give an uncertainty of 29% when subtracted.

Example 3

(Uncertainty in multiplication or division of values.)
These are very common situations. A plane travels at a speed of $(250 \pm 10)\,\text{m s}^{-1}$ for a time of $(18\,000 \pm 100)\,\text{s}$. Determine the distance travelled and its uncertainty.

Answer The maximum possible distance
$= 260\,\text{m s}^{-1} \times 18\,100\,\text{s} = 4.71 \times 10^6\,\text{m}$.

$250\,\text{m s}^{-1} \times 18\,000\,\text{s} = 4.50 \times 10^6\,\text{m}$ so the uncertainty is $0.2 \times 10^6\,\text{m}$. The answer should be written as $(4.5 \pm 0.2) \times 10^6\,\text{m}$.

You can add percentage uncertainties here because it is a multiplication. The percentage uncertainty in the speed is 4%, the percentage uncertainty in the time is 0.6% and the percentage uncertainty in the distance is, therefore, 4.6% and 4.6% of 4.5 is 0.2.

Example 4

(Uncertainty in values raised to a power.)
Determine the value of the kinetic energy, and its uncertainty, of a cyclist of mass $(63 \pm 1)\,\text{kg}$ when travelling with speed $(12.0 \pm 0.5)\,\text{m s}^{-1}$.

Answer Here the expression is
kinetic energy $= \frac{1}{2} \times m \times v \times v$. The $\frac{1}{2}$ has no uncertainty. You must not divide your uncertainty figure by 2. The percentage uncertainties of the other three terms must be added together. This has the effect of doubling the uncertainty for v, since it is squared. A cubic term would involve multiplying its uncertainty by 3. A square root is a power of a half, so uncertainty in a square root is halved.

Percentage uncertainty in $m = 1.5\%$, uncertainty in $v = 4\%$ so in v^2 is 8%. This gives a total percentage uncertainty of 9.5%, round this up to 10%, therefore the result is

$$\text{kinetic energy} = (4500 \pm 500)\,\text{J}$$

Note that in quoting the uncertainty only one significant figure is used.

Chapter Summary

- ✓ When taking experimental readings, always record actual readings as soon as you take them.
- ✓ Keep the number of significant figures determined by the instrument you are using.
- ✓ Plot graphs on as large a scale as possible but do not use awkward scales on the axes.
- ✓ An instrument with incorrect calibration will result in a systematic uncertainty.
- ✓ All readings, even those given by a digital display, will additionally have random uncertainties as a result of the way the readings are taken.

Progress Check

2.1 An experiment was performed to determine the resistivity ρ of copper. The resistance R of a length of wire is related to its length l and area of cross-section A by the equation

$$R = \frac{\rho l}{A}$$

The resistance of 1 metre length of copper wire of different diameters was measured, with the following results:

Length of wire l/m	Diameter of wire d/m	Resistance of wire R/ohm
1.000	0.559×10^{-3}	0.0704
1.000	0.315×10^{-3}	0.225
1.000	0.234×10^{-3}	0.402
1.000	0.152×10^{-3}	0.952
1.000	0.122×10^{-3}	1.47
1.000	0.102×10^{-3}	2.09

Plot a suitable graph and use the graph to determine the resistivity of copper. Estimate the uncertainty in the value you obtain.

2.2 A cuboid of metal has a measured mass of (4.70 ± 0.2) kg. Its dimensions are: length (50.5 ± 0.2) cm, width (7.60 ± 0.08) cm, depth (5.02 ± 0.02) cm.

Deduce (a) the volume of the cuboid, together with its uncertainty, and (b) the density of the metal of the cuboid.

2.3 Explain why the following statements of uncertainty are inappropriate. Give a possible correction.
(a) $g = 9.81 \pm 0.3$
(b) $g = 9.810794 \pm 0.3$
(c) $g = 9.810794 \pm 0.34781$
(d) $g = 9.8 \pm 0.369$
(e) $g = 9.81 \pm 0.39$

Examination Questions I

1. (a) Two of the SI base quantities are mass and time. State three other SI base quantities. [3]

(b) A sphere of radius r is moving at speed v through air of density ρ. The resistive force F acting on the sphere is given by the expression

$$F = Br^2 \rho v^k$$

where B and k are constants without units.

(i) State the SI base units of F, ρ and v. [3]
(ii) Use base units to determine the value of k. [2]

(**Cambridge International AS and A Level Physics 9702 Paper 21 Question 1 October/November 2010**)

2. The volume of fuel in the tank of a car is monitored using a meter as illustrated in Figure 1.

Figure 1 Fuel meter

The meter has an analogue scale. The meter reading for different volumes of fuel in the tank is shown in Figure 2.

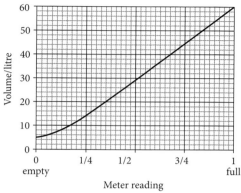

Figure 2

The meter is calibrated in terms of the fraction of the tank that remains filled with fuel.
(a) The car uses 1.0 litre of fuel when travelling 14 km. The car starts a journey with a full tank of fuel.
   (i) Calculate the volume, in litres, of fuel remaining in the tank after a journey of 210 km. [2]
   (ii) Use your answer to (i) and Figure 2 to determine the change in the meter reading during the 210 km journey. [1]
(b) There is a systematic error in the meter.
   (i) State the feature of Figure 2 that indicates that there is a systematic error. [1]
   (ii) Suggest why, for this meter, it is an advantage to have this systematic error. [1]

(Cambridge International AS and A Level Physics 9702
Paper 21 Question 1 October/November 2009)

3. Make reasonable estimates of the following quantities.
(a) the frequency, in Hz, of an audible sound wave [1]
(b) the wavelength, in nm, of ultraviolet radiation [1]
(c) the mass, in grams, of a plastic 30 cm ruler [1]
(d) the density of air, in kg m^{-3} at atmospheric pressure [1]

(Cambridge International AS and A Level Physics 9702
Paper 02 Question 1 May/June 2008)

4. (a) The current in a wire is I. Charge Q passes one point in the wire in time t. State
   (i) the relation between I, Q and t, [1]
   (ii) which of the quantities I, Q and t are base quantities. [2]
(b) The current in the wire is due to electrons, each with charge q, that move with speed v along the wire. There are n of these electrons per unit volume. For a wire having a cross-sectional area S, the current I is given by the equation

$$I = nSqv^k,$$

where k is a constant.
   (i) State the units of I, n, S, q and v in terms of the base units. [3]
   (ii) By considering the homogeneity of the equation, determine the value of k. [2]

(Cambridge International AS and A Level Physics 9702
Paper 02 Question 1 October/November 2008)

Kinematics 3

Distance and displacement

The distance you travel by a car on a journey, or since the car was bought, is recorded on the instrument panel. The distance will be given in miles or kilometres, usually to the nearest tenth of a unit. This recorded distance makes no mention of the direction in which any distance travelled has taken place. In SI units, a distance such as this would be recorded using the standard unit of length, the metre. The metre is defined in a very accurate way, in terms of the speed of light, but you need to think of it just as being a very accurately defined length, and metre rules approximate to that accurately defined distance.

The term **displacement** differs from distance in the sense that it is not only giving a distance but is also stating the direction in which any movement has taken place.

Displacement is a vector quantity while distance is a scalar quantity.

When a ball is thrown vertically upwards a distance of 3.0 m, its displacement from its starting point, when it reaches the top of its movement, is 3.0 m upwards. By the time it falls back to its point of throw, its displacement is zero. On the way down only, its displacement from the top is −3.0 m upwards.

When a ship sails a distance of 3700 km between Mumbai and Kolkata, its displacement from its starting point on its arrival in Kolkata will be 1700 km in a direction N 75° E. This difference arises from the fact that the ship will have to travel right around the south of India, a much greater distance than a straight overland distance.

Speed and velocity

As with distance and displacement, one of these terms, velocity, is a vector and other, speed, is a scalar quantity. Therefore, whenever velocity is used a direction must be given.

Speed is defined as the distance travelled per unit time. It is a scalar quantity.

Velocity is defined as displacement per unit time. It is a vector and so the direction must be stated.

The defining equation for both of these terms is:

$$v = \frac{s}{t}$$

where v is the speed or velocity,
s is the distance or displacement, and
t is the time interval.

Example 1

What is the average speed on a journey of a car in which it travels 620 km in 8 h 25 m?

Answer Distance $(s) = 620\,\text{km} = 6.2 \times 10^5\,\text{m}$

Time $(t) = 8\,\text{h}\ 25\,\text{min} = (8 \times 60) + 25 = 505\,\text{min}$

$505\,\text{min} = 505 \times 60 = 3.03 \times 10^4\,\text{s}$

∴ average speed =

$$\frac{s}{t} = \frac{6.20 \times 10^5\,\text{m}}{3.03 \times 10^4\,\text{s}} = 20.5\,\text{m s}^{-1}$$

Teacher's Tip

Many careless mistakes are made when using equations such as $v = s/t$. Some of these mistakes can be eliminated if you put units into the working equation. For example, a train travelling at 136 km h^{-1} for 6 hours travels a distance of

$$136\,\frac{\text{km}}{\text{h}} \times 6\text{h} = 816\,\text{km}$$

It is clear that the unit of time, the hour, cancels out from the top and the bottom, leaving the answer in kilometres. A corresponding answer for velocity can be worked out in exactly the same way, but the answer needs to have a direction included. It could be 609 km due south.

Acceleration

Acceleration is a vector and is defined as the rate of change of velocity.

The average acceleration a of an object is, therefore, given by

$$a = \frac{v - u}{t}$$

where v is the final velocity, u is the starting velocity and t is the time interval.

The SI unit of acceleration is $\text{m s}^{-1} \div \text{s}$ or m s^{-2}.

Graphs for motion

Distance–time graphs

A distance–time graph can be used to find the speed of an object. Figure 3.1 shows a distance–time graph for an object travelling with speed 6.0 m s^{-1}.

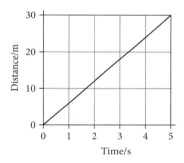

Figure 3.1 A distance–time graph

After 1 s the object has travelled 6.0 m, after 2 s 12 m and so on until after 5 s it has travelled 30 m. The object is travelling at a constant speed.

Figure 3.2 gives another graph where the object also travels 30 m in 5 s but it has covered a greater distance in the last second than it did in the first second. Its speed is not constant.

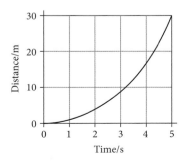

Figure 3.2

To calculate the object's speed after 4 s of travel, the distance travelled in a small interval of time needs to be taken. This could be from 3.9 s to 4.1 s or even 3.99 s to 4.01 s. Each of these is getting closer to the gradient of the graph at a time of 4.0 s.

The slope (gradient) of a distance–time graph gives the speed.

The slope (gradient) of a displacement–time graph gives the velocity, provided the direction of the change in displacement is given.

Velocity–time graphs

As acceleration is the rate of change of velocity, the slope (gradient) of a velocity–time graph will be the acceleration.

Consider an object accelerating uniformly in a straight line from a velocity of 8.0 m s^{-1} to a velocity of 23.0 m s^{-1} in a time of 5.0 s. A graph of this motion is shown in Figure 3.3.

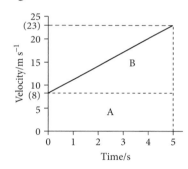

Figure 3.3

The slope of the graph, the acceleration, is given by

$$\text{acceleration} = \frac{\text{increase in velocity}}{\text{time}}$$

$$= \frac{(23.0 - 8.0)\text{ m s}^{-1}}{5.0 \text{ s}}$$

$$= \frac{15 \text{ m s}^{-1}}{5.0 \text{ s}} = 3.0 \text{ m s}^{-2}$$

However, this is not the only information that this graph of Figure 3.3 supplies. If the object had remained at a constant velocity of 8.0 m s^{-1} for all of the 5.0 s of travel, it would have had a displacement of $8.0 \text{ m s}^{-1} \times 5.0 \text{ s} = 40 \text{ m}$. This is shown as area A, on Figure 3.3. Extending this idea to the accelerated motion, the total displacement will be area A plus area B.

Area A $= 40$ m

Area B $= \frac{1}{2} \times$ base $\times$ height of the triangle

$$= \frac{1}{2} \times 5.0 \text{ s} \times 15 \text{ m s}^{-1}$$

$$= 37.5 \text{ m}$$

Total displacement $= 40$ m $+ 37.5$ m

$$= 77.5 \text{ m}$$

Derivation of equations of motion for uniformly accelerated motion in a straight line

In this section, the symbols used have the following meanings:

    s the displacement,

    u the velocity at the start of the motion,

    v the velocity at the end of the motion,

    t the total time for the acceleration and

    a the acceleration.

Directly from the definition of acceleration as the increase in velocity per unit time, we get,

$a = \dfrac{v - u}{t}$ which can be written as

$at = v - u$ OR $v = u + at$ **Equation I**

Figure 3.4 is a velocity–time graph that shows these terms as used with uniform acceleration and some connections between them.

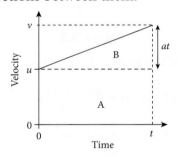

Figure 3.4 A velocity–time graph

Area A is ut,

Area B is $\frac{1}{2} \times t \times at = \frac{1}{2} at^2$

This gives the total displacement s the area beneath the graph

$$s = ut + \frac{1}{2} at^2 \qquad \textbf{Equation II}$$

The total area under the graph could equally be given by

$$s = vt - \frac{1}{2} at^2 \qquad \textbf{Equation III}$$

or the average value of the velocity multiplied by the time, namely

$$s = \frac{u + v}{2} \times t \qquad \textbf{Equation IV}$$

If you look at Equations I to IV, you may notice that Equation I omits s, Equation II omits v, Equation III omits u and Equation IV omits a. All the equations require t, but this term may not be given. An equation that does omit t can be obtained by some difficult algebra.

$$v^2 = u^2 + 2as \qquad \textbf{Equation V}$$

The five equations all refer to uniformly accelerated motion in a straight line. In other words, they do not apply if the acceleration is changing or if the object is going round a corner. It is worthwhile for you to be able to quote all of these equations. Two of them are given on the Data and Formulae page of the exam paper.

Teacher's Tip

Whenever you use any of these equations always carefully check the signs. For example, if movement upwards is positive then movement downwards is negative.

Example 2

A ball is thrown vertically upwards with a velocity of 28 m s^{-1} from a point 2.8 m above the ground. Calculate

    (a) the maximum height reached, and

    (b) the time taken before it reaches the ground.

The acceleration due to gravity is 9.8 m s^{-2}. Air resistance can be neglected.

Answer (a) $u = 28 \text{ m s}^{-1}$, $v = 0$, $a = g = -9.8 \text{ m s}^{-2}$

Note the minus sign; u is taken as positive for upwards so g must be negative as the acceleration due to gravity is downwards.

Here s is required, so use equation $v^2 = u^2 + 2as$ to get

$$0 = 28^2 + (2 \times (-9.8) \times s)$$

This gives $28^2 = 2 \times 9.8 \times s$

So, $s = \dfrac{28^2}{19.6} = 40$ m

(b) The time taken to reach the top can be found using $v = u + at$

$$0 = 28 + (-9.8\,t)$$
$$t = 28/9.8 = 2.86\,s$$

The time to fall a total distance of 42.8 m can now be found using $s = ut + \frac{1}{2}at^2$ with all values in the downward direction

$$42.8 = 0 + \frac{1}{2} \times 9.8 \times t^2$$

$$t^2 = 2 \times 42.8/9.8 = 8.73$$
$$\text{so } t = 2.96$$

From the start the total time will be $(2.86 + 2.96)\,s = 5.82\,s$

Part (b) could have been done in one step using $s = ut + \frac{1}{2}at^2$ and getting

$$-2.8 = 28t + \frac{1}{2}(-9.8)t^2$$

But this does involve solving a quadratic equation. What would the negative value of t give?

Weight

The weight of any object is the gravitational pull on the object. Our human body does not have any sense organs that detect this pull but everybody knows that there is a pull towards the Earth because if we drop something it moves towards the Earth until it hits something. When you stand on the Earth you can feel the contact force of the Earth acting upwards on you, because your body does have a sense of touch. The forces acting on you when you fall or when you stand on the ground are shown in Figures 3.5(a) and (b).

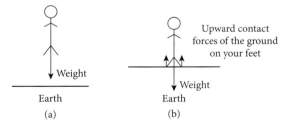

(a)   (b)

Figure 3.5 Forces acting on you (a) when you fall and (b) when you stand on the ground

The forces involved in these diagrams will be considered in more detail in Chapter 4 but, at present, note that when falling in mid-air your weight causes you to accelerate downwards. At this stage you have no feeling for your weight, though you might feel a

force from the air you are passing through. Similarly an astronaut in the space shuttle has no feeling for weight. In simulated free fall in a plane, people seem to be weightless. This, too, is because we cannot feel weight.

When you are standing on the Earth you are not accelerating because the support force on you, provided by contact with the Earth balances your weight. Your weight is the same in both Figure 3.5(a) and Figure 3.5(b).

The weight of an object is defined as the product of the object's mass and the acceleration of free fall g. So, if your mass is 68.0 kg and the acceleration of free fall is 9.81 m s^{-2} then your weight is given by,

$$\text{Weight} = \text{mass} \times \text{acceleration of free fall}$$
$$= 68.0 \times 9.81 = 667\,N.$$

Note that weight, being a force, will always be measured in newtons. Your weight will vary slightly from place to place on the Earth because the acceleration of free fall varies from place to place on the Earth's surface.

Measurement of the acceleration of free fall, g

One way in which g can be measured in the laboratory is to release a ball as a timer is started. After falling through a distance s, the timer stops and records a time t for the fall.

Using $s = ut + \frac{1}{2}at^2$, gives

$$s = 0 + \frac{1}{2}gt^2$$

and hence $g = 2s/t^2$

One arrangement that will achieve this is shown in Figure 3.6.

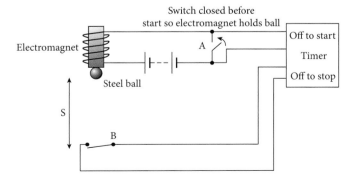

Figure 3.6 Laboratory set-up to measure g

When switch A is turned off the steel ball starts to fall and the timer starts. The ball falls onto switch B and when it breaks the circuit the timer stops.

Some problems with the method are:

- the ball is inclined to stick on the electromagnet after switching off, so the current in the electromagnet must be only just large enough to hold the ball, and
- air resistance increases as the ball falls, reducing the acceleration.

An improved method, using light gates, is suggested in Progress Check Question 3.10.

The effect of air resistance on a falling body

So far in this chapter, air resistance has largely been ignored. In practice there are situations in real life where air resistance is vitally necessary, a parachute being the best example. Air resistance on a falling sphere increases with velocity. It is a force that acts upwards. This is also true for most other falling bodies, but area of cross-section also affects the magnitude of air resistance. Sky divers, for example, usually spread themselves to give maximum air resistance because it increases the time they can be in free fall before they need to open their parachutes.

Figure 3.7 shows how air resistance increases as downward velocity increases.

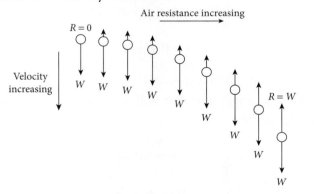

Figure 3.7

This causes the resultant downward force on the falling body to decrease and so there is less acceleration. Provided the length of drop is sufficient, air resistance increases to become an upward force equal in magnitude to the body's weight, at which point the object has zero acceleration and constant velocity.

The expression **terminal velocity** is used for this situation. For a falling person this happens at a velocity of around 50 to $60\,\mathrm{m\,s^{-1}}$. A parachutist, in contrast, is slowed down by his parachute and usually hits the ground when travelling at about $2–3\,\mathrm{m\,s^{-1}}$. Graphs showing how the downward acceleration and velocity change with time are given in Figures 3.8(a) and (b).

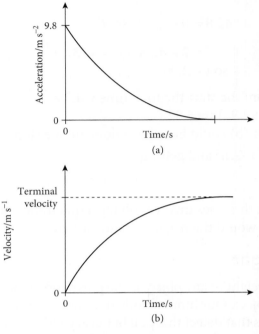

Figure 3.8

Objects moving under gravity in two dimensions

Anything moving through the air near the Earth's surface is often moving sideways as well as up or down. When a golf ball is hit cleanly with a golf club, it will start by moving forwards and upwards and, before it hits the ground, by moving forwards and downwards. This is shown in Figure 3.9, where air resistance has again been ignored.

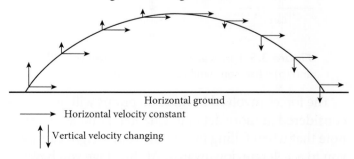

Figure 3.9 The path of a golf ball when air resistance is ignored

In this idealised case, once the ball has lost contact with the club there will be zero horizontal force on the ball. Its horizontal velocity, therefore, remains constant. This is shown by black arrows of constant length. Vertically, however, the weight of the ball will cause a downward acceleration of g. Its vertical velocity, therefore, falls at a constant rate of $9.81\,\mathrm{m\,s^{-2}}$ to 0 at the top of the flight and then increases at the same rate bringing the ball back to the ground.

The following example shows how to calculate the range of a golf ball in the absence of air resistance. Air resistance will decrease the range of the ball and the maximum height it reaches.

Example 3

A golfer strikes a ball so that the ball has a velocity of $64\,\mathrm{m\,s^{-1}}$ at an angle of $37°$ to the horizontal. In the absence of air resistance, calculate for horizontal ground,

(a)   the maximum height reached,
(b)   the time taken to reach maximum height, and
(c)   the distance the ball travels horizontally before hitting the ground for the first time.

Answer Start by finding the horizontal and vertical components of the initial velocity, using Figure 3.10.

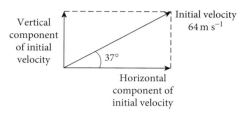

Figure 3.10

Horizontal component $= 64\cos 37° = 51.1\,\mathrm{m\,s^{-1}}$
Vertical component $= 64\sin 37° = 38.5\,\mathrm{m\,s^{-1}}$

(a)   Use $v^2 = u^2 + 2as$ for the vertical motion only, so $v = 0$ at the top of the flight. This gives
$$0 = (38.5)^2 - 2 \times 9.81 \times s$$
where s is the vertical rise.
Therefore $2 \times 9.81 \times s = 38.5^2$ and $s = 75.5\,\mathrm{m}$.

(b)   The time for this vertical rise can be obtained from $s = vt - \dfrac{1}{2}at^2$
$75.5 = 0 - \dfrac{1}{2} \times (-9.81) \times t^2$ and
so $t^2 = 2 \times 75.5/9.81 = 15.4$ and $t = 3.93\,\mathrm{s}$

(c)   Since both halves of this path are symmetrical, the time taken to return to the ground will also be $3.93\,\mathrm{s}$. The total time is, therefore, $7.86\,\mathrm{s}$. At a constant horizontal velocity of $51.1\,\mathrm{m\,s^{-1}}$, the ball will travel a total horizontal distance of
$$51.1\,\frac{\mathrm{m}}{\mathrm{s}} \times 7.86\,\mathrm{s} = 400\,\mathrm{m}\ (\text{to 2 significant figures}).$$

Chapter Summary

✓   Speed is a scalar and is distance travelled per unit time.
✓   Velocity is a vector and is speed in a stated direction.
✓   Acceleration is the rate of change of velocity. It is a vector.
✓   Equations of motion for uniform acceleration:

1. $v = u + at$

2. $s = ut + \dfrac{1}{2}at^2$

3. $s = vt - \dfrac{1}{2}at^2$

4. $s = \dfrac{u+v}{2} \times t$

5. $v^2 = u^2 + 2as$

✓   The gradient of a distance–time graph gives the speed (or velocity).
✓   The gradient of a velocity–time graph gives the acceleration.
✓   The area beneath a velocity–time graph gives the distance.
✓   The pull of gravity on an object is its weight.
✓   For motion in two dimensions, horizontal velocity is usually considered to be constant; vertical velocity will have acceleration due to gravity downwards. These two velocities can be considered separately.

Progress Check

3.1 A car travels a distance of 720 km in moving 480 km south and 370 km west as shown in Figure 3.11. What is the displacement of the car from its starting point after completing the journey?

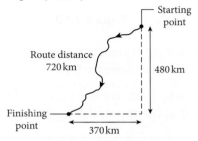

Figure 3.11

3.2 A plane travels 2000 km east and 150 km south on a flight. What is the displacement of the plane from its starting point at the end of the journey?

3.3 When travelling in a straight line, a train increases its velocity from $3\,\text{m}\,\text{s}^{-1}$ to $50\,\text{m}\,\text{s}^{-1}$ in a time of 107 s. What is its average acceleration during this time?

3.4 In an X-ray tube an electron has acceleration of $8.4 \times 10^{16}\,\text{m}\,\text{s}^{-2}$ from rest to a velocity of $3.8 \times 10^{7}\,\text{m}\,\text{s}^{-1}$. How long does the acceleration take?

3.5 What is the minimum time it will take for a racing car to increase its speed from $28\,\text{m}\,\text{s}^{-1}$ to $75\,\text{m}\,\text{s}^{-1}$ if the maximum grip between the car and the racetrack enables a maximum acceleration of $17\,\text{m}\,\text{s}^{-2}$?

3.6 In a sprint, an athlete maintains a constant acceleration of $7.8\,\text{m}\,\text{s}^{-2}$ for the first 1.5 s of the race. Calculate:
(a) the velocity of the athlete after 1.5 s,
(b) the displacement of the athlete after the 1.5 s.

3.7 In an old castle there is a well that is so deep that when a bucketful of water is dropped down the well it takes 4.0 s before the dropped water hits the water in the well. The acceleration due to gravity is $9.8\,\text{m}\,\text{s}^{-2}$.
Estimate:
(a) the speed of the dropped water when it hits the water in the well,
(b) the depth of the well.
Explain two factors that make your answers unreliable.

3.8 A railway company is asked to allow a high-speed train to make a stop at a station where it had previously not

stopped. Two minutes must be allowed for the train to be stationary. Consider a train travelling at $60\,\text{m}\,\text{s}^{-1}$ before braking with a deceleration of $2.0\,\text{m}\,\text{s}^{-2}$. (Deceleration is negative acceleration.) After stopping it can accelerate at a rate of $1.2\,\text{m}\,\text{s}^{-2}$. Calculate
(a) the time taken for the train to stop,
(b) the time taken for the train to accelerate back to top speed,
(c) the distances the train takes to stop and to speed up,
(d) the delay time of the train as a result of stopping at the station.

3.9 A motorist travelling at $25\,\text{m}\,\text{s}^{-1}$ is 40 m behind another motorist also travelling at $25\,\text{m}\,\text{s}^{-1}$. The first motorist accelerates in 6.0 s to $30\,\text{m}\,\text{s}^{-1}$ and maintains this speed difference until he is 50 m in front of the other motorist, who keeps to his original speed. Deduce
(a) the total time this takes,
(b) the distance the overtaking motorist has travelled.

3.10 A steel ball bearing is dropped from above gate 1 and is timed as it passes through the three light gates shown in Figure 3.12.

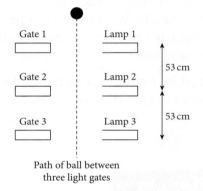

Figure 3.12

The separation between each pair of light gates is 53.0 cm. The time interval between gates 1 and 2 is 0.197 46 s and between gates 2 and 3 is 0.124 34 s.

(a) Write equations using $s = ut + \dfrac{1}{2}at^2$ for
  (i) the time between gates 1 and 2,
  (ii) the total time between gates 1 and 3.
(b) Eliminate u, the speed of the ball at gate 1 and solve the equation to find g.

Dynamics

4

Introduction

You need some background knowledge about motion to understand dynamics. In the seventeenth century Sir Isaac Newton transformed ideas about motion. He stated three laws of motion that are now known as Newton's laws of motion. The most important difference between pre-Newton ideas and his own ideas was that Newton realised that increased force resulted in increased acceleration and that zero force resulted in zero acceleration. Previously zero force was assumed to be the condition for zero velocity. It may appear obvious that force is required for motion but it is not so. The Earth, for example, is travelling at about 30 kilometres per second in its orbit around the Sun. Nothing is pushing it to keep it at this speed and it has been travelling with a speed like this for the last 4 500 000 000 years. Similarly an artificial space probe, far out in space might be travelling with constant velocity of $5 \, \text{km s}^{-1}$ for years. It only requires its rocket motor to be switched on when it is required to change its velocity.

Teacher's Tip

Zero resultant force implies constant velocity and zero acceleration. A resultant force will cause an acceleration in the direction of the resultant force.

Newton's laws of motion

The formal statements of the laws are as follows.

Newton's first law

Every object continues in its state of rest or state of uniform motion in a straight line unless acted upon by a resultant external force.

Newton's second law

The rate of change of momentum of a body is proportional to the resultant force acting on it.

More detail about momentum will be given shortly. Here it refers to the product of the mass and velocity of an object. It is a vector quantity.

Newton's first law is actually the special case of the second law when the resultant force is zero. In that case there will be no rate of change of momentum, so there will be a constant velocity.

Newton's third law

In its traditional wording, it is:

If body A exerts a force on body B then body B exerts an equal and opposite force on body A.

A different version of this law will be given in a Teacher's Tip on page 24.

Mass

Whereas weight is a force and is, therefore, measured in newtons, mass is not a force. Mass is a measure of how difficult it is to accelerate a body. It is often referred to as the inertia of a body or its reluctance to accelerate. Mass is measured in the familiar unit, the kilogram.

If an object has a mass of 100 kg, it will be 100 times more difficult to accelerate it than the standard 1 kilogram mass. Another way of looking at this is that if a force can give the standard kilogram a certain acceleration, then the same force on a 100 kg mass will cause one hundredth of this acceleration.

One important point about an object's mass is that it is constant throughout the Universe. The weight of a 5.000 kilogram mass on Earth may vary from 49.15 N at the North Pole to a lower force of 48.90 N at the equator. On the Moon the weight would be about 8.0 N only. It would be very easy to lift the mass on the Moon but if you kicked it, that is, accelerated it, the feel of it on your toes would be exactly the same as if you kicked it on the Earth. In all these situations, the mass remains the same at 5.000 kg.

It is confusing that in everyday life, weights are given in kilograms. Postal services in many countries, for example, charge for parcels according to weight— and then give weights in kilograms. For your physics course it is best to remember the difference between mass and weight as shown in the Teacher's Tip.

Teacher's Tip

- The mass of an object is always measured in kilograms.
- The gravitational force pulling an object towards the Earth, its weight, is always measured in newtons.

If your own mass is 70 kg, your weight is 70 kg × 9.81 m s^{-2} = 687 N.

Note that the unit for g, the acceleration of free fall due to gravity, is not only m s^{-2} but since acceleration can be calculated from force divided by mass, the unit of acceleration can also be written as

$$\frac{N}{kg}.$$

Therefore, 9.81 m s^{-2} is 9.81 newtons per kilogram, and when written this way it is referred to as the Earth's gravitational field strength. **Gravitational field strength is defined as the force per unit mass acting due to gravity.**

Linear momentum

Momentum was stated earlier to be the product of a body's mass m and velocity v. The symbol normally used for momentum is p, so

$$p = m \times v$$

(There is another momentum called angular momentum. It involves rotation and is not included in this physics course. Therefore, whenever you see the word momentum in this course you can assume it is linear momentum for an object travelling in a straight line.)

Newton's second law states that the rate of change of momentum of an object is proportional to the resultant force acting on the object.

This gives $\quad F = k \times \dfrac{\text{change in momentum}}{\text{change in time}}$ **Equation I**

where k is a constant.

For those of you studying calculus this is $F = k\dfrac{dp}{dt}$.

For a constant mass this becomes

$$F = k \times \frac{m \times \text{change in } v}{\text{change in } t}$$

Since change in v/change in t is the acceleration we get

$$F = kma \qquad\qquad\qquad \textbf{Equation II}$$

You may be familiar with this equation, apart from the k term in it. Making k equal to 1 comes about from the definition of the unit of force, the newton.

A force of 1 newton (N) is the force that causes a mass of 1 kilogram to have an acceleration of 1 m s^{-2}.

$$\text{So, } 1\,N = k \times 1\,kg \times 1\,m\,s^{-2}$$

This makes $k = 1$ so long as the units used are newtons, kilograms and metres second^{-2}. It also means that force in newtons can be defined as being equal to the rate of change of momentum.

With $k = 1$, Equation II becomes the familiar, $F = m \times a$.

In this equation F and a are vectors and m is a scalar. This means that F and a must always be in the same direction. A resultant force on an object will accelerate the object only in the direction that the force is acting. This reinforces the comment made in Chapter 3 about a ball travelling through the air (see Figure 3.9). In Figure 4.1 the ball is following a curved path.

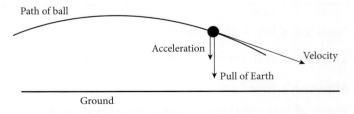

Figure 4.1

The velocity of the ball is at a tangent to the curve, but the force acting on the ball is the gravitational attraction of the Earth pulling vertically downwards, so the acceleration must also be vertically downwards.

Equation I gives a more meaningful SI unit for momentum than the artificial $kg\,m\,s^{-1}$. Rearranging the equation gives

change in momentum = force × time

and, therefore, an SI unit of momentum is the newton second, N s.

Newton's third law

This law effectively states that forces always come in pairs. A's push on B is always accompanied by B's push on A, and that these two forces are equal in magnitude and opposite in direction. The two forces are also always of the same type and **never** act on the same object.

For example, when a tennis racket hits a tennis ball, the contact force of the racket on the ball equals the contact force of the ball on the racket.

This does not mean that they somehow cancel one another out.

If the contact force on the ball is 60 N forwards then it accelerates forwards at a rate dependent on its mass. The contact force on the racket is 60 N backwards and it will decelerate at a rate depending on its mass, and any other forces acting on it.

Now consider an apple falling from a tree. (This is an appropriate example because Newton, by common agreement, is assumed to have written his laws after thinking about a falling apple!) Figure 4.2 shows the Earth and the apple.

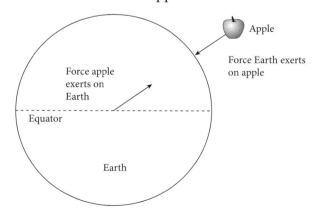

Figure 4.2 As an apple falls the force the Earth exerts on it is equal and opposite to the force the apple exerts on the Earth. (The figure is not drawn to scale!)

The gravitational force of the Earth on the apple downwards equals the gravitational force of the apple on the Earth upwards.

The forces

- are equal in magnitude,
- are opposite in direction,
- are both gravitational
- and act on different objects.

The downward force on the small mass of the apple causes its acceleration, the force of the same magnitude acting upwards on the vast mass of the Earth has virtually no effect on the Earth's movement.

Now consider the situation at the instant the apple hits the ground. Figures 4.3(a) and (b) show so-called free-body diagrams for both the Earth and the apple. The apple is touching the Earth but the diagrams get confused with one another if they are shown touching.

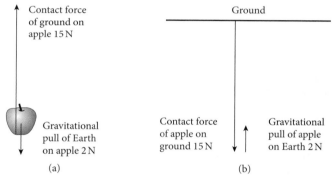

Figure 4.3

The gravitational forces are exactly the same as has just been discussed. They are now taken to be 2 N in magnitude. The difference is that now there is an upward contact force of the ground on the apple, taken as 15 N, and consequently a downward contact force of 15 N of the apple on the ground. The apple is decelerated by a resultant upward force of 13 N. The Earth is almost unaffected by the 15 N downward contact force on it.

Once the apple has stopped, the free-body force diagrams are shown in Figures 4.4(a) and (b).

These diagrams are very similar to those in Figures 4.3(a) and (b). The only difference is that the 15 N forces have dropped in magnitude down to 2 N. The resultant force on the apple is zero and so at rest on the ground it has zero acceleration.

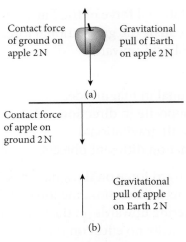

Figure 4.4

In studying this topic it is important to note that contact forces can vary; the gravitational attraction does not, for a given object in a given place. When walking, for example, you vary the contact force between your shoes and the ground in a complicated way. There are only a few special moments when the magnitude of the contact force happens to be equal to the magnitude of your weight.

Teacher's Tip

Learn Newton's third law in a longer, but more precise form.

If body A exerts a force on body B then body B exerts a force on body A that is equal in magnitude, opposite in direction, and the two forces are of the same type.

So, it is incorrect to apply Newton's third law to two forces acting on the same body that might happen to be equal and opposite to one another even though they are different types of force. Newton's third law says nothing about a gravitational force being equal and opposite to a contact force. The two different forces may be equal and opposite, but this is not related to Newton's third law.

Conservation of momentum

The deduction of the principle from Newton's third law

Consider a collision between two blocks of matter far out in space. The blocks can be of any size, any shape, any mass, any velocity, any strength and any stickiness. After the collision, the two blocks may stick together, may bounce off one another or may break up into thousands of bits. To simplify things the following analysis assumes that the blocks hit one another head on but the analysis is equally true if done for two or three dimensions rather than one. Figure 4.5 shows the arrangement with A, of mass M, moving in one direction with velocity U. It also shows B, of mass m, moving in the opposite direction with velocity u.

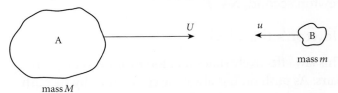

Figure 4.5

On hitting B, A will exert a force on it which might vary with time as shown in Figure 4.6(a).

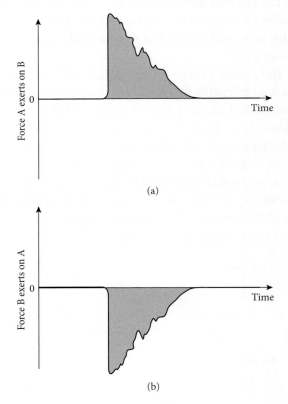

Figure 4.6

The area beneath this graph is a product of the average force exerted F and the time t. $F \times t$ is the change in momentum of B.

Newton's third law states that if body A exerts a force on body B, then body B exerts an equal and opposite force on body A. The force that B exerts on A is, therefore, shown in Figure 4.6(b). The two graphs must be exactly mirror images of one another. The area beneath the top graph shows the gain in the momentum of B. The area beneath the bottom graph shows that all the momentum gained by B is exactly matched by the momentum lost by A. It is a loss of momentum of A because the force on A is in the opposite direction to its motion. The force on A slows A down.

Gain of momentum of B = loss of momentum of A.

The total momentum of the two bodies is unchanged.

This is a fundamental principle of physics that has never been known to have been broken. It is called the **principle of conservation of linear momentum**.

The use of the principle of conservation of momentum

A formal statement of the principle of conservation of linear momentum is as follows.

In any collision between bodies the total momentum remains constant provided that there is no resultant external force acting.

The principle holds however many systems are involved but, for example, when a collision takes place between two cars, not only are the cars involved but the ground has forces exerted on it as well and so does the air surrounding the collision as air resistance might be involved. The following example shows how this difficulty can be minimised and how the principle of conservation of momentum can be used.

Example 1

A car of mass 950 kg is at rest and a car of mass 1200 kg travelling at an unknown velocity u hits it from behind. From skid markings on the road an investigator deduces that the speed of both vehicles immediately after the collision was 7.3 m s^{-1}. Calculate the value of u.

Answer It is always worthwhile with these problems to sketch a diagram on which known details can be added. It is all too easy to confuse

velocity v and velocities u and U and get masses m and M the wrong way round. A typical sketch is given in Figure 4.7.

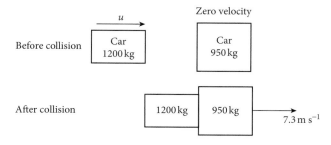

Figure 4.7

Using the principle of conservation of momentum

Total momentum before collision	=	total momentum after collision

$$(1200 \times u) = (1200 + 950) \times 7.3$$

Therefore, $u = (2150 \times 7.3)/1200 = 13.1$ m s^{-1}.

One interesting point about this collision is that although momentum is conserved in the collision, kinetic energy is not conserved. This must be the case, since even if no other energy is lost there will be a lot of sound energy produced in the crash. You are probably familiar with kinetic energy being $\frac{1}{2}mv^2$. This will be considered in more detail later but here,

Kinetic energy of 1200 kg car before the collision

$$= \frac{1}{2} \times 1200 \times 13.1^2 = 103 \text{ kJ}$$

Kinetic energy of both cars after the collision

$$= \frac{1}{2} \times (1200 + 950) \times 7.3^2 = 57 \text{ kJ}$$

So, 46 kJ has been lost in heating the road and the cars and in producing sound energy.

Elastic and inelastic collisions

A collision such as the one detailed in the example above is known as an **inelastic collision** because kinetic energy has been lost. In an **elastic collision** there is no loss of kinetic energy. A special situation arises with an elastic collision.

Consider the following elastic collision in a straight line between body A of mass m and velocity u with body B of mass M and velocity U as shown in Figure 4.8. The velocities after the collision are v and V.

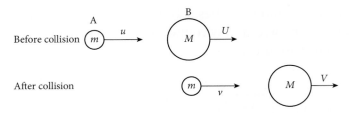

Figure 4.8

Equating total momentum before the collision with momentum after gives

$$mu + MU = mv + MV$$

The corresponding equation for kinetic energy will be

$$\tfrac{1}{2}mu^2 + \tfrac{1}{2}MU^2 = \tfrac{1}{2}mv^2 + \tfrac{1}{2}MV^2$$

To simplify these two equations is not as easy as it might seem. It can be made easier by putting all the terms with an m in them on the left-hand side of the equations and all the terms with M in them on the right. The $\tfrac{1}{2}$ may be cancelled from the kinetic energy equation giving

$$mu - mv = MV - MU \quad \text{or}$$
$$m(u - v) = M(V - U) \text{ and} \qquad \textbf{Equation I}$$
$$mu^2 - mv^2 = MV^2 - MU^2 \quad \text{or}$$
$$m(u^2 - v^2) = M(V^2 - U^2) \qquad \textbf{Equation II}$$

Now divide the Equation II by Equation I to get

$$\frac{m(u^2 - v^2)}{m(u - v)} = \frac{M(V^2 - U^2)}{M(V - U)}$$

Both m and M cancel out and both top lines are differences of two squares so

$$\frac{(u+v)(u-v)}{(u-v)} = \frac{(U+V)(U-V)}{(U-V)}$$

giving

$$(u + v) = (U + V)$$
$$\text{or } (u - U) = (V - v)$$

The term on the left is the relative velocity of approach, i.e. how fast mass m is catching up mass M. The term on the right is the relative velocity of separation, i.e. how fast M is moving away from mass m.

For elastic collisions only, the velocity of approach equals the velocity of separation.

Example 2

On a linear air track, a mass of 120 g is travelling to the right with a velocity of 83 cm s^{-1}. It collides elastically with a mass of 200 g travelling with velocity 47 cm s^{-1} in the opposite direction, as shown in Figure 4.9.

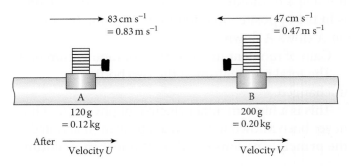

Figure 4.9

With what velocity do the masses travel after the collision?

Answer Before collision total momentum to right
$$= (0.12 \times 0.83) - (0.20 \times 0.47)$$

After the collision total momentum to right $= (0.12 \times U) + (0.20 \times V)$

These two terms are equal by the principle of conservation of energy, so

$$(0.0996 - 0.0940) = 0.0056 = 0.12U + 0.20V$$

Sometimes it is worthwhile multiplying both sides of an equation by a large number to get rid of all the zeroes. Multiplying through by 100 gives

$$(9.96 - 9.40) = 0.56 = 12U + 20V$$

Neither U nor V can be obtained from this equation but using the fact that the velocity of approach equals the velocity of separation gives

$$(0.83 + 0.47) = V - U$$

By substituting into the first equation we get

$$12U + 20(1.30 + U) = 0.56$$
$$12U + 26 + 20U = 0.56 \quad \text{so} \quad 32U = -25.44 \text{ and}$$
$$U = -0.795 \text{ m s}^{-1} = -80 \text{ cm s}^{-1} \text{ to 2 sig figs. and}$$
$$V = 0.505 \text{ m s}^{-1} = 51 \text{ cm s}^{-1} \text{ to 2 sig figs.}$$

Chapter Summary

- ✓ Newton's first law. Every object continues in its state of rest or state of uniform motion in a straight line unless acted upon by a resultant external force.
- ✓ Newton's second law. The rate of change of momentum of a body is proportional to the resultant force acting on it.
- ✓ Newton's third law. If body A exerts a force on body B then body B exerts an equal and opposite force on body A.
- ✓ Mass is a measure of how difficult it is to accelerate a body. It is measured in kilograms.

- ✓ Weight is the force of gravitational attraction acting on a body. It is measured in newtons.
- ✓ Momentum is the product of an object's mass and velocity. It is measured in N s. To determine the time t an object takes to stop when a force F is applied, use its momentum in the equation $mv = Ft$.
- ✓ The principle of conservation of momentum states that in all collisions the total momentum is constant provided that there is no resultant external force acting.

Progress Check

4.1 (a) Calculate the weight of a new-born baby of mass 3.72 kg.

(b) Calculate the mass and the weight on the Earth of a satellite that has a weight on the Moon of 1130 N. The gravitational field of the Moon at its surface is 1.62 N kg^{-1}.

4.2 For each of the following situations, which quantity, mass or weight, is mainly involved? Give reasons for your answers.

(a) Buying a loaf of bread
(b) Lifting a group of people in a lift
(c) Starting a Grand Prix racing car in a race
(d) Posting a parcel
(e) Hitting a wall in an accident in a car
(f) Checking the load in a helicopter
(g) Rock climbing

4.3 In using the equation $F = kma$, what value will k have if the mass is measured in grams, the acceleration is measured in cm s^{-2} and F is to be found and measured in newtons?

4.4 Draw free-body force diagrams for

(a) a person standing on level ground and a case held in their hand,
(b) a person driving a car and the car accelerating in a straight line,
(c) a car and a caravan, with the car accelerating.

4.5 A cannonball has mass 25 kg and it is fired horizontally with velocity 75 m s^{-1} from a cannon of mass 320 kg. Calculate the initial velocity of recoil of the cannon.

4.6 A head-on elastic collision takes place between a stationary nucleus of uranium, mass 235 u, and a neutron, mass 1.00 u. The neutron was travelling with velocity 4.70×10^6 m s^{-1}. Calculate the speed of the two particles after the collision.

[**Note:** Provided all the mass units are the same in the conservation of momentum equation, there is no need to convert masses in u to masses in kilograms because the conversion factor would cancel out throughout your equation.]

Forces, Density and Pressure 5

Types of force

A force is often described as a push or a pull, but if we want to know more about this term, then first we have to learn how a force can be produced.

Outside of the nucleus of an atom, there are three ways in which a force can be generated. It can be generated:

- on a mass in a gravitational field,
- on a charge in an electric field, and
- on an electric current in a magnetic field.

The first of these three has been mentioned in Chapter 4. A mass m in a gravitational field g experiences a force mg. For example, in the Earth's gravitational field of $9.81\,\text{N}\,\text{kg}^{-1}$ a $20.0\,\text{kg}$ mass will experience a force of $20.0\,\text{kg} \times 9.81\,\text{N}\,\text{kg}^{-1} = 196.2\,\text{N}$ in the direction of the field.

The other two types of force will be considered in more detail later in the book but, for the sake of completeness they are given here and described in outline.

A charge q in an electric field E experiences a force qE. For example, a charge of 3.6 microcoulombs (μC) in an electric field of $23\,000\,\text{N}\,\text{C}^{-1}$ experiences a force given by

$F = qE = 3.6 \times 10^{-6}\,\text{C} \times 23\,000\,\text{N}\,\text{C}^{-1} = 0.083\,\text{N}$ in the direction of the field.

A current I flowing through a wire of length l when placed at right angles to a magnetic field of flux density B will experience a force F given by $F = BIl$.

For example, a current of 6.2 A flowing through a 3.0 cm length of wire, when placed at right angles to a magnetic field of flux density 0.026 tesla (T) will experience a force F given by

$F = BIl = 0.026\,\text{T} \times 6.2\,\text{A} \times 0.030\,\text{m} = 0.0048\,\text{N}$

This force will be at right angles to both the current and the magnetic field.

The definitions for gravitational field and electric field are directly comparable. The definition for magnetic field is more complicated, particularly concerning direction.

These three causes of force appear to omit ordinary forces between touching objects like knocks, hits, pushes, tensions, etc. This is because all of these forces are actually electrical forces. It is the electrical force that holds all solid objects together. All atoms contain charged particles and solid objects remain solid because of the attractive force between these particles. All forces of contact are, in fact, electrical forces, even though you do not regard touching a table as having an electric shock.

Forces in fluids

Swimming is possible because the water you swim in provides an upward force on you. This becomes very clear when you snorkel on the surface of deep water. When you look down to the bottom of the sea, provided the water is clear and perhaps the Sun is shining, it almost looks as if you are in danger of falling from a great height, but you know that the water is holding you up. The support force acting on you is a contact force from the water and is called an **upthrust**. Upthrust is the force that allows all boats to float. A boat in equilibrium will have an upthrust on it that is equal and opposite to its total weight. If it rises a little, then the weight will be greater than the upthrust and if it falls a little, then the upthrust will be greater than the weight. So, when out of equilibrium, the resultant force will tend to push it back into equilibrium.

The origin of upthrust is due to the increase in pressure in a liquid with depth. More detail will be given about pressure later in the chapter but its definition is that pressure is force per unit area. Be careful with the use of the word *pressure* because in everyday speech people often use the term 'pressure' when they should have correctly used 'force'. Pressure is correctly measured in the unit newtons per square metre unit or the pascal.

$1\,\mathrm{N\,m^{-2}}$ is a pressure of 1 pascal, 1 Pa.

Atmospheric pressure is about 100 000 Pa. Meteorologists (scientists who study the weather and climate) use the unit 1 bar for 100 000 Pa and often measure atmospheric pressure as, say, 998 mbar (= 0.998 bar).

A cube submerged in a liquid will have forces acting on it due to the pressure of the liquid. This is shown in Figure 5.1.

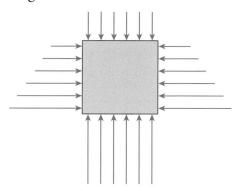

Figure 5.1 Forces acting on a solid submerged in a liquid

The sideways forces cancel out; the upward forces are greater than the downward forces, so there is a resultant of all these forces in an upward direction. This resultant is the upthrust.

Resistive forces

When there is movement of an object across a surface, there is usually a force on the object that is in the opposite direction to its motion. The force on the object is called **friction** when the object is moving across a solid. When the object is moving through a fluid, the terms **viscous force** or **drag** are used. **Fluid** means 'something that can flow' and so a fluid substance is a liquid or a gas. In air, the term **air resistance** is frequently used and **fluid friction** is another term used generally for viscous forces.

Generally the magnitude of viscous force increases with speed but only under special non-turbulent conditions is viscous force proportional to speed. Friction between solids is usually independent of speed once the object is moving. You must have noticed that it is easier to keep something moving than it is to get it moving in the first place. This is because the frictional force on a stationary object is greater than that on the same object when it is moving.

Friction is frequently considered to be a nuisance. However, friction is an absolutely essential force for almost everything. Life, as we know it, would not exist without friction. All clothing is held together by friction. All houses require friction to remain standing. Nails, screws, nuts and bolts all hold together because of friction. Cars not only require tyres to grip a road using friction, they are held together by friction. Even mountains would not exist if there was no such force as friction.

Centre of gravity

Any large object may be made up of many parts and each part made of innumerable numbers of molecules. It is almost impossible to make any calculation about the overall acceleration of the object by considering each molecule separately. This problem is overcome by using the concept of the **centre of gravity** of an object.

The centre of gravity of an object is defined as the single point where the weight of the object may be considered to act. For most regular objects, the centre of gravity (C of G) of the object is at its geometrical centre, as shown in Figure 5.2.

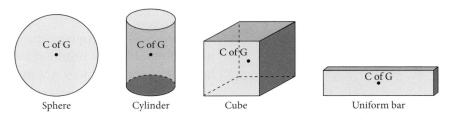

Figure 5.2 For regular objects, centre of gravity is the geometrical centre

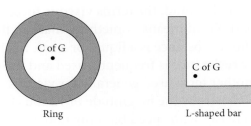 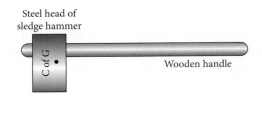

Figure 5.3 For some objects, centre of gravity lies outside of the object

For some objects the centre of gravity may be difficult to find or may even be outside of the body altogether, as shown in Figure 5.3.

Note that the weight of an object does not act at the centre of gravity. It acts on all the molecules that make up the object. It is just that for the sake of calculations, the same answer is obtained by assuming that the whole weight does act at the centre of gravity.

Turning forces

So far with the study of Newton's laws of motion, it has been stated that a resultant force will cause an acceleration of a body. This is true, but a force may also cause rotation of the body.

There is a series of terms associated with turning forces. These are now defined with the warning that they need to be used with care.

The **moment of a force** is the product of the force and its perpendicular distance from the axis of rotation. This is illustrated in Figures 5.4(a) and (b).

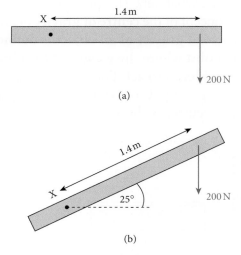

Figure 5.4

Here, in Figure 5.4(a) a beam is pivoted at X with a 200 N force applied to it at a distance of 1.4 m from its axis of rotation. The clockwise moment of the force is 200 N × 1.4 m = 280 N m.

When the force is not at right angles to the beam, in Figure 5.4(b) it is the perpendicular distance from the line of action of the force to the pivot that is needed.

With an angle of 25° the clockwise moment becomes

$$200\,\text{N} \times 1.4 \times \cos 25° = 254\,\text{N m}.$$

A **couple** is a pair of equal forces that tend to produce rotation only. They will, therefore, not produce any linear acceleration. See Figure 5.5.

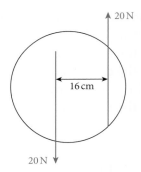

Figure 5.5

The torque of a couple is equal to one of the forces multiplied by the perpendicular distance between them. For Figure 5.5 the torque is 20 N × 0.16 m = 3.2 N m.

Equilibrium

A body is said to be in equilibrium when there is no resultant force or resultant torque acting on the body. Note that this does not mean that the body is not moving. When you are travelling at 800 kilometres per hour in a comfortable airline seat during a smooth flight, you are in equilibrium. This is because you are not rotating and you are not accelerating. The resultant force on you is zero and the resultant torque on you is also zero. Under these conditions, normal actions such as pouring a drink into a glass can be performed in the same way as if you were sitting at home. The problem in a plane only comes about when the plane meets air disturbance, where a resultant force may be caused. You are then no longer in equilibrium.

The triangle of forces

Consider a child on a swing having been pulled backwards before starting the swing. A force diagram for the situation is shown in Figure 5.6.

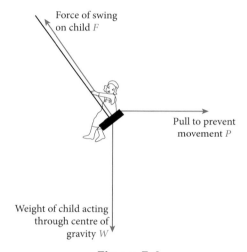

Figure 5.6

For these three forces to provide equilibrium, they must act through a single point so that there is no resultant torque. They must also have a resultant force of zero so the forces must add vectorially to zero. This they will do provided they add to form a closed triangle, called a vector triangle. This is shown in Figure 5.7.

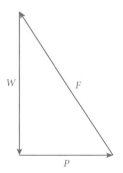

Figure 5.7

The principle of moments

This principle states that if the sum of the clockwise moments about any point in a system equals the sum of the anticlockwise moments about the same point, then the system will not rotate. (Strictly it will not change its rate of rotation.)

This is an equivalent statement for rotation as Newton's first law is for linear motion.

Example 1

The jib of a tower crane is in equilibrium and is illustrated in Figure 5.8 with the loading forces acting on it at specified distances.

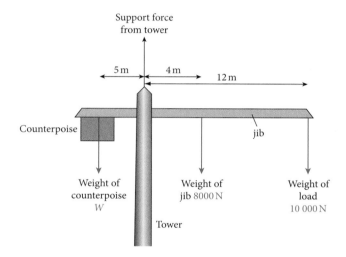

Figure 5.8

Calculate (a) the weight necessary for the counterpoise and (b) the support force provided by the tower.

Answer (a) The clockwise moments about the tower:

moment provided by the weight of the jib
    $= 8000 \, \text{N} \times 4.0 \, \text{m} = 32\,000 \, \text{N m}$
moment provided by the load
    $= 10\,000 \, \text{N} \times 12 \, \text{m} = 120\,000 \, \text{N m}$
Total clockwise moment
    $= 32\,000 \, \text{N m} + 120\,000 \, \text{N m} = 152\,000 \, \text{N m}$
The anticlockwise moment is provided by the counterpoise weight.

This is $W \times 5 \, \text{m}$

For equilibrium,

clockwise moments = anticlockwise moments so

$5W = 152\,000$ and therefore

$W = 152\,000/5$

$\quad = 30\,400\,\text{N}$

(b)   The total downward force = the total upward force when in equilibrium, so

$30.4\,\text{kN} + 8\,\text{kN} + 10\,\text{kN}$

= support force provided by the tower

= 48.4 kN.

Density

Density is defined as the mass per unit volume of a substance. In equation form, this becomes

$$\text{density} = \frac{\text{mass}}{\text{volume}}, \quad \text{or in symbols} \quad \rho = \frac{m}{V}$$

In SI units, density is measured in kilograms per cubic metre. The symbol for density, ρ is the Greek letter rho.

Example 2

A cold water tank providing water for use in a house, has internal dimensions of width = 64 cm, length = 92 cm. It contains water to a depth of 56 cm. The mass of water in the tank is 330 kg. (This is about a third of a tonne.) Calculate the density of water.

Answer   Volume of water = $0.64\,\text{m} \times 0.92\,\text{m} \times 0.56\,\text{m}$

$= 0.33\,\text{m}^3$

Density of water = mass/volume

$= 330\,\text{kg}/0.33\,\text{m}^3 = 1000\,\text{kg}\,\text{m}^{-3}$

Note from this example that the density of water is **not** $1\,\text{kg}\,\text{m}^{-3}$. A cubic metre of water is a large quantity of water. It has a mass of a tonne, a thousand kilograms.

Densities of some common materials, in decreasing values, are given in Table 5.1.

Table 5.1

Phase	Material	Density/kg m⁻³
solid	gold	19 300
solid	lead	11 300
solid	copper	8930
solid	iron	7870
solid	concrete	2400
liquid	water	1000
solid	ice	920
solid	wood (oak)	650
gas	air (at standard pressure and 273 K)	1.3
gas	steam (at standard pressure and 373 K)	0.80
gas	hydrogen (at standard pressure and 273 K)	0.090

Pressure

Pressure is defined as the normal force per unit area. The unit of pressure is the pascal, Pa, and is 1 newton per metre squared.

(Old non-SI units are still used frequently for pressure. If you ever have your blood pressure taken, it will be measured in millimetres of mercury because before using electronic devices doctors used to use a pressure instrument called a manometer, in which there is mercury in a glass U-shaped tube. Meteorologists use the unit millibar for pressure. One bar is approximately equal to atmospheric pressure and is exactly 100 000 newtons per square metre, so a millibar is 100 newtons per square metre. High atmospheric pressure might be 1024 mB and in a depression might fall to 940 mB.)

Atmospheric pressure

The Earth's atmosphere is a relatively thin layer of mostly nitrogen and oxygen gases. The pressure exerted on a particular object on the Earth is due to the continual bombardment the object receives from molecules surrounding it. Each collision results in a molecule's momentum changing. The rate of change of momentum is force. Add all the small forces together and the result is the total force on the object. The fact that you do not feel atmospheric pressure is because the pressure inside your body is nearly the same as that outside it. The resultant force on you caused by atmospheric pressure is, therefore, almost zero. Where you do notice pressure is when you are swimming. Here, the pressure in the water increases considerably with depth. The pressure, even only 30 cm below the surface of water is considerably greater than that at the surface. This means that the force on you due to water pressure upwards is greater than that downwards. This results in buoyancy.

Pressure due to a column of liquid of constant density

Consider a cylinder of liquid of density ρ. The height of the cylinder is h and its area of cross-section is A, as shown in Figure 5.9.

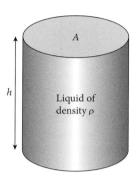

Figure 5.9

The total volume of liquid $= hA$
So the total mass m of the liquid $=$ density $\times$ volume
$$= \rho \times hA$$
The weight of liquid $= mg = \rho h A g$

This is the force F acting downwards on its base and the pressure on the base is F/A.
So,

$$p = \frac{F}{A} = \frac{\rho h A g}{A} = \rho g h$$

If the difference in pressure between two points in a liquid, a vertical distance Δh apart, is required then the difference in pressure is given by

$$\Delta p = \rho g \Delta h$$

Standard pressure

Sometimes pressure may be measured in atmospheres. Standard pressure is one atmosphere and to convert this to a pressure in pascals, you will need to use the above equation. An older standard of pressure was equal to the pressure of 76 cm of mercury. This was used because many old barometers used a glass tube, sealed at its upper end, containing mercury and with a vacuum above the mercury.
The pressure of 76 cm of mercury is
$$0.76 \, \text{m} \times 13\,600 \, \text{kg m}^{-3} \times 9.81 \, \text{m s}^{-2}$$
$$= 1.014 \times 10^5 \, \text{Pa}$$

Chapter Summary

- ✓ Forces outside of the nucleus are either on a mass in a gravitational field OR on a charge in an electrical field OR on an electric current in a magnetic field.
- ✓ Pressure is force per unit area. It is measured in pascals (Pa). $1 \, \text{Pa} = 1 \, \text{N m}^{-2}$.
- ✓ The centre of gravity of an object is the point where the weight of an object may be considered to act.
- ✓ The moment of a force is the product of the force and its perpendicular distance from the axis of rotation.

- ✓ An object is said to be in equilibrium when the resultant force on it is zero and the sum of the moments on it is zero.
- ✓ Density is mass per unit volume. Its SI unit is kilograms per cubic metre.
- ✓ Pressure is force per unit area. Its SI unit is the pascal. $1 \, \text{Pa} = 1$ newton per square metre.
- ✓ The pressure due to a column of liquid is given by
  pressure $= \rho g h$
  $=$ density $\times$ acceleration $\times$ height
  of liquid   due to gravity   of column

Progress Check

5.1 Calculate:
  (a) the charge on an electron from the information that in an electric field of magnitude 400 000 N C⁻¹ it experiences a force of 6.4×10^{-14} N,
  (b) the current needed in a wire, 20 cm long and placed at right-angles to a magnetic field of flux density 0.84 T, for the force on the wire to be 0.040 N.

5.2 Using SI units the viscous drag P on a parachute is given by the empirical equation $P = 4.7 \times 10^2 \, v$, where v is the descent velocity.
  (a) What is the unit of the numerical value 4.7×10^2?
  (b) Determine the maximum descent velocity of a girl of mass 63 kg. The mass of the parachute is 13 kg.

5.3 A plane in flight has vertical forces acting on it as shown in Figure 5.10.
What conditions must apply for the plane to be in equilibrium? Give your answer in terms of the magnitude of the forces *M*, *T* and *W* and the distances *x* and *y*.

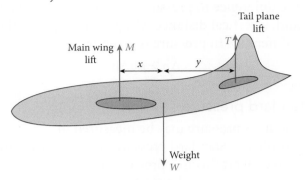

Figure 5.10

5.4 (a) Sketch a vector triangle for each of the three systems shown in Figure 5.11. Each system is in equilibrium.
(b) Use your sketch to calculate the value(s) of the unknown force(s).
(c) Draw scale diagrams of the vector triangles to check your answers to (b).

5.5 In a simple weighing machine a load of 80 N was balanced by moving a sliding weight along a bar until equilibrium was found. Figure 5.12 shows the arrangement and the relevant distances.

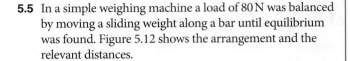
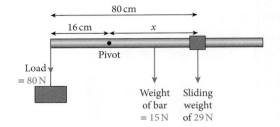

Figure 5.12

(a) What distance *x* will balance the load?
(b) What is the maximum load that can be measured by this weighing machine?

5.6 A girder is pivoted at X and has the forces shown in Figure 5.13 acting upon it.

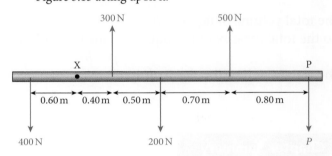

Figure 5.13

Calculate the force necessary at P to prevent rotation.

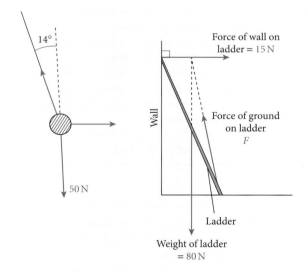
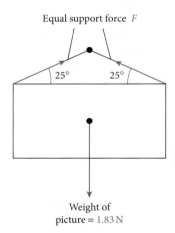

Figure 5.11

5.7 A forearm and hand of weight 18 N is held
horizontally and is carrying in the hand a weight of
30 N. The arm is kept horizontal by a tension applied
by a tendon attached to the biceps muscle at one end
and to a bone in the arm at the other. The tendon is
at an angle of 76° to the horizontal and attached a
distance of 4.0 cm from the point where the arm is
pivoted, as shown in Figure 5.14.

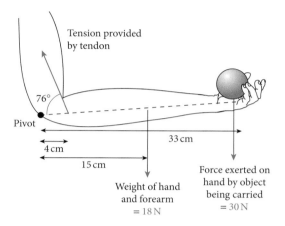

Figure 5.14

Calculate the tension in the tendon.

5.8 The loading of a bridge does not cause rotation but
the principle of moments can still be used to calculate
loading forces. One such system is shown in
Figure 5.15.
(a) Take moments about A and hence find the value of
    the support force at B.
(b) Making use of the fact that the total of all the
    downward forces must equal the total of all the
    upward forces, deduce the value of A.

5.9 A school hall has dimensions 30 m × 15 m × 5 m.
Calculate the mass of air in the hall. Express your answer
to 1 significant figure. (Density of air = 1.3 kg m^{-3})

5.10 Calculate the mass of a coin made of copper. Its diameter
is 3.0 cm and its thickness is 1.6 mm.
(Density of copper = 8930 kg m^{-3})

5.11 Estimate the mean spacing of gold atoms. One gold atom
has a mass of 3.27×10^{-25} kg.
(Density of gold = 19 300 kg m^{-3})

5.12 A hydrogen balloon is spherical and has a radius of 5.1 m.
The fabric of the balloon has mass 60 kg. Calculate
(a) the mass of hydrogen filling the balloon,
(b) the mass of air having the same volume,
(c) the mass of the load the balloon can support. This
    is given by answer (b) – answer (a) – the mass of
    the fabric of the balloon. (Density of hydrogen
    in balloon = 0.090 kg m^{-3}, density of air outside
    balloon = 1.3 kg m^{-3})

5.13 A blood pressure reading is 130/86. The two figures
are the systolic (maximum) and diastolic (minimum)
pressures in millimetres of mercury. Convert these two
pressures into kilopascals (kPa). (Density of mercury is
13 600 kg m^{-3}.)

5.14 The density of air at sea level is 1.29 kg m^{-3}. Atmospheric
pressure at a particular place is 9.76×10^4 Pa on a certain
day. Assuming that all the atmosphere has the same
density, calculate the height of atmosphere required for
this pressure. Explain why planes can actually fly at an
altitude of 11 km.

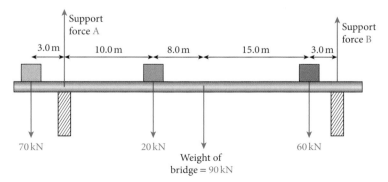

Figure 5.15

5.15 An object in the shape of a cube of side 200 mm is placed in a liquid of density 1.8×10^3 kg m^{-3}. Its top surface is horizontal and is 350 mm below the surface, as shown in Figure 5.16.

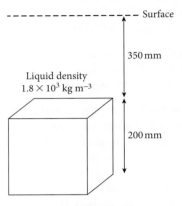

Figure 5.16

(a) Calculate
  (i)   the pressure from the liquid, at the top surface,
  (ii) the pressure from the liquid, at the bottom surface,
  (iii) the downward force caused by the liquid on the top surface,
  (iv) the upward force caused by the liquid on the bottom surface,
  (v)   the net upthrust on the cube.
(b) Archimedes' Principle states that the upthrust on a body in a fluid is equal to the weight of fluid displaced. Show that this is true for your calculation in (a) (v).
(c) What condition needs to be satisfied for the cube to float up to the surface?

Examination Questions II

1. (a) Distinguish between the moment of a force and the torque of a couple.   [4]

   (b) One type of weighing machine, known as a steelyard, is illustrated in Figure 1.

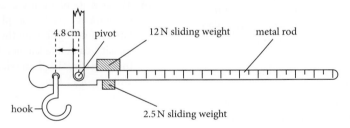

Figure 1

The two sliding weights can be moved independently along the rod.

With no load on the hook and the sliding weights at the zero mark on the metal rod, the metal rod is horizontal. The hook is 4.8 cm from the pivot.

A sack of flour is suspended from the hook. In order to return the metal rod to the horizontal position, the 12 N sliding weight is moved 84 cm along the rod and the 2.5 N weight is moved 72 cm.
   (i) Calculate the weight, in N, of the sack of flour.   [2]
   (ii) Suggest why this steelyard would be imprecise when weighing objects with a weight of about 25 N.   [1]

(Cambridge International AS and A Level Physics 9702
Paper 02 Question 3 October/November 2008)

Work, Energy and Power

6

Work and energy

Work and energy are closely related to one another and both are measured, using the SI system of units, in joules.

Work

Work is defined as the product of a force and the distance moved in the direction of the force.

It is a scalar quantity, so does not have direction associated with it even though direction is mentioned in its definition. [This is a case where two vectors, force and distance in the direction of the force, are multiplied together to give a scalar product.]

The unit of work, the joule, is defined as the work done when a force of one newton moves its point of application a distance of one metre in the direction of the force.

Two straightforward examples are given to show this in practice.

Example 1

A crane lifts a boat of weight 5000 N from a height of 0.20 m above the surface of the water to a height of 3.70 m above the water at a constant speed. What work is done by the crane?

Answer The crane exerts a constant force of 5000 N on the boat while it rises a height of (3.70 − 0.20) m at a constant speed.

Work done by the crane on the boat

$$= \text{force} \times \text{distance moved upwards}$$
$$= 5000\,\text{N} \times 3.50\,\text{m} = 17\,500\,\text{J}$$

Example 2

An escalator lifts a family of total weight 2200 N a distance of 8.0 m at an angle of 37° to the horizontal, as shown in Figure 6.1.

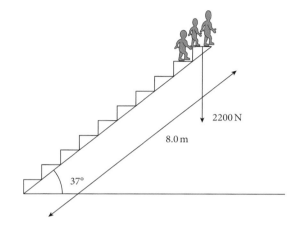

Figure 6.1

What work is done by the escalator on the family?

Answer The family is moved a vertical height of $8.0 \times \sin 37° = 4.81$ m

$$\text{Work done on the family} = 2200\,\text{N} \times 4.81\,\text{m}$$
$$= 10\,600\,\text{J}$$

Note that the step each member of the family stands on is pushing that family member vertically upwards. The horizontal movement of the family member does not involve any work being done.

Energy

Energy is defined as the stored ability to do work. A truck travelling along a horizontal motorway may have a kinetic energy of 18 MJ (18 000 000 J). When it comes to a slip road that has an upward gradient, it will use some of this stored energy to enable it to climb the slope, as well as to waste some of the energy in heating the road surface, the air around the truck and maybe the brakes. If it uses up all its stored energy, the kinetic energy it had, it will have stopped. This process may be reversed when rejoining the motorway. The gravitational potential energy the truck now has can be used to do work on the truck on the downward gradient slip road in order to increase its speed.

Motorway designers always try to make slip roads upwards for getting off and downwards for getting on. The natural slope of the land does not always make this possible.

Conservation of energy

In the nineteenth century, **James Prescott Joule**, an English physicist performed a remarkable series of accurate experiments in which he converted one form of energy into another. In one such experiment, he converted the gravitational potential energy of falling masses to turn a paddle wheel in some well-insulated water. Joule found that the loss of gravitational potential energy always equalled the gain in thermal energy of the water, once he had taken into account such factors as the thermal energy gained by the container, the lagging and the thermometer and the kinetic energy the weight had when it hit the ground. Joule actually made his own thermometers for doing these experiments and they were accurate to a hundredth of a degree Celsius. It took many years before the implication of Joule's work was fully accepted. It is now expressed as the principle of conservation of energy. This states that:

Energy can be converted from one form into another but can never be destroyed.

Categorising different forms of energy is important because in many ways all the different forms are related to work done in a physical field or to kinetic energy of movement. Table 6.1 may be helpful in understanding the connections between the different labels attached to energy.

Table 6.1

Term used	Comment
Gravitational potential energy	Energy gained as a result of moving upwards in a gravitational field
Electrical potential energy	Energy gained as a result of a charge moving against the force provided by an electric field
Elastic potential energy	Energy gained by stretching or squashing a material
Kinetic energy	Energy as a result of movement

Chemical energy	Energy associated with the arrangement of atoms in molecules
Thermal energy	Energy gained as a result of an increase in temperature
Internal energy	Energy gained as a result of an increase in the random movement of atoms/molecules'
Sound energy	Transmitted energy as a result of organised movement of atoms/molecules in a sound wave
Radiation energy, e.g. light, infra red, radio, etc.	Transmitted energy as a result of electromagnetic waves no movement of atoms/molecules is needed
Nuclear energy	Energy as a result of the nuclear structure of atoms

Examples of work done or energy supplied

While both work and energy are always calculated from the basic equation of

work = force × distance moved in the direction of the force, there are some situations that are so common in practice that it is useful to be able to quote certain answers.

Gravitational potential energy (E_p)

The work done in lifting an object of mass m, at constant speed, a height Δh in a downward gravitational field of magnitude g is given by,

$$\Delta E_p = \text{weight} \times \text{distance moved} = mg \times \Delta h$$

$$\Delta E_p = mg\Delta h$$

Electrical potential energy (e.p.e.)

The work done in moving a charge q a distance x against an electric field of field strength E^* is given by

$$\text{work} = \text{force} \times \text{distance} = Eq \times x = Eqx$$

This is shown in Figure 6.2 where a positive charge q is moved from A to B against the force caused by the electric field.

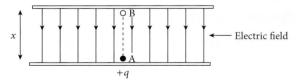

Figure 6.2

The charge, therefore, has Eqx of extra electrical potential energy at B than at A.

---

*Electric field will be covered in Chapters 10 and 23.

Elastic potential energy

This is similar to gravitational and electrical potential energy but, in the case of springs the force will not be constant as the spring is stretched. The graph of force against extension for an elastic change is shown in Figure 6.3.

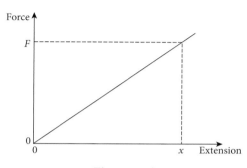

Figure 6.3

The work done in stretching the spring a distance x will be

the average force × distance moved $= \frac{1}{2} F \times x$.

This is $\frac{1}{2} Fx$ and it is also given by the area beneath the graph.

Elastic potential energy in a gas

The air in a bicycle tyre is under pressure. This air could do work so it has stored energy. All pneumatic systems use compressed air to do work.

Remember that pressure = force/area, so force due to pressure = pressure × area = pA

If a gas expands and does work against a surface of area A and at constant external pressure p, then the

$$\text{work done} = \text{force} \times \text{distance moved}$$
$$= pA \times \text{distance moved}$$

but $A \times$ distance moved = the change in the volume ΔV

The energy supplied by the gas is, therefore, $p \, \Delta V$.

This analysis can be extended to situations where the pressure is not constant, but the mathematics is more involved. The work done by a gas is, however, always the area beneath a graph of pressure against volume as shown in Figure 6.4.

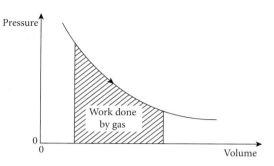

Figure 6.4

Kinetic energy

This is the work an object can do against a resistive force as a result of its speed. It is also, therefore, the work that needs to be done on the object to reach that speed in the first place.

Consider an object of mass m at rest. When a force F acts on it to give it an acceleration a so that it reaches a speed v in a distance s, then the work W done by the force is given by

$$W = Fs \quad \text{and also} \quad F = ma.$$

Since the object accelerates uniformly from rest, the equation of motion

$$v^2 = u^2 + 2as \quad \text{becomes} \quad v^2 = 2as$$

Combining these equations gives

$$W = Fs = mas = \frac{mv^2}{2} = \frac{1}{2} mv^2$$

Note that kinetic energy is often given the symbol E_k. It is always a force × a distance and so in SI units will always be measured in joules.

Example 3

A loaded truck has mass 40 tonnes (40 000 kg) and is travelling with a speed of $20 \, \text{m s}^{-1}$. Calculate its kinetic energy and use the kinetic energy to deduce the stopping force needed to stop the truck in 1000 m, 100 m and 10 m.

Answer The kinetic energy of the truck is $\frac{1}{2} \times 40\,000 \times 20^2 = 8.0 \times 10^6 \, \text{J}$.

Since this is the braking force × the stopping distance then,

for a stopping distance of 1000 m the braking force needs to be 8000 N, for a stopping distance of 100 m the braking force needs to be 80 000 N,

for a stopping distance of 10 m the braking force needs to be 800 000 N.

You can see as the distance decreases, the force increases. This is why, in cases of serious accidents where vehicles stop in very short distances, much damage is caused.

Internal energy

Internal energy is the sum of the random potential and kinetic energy of all the molecules in the mass of matter being considered. Since molecules vibrate they are continually changing potential energy into kinetic energy and vice versa. Later in this book you will be able to deduce that the mean internal energy of any molecule at temperature T is given by $\frac{3kT}{2}$,

where k is a constant called the **Boltzmann constant**.

Chemical energy

When a chemical reaction occurs there is a rearrangement of the atoms in the reaction and often there is a release of energy. In a torch battery, the chemical reaction enabling a current to be produced reduces the chemical energy within the battery and causes the current.

Mechanical energy

This term is usually used in a rather vague way and is often applied to vehicles, aircraft and many types of machines. It often implies a mixture of energies such as kinetic and potential energy.

Power

Power is defined as the rate of doing work. That is the work done per unit time.

Average power $= \frac{\text{work done}}{\text{time taken}}$; in symbols $P = \frac{W}{t}$

The unit of power is the watt. One watt is one joule per second.

A problem here is what W represents. When it is in roman script W it represents the unit, watt. When it is in italic script W it represents work done. (There are not enough letters in the alphabet to give every quantity a different letter so you will have to be

particularly careful, especially with W and W. There is no problem if you write 'work' or 'watt'.)

Power in terms of velocity

When you are moving a bicycle with a speed of $10\,\text{m s}^{-1}$ and the driving force provided by you is 30 N, then the work done by you per second is given by

force × distance moved per second $= 30\,\text{N} \times 10\,\text{m s}^{-1}$

$$= 300\,\text{N m s}^{-1} = 300\,\text{J s}^{-1}$$

That is, your useful power output is 300 W.

You will not be able to keep up this power for long. Even a fit person would have difficulty sustaining a power of 100 W continuously.

From this calculation you can see that

force × velocity = power,   in symbols $F \times v = P$

Efficiency

The truck in Example 3 was travelling at $20\,\text{m s}^{-1}$ and had a mass of 40 tonnes. Its kinetic energy was 8.0 MJ. In ideal circumstances, 8.0 MJ would be required to get the truck up to that speed. In the real world, however, there are many ways in which energy can be wasted. Air resistance, drag on the tyres, internal friction in the gear box and other mechanical systems all result in energy being wasted in heating parts of the truck and the surroundings. Then there are inefficiencies in the engine itself when the chemical energy of the fuel has to be converted into work done by the engine.

Definition of Efficiency

Efficiency is defined by the following equation and it is normally quoted as a percentage.

$$\text{Efficiency} = \frac{\text{Useful energy output}}{\text{Total energy input in the same time}} \times 100\%$$

For internal combustion engines, the efficiency of diesel engines is usually greater than that for petrol engines. Typical figures for a well-tuned engine are around 55% for diesel engines and 40% for petrol engines. Theses figures may seem low but the laws of thermodynamics place limits on the maximum efficiency possible for an engine. The limits are determined by the temperature in the engine and the temperature of the surroundings. There is difficulty in converting disorganised energy, such as the kinetic energy of molecules moving in all directions in a hot gas, into ordered energy, such as a car moving along a road.

Figure 6.5 is a diagram known as a Sankey diagram. It shows how the power of a car's engine may be distributed between various useful and wasteful powers. The width of each arrow indicates the quantities of power. Sankey diagrams are not directly specified in the syllabus, but some students might find the ideas contained in these diagrams useful in understanding energy losses in practical devices.

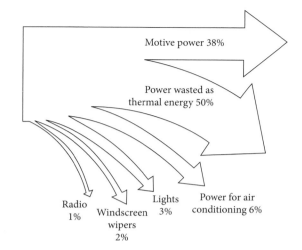

Figure 6.5

Chapter Summary

✓ Work is defined as the product of the force and the distance travelled in the direction of the force. It is measured in joules.

✓ Energy is defined as the stored ability to do work. It too, is measured in joules.

✓ Power is defined as the rate of doing work. It is measured in watts. $1\,\text{W} = 1\,\text{J}\,\text{s}^{-1}$

✓ Efficiency is the useful energy out of a system divided by the total energy input to the system. Often given as a percentage.

Table of different energy types.

Type of energy	Explanation	Equation for calculation
gravitational potential energy	energy an object can provide as a result of its change in position in a gravitational field	$\Delta E_{\text{p}} = mg\Delta h$
electrical potential energy	energy an object can provide as a result of its change in position in an electrical field	$E_{\text{e}} = Eqx$
kinetic energy	the energy an object can provide as a result of its change in speed	$E_{\text{k}} = \frac{1}{2}mv^2$
thermal energy	the energy an object can provide as a result of a change in its temperature	$Q = ms\Delta\theta$
elastic potential energy in a spring	the energy an object can provide from a stretched spring (or elastic)	$E = \frac{1}{2}Fx$
elastic potential energy in compressed gas	the energy that can be provided from a squashed gas	$E = p\Delta V$
internal energy	the sum of the potential and kinetic energies of the molecules in a gas	$E = \frac{3kT}{2}$
chemical energy	the energy available from rearranging the atoms in a reaction	

Progress Check

6.1 A person of mass 60 kg goes upstairs, a vertical distance of 2.8 m, in 4.7 s. Determine the work done and the minimum power output of the person.

6.2 A vehicle has a kinetic energy of 48 000 J.
   (a) Calculate the distance it will travel against a constant stopping force of 600 N.
   (b) The mass of the vehicle is 800 kg. Calculate its initial speed.

6.3 A car of mass 1200 kg is going to overtake another car and hence wants to increase its speed from 25 m s^{-1} to 30 m s^{-1}. Deduce
   (a) the increase in kinetic energy required for this,
   (b) the force necessary for the acceleration if it is to be completed in a distance of 100 m.

6.4 Explain why the work that has to be done on a train to accelerate it from zero speed to 10 m s^{-1} is not the same as the work done on it to increase its speed from 40 m s^{-1} to 50 m s^{-1}.

6.5 A person of mass 80 kg, travelling in a car at a speed of 25 m s^{-1}, is stopped in a distance of 43 m.
   (a) Calculate the force on the person during this braking period.
   (b) The brakes cause the wheels to turn less quickly, resulting in a drag force on the car. What two or three forces cause the drag on the person?

6.6 Calculate the increase in the potential energy of a person of mass 100 kg when going to the top of the Eiffel Tower, a height of 330 m.

6.7 (a) Calculate the minimum power necessary for an elevator to raise a mass of ten people of average mass 80 kg at a speed of 4.3 m s^{-1}.
   (b) Explain why the mass of the elevator itself is not required.

6.8 A ball, of mass 1.30 kg is thrown vertically upwards with a speed of 18.6 m s^{-1}.
   In rising, it reaches a height of 15.0 m. Calculate the work done by the ball against air resistance.

6.9 Copy and complete the following table to show the device, the type of energy supplied to the device, the type of energy wanted from the device and the energy wasted by the device. The last two rows are for any two additional devices.

Device	Energy supplied	Energy wanted	Energy wasted
car	chemical	kinetic/potential	thermal
television	electrical	light/sound	thermal
	electrical	kinetic	
loudspeaker			
microphone			
		potential	
candle			
	kinetic	electrical	
	nuclear		
	potential		

Examination Questions III

1. (a) State what is meant by *work done*. [1]

(b) A trolley of mass 400 g is moving at a constant velocity of 2.5 m s⁻¹ to the right as shown in Figure 1.

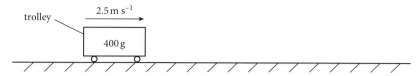

Figure 1

Show that the kinetic energy of the trolley is 1.3 J. [2]

(c) The trolley in **(b)** moves to point P as shown in Figure 2.

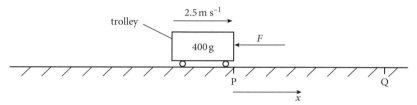

Figure 2

At point P the speed of the trolley is 2.5 m s⁻¹.

A variable force F acts to the left on the trolley as it moves between points P and Q.

The variation of F with displacement x from P is shown in Figure 3.

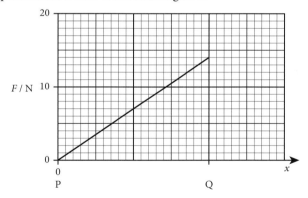

Figure 3

The trolley comes to rest at point Q.
(i) Calculate the distance PQ, in m. [3]

(ii) On Figure 4, sketch the variation with x of velocity v for the trolley moving between P and Q.

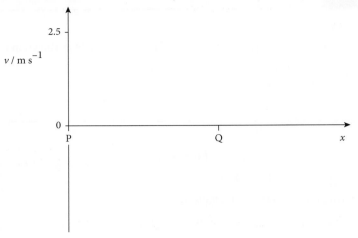

Figure 4   [2]

(Cambridge International AS and A Level Physics 9702 Paper 21 Question 3 October/November 2013)

2. (a) (i) Define *acceleration*.   [1]
            (ii) State Newton's first law of motion.   [1]

    (b) The variation with time t of vertical speed v of a parachutist falling from an aircraft is shown in Figure 5.

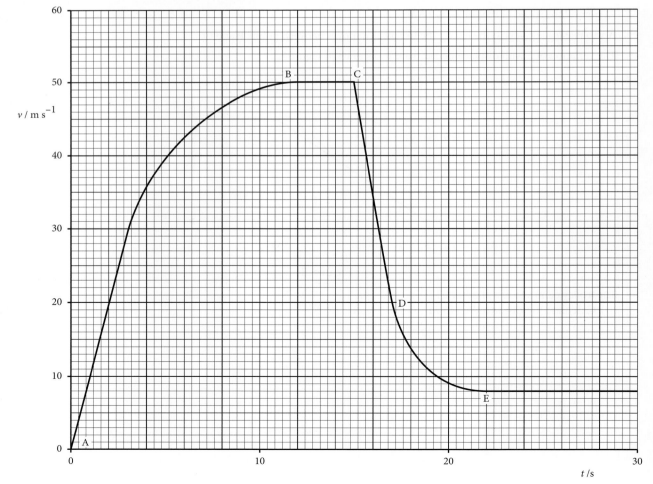

Figure 5

(i) Calculate the distance travelled by the parachutist, in m, in the first 3.0 s of the motion. [2]
(ii) Explain the variation of the resultant force acting on the parachutist from $t = 0$
(point A) to $t = 15$ s (point C). [3]
(iii) Describe the changes to the frictional force on the parachutist
1. at $t = 15$ s (point C), [1]
2. between $t = 15$ s (point C) and $t = 22$ s (point E). [1]
(iv) The mass of the parachutist is 95 kg.
Calculate, for the parachutist between $t = 15$ s (point C) and $t = 17$ s (point D),
1. the average acceleration, in m s^{-2}, [2]
2. the average frictional force, in N. [3]

**(Cambridge International AS and A Level Physics 9702
Paper 21 Question 1 October/November 2012)**

3. (a) (i) State the SI base units of volume. [1]
(ii) Show that the SI base units of pressure are kg m^{-1} s^{-2}. [1]

(b) The volume V of liquid that flows through a pipe in time t is given by the equation

$$\frac{V}{t} = \frac{\pi P r^4}{8Cl}$$

where P is the pressure difference between the ends of the pipe of radius r and length l.

The constant C depends on the frictional effects of the liquid.

Determine the base units of C. [3]

**(Cambridge International AS and A Level Physics 9702
Paper 21 Question 1 May/June 2012)**

4. A ball is thrown against a vertical wall. The path of the ball is shown in Figure 6.

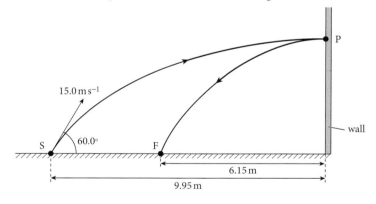

Figure 6

The ball is thrown from S with an initial velocity of 15.0 m s^{-1} at 60.0° to the horizontal. Assume that air resistance is negligible.
(a) For the ball at S, calculate
(i) its horizontal component of velocity, in m s^{-1}, [1]
(ii) its vertical component of velocity, in m s^{-1}. [1]

(b) The horizontal distance from S to the wall is 9.95 m. The ball hits the wall at P with a velocity that is at right angles
to the wall. The ball rebounds to a point F that is 6.15 m from the wall.

Using your answers in (a),
(i) calculate the vertical height gained by the ball, in m, when it travels from S to P, [1]
(ii) show that the time taken for the ball to travel from S to P is 1.33 s, [1]
(iii) show that the velocity of the ball immediately after rebounding from the wall is about 4.6 m s^{-1}. [1]

(c) The mass of the ball is 60×10^{-3} kg.
    (i) Calculate the change in momentum of the ball, in N s, as it rebounds from the wall. [2]
    (ii) State and explain whether the collision is elastic or inelastic. [1]

(Cambridge International AS and A Level Physics 9702
Paper 21 Question 3 October/November 2011)

5. (a) Distinguish between *gravitational potential energy* and *electric potential energy*. [2]

  (b) A body of mass m moves vertically through a distance h near the Earth's surface. Use the defining equation for work done to derive an expression for the gravitational potential energy change of the body. [2]

  (c) Water flows down a stream from a reservoir and then causes a water wheel to rotate, as shown in Figure 7.

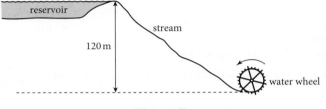

Figure 7

As the water falls through a vertical height of 120 m, gravitational potential energy is converted to different forms of energy, including kinetic energy of the water. At the water wheel, the kinetic energy of the water is only 10% of its gravitational potential energy at the reservoir.
    (i) Show that the speed of the water as it reaches the wheel is $15\,\mathrm{m\,s^{-1}}$. [2]
    (ii) The rotating water wheel is used to produce 110 kW of electrical power. Calculate the mass of water flowing per second through the wheel, in $\mathrm{kg\,s^{-1}}$, assuming that the production of electric energy from the kinetic energy of the water is 25% efficient. [3]

(Cambridge International AS and A Level Physics 9702
Paper 21 Question 4 October/November 2011)

Deformation of Solids 7

Introduction

The application of a pair of squeezing or stretching forces to a solid will cause a change in the shape of a solid. This chapter will deal only with solids, because for liquids and gases, changes in shape are dependent on the container holding them.

Tension and compression

When a solid rod has two forces applied to it in the way shown in Figure 7.1(a), its length increases by a small amount and the rod is said to undergo tensile deformation. If the forces are reversed and the rod is squeezed, as shown in Figure 7.1(b), its length decreases a little and it is said to undergo compressive deformation.

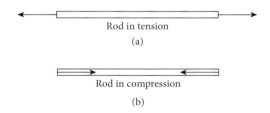

Rod in tension

(a)

Rod in compression

(b)

Figure 7.1

The fact that the rod can be deformed in these ways implies two things for the rod:

- separation of molecules in the rod can be affected by external forces applied to it, and
- percentage changes in the separation of molecules are usually very small.

In everyday life, the changes in shapes of most solids are not noticed. When you put your dinner plate down on a table you do not notice that the table has sagged a little under the weight; when you sit on a swing you do not notice that the steel chain holding the seat has stretched as a result. As you drive a car over a suspension bridge you are not aware that the chains supporting the bridge have become longer, or

that when you reach the other side of the bridge, the chains go back to their original length.

Changes in the separation distance between molecules in the examples quoted above are small and reversible. Any change in the shape of a solid as a result of forces being applied to it and which returns to its original shape when the forces are removed is said to be an **elastic deformation**. Elastic deformation is very common with most objects we use daily and is usually so small that it is not noticed.

Springs

The effects described in the previous section can be exaggerated if the solid is not a straight rod but is coiled into a spring. It then becomes easier to measure any extension or compression that takes place. Figure 7.2 shows on the left-hand side a spring without any load on it attached to a horizontal support. The right-hand side shows the effect of attaching a load to the spring.

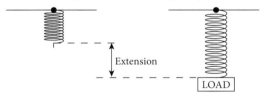

Extension

LOAD

Figure 7.2

As a result of placing the load on the spring, a pair of forces causes the extension to occur. The first of these forces is the downward force the load exerts on the spring. This will be equal to the weight of the load provided the load is at rest. The second force is the upward force the support exerts on the spring. Once the spring is at rest these two forces are equal.

When an experiment is carried out, a graph of extension against load might be as shown in Figure 7.3. Note that when a pair of forces, each of magnitude F, stretches a spring, the tension in the spring is said to be F and not $2F$.

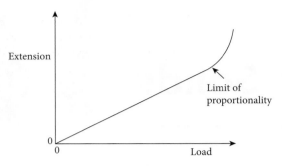

Figure 7.3

For tensions up to a certain value the graph is a straight line. The final point on the straight line is called the **limit of proportionality**, for the obvious reason that the extension is proportional to the tension up to that point. After this point the extension increases at a greater rate.

Hooke's law

For the straight line portion of the graph Hooke's law applies. This states that for tensions up to a certain value, the extension is proportional to the tension. Within this range the value of the tension per unit extension is called the **spring constant**.

When the experiment is carried out over the full range of tension, it is found, on removing the load so the tension falls to zero, that the spring has been permanently stretched. This deformation starts at values of tension close to the limit of proportionality. The **elastic limit** is the point at which permanent deformation starts. Beyond the elastic limit, the spring is said to show plastic deformation.

Elastic and plastic deformation of a material

The terms **elastic** and **plastic** can be applied generally to all deformations. An elastic deformation of a material is one in which the material regains its original shape once the deforming forces are removed. A plastic deformation is one where a permanent change in shape takes place.

In many respects the manufacturing of an object, such as a frying pan, involves using large forces to mould a piece of metal permanently into a suitable shape. The manufacturer makes a plastic deformation of the sheet of metal. In use, the frying pan undergoes only elastic deformation. Its permanent shape remains the same perhaps

for many years (unless it has been dented by being knocked or dropped).

In terms of molecules, an elastic deformation means that any change in the mean separation of the molecules is zero once the deforming forces are removed. For a plastic deformation, the molecules are rearranged within the material. Diagrammatically this is shown in Figure 7.4.

Figure 7.4

Teacher's Tip

Elastic deformation of an object is reversible. Articles used in daily life undergo frequent, small elastic deformations.
Plastic deformation is permanent. In manufacture, basic materials are deliberately shaped by plastic deformation. (If you make a dent in something by dropping it accidentally you have caused a plastic deformation.)

The Young modulus

This oddly named quantity is used for solids, often as wires, to indicate how much the solid distorts when subjected to tensile forces. Wires come in many different lengths and diameters so the Young modulus must involve the length and area of cross-section of any wire. It does so by using two additional terms. These are **stress** and **strain**.

Stress is the tensile force per unit area, and strain is the extension per unit original length.

The Young modulus E is defined as the ratio of stress to strain for an elastic deformation. This gives

$$\text{Young modulus} = \frac{\text{stress}}{\text{strain}} = \frac{\dfrac{\text{tensile force}}{\text{area of cross-section}}}{\dfrac{\text{extension}}{\text{original length}}}$$

$$= \frac{\dfrac{F}{\pi r^2}}{\dfrac{e}{L}} = \frac{FL}{\pi r^2 e}$$

The measurement of the Young modulus

Figure 7.5 shows one arrangement that can conveniently be used to measure the Young modulus of the metal of a copper wire.

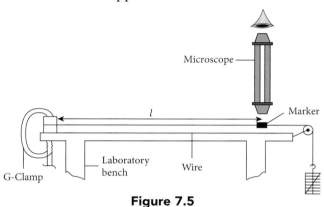

Figure 7.5

A long length of copper wire is clamped at one end and the other end passes over a pulley and is attached to a set of hanger weights. The wire needs to be free of kinks so the hanger by itself needs to pull the wire taut. A marker is placed on the wire near the pulley and the edge of the marker is viewed through a travelling microscope. This is a standard microscope mounted on a moveable arm which is attached to one side of a vernier scale. The other side of the vernier is attached to the framework of the microscope so that, as the microscope moves, different vernier readings enable the distance of movement of the microscope to be calculated. Typical readings taken for such an experiment are given in Table 7.1.

Table 7.1

Mass added to hanger (g)	Tensile force (N)	Reading on vernier scale (mm)	Total extension caused by tensile force (mm)
0	0	3.26	0
100	0.98	5.39	2.13
200	1.96	7.78	4.52
300	2.94	9.89	6.63
400	3.92	12.90	9.64
500	4.91	15.03	11.77
600	5.89	17.15	13.89
700	6.87	19.30	16.04
800	7.85	21.42	18.16
900	8.83	25.93	22.67
1000	9.81	32 ?	29 ?

A sketch graph of force against extension is shown for these readings in Figure 7.6. (For a reason given later, this graph is unusual in the sense that the quantity the experimenter changes, the independent variable, is on the y-axis and the quantity that changes as a consequence, the dependent variable, is on the x-axis.)

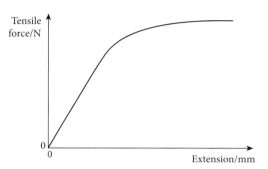

Figure 7.6

As you can see from the table, after the tensile force exceeds 7.85 N, the wire stretches considerably. This is because it becomes plastic. All the readings for the Young modulus need to be taken from the straight line part of the graph. The question marks in the table are because at this stage values do not stay constant. The wire shows creep: it stretches under a constant tensile force.

The calculation requires two additional items of data. They are:

radius r of wire = 0.125 mm/2 = 0.0625 mm
$$= 6.25 \times 10^{-5}\,\text{m}$$

length l of wire = 3.324 m

Note carefully from Figure 7.5 where this distance is measured. It is not the total length of wire. It is the distance from the clamp to the edge of the marker.

Now the area A of cross-section can be calculated.
$$A = \pi r^2 = \pi \times (6.25 \times 10^{-5})^2 = 1.227 \times 10^{-8}\,\text{m}^2$$
So the Young modulus for copper is given by
$$E = \frac{Fl}{Ae} = \frac{F}{e} \times \frac{3.324\,\text{m}}{1.227 \times 10^{-8}\,\text{m}^2}$$
where $\frac{F}{e}$ is the gradient of an accurately drawn graph giving
$$E = \frac{7.75\,\text{N}}{0.0180\,\text{m}} \times \frac{3.324\,\text{m}}{1.227 \times 10^{-8}\,\text{m}^2}$$
$$= 1.17 \times 10^{11}\,\text{N m}^{-2}$$

The unit $N\,m^{-2}$ is the unit of pressure, the pascal Pa.

Values of the Young modulus for other materials are given in Table 7.2.

Table 7.2

Material	Young modulus (Pa)
Aluminium	7.1×10^{10}
Glass	8.0×10^{10}
Iron	21×10^{10}
Lead	1.8×10^{10}
Tin	4.0×10^{10}
Polypropylene	0.12×10^{10}

One final point on this calculation. Most mistakes made in carrying out this calculation are not due to lack of understanding of the principles of the topic but due to

- using diameter rather than radius of the wire,
- getting the powers of 10 incorrect, e.g. by using millimetres instead of metres. This will show in getting a result that is not of the order of 10^{10}, and
- assuming that all the wire is under test rather than that between the clamp and the marker.

Teacher's Tip

Always double check powers of 10 when making this type of calculation. Often a power of 10 calculation error will result in a nonsense answer. For example, you are unlikely to have a wire with a diameter of 0.25 m, so always think about the meaning of any answer you obtain and start trying to find the mistake by looking for a power of 10 mistake. Here the wire's diameter is probably 0.25 mm, so 0.000 25 m.

Categories of materials

So far in this chapter the emphasis has been on metal wires behaving elastically, but many different materials are used in a large variety of manufacturing processes. One important quantity for any material is called its **ultimate tensile stress**. This is the maximum tensile stress that can be applied to the material before it breaks.

Materials can be put into categories according to their behaviour under stress. The following shapes of force–extension graphs correspond to different behaviour. Some materials can occur in several categories depending on the method of

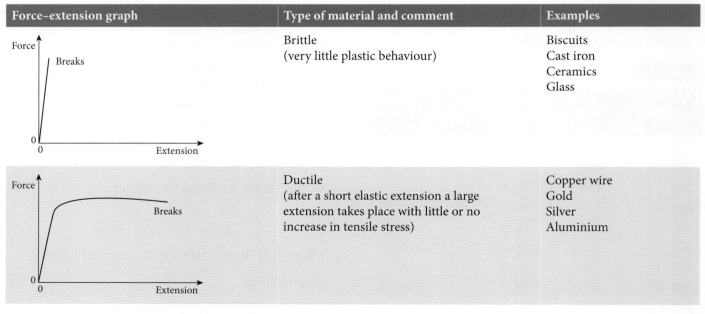

Force–extension graph	Type of material and comment	Examples
Force ↑, Breaks, 0 — Extension	Brittle (very little plastic behaviour)	Biscuits Cast iron Ceramics Glass
Force ↑, Breaks, 0 — Extension	Ductile (after a short elastic extension a large extension takes place with little or no increase in tensile stress)	Copper wire Gold Silver Aluminium

(Continued)

(Continued)

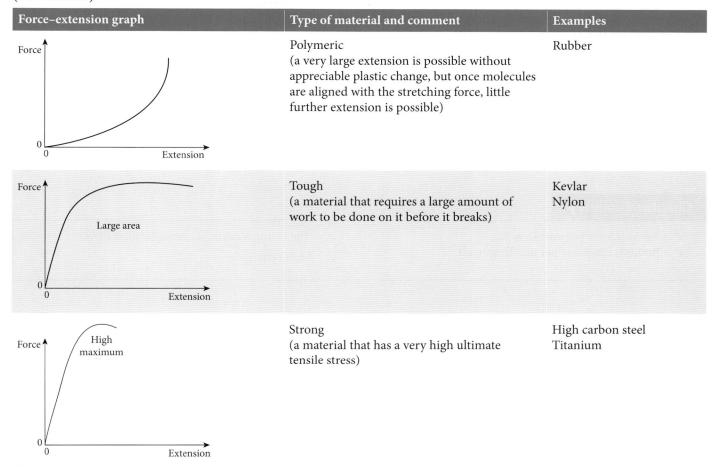

Force–extension graph	Type of material and comment	Examples
Force / Extension (curve rising steeply)	Polymeric (a very large extension is possible without appreciable plastic change, but once molecules are aligned with the stretching force, little further extension is possible)	Rubber
Force / Extension (curve with "Large area")	Tough (a material that requires a large amount of work to be done on it before it breaks)	Kevlar Nylon
Force / Extension (curve with "High maximum")	Strong (a material that has a very high ultimate tensile stress)	High carbon steel Titanium

manufacturing and the environment in which they are used. For example, a material with fine cracks in it will be less strong than one without cracks.

Strain energy

Work needs to be done on a wire to stretch it. If the wire is behaving elastically, then the amount of work done on it to stretch it will result in the wire having elastic potential energy called the **strain energy**.

The amount of work done on a wire during an elastic extension will be the average force multiplied by the extension. Figure 7.7 shows that this is also the area beneath the force–extension graph and explains why these graphs are drawn with extension on the x-axis.

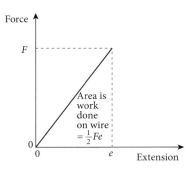

Figure 7.7

Once plastic extension takes place, the work done is still equal to the area beneath the graph, but this results in the material warming up so the energy stored as elastic potential energy does not increase any further. Note that plastic deformation graphs will usually only be able to be drawn when working in one direction. Figure 7.8 shows that the work done in stretching a material and then reducing the tensile stress to zero involves work being done equivalent to areas A + B. Only energy equivalent to area B can be used to do work when the tensile stress is returned to zero.

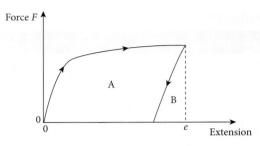

Figure 7.8

Chapter Summary

✓   Stress is force per unit area, F/A

✓   Strain is extension per unit length, e/L

✓   The Young Modulus is stress/strain = FL/Ae

✓   Strain energy = $\frac{1}{2}Fe$

Progress Check

7.1 A spring has a spring constant of $180\,\text{N}\,\text{m}^{-1}$.
A mass of $0.360\,\text{kg}$ is suspended by the spring.
   (a) Calculate the extension of the spring.
   (b) The elastic limit and the limit of proportionality for the spring both occur at an extension of $12.5\,\text{cm}$. Calculate the mass that can be suspended from the spring before plastic distortion occurs.

7.2 A steel wire has a Young modulus of $2.10 \times 10^{11}\,\text{Pa}$, an area of cross-section of $4.76 \times 10^{-6}\,\text{m}^2$ and a length of $3.27\,\text{m}$. A tension of $200\,\text{N}$ is applied to it. Calculate the stress in the wire, the strain in the wire and the extension produced.

7.3 Suggest a suitable material for the following applications. Give your answer in a similar way to the following example:

Making the support cables for a suspension bridge: a strong material such as steel with a high tensile stress
   (a) Holding together a bundle of letters
   (b) Making the sole of a shoe
   (c) Forming the bodywork of a car
   (d) As a tow rope
   (e) As body armour
   (f) As a building brick

7.4 A shock absorber in the suspension of a truck contains a spring of spring constant $60\,\text{kN}\,\text{m}^{-1}$. Under normal use conditions, it is compressed by a distance of $20\,\text{cm}$. How much energy will it absorb when the truck goes over a bump and the spring is compressed by a further $11\,\text{cm}$?

1. (a) Define electrical *resistance*. [1]

(b) A circuit is set up to measure the resistance R of a metal wire. The potential difference (p.d.) V across the wire and the current I in the wire are to be measured.

(i) Draw a circuit diagram of the apparatus that could be used to make these measurements. [3]

(ii) Readings for p.d. V and the corresponding current I are obtained. These are shown in Figure 1.

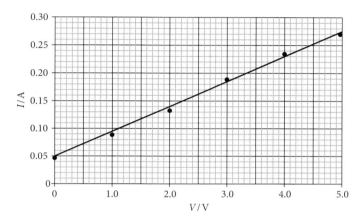

Figure 1

Explain how Figure 1 indicates that the readings are subject to

1. a systematic uncertainty, [1]
2. random uncertainties. [1]

(iii) Use data from Figure 1 to determine R. Explain your working. [3]

(c) In another experiment, a value of R is determined from the following data:

Current $I = 0.64 \pm 0.01$ A and p.d. $V = 6.8 \pm 0.1$ V.

Calculate the value of R, in Ω, together with its uncertainty. Give your answer to an appropriate number of significant figures. [3]

**(Cambridge International AS and A Level Physics 9702
Paper 21 Question 2 October/November 2012)**

2. (a) Define *pressure*. [1]

(b) Explain, in terms of the air molecules, why the pressure at the top of a mountain is less than at sea level. [3]

(c) Figure 2 shows a liquid in a cylindrical container.

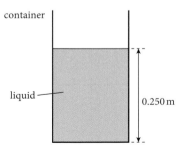

container

liquid

0.250 m

Figure 2

The cross-sectional area of the container is $0.450\,\text{m}^2$. The height of the column of liquid is $0.250\,\text{m}$ and the density of the liquid is $13\,600\,\text{kg}\,\text{m}^{-3}$.

(i) Calculate the weight of the column of liquid, in N. [3]
(ii) Calculate the pressure on the base of the container, in Pa, caused by the weight of the liquid. [1]
(iii) Explain why the pressure exerted on the base of the container is different from the value calculated in (ii).

[1]

(Cambridge International AS and A Level Physics 9702 Paper 21 Question 3 October/November 2012)

3. One end of a spring is fixed to a support. A mass is attached to the other end of the spring.

The arrangement is shown in Figure 3.

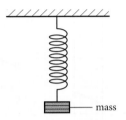

Figure 3

(a) The mass is in equilibrium. Explain, by reference to the forces acting on the mass, what is meant by equilibrium. [2]

(b) The mass is pulled down and then released at time $t = 0$. The mass oscillates up and down. The variation with t of the displacement of the mass d is shown in Figure 4.

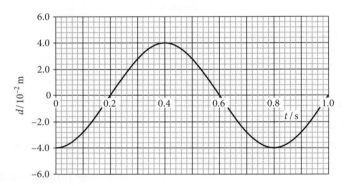

Figure 4

Use Figure 4 to state a time, in s, one in each case, when
 (i) the mass is at maximum speed, [1]
(ii) the elastic potential energy stored in the spring is a maximum, [1]
(iii) the mass is in equilibrium. [1]

(c) The arrangement shown in Figure 5 is used to determine the length l of a spring when different masses M are attached to the spring.

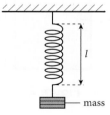

Figure 5

The variation with mass M of l is shown in Figure 6.

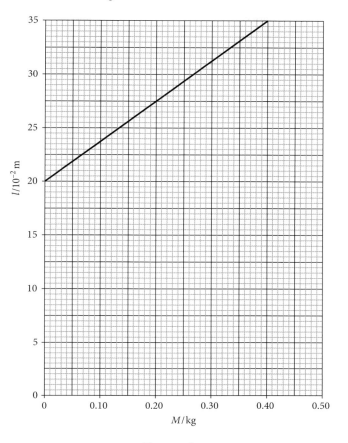

Figure 6

 (i) State and explain whether the spring obeys Hooke's law. [2]
(ii) Show that the force constant of the spring is $26\,\mathrm{N\,m^{-1}}$. [2]
(iii) A mass of $0.40\,\mathrm{kg}$ is attached to the spring. Calculate the energy stored in the spring, in J. [3]

**(Cambridge International AS and A Level Physics 9702
Paper 21 Question 3 May/June 2012)**

Waves

Introduction

Everyone is familiar with waves, but the mental image of waves inevitably centres on water waves on a beach – and these waves are not at all typical of the vast majority of waves. The reason that waves break on a beach is because as they get into shallow water, their speed decreases. This also means that the crest of a water wave moves faster than the trough and so eventually the crest becomes unstable. This might be good fun to play in, but other waves do not break in this way. In this chapter the waves that we shall study are waves that are essential for life or are useful in other ways. Those that are essential for life are light waves from the Sun that are used by plants in photosynthesis and infra-red waves, also from the Sun, that keep the Earth's temperature at about 290 K. Then there are sound waves that enable audio communication between people and waves, such as radio waves and microwaves that have become so important during the last century or so.

All waves have some features in common despite their differences.

Wave motion

It is obvious that waves move. The direction of movement and what is actually moving is not so obvious. If a slinky spring is placed on the floor with one end fixed and the other end oscillated once sideways, a wave pattern moves forward along the slinky although the individual coils of the slinky are only moving from side to side. Figure 8.1 shows this and also shows the problem of illustrating a moving pattern on a piece of paper.

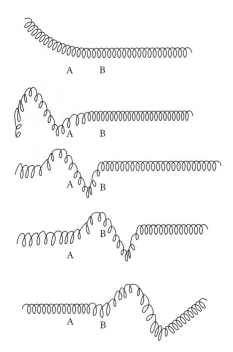

Figure 8.1

In order to understand wave movement it is important to remember that, in the case of wave movement along a slinky, each coil copies the pattern of movement of the coil just before it, but with a small time delay. Using Figure 8.1 again, coil B moves with the same pattern of movement as coil A but it is a fraction of a second behind A. The net result is that the pulse moves forward. The same principle applies with all wave movement.

Water waves in a ripple tank, and air particles in a trumpet, see Fig. 8.2, all rely on adjacent particles copying the movement of particles behind them and hence propagating the wave. The particles oscillate, the wave moves forward. It is, of course, energy that is moving forward.

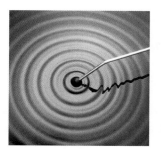

(a) Water waves in a ripple tank

(b) A trumpet being played

Figure 8.2

Wave terminology

Figure 8.3 represents a snapshot of a standardised wave at one instant of time. Figure 8.4 represents, for the *same* wave, how the oscillation at point X on Figure 8.3 varies with time.

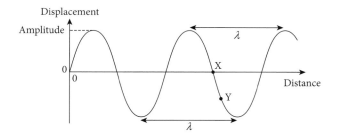

Figure 8.3

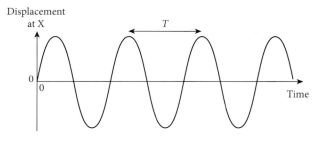

Figure 8.4

Both of these graphs show the displacement of a particle within the wave. The **displacement** of a particle is its movement from the rest position. Its value may be positive or negative. The **amplitude** of a wave is the maximum value of the displacement. It will always be positive.

The *x*-axis of Figure 8.3 is distance. The distance between adjacent crests of this graph is the **wavelength** (λ). The wavelength is also the distance between any two adjacent points having the same pattern of movement.

The *x*-axis of Figure 8.4 is time. The time taken for one complete cycle of oscillation is called the **period** (T) of the wave. The **frequency** (f) is the number of waves occurring per unit time. The unit of frequency is the hertz, Hz. One hertz is 1 wave per second.

If $T = 0.10$ s then 10 waves per second are formed and the frequency is 10 Hz.

The period is always the reciprocal of the frequency, $T = 1/f$.

The standard multipliers of hertz are often used with frequencies. Radio waves, for example, have a large range of frequencies and may be measured in kHz, MHz or GHz, that is in thousands, millions or billions of cycles per second. Light has a much higher frequency than this, but is restricted to quite a small range of frequencies namely, 4.3×10^{14} Hz for red to 7.5×10^{14} Hz for violet.

Phase difference

Figure 8.5 shows in black how particles at X in Figure 8.3 move with time.

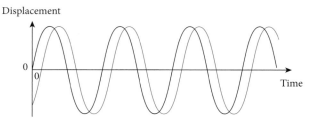

Figure 8.5

It also shows in purple how particles at Y move with time. The two graphs have the same amplitude, period and frequency but are said to be **out of phase** with one another. The movement at Y is a fixed time after the corresponding movement at X. There is no meaning to the expression "the phase of a wave".

Phase difference between two waves does make sense. Phase difference can be measured as a fraction of a complete cycle rather than as a time. One complete cycle of a wave can be regarded as an angle of 2π radians. (You will learn about the reasoning behind this later in the course if you have not studied radian measure for angles already.) The black movement in Figure 8.5 is one-eighth of a cycle in front of (*not* behind – it takes place earlier) the purple movement, so we say that the black movement is out of phase with the purple movement and leading by an angle of $\pi/4$ radians. Note that it could equally well be lagging by $7\pi/4$ radians.

> ### Teacher's Tip
>
> Make sure you convert phase angles to radians and fractions of a cycle correctly. This table gives some of the values and shows the way the different measures are related.
>
> | Fraction of a cycle | 0 | $\frac{1}{8}$ | $\frac{1}{4}$ | $\frac{1}{2}$ | $\frac{3}{4}$ | 1 |
> |---|---|---|---|---|---|---|
> | angle in degrees | 0 | 45 | 90 | 180 | 270 | 360 |
> | angle in radians | 0 | $\frac{1}{4}\pi$ | $\frac{1}{2}\pi$ | π | $1\frac{1}{2}\pi$ | 2π |

One final point on phase difference is that when two waves are as shown in Figure 8.6, they are said to be in anti-phase with one another. They are π radians out of phase with one another.

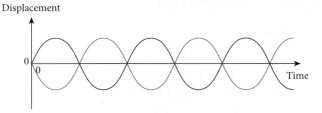

Figure 8.6

Wave speed

If the wavelength of a particular wave is 6.0 metres and 30 waves pass a point every second, then the speed of travel of the waves must be $6.0\,\text{m} \times 30\,\text{s}^{-1} = 180\,\text{m}\,\text{s}^{-1}$.

This is an example of the general equation for wave speed and can be written as

$$\text{Speed} = \frac{\text{wavelength}}{\text{period}} = \text{frequency} \times \text{wavelength}$$

$$\text{Or} \quad v = \frac{\lambda}{T} = f\lambda$$

Be careful when using this equation to get the powers of 10 correct, as frequency and wavelength are often given with prefixes, micro, milli, kilo, ..., etc.

Example 1

Find the speed of a microwave that has a wavelength of 6.0 cm and a frequency of 5.0 GHz.

Answer $f = 5.0\,\text{GHz} = 5.0 \times 10^9\,\text{Hz}$

$\lambda = 6.0\,\text{cm} = 0.060\,\text{m} = 6.0 \times 10^{-2}\,\text{m}$

$v = f\lambda = 5.0 \times 10^9\,\text{Hz} \times 6.0 \times 10^{-2}\,\text{m} = 30 \times 10^7\,\text{m}\,\text{s}^{-1}$

$= 3.0 \times 10^8\,\text{m}\,\text{s}^{-1}$

As you might have expected, microwaves, like light, travel at the speed at which all electromagnetic waves travel in a vacuum.

Energy transfer by a progressive wave

Waves are said to be progressive when they transfer energy from the source of the wave. In the introduction to this chapter, it was mentioned that infra-red waves from the Sun spread out and some of the total energy emitted by the Sun reaches the Earth. The infra-red waves are progressive waves because they transfer energy from the Sun to the Earth.

The same is true for a sound wave generated by a loudspeaker. When you hear the sound, it is because energy transference has taken place, by means of the sound wave, from the loudspeaker to your ear.

Wave intensity

The **intensity** of a wave is the power supplied by the wave per unit area of the receiver. The intensity of some useful waves seems very small. For example, a young person can hear a sound at a frequency of 1 kHz when the intensity at his or her ear is only $10^{-12}\,\text{W}\,\text{m}^{-2}$. Since the area of sound collected by the ear is roughly $10^{-3}\,\text{m}^2$, this means that the power received by the ear is only

$$10^{-12}\,\text{W}\,\text{m}^{-2} \times 10^{-3}\,\text{m}^2 = 10^{-15}\,\text{W}.$$

A millionth of a billionth of a watt!

Example 2

The footprint of the transmitted TV signal from a satellite can be as much as a circle of radius 2000 km as shown in Figure 8.7. If the power transmitted in the signal is 1.8 kW, what is the power received by a dish aerial of area 0.10 m²?

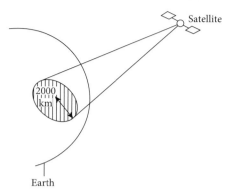

Figure 8.7

Answer The area of the footprint $= \pi \times (2.0 \times 10^6)^2$
$$= 1.26 \times 10^{13}\,\text{m}^2$$

Intensity at Earth's surface $= 1800\,\text{W}/1.26 \times 10^{13}\,\text{m}^2$
$$= 1.4 \times 10^{-10}\,\text{W m}^{-2}$$

Therefore, power received by the dish
$$= 1.4 \times 10^{-10}\,\text{W m}^{-2} \times 0.10\,\text{m}^2$$
$$= 1.4 \times 10^{-11}\,\text{W} = 14\,\text{pW (14 picowatts)}$$

The relationship between the amplitude and the intensity of a wave

Any wave involves oscillation and the average speed in any oscillation depends on the frequency and the amplitude of the oscillation. For a wave of any given frequency, the average speed is directly proportional to the amplitude. Since the kinetic energy of any particle oscillating in a wave is proportional to v^2, the kinetic energy of all the particles in a wave and hence the intensity of the wave is proportional to the amplitude squared.

$$\text{intensity} \propto (\text{amplitude})^2$$

This is true for all waves and is the reason why so much damage is caused by water waves in a storm. If the waves have amplitude ten times their usual value, the intensity of the waves is one hundred times normal and this can be very destructive.

Transverse and longitudinal waves

The direction in which water particles move in a water wave in a ripple tank is up and down, i.e. at right-angles to the direction of motion of the wave.

This type of wave is called a **transverse** wave. Other examples of transverse waves are all the waves in the electromagnetic spectrum, including waves such as radio waves, microwaves, X-rays and light. In other types of wave, the direction of vibration of the particles is in the direction in which the wave is travelling. These waves are called **longitudinal** waves.

A slinky spring is useful for illustrating the differences between these two categories of waves as shown in Figures 8.8(a) and 8.8(b).

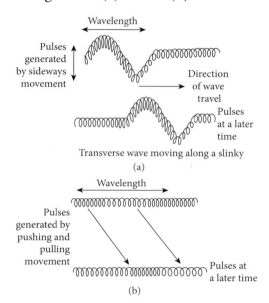

Figure 8.8

The normal wave terminology can be used for both categories of waves. Each has a frequency, a wavelength, a velocity, an amplitude and a period. The real problem with longitudinal waves is that they are difficult to draw convincingly. Diagrams often make them look like transverse waves, as in Figure 8.9. Note that on this diagram the label on the vertical axis is the *horizontal* displacement. Sound waves are longitudinal waves and so are pressure waves travelling through fluids.

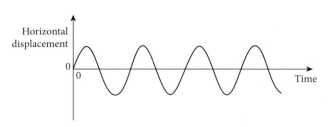

Figure 8.9

When an earthquake occurs on the far side of the Earth from a seismic recording station, the only waves following a direct route from the earthquake to the station are longitudinal waves. This is because transverse shock waves cannot travel through a liquid and the greater part of the core of the Earth is liquid. Observations of waves such as these enabled scientists to determine the structure of the interior of the Earth.

Sound waves

As with the slinky shown in Figure 8.8(b), a sound wave consists of a region where pressure is increased, so that molecules are pushed closer together (**compression**), followed by a region where molecules are further apart (**rarefaction**). This is shown in Figure 8.10. The effect of a sound wave entering your ear is, therefore, a succession of high and low pressure regions. With high pressure your eardrum is pushed inwards a little and with low pressure your eardrum moves out a little.

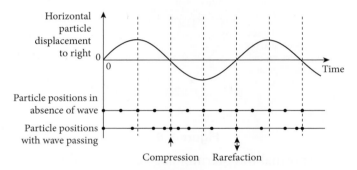

Figure 8.10

Experimental techniques

To determine the frequency of a sound wave using a calibrated oscilloscope

The calibration on an oscilloscope normally gives ranges of values for the speed with which the spot moves in the x-direction when forming the trace. Set the speed to a value such as 1 millisecond per centimetre (1 ms per cm) of grid on the screen.

Connect a microphone to the y-input and place the microphone near the source of sound you are using. The source needs to have a reliably constant frequency. If it is not an electronically generated sound, it needs to be generated for an appreciable

time. A percussion note is not suitable but a long note played on a woodwind instrument, such as an oboe, works well. Adjust the gain of the oscilloscope so that, with the source you are using the wave trace occupies at least half the height of the screen.

Calculate the frequency of the source when the screen appears as shown in Figure 8.11(a) and calculate the two frequencies present when the screen appears as shown in Figure 8.11(b).

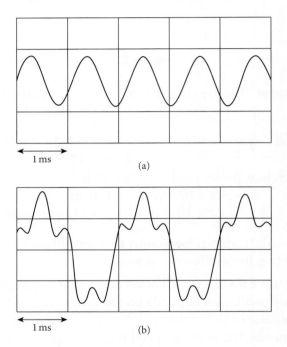

Figure 8.11

To determine the wavelength of a sound wave using a stationary wave

In the next chapter more detail will be given about stationary waves but, for this experiment, to measure the wavelength of a sound wave you need to know that when the air column inside a pipe produces a sound, the note is determined by a relationship between the length of the pipe and the wavelength of the sound. This is why musical instruments require fingering to adjust the lengths of strings and tubes.

Nearly fill a long measuring cylinder with water and place a tube, open at both ends into it as shown in Figure 8.12.

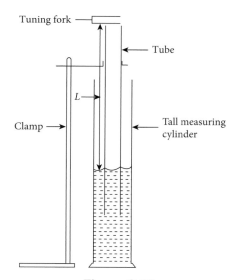

Figure 8.12

Holding the tube loosely in the clamp, hit a tuning fork on a cork and place it over the tube as you adjust the length L of the tube above the water. There are positions of the tube where the sound of the tuning fork is particularly clear. This takes a bit of practice. The sound is not particularly loud but it is definitely audible and you have to get the position quite accurately: a few millimetres either way and the sound cannot be heard. A stationary wave has been set up in the air in the tube and this occurs when the length of the air column in the tube is equal to $\frac{1}{4}\lambda$

or $\frac{3}{4}\lambda$. The distance between these two positions is, therefore, $\frac{1}{2}\lambda$ and twice this value will give the wavelength of the sound from the tuning fork.

The electromagnetic spectrum

All electromagnetic waves travel at the same speed in a vacuum. The speed is approximately $3.00 \times 10^8 \,\mathrm{m\,s^{-1}}$.

(The speed is now exactly, by definition, $2.997\,924\,58 \times 10^8 \,\mathrm{m\,s^{-1}}$. Giving the definition this way actually defines the metre itself.)

During your course it is important that you learn the order of magnitude of the wavelengths of the principal radiations of the electromagnetic spectrum. These are given in Table 8.1 together with some extra information for reference. Note that there are considerable overlaps of wavelength. For example, short wavelength X-rays have a shorter wavelength than long wavelength γ-rays even though γ-rays are generally regarded as having shorter wavelength than X-rays. It is the method of production or detection that is used to categorise these waves. X-rays are produced from electrons losing energy but γ-rays are produced from the nucleus of atoms.

Table 8.1

Category	Wavelength (m)	Frequency (Hz)	Source	Some of its uses
Gamma rays (γ)	$10^{-16} \rightarrow 10^{-10}$	$10^{24} \rightarrow 10^{18}$	From nuclear reactions	Cancer treatment
X-rays	$10^{-12} \rightarrow 10^{-8}$	$10^{20} \rightarrow 10^{16}$	Stopping high speed electrons	Cancer treatment, X-ray images, CT scans, checking items in packs at the end of a production line
Ultra-violet	$10^{-8} \rightarrow 4 \times 10^{-7}$	$10^{16} \rightarrow 7 \times 10^{14}$	Sun, special lamps	Sunburn/tanning, fluorescence
Light	$4 \times 10^{-7} \rightarrow 7 \times 10^{-7}$	$7 \times 10^{14} \rightarrow 4 \times 10^{14}$	Sun lamps	Vision, photography
Infra-red	$7 \times 10^{-7} \rightarrow 10^{-3}$	$4 \times 10^{14} \rightarrow 10^{11}$	Hot bodies	Radiators, hot plates, night vision photos
Microwaves	$10^{-4} \rightarrow 10^{-1}$	$10^{12} \rightarrow 10^{9}$	A cavity with electrons passing its opening	Microwave cookers, radar, mobile phones, satellite navigation
Radio waves	$10^{-2} \rightarrow 10^{+4}$	$10^{10} \rightarrow 10^{4}$	Accelerated electrons in an aerial	Radio and television

The Doppler effect

When a source of waves moves relative to a stationary observer, the pattern of wavefronts changes from the series of concentric circles obtained when the source is stationary. The new pattern is shown in Figure 8.13.

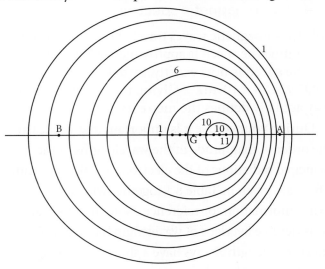

Figure 8.13 The pattern of wavefronts made by waves spreading out from a source moving towards the right.

The source of these waves moves from position 1; the wavefront emitted from this position is labelled 1 and is the largest circle of the diagram. The 11th wavefront is just about to be formed at position 11.

An observer at A will notice that the wavelength of the waves passing them is less than the actual wavelength. This will result in a change in the frequency observed.

We can derive an equation to enable us to calculate the apparent frequency, but you do not need to remember this derivation. However, you do need to be able to apply the equation. In this analysis the source when not moving would have –

a wavelength λ_s,

a frequency f_s,

resulting in a time period $T = \dfrac{1}{f_s}$.

With the source moving the distance between wavefronts, the observed wavelength λ_o is

(λ_s – distance the source moves in a time T)

$$\lambda_o = \left(\lambda_s - \frac{v_s}{f_s}\right)$$

where v_s is the velocity of the source of the waves.

The observed frequency f_o is therefore

$$f_o = \frac{v}{\lambda_o} = \frac{v}{\left(\lambda_s - \dfrac{v_s}{f_s}\right)} = \frac{v}{\left(\dfrac{v}{f_s} - \dfrac{v_s}{f_s}\right)}$$

Rearranging this equation gives

$$\left(\frac{v}{f_s} - \frac{v_s}{f_s}\right) = \frac{v}{f_o} \quad \text{so} \quad f_o = \frac{v}{v - v_s} f_s$$

This equation applies when a source is approaching the observer. When the source is moving away from the observer the equation becomes

$$f_o = \frac{v}{v + v_s} f_s$$

Example 3

An express train travelling at $30\,\text{m s}^{-1}$ sounds a horn of frequency $500\,\text{Hz}$ as it passes through a station. What frequency does a person on the station platform hear when (a) the train is approaching and (b) when it is leaving the station? The speed of sound is $330\,\text{m s}^{-1}$.

Answer

(a) Observed frequency on approach $= f_o$.

$$f_o = \frac{v}{v - v_s} f_s$$

$$f_o = \frac{330}{330 - 30} \times 500$$

$$f_o = \frac{330 \times 500}{300} \times 550\,\text{Hz}$$

(b) When leaving

$$f_o = \frac{330}{330 + 30} \times 500$$

$$f_o = \frac{330 \times 500}{360} \times 470\,\text{Hz}$$

Example 4

Light from a distant galaxy has a wavelength of $587\,\text{nm}$ when measured on the Earth. From the pattern of visible lines in the spectrum, this is known to be part of the hydrogen spectrum, which has a wavelength of $486\,\text{nm}$ on the Earth. How fast is the galaxy moving? Speed of light $= 3.0 \times 10^8\,\text{m s}^{-1}$.

Answer

Since the wavelength has increased, the frequency must have decreased and so the galaxy is moving away from the Earth. Using

$$\frac{f_o}{f_s} = \frac{c}{c+v_s} = \frac{\lambda_s}{\lambda_o}$$

so $\dfrac{3.00 \times 10^8}{3.00 \times 10^8 + v_s} = \dfrac{486}{587}$

and $\dfrac{3.00 \times 10^8 + v_s}{3.00 \times 10^8} = \dfrac{587}{486} = 1.208$

This gives $1 + \dfrac{v_s}{3.00 \times 10^8} = 1.208$

and finally $v_s = 3.00 \times 10^8 \times 0.208$

$$= 6.2 \times 10^7 \, \text{m s}^{-1}$$

Chapter Summary

✓ The speed of a wave is given by its frequency × its wavelength $v = f \times \lambda$.
✓ The intensity of a wave is proportional to its amplitude squared.
✓ Waves can be longitudinal – where the oscillation of particles takes place in the direction of travel, e.g. a sound wave OR transverse – where the oscillation takes place at right angles to the direction of travel, e.g. water waves.
✓ All electromagnetic waves, from radio waves, through light waves to gamma rays, travel at a speed of $300\,000 \, \text{km s}^{-1}$ through space.

✓ The Doppler effect equations calculate the observed frequency of waves emitted by a moving source, based on the speed of the source.

Source moving towards observer

$$f_o = \frac{v}{v - v_s} f_s$$

Source moving away from observer

$$f_o = \frac{v}{v + v_s} f_s$$

Progress Check

The speed of electromagnetic radiation is $3.00 \times 10^8 \, \text{m s}^{-1}$.

8.1 How long does light take to reach the Earth from the Sun? The distance of the Earth from the Sun is $1.50 \times 10^{11} \, \text{m}$.

8.2 The Great Nebula in Andromeda is 2.2×10^6 light years from the Earth. Calculate its distance from the Earth in metres.

8.3 A particular radio wave has a wavelength of $240 \, \text{m}$. Calculate its frequency.

8.4 A radio transmitter radiates a power of $2.8 \, \text{kW}$ uniformly in all directions. Calculate the power received by a dish aerial of area $0.23 \, \text{m}^2$, directly facing the transmitter when at a distance of $83 \, \text{km}$ from the transmitter. (Remember that: the surface area of a sphere of radius r is equal to $4\pi r^2$)

8.5 A ripple spreading on a pond has total energy of $0.42 \, \text{J}$.
    Calculate
    (a) the energy per unit length of the ripple when the radius of the ripple is (i) $0.30 \, \text{m}$ and (ii) $1.20 \, \text{m}$.
    (b) the ratio of the amplitudes of the ripple when the radius is $0.30 \, \text{m}$ to that when the radius is $1.20 \, \text{m}$.

8.6 (a) Draw diagrams to show possible arrangements of nodes and antinodes in sound waves in an open pipe. When the frequency of the lowest note is $70 \, \text{Hz}$, what other frequencies can be produced in the pipe?
    (b) Explain how your answer to (a) would change if a pipe of the same length but closed at one end, replaced the open pipe.

8.7 A car travelling with speed $130 \, \text{km}$ per hour passes a camera that measures the speed of the car. The camera transmits electromagnetic waves of frequency $8.0 \times 10^8 \, \text{Hz}$. The reflected waves from the car have a different frequency from this as a result of the Doppler effect.

Calculate the difference between the frequencies of the transmitted waves and the reflected waves.

The camera effectively uses rays from the electromagnetic image of the car. At what speed is the image of the car moving with respect to the camera?

Superposition

9

Introduction

Interesting things happen when waves interact with one another. Some people put water wave interaction as the cause of mysterious happenings in the Bermuda Triangle and for the strange loss of shipping that, over the years, has taken place off the eastern coast of South Africa.

In this chapter the study is of carefully controlled wave behaviour and generally considers the interaction of just two waves. For any number of waves of the same type added together, the resultant total displacement is always the sum of the displacements of all the waves separately. If, for example, six waves meet at a point at one instant and, individually would cause displacements of 2, 4, −2, 4, 0 and −3 units of distance separately, then the actual movement at that point will be
$2 + 4 − 2 + 4 + 0 − 3 = 5$ units.

Stationary waves

The idea of a 'stationary wave' sounds like a contradiction, but in fact stationary waves are very common. The term does not mean that no movement is taking place but rather that the pattern of movement remains fixed. This is shown in Figure 9.1 where a cellist can cause stationary waves to be set up on the strings of a cello.

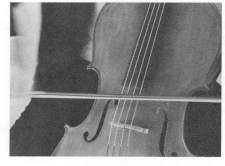

Figure 9.1 A cellist uses the bow to cause stationary waves to be set up on the strings of a cello.

A stationary wave, sometimes called a standing wave, may be set up when two waves of the same frequency and amplitude travel in opposite directions through one another. The formation of the wave is illustrated in Figure 9.2 and the sequence of the diagram needs to be studied carefully. Waves A and B are of the same type and have the same frequency and amplitude. The only difference between them is that A moves from left to right and wave B moves from right to left.

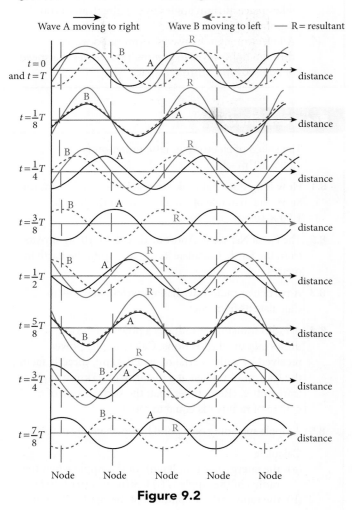

Figure 9.2

The resultant wave formed in this case has some points on it where no movement ever takes place.

These points are called **nodes**. There are other points where there is a maximum displacement. These points are called **antinodes**. The distance between two nodes or two antinodes is half a wavelength. The distance between a node and an antinode is a quarter of a wavelength. The strings on the cello in Figure 9.1 can form stationary waves. The two nodes are at either end of each string: the antinode is in the middle of the string. This stationary wave is set up because the waves set up in the string by the bow travel along the string and are reflected at each end. Within the string, therefore, are waves moving upwards and downwards. This is just the condition for the formation of a stationary wave.

When a vibrating string is illuminated by a stroboscopic lamp, some fascinating images are seen (Figure 9.3).

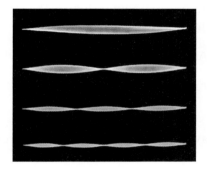

Figure 9.3 Photograph taken with a stroboscopic lamp of a vibrating string

It is possible to have several antinodes on the string and if the stroboscopic frequency is not quite equal to the wave frequency the image moves in a slow, bizarre manner.

Teacher's Tip

The left-hand diagram in Fig. 9.4 shows one moment in which a longitudinal stationary wave is formed. The pressure at a node is high as particles either side of the node squash in towards it. Half a cycle later it will be low, as the particles near the node move in the opposite direction. This means that at nodes in a stationary longitudinal wave the pressure varies by a large amount. At the antinodes, where the particles are moving quickly, but not squashing up on one another, the pressure remains nearly constant.

Examples of stationary waves

Virtually all musical instruments use stationary waves to create sounds of definite frequency. All the brass and woodwind instruments create stationary sound waves in the air inside a tube. An organ may have several thousand pipes within which stationary waves of fixed frequency can be formed. In a pipe closed at one end, an antinode forms at the open end and a node at the closed end. In between, one way the air particles can vibrate up and down the pipe is as shown in Figure 9.4.

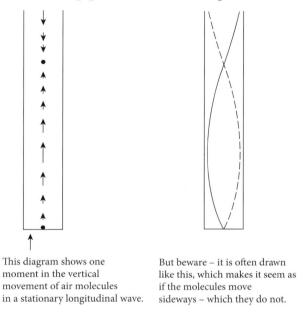

This diagram shows one moment in the vertical movement of air molecules in a stationary longitudinal wave.

But beware – it is often drawn like this, which makes it seem as if the molecules move sideways – which they do not.

Figure 9.4

Stationary electromagnetic waves are set up in microwave ovens and in lasers. A straightforward demonstration of stationary microwaves also enables the wavelength of electromagnetic microwaves to be measured. The arrangement is shown in Figure 9.5.

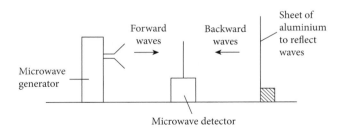

Figure 9.5

The microwave transmitter sends the wave towards a metal plate that reflects it back along itself. A small adjustment to the separation of the transmitter and reflector allows the formation of the stationary wave and nodes and antinodes can be detected by the detector. The distance between antinodes is half a wavelength.

Diffraction

When water waves meet a small obstacle the shadow of the obstacle soon disappears, as can be seen in Figure 9.6(a). If the waves meet an opening they spread out. An example of this is shown in the diagram of Figure 9.6(b) where sea waves are entering a harbour.

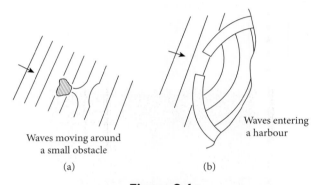

Waves moving around a small obstacle

(a)

Waves entering a harbour

(b)

Figure 9.6

The ability of waves to bend around corners is known as **diffraction**. The amount of diffraction that occurs depends to a large extent on the relative size of the obstacle to the wavelength of the waves. The reason that you cannot see around corners but you can hear around them is because the wavelength of light is very small. The wavelength of sound is about ten million times larger than the wavelength of light. Figures 9.7(a) and (b) show ripples on the surface of water meeting a small opening and a large opening.

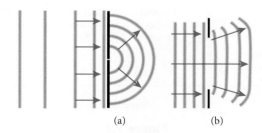

(a)   (b)

Figure 9.7 Ripple tank waves meeting (a) small and (b) large opening

Interference

As a result of diffraction it is possible to get waves from a single source to be split into two or more separate sections and then to combine these sections back together again. It probably seems to be a rather pointless exercise but actually some surprising effects take place. These effects can be very useful, especially with light. Light waves are extraordinarily complex. They have many different wavelengths and there is a large number of breaks in the wave pattern itself. To demonstrate interference, we need light waves that are **monochromatic** (they share a single wavelength) and **coherent** (the wave patterns would appear identical if we laid them on top of one another). The important point with two coherent waves is that they have a constant phase difference between them. In diagrammatic form two coherent waves would be as shown in Figure 9.8. This figure would last for about 10^{-13} s.

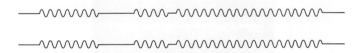

Figure 9.8

The two waves in Figure 9.9 are not coherent.

Figure 9.9

Two coherent light waves can be made to overlap one another using the arrangement shown in Figure 9.10.

When the coherent and monochromatic waves arrive at a screen, the wave from one of the double slits has generally not travelled the same distance as the wave from the other slit. If one wave had travelled half a wavelength further than the other, then a peak of one wave will meet a trough of the other wave and they will cancel one another out to give a dark patch on the screen. The path difference between the two waves of light is shown in Figure 9.11 together with the resulting pattern, a series of horizontal light and dark lines called **fringes**.

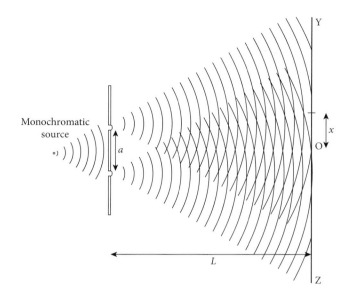

Figure 9.10

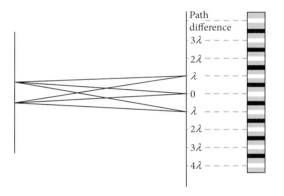

Figure 9.11

Theory for the separation of the fringes

Figure 9.12 just concentrates on the formation of the first fringe after the one at the centre.

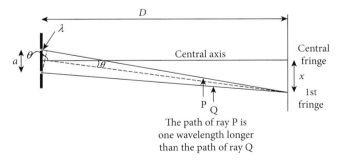

The path of ray P is one wavelength longer than the path of ray Q

Figure 9.12

The figure shows θ, the angle of deflection and it exaggerates it. For the small angles involved we can use the small angle approximation that $\sin\theta \approx \tan\theta \approx \theta$ in radians.

$$\tan\theta = \frac{x}{D}$$

For the triangle given by the central axis, the fringe separation and the dotted line, $\tan\theta = x/D$
For the small triangle near the double slits we get

$$\sin\theta = \frac{\lambda}{a}$$

Equating $\sin\theta$ with $\tan\theta$ gives

$$\frac{\lambda}{a} = \frac{x}{D} \quad \text{and hence } \lambda = \frac{ax}{D}.$$

This experiment was carried out by Thomas Young in 1801 and showed that light was a wave motion with wavelength around 5×10^{-7} m.

Corresponding experiments can be performed with water waves in a ripple tank and a photograph of the result is given in Figure 9.13.

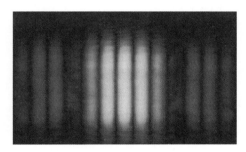

Figure 9.13

When the experiment is carried out with microwaves of wavelength 3.0 cm, the number of fringes is much reduced but an arrangement as shown in Figure 9.14 will produce a series of greater and lesser intensity of the microwaves as the detector is moved round.

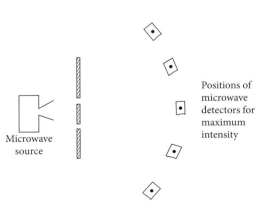

Positions of microwave detectors for maximum intensity

Figure 9.14

The diffraction grating

To improve the accuracy of measurements of wavelengths of light, it is necessary to have more than two coherent beams of monochromatic light. This can be achieved with a diffraction grating. The grating is transparent and typically crossed by as many as 500 straight, dark lines per millimetre. Gratings are produced now using photographic techniques. (A similar procedure is used in the production of CDs and this is why CDs show strong colouring when white light falls on them.)

A small part of a diffraction grating is shown in Figure 9.15 with parallel waves of light from a monochromatic source approaching the slits from the left-hand side. Light on all the slits is coherent since it all starts from the same source.

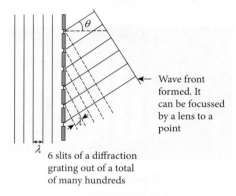

6 slits of a diffraction grating out of a total of many hundreds

Figure 9.15

In the diagram the light being considered is emerging from the slits at an angle θ. This angle is chosen so that $d\sin\theta = \lambda$. This not only means that the bottom ray travels a distance λ further than the bottom but one ray, but that it travels 2λ further than the next one up and 3λ further than the next one, … and so on. Therefore, if all the rays are brought to a focus by the lens, at this angle there will be a very bright line on a screen at the focus of the lens. At any other angle less than θ, there will be no possibility of rays reinforcing one another since, over, say 500 slits there will always be one ray to cancel out any other. If, however, the angle is increased so that the distance marked λ can be marked 2λ, then again reinforcement is possible. Likewise 3λ will give reinforcement. This can go on as long as the slit separation d is smaller than $n\lambda$, where n is an integer.

Theory for the diffraction grating

For the first order, $d\sin\theta = \lambda$.
For the second order, $d\sin\theta' = 2\lambda$.
For the third order, $d\sin\theta'' = 3\lambda$.

An equation covering all the orders is, therefore, given by
$$d\sin\theta = n\lambda,$$
where d is the grating spacing,
$\quad$ θ is the angle of diffraction
$\quad$ n is the order, and
$\quad$ λ is the wavelength.

With light consisting of two or more colours, each colour will have its own pattern, as shown in Figure 9.16.

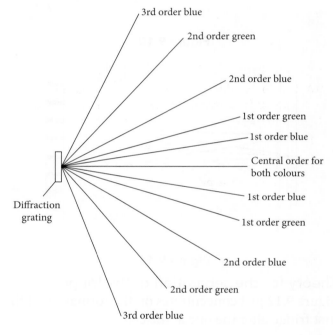

Figure 9.16

Teacher's Tip

Note that when considering diffraction, interference and the diffraction grating it is important that the waves are uniform. That is they have equally spaced wavefronts and are the same wave shape. In all the examples drawn here it is assumed that they are all sine waves of identical shape and wavelength. In practice, this will not always be possible but if the difference between sets of waves gets too large the effect described soon becomes impossible to see.

Chapter Summary

✓ Stationary waves can be set up when waves of the same type travel in opposite directions through one another. They will have:
  ✓ nodes, where the amplitude of the resultant wave is zero and, for sound, where the pressure variation is large, and
  ✓ antinodes, where the amplitude of the resulting wave is large but, for sound the pressure variation is small.

✓ Diffraction occurs where waves spread out when passing through an opening, when the dimensions of the opening are comparable with the wavelength of the waves.
✓ Interference patterns caused by waves travelling through double slits enable the wavelength λ to be found using the equation $\lambda = ax/D$ where a is the slit width, x is the distance between maxima and D the distance to the screen.
✓ The corresponding equation for a diffraction grating is $n\lambda = d\sin\theta$.

Progress Check

9.1 Give two practical situations in which stationary waves are useful. Your examples should be with different types of wave.

9.2 Distinguish between *interference* and *diffraction*.

9.3 In a double-slit experiment, light of wavelength 5.3×10^{-7} m is passed through a pair of slits separated by a distance of 0.20 mm. The resulting fringes are viewed on a screen at a distance of 0.89 m from the slits.
  (a) State the colour of the fringes.
  (b) Calculate the separation of the fringes.
  (c) Deduce the path difference between light that travels from one of the slits to the fourth bright fringe from the centre of the pattern and the light that travels to the same fringe but starts from the other slits.

9.4 A diffraction grating has 400 lines per millimetre and is illuminated by narrow beams of red light of wavelength 7.2×10^{-7} m and blue light of wavelength 4.8×10^{-7} m.
  (a) Draw a diagram to show the whole pattern of the light beams formed.
  (b) What will be observed at a diffraction angle of 35°?

9.5 Put the following radiations in order of increasing frequency.
  X-rays, ultra-violet, radio, γ-rays, red light, microwaves, infra-red, violet light

Examination Questions V

1. A long rope is held under tension between two points A and B. Point A is made to vibrate vertically and a wave is sent down the rope towards B as shown in Figure 1.

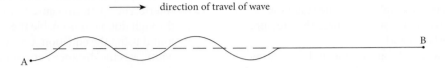

Figure 1 (not to scale)

The time for one oscillation of point A on the rope is 0.20 s. The point A moves a distance of 80 mm during one oscillation. The wave on the rope has a wavelength of 1.5 m.

(a) (i) Explain the term *displacement* for the wave on the rope. [1]
   (ii) Calculate, for the wave on the rope,
      1. the amplitude, in mm, [1]
      2. the speed, in m s^{-1}. [3]

(b) On Figure 1, draw the wave pattern on the rope at a time 0.050 s later than that shown. [2]

(c) State and explain whether the waves on the rope are
   (i) progressive or stationary, [1]
   (ii) longitudinal or transverse. [1]

(Cambridge International AS and A Level Physics 9702 Paper 21 Question 5 October/November 2013)

2. (a) State what is meant by
   (i) the *frequency* of a progressive wave, [2]
   (ii) the *speed* of a progressive wave. [1]

(b) One end of a long string is attached to an oscillator. The string passes over a frictionless pulley and is kept taut by means of a weight, as shown in Figure 2.

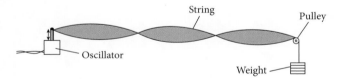

Figure 2

The frequency of oscillation is varied and, at one value of frequency, the wave formed on the string is as shown in Figure 2.
   (i) Explain why the wave is said to be a *stationary wave*. [1]
   (ii) State what is meant by an *antinode*. [1]
   (iii) On Figure 3, label the antinodes with the letter A. [1]

(c) A weight of 4.00 N is hung from the string in **(b)** and the frequency of oscillation is adjusted until a stationary wave is formed on the string. The separation of the antinodes on the string is 17.8 cm for a frequency of 125 Hz.
   The speed v of waves on a string is given by the expression

   $$v = \sqrt{\frac{T}{m}},$$

   where T is the tension in the string and m is its mass per unit length.
   Determine the mass per unit length of the string in kg m^{-1}. [5]

(Cambridge International AS and A Level Physics 9702 Paper 02 Question 5 May/June 2008)

3. (a) Explain what is meant by the *diffraction* of a wave. [2]

(b) (i) Outline briefly an experiment that may be used to demonstrate diffraction of a transverse wave. [3]

(ii) Suggest how your experiment in (i) may be changed to demonstrate the diffraction of a longitudinal wave. [3]

(Cambridge International AS and A Level Physics 9702 Paper 02 Question 6 October/November 2008)

4 (a) A laser is used to produce an interference pattern on a screen, as shown in Figure 3.

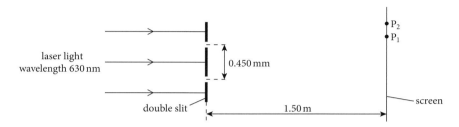

Figure 3 (not to scale)

The laser emits light of wavelength 630 nm. The slit separation is 0.450 mm. The distance between the slits and the screen is 1.50 m. A maximum is formed at P_1 and a minimum is formed at P_2.

Interference fringes are observed only when the light from the slits is coherent.

(i) Explain what is meant by *coherence*. [2]

(ii) Explain how an interference maximum is formed at P_1. [1]

(iii) Explain how an interference minimum is formed at P_2. [1]

(iv) Calculate the fringe separation, in m. [3]

(b) State the effects, if any, on the fringes when the amplitude of the waves incident on the double slits is increased. [3]

(Cambridge International AS and A Level Physics 9702 Paper 21 Question 6 May/June 2012)

Electric Fields: Part A

10

Electric field definition

In physics, all fields – gravitational, magnetic and electrical are vectors. They all indicate that there is a force on something. In the case of electric fields, it is a charge that the force is exerted on. Electric field strength E is the force acting per unit positive charge for a stationary point charge. Put into equation form this becomes

$$\text{Electric field strength} = \frac{\text{Force}}{\text{Charge}} \quad \text{or} \quad E = \frac{F}{Q}.$$

Electric field strength is a vector, so its direction as well as its magnitude is important. The direction of the electric field will be in the same direction as the force provided the charge is positive. A negative charge will result in a force in the opposite direction to the electric field. Electric field strength has units newtons per coulomb, $N\,C^{-1}$.

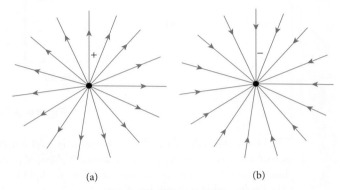

(a)   (b)

Figure 10.1

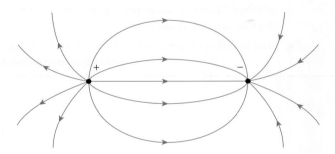

Figure 10.2

Teacher's Tip

Always keep in mind that it is the electrical attraction between, and within, molecules that holds matter together. Your body is held together in one piece because of forces between billions of billions of molecules. Gravitational forces are far, far too weak to keep you whole.

Electric field diagrams

The electric field surrounding a point positive charge is shown in Figure 10.1(a). A similar figure, Figure 10.1(b) shows the same pattern of lines but the opposite direction for a negative charge.

If a positive point charge is placed near a negative point charge, then the combined field is as shown in Figure 10.2.

Other field shapes are shown in Figures 10.3(a) and (b).

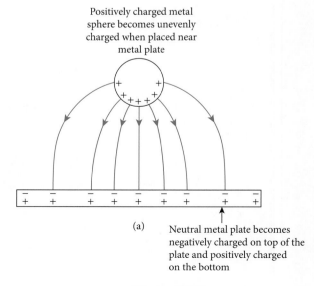

Positively charged metal sphere becomes unevenly charged when placed near metal plate

(a)

Neutral metal plate becomes negatively charged on top of the plate and positively charged on the bottom

Figure 10.3

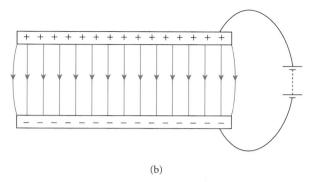

(b)

Figure 10.3

Field lines will be close together where the field is strongest. Field lines to a conductor always meet the surface at a right angle.

Potential difference

You must have heard the term 'voltage' many times when considering different types of electrical problems. The full name for voltage is potential difference (p.d.). This will be formally defined in chapter 11. For this chapter you need to know that the potential difference between two points, V, is the work done in transferring a unit positive charge between the two points. In equation form this gives

$V = \dfrac{W}{Q}$ where Q is the charge and W is the work done.

Figure 10.3(b) shows that a nearly uniform electric field exists between charged parallel plates. Consider a pair of parallel charged plates and a point charge $+Q$, placed in the centre of the −ve plate, as shown in Figure 10.4.

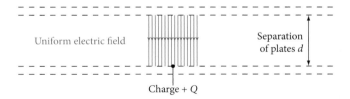

Uniform electric field   Separation of plates d

Charge $+ Q$

Figure 10.4

From the definition of electric field strength the force on the charge is given by

$$E = \frac{F}{Q} \quad \text{so } F = EQ$$

If work is done to move the charge at constant speed from the bottom plate to the top plate then,

$W = EQ \times d$ [since, work = force × distance moved in the direction of the force]

Since also from the potential difference $V = W/Q$ we get

$$\frac{W}{Q} = V = Ed \quad \text{and hence} \quad E = \frac{V}{d}$$

This gives two statements that enable a uniform electric field between a pair of plates to be found.

- From the definition of electric field strength: $E = F/Q$
- From the definition of potential difference: $E = V/d$.

There are many practical situations involving uniform electric fields where both of these equations are required – so it is worthwhile remembering both of them.

The movement of charges in electric fields

The movement considered here is for the movement of charge, often electrons, in a vacuum. This is particularly important in practical situations such as X-ray tubes and cathode-ray tubes in oscilloscopes and in old televisions. The movement of charge in a vacuum can be controlled by both electric and magnetic fields. Betatrons, cyclotrons, microwave cookers, photomultiplier tubes and other devices, such as the CERN Large Hadron Collider, see Fig. 10.5, all make use of electric field control systems.

Figures 10.5 CERN Large Hadron Collider

In the absence of an electric or magnetic field, electrons will travel with constant velocity. The gravitational force on a moving electron is so small it barely has any effect at all, especially since electrons are likely to be moving very fast. The effect of a magnetic force on a moving electron will be considered in Chapter 24.

Three situations will be considered here for an electron.

(i) An electron initially stationary in a uniform electric field. The force on the electron will cause a constant acceleration in the opposite direction to the direction of the field, because the electron has a negative charge. This is shown in Figure 10.6.

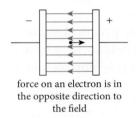

force on an electron is in the opposite direction to the field

Figure 10.6

(ii) An electron inside a closed metal container. The electric field in such a container is zero. The electron will have zero force acting on it, so it will have a constant velocity.

(iii) An electron entering a region in which there is a uniform electric field at right angles to its initial velocity, as shown in Figure 10.7. The force on the electron will be in the opposite direction to the field so the electron will accelerate downwards. There is no force forwards or backwards however, so the velocity of the electron in the forwards direction is unchanged. The situation is comparable to the gravitational movement of a ball thrown horizontally. It goes forward with constant velocity while accelerating downwards. The paths of both the electron and the ball are parabolic (Figure 10.7).

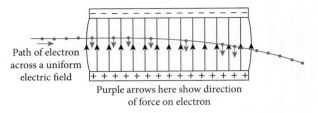

Path of electron across a uniform electric field

Purple arrows here show direction of force on electron

Figure 10.7

Example 1

Electrons are accelerated from rest in a uniform field of electric field strength $8.0 \times 10^4 \, \text{N C}^{-1}$ (or $8.0 \times 10^4 \, \text{V m}^{-1}$) for a distance of 3.0 cm in a vacuum. They then enter a chamber of length 40 cm where there is no electric field, as shown in Figure 10.8.

Calculate

(a) the potential difference between A and B,

(b) the speed of the electrons at B and,

(c) the time taken for the electrons to travel from B to C.

The electronic charge $e = 1.6 \times 10^{-19} \, \text{C}$: mass of electron $= 9.1 \times 10^{-31} \, \text{kg}$

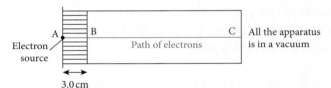

3.0 cm

Figure 10.8

Answer

(a) $V_{AB} = E \times d = (8.0 \times 10^4 \, \text{V m}^{-1}) \times 0.030 \, \text{m}$
$= 2400 \, \text{V}$

(b) Energy of charge $1.6 \times 10^{-19} \, \text{C}$ accelerated through a p.d. of 2400 V
$= Q \times V$
$= 3.84 \times 10^{-15} \, \text{C} \times 2400 \, \text{J/C} = 3.84 \times 10^{-6} \, \text{J}$.
This is the kinetic energy of the electron, so

$3.84 \times 10^{-15} \, \text{J} = \frac{1}{2} \times 9.1 \times 10^{-31} \, \text{kg} \times v^2$

$v = \sqrt{\dfrac{2 \times 3.4 \times 10^{-15}}{9.11 \times 10^{-31}}} = 9.2 \times 10^7 \, \text{m s}^{-1}$

(c) Time from B to C at constant speed

$= \dfrac{\text{distance}}{\text{speed}} = \dfrac{0.40 \, \text{m}}{9.2 \times 10^7 \, \text{m s}^{-1}} = 4.3 \times 10^{-9} \, \text{s}$

Chapter Summary

✓ Electric field strength is force per unit charge. $E = F/Q$. The unit is newtons per coulomb.

✓ Electric field strength has been shown in this chapter to be equal to the potential gradient so, $E = V/d$. You will often see its value quoted in volts per metre. Volts per metre is identical to newtons per coulomb. (See question 10.1 below.)

✓ Electric fields can be represented by field lines that point from positive charges to negative charges.

✓ Electric fields between parallel, oppositely charged metal plates are uniform and are shown by evenly spaced, straight, parallel field lines.

✓ Electric charges moving through external electric fields experience a force and may accelerate and change direction of travel.

Progress Check

10.1 Show that the unit volts per metre, $V\,m^{-1}$ is identical to the unit newtons per coulomb, $N\,C^{-1}$. Both of these units can be used for electric field strength.

10.2 Calculate the force on a charge of 5.3 mC when placed in an electric field of field strength $22\,000\,V\,m^{-1}$.

10.3 An electron is accelerated from rest in a uniform electric field between two parallel plates in a vacuum. The plates are a distance 5.0 cm apart and have a potential difference between them of 800 V. Calculate,

(a) (i)   the electric field strength between the plates,
     (ii) the force on the electron, (of charge $1.6 \times 10^{-19}\,C$)
     (iii) the acceleration of the electron, (of mass $9.1 \times 10^{-31}\,kg$)
     (iv) the speed of the electron when it reaches the positive plate, assuming it left the negative plate with zero velocity,
     (v)   the kinetic energy of the electron on reaching the positive plate.

(b) Explain how your answers to the five parts of (a) would differ if the plates were separated by a distance of 10 cm but other details were to the same values.

(c) What is a much quicker way of finding answer (a)(v)?

10.4 (a) A charge of +45 µC placed a distance of 2.3 m from a charge of +12 µC experiences a repulsive force of 0.92 N. Calculate the force between the two charges when their separation increases to 4.6 m. (The force between isolated charges follows an inverse square law in the same way that gravity does.)

(b) Use the information from (a) to determine the force between a proton and an electron in a hydrogen atom. The radius of a hydrogen atom can be taken to be 46 pm.

Current of Electricity

11

This chapter will introduce the basic quantities of electricity. As usual, it is important that you can use these quantities with accuracy and understanding.

Charge and current

Introduction

The terms 'charge' and 'current' are not usually difficult to understand. Everyone is familiar with the idea of electric charge, if only from rubbing a balloon on clothing and using the charge it acquires to get it to attach itself to the ceiling. The sense of excitement from standing too close to a Van de Graaff machine may also be a familiar way of feeling the presence of electric charge.

The idea that all solids are solid because of electric charges holding them together is less well appreciated. Every single atom exists because it has positively charged protons in the nucleus and negatively charged electrons surrounding the nucleus. When atoms combine chemically into molecules, they do so because of electrical attraction and repulsion between charges. The reason the floor supports you is because of electrical repulsion between the molecules in the soles of your feet and those in the floor itself. All contact forces are due to attraction or repulsion of electric charges.

Conductors and insulators

Any object with equal numbers of positively-charged protons and negatively-charged electrons is said to be uncharged, as the positive charge on a proton is exactly equal and opposite to the negative charge on an electron. However, different uncharged substances behave differently towards the movement of electrons within them. In a material that conducts electricity, electrons are able to drift easily, but surprisingly slowly,

through the material. In an insulator the electrons are so firmly bound to the molecules of the insulator that movement is almost impossible. This is illustrated in Figures 11.1(a) and 11.1(b). Figure 11.1(a) represents a conductor in which some of the electrons, shown in purple, are not attached to any particular atom. These electrons, called the **conduction electrons**, are able to drift from atom to atom. The drift of electrons is a current of charge, called an **electric current**. Conductors used in electrical circuits are usually metals such as copper. Figure 11.1(b) represents an insulator in which all electrons are firmly attached to a molecule or atom and are, therefore, not able to drift through the material. Insulators are materials such as plastics, glass, cotton and rubber.

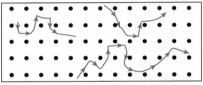

(a) A conductor in which some electrons are free to drift through the material

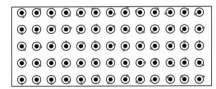

(b) An insulator with all electrons fixed to molecules

Figure 11.1

Definitions

The unit of electric current, the ampere A, is one of the base units of the SI system of units. As such it is defined with great care from the magnetic effect it causes. For A Level its definition is not required, but it is essential that you realise that an electric current is a rate of flow of charged carriers. The charge carriers in metals are electrons but other charge carriers can be protons or positive or negative ions. Each of these carriers has a fixed charge. The charge on a carrier is said to be **quantised**. A current of 10 A implies that the rate of flow of charged carriers is ten times the rate of flow of charged carriers in a current of 1 A. Note that this does not necessarily mean that the carriers in a current of 10 A are flowing ten times faster, it might mean that there are ten times the number of carriers all travelling at the same speed. It could also be five times the number of carriers travelling at twice the speed.

Charge Q is defined by the equation $Q = It$, where I is the current and t is the time.

The unit of charge is the coulomb (C). A coulomb of charge is the charge provided by a current of one ampere for one second. Note that it is NOT one ampere per second. The current is multiplied by the time, not divided by it.

Using these definitions (and some very skilled experimental work) it is possible to measure the charge on an electron to be -1.6022×10^{-19} C. One ampere, therefore, will be a rate of flow of 6.2414×10^{18} electrons per second past any point in the circuit: over six million million million electrons per second for just one ampere. Just how large this number is, can perhaps be appreciated by the fact that it is ten times larger than the number of seconds between the Big Bang at the formation of the Universe and the present.

Example 1

(a) What charge is provided by a current of 15 A to a cooker in one hour?
(b) How many electrons pass any point in the cooker heater in this time, assuming the current is constant?

Answer (a) Charge = current × time =
$$15\,\text{A} \times 3600\,\text{s} = 54\,000\,\text{C}$$
(b) Number of electrons = $54\,000\,\text{C}/1.6 \times 10^{-19}\,\text{C}$
$$= 3.4 \times 10^{23}$$

Current and charge carriers

Consider a wire of cross-sectional area A with a current I passing through it. The mean speed of the moving electrons is v (Figure 11.2).

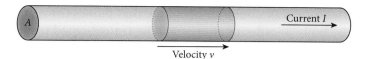

Figures 11.2 Wire of cross-sectional area A

In one second, an electron moves a distance v along the wire. If the number of electrons per unit volume of wire is n, then the number of electrons in the shaded cylinder of Figure 11.2 is nAv. Therefore, the total charge on this volume of electrons is $nAve$, where e is the charge on one electron.

This charge is the total charge passing a single point in the wire in 1 second, and so it is the same as the current I. Therefore:
$$I = nAve$$

If charge carriers other than electrons are considered, each having a charge q, then a more general form of this equation is $I = nAvq$.

Potential difference

Potential difference (p.d.) is measured in volts and is, therefore, often referred to as 'the voltage'. The variety of terms used is perhaps why the understanding of potential difference is frequently poor. A formal definition of potential difference is as follows.

The potential difference between two points is the quantity of energy transformed from electrical energy to other forms of energy in moving a unit positive charge between these two points.

In equation form this becomes:

$$\text{potential difference } (V) = \frac{\text{energy transformed}}{\text{charge}}$$

$$\text{or } V = \frac{W}{Q}$$

Note that, as always, a quantity is defined in terms of other quantities, but once the quantity is defined the definition of the unit for that quantity follows a similar pattern.

The definition of the volt is: **one volt is one joule per coulomb.**

Potential difference is, therefore, a measure of energy transfer. A bulb in a torch may have 3 volts between its positive and negative terminals. This says that for every coulomb of charge that passes through the bulb, 3 joules of energy will be transformed from electrical energy into heat and light energy. If the current in the bulb is A amp, then a coulomb

of charge will pass in 4 seconds and the 3 joules of energy will be supplied in 4 seconds. This enables the power of the bulb to be found as $\frac{3}{4}$ W.

A mains lamp may be working with a potential difference of 240 V between its terminals. The much greater 240 J is being supplied with each coulomb, so fewer coulombs of charge are required for the same energy.

Example 2

A motor working from a mains supply of 240 V provides 900 W of power for 80 s. It has a current of 4.0 A in it. What can be determined from this information?

Answer Charge through motor $= It = 4.0\,\text{A} \times 80\,\text{s}$
$$= 320\,\text{C}$$
Energy supplied to motor $= 240\,\text{V} \times 320\,\text{C} = 76\,800\,\text{J}$
Power supplied to motor $= 76\,800\,\text{J}/80\,\text{s} = 960\,\text{W}$
Work done by motor $= 900\,\text{W} \times 80\,\text{s} = 72\,000\,\text{J}$
Efficiency of motor = work done/energy supplied
$$= 72\,000\,\text{J}/76\,800\,\text{J} = 0.94 = 94\%$$

This last value could equally well have been given by power output divided by power input, namely 900 W/960 W = 94%.

Resistance

The formal definition of resistance is the statement: **resistance is the potential difference per unit current, $R = V/I$.**

It is, therefore, measured in volts per ampere. One volt per ampere is given the name ohm, symbol Ω. If a supply of 240 V is providing a current of 5.0 A through a component, the resistance of the component is 240 V/ 5.0 A = 48 Ω.

Equation summary

Symbols used	
time	t
energy, work	W
power	P
current	I
charge	Q
potential difference	V
resistance	R

Defining equations

$$P = \frac{W}{t}$$

$$Q = It$$

$$V = \frac{W}{Q}$$

$$R = \frac{V}{I}$$

These defining equations can be manipulated into many different equations but until you are thoroughly familiar with them you are recommended to use just the defining equations. Some of the more useful deduced equations are given here.

$$P = VI = I^2R = \frac{V^2}{R}$$

$$W = VIt = I^2Rt = \frac{V^2}{R}t$$

Teacher's Tip

If you get stuck with an electricity problem, try using the following four changes.
Read   1 watt as 1 joule per second,
          1 ampere as 1 coulomb per second,
          1 volt as 1 joule per coulomb and
          1 ohm as 1 volt per ampere.

These alterations often give more meaning to a problem. An amount of 9 joules per coulomb to a lamp bulb suggests more than just a potential difference and immediately points in the direction of energy supply.

Current–potential difference (*I–V*) characteristics

Different materials respond differently to potential difference. Three different situations will be considered.

1. A wire at a constant temperature

Figure 11.3 shows how the current increases as the potential difference is increased. Under these conditions the graph is a straight line and, therefore, the resistance is constant.

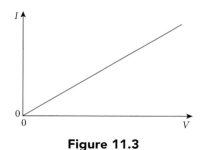

Figure 11.3

2. A filament lamp

Figure 11.4 shows that when the temperature of a wire changes, as in a filament lamp, the current is not directly proportional to the potential difference.

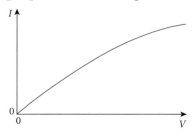

Figure 11.4

The hotter the filament becomes the smaller is the increase in the current for a given increase in potential difference. Under these conditions the resistance increases with temperature.

3. A semiconductor diode

You are already familiar with the terms 'conductor' and 'insulator' when referring to the ability of a material to have a flow of charge carriers through it. However there are some materials, such as germanium and silicon, which do conduct electricity but which have a considerably higher resistance than metals. These materials are called **semiconductors** and they are used extensively in electronic circuits.

One device, made of semiconductor material, allows current in it in one direction only. It is called a semiconductor diode. Figure 11.5 shows that there will be no current in the device for a potential difference applied in one direction, and even in the other direction there will be no current in it until the potential difference reaches a certain value, after which the current increases rapidly. A semiconductor diode, therefore, has infinite resistance until there is a current, after which its resistance falls rapidly.

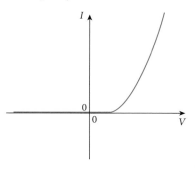

Figure 11.5

Temperature characteristics

The resistance of a filament lamp has been seen to vary with temperature. A typical resistance – temperature graph for a filament lamp is shown in Figure 11.6. At room temperature the resistance is not zero and it increases almost uniformly as the temperature rises.

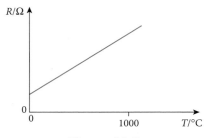

Figure 11.6

Ohm's law

For the particular case of a metallic conductor, this law will apply. The law states that the current in a metallic conductor is proportional to the potential difference between its ends, provided physical conditions, such as temperature, remain constant.

The law formalises the fact, stated earlier, that for a metal at a constant temperature, the graph of I against V will be a straight line through the origin, so the resistance of the metal will be constant.

Electrical resistivity

Other factors that affect the resistance R of any material are the length of the material and its cross-section area. The greater the length l of a piece of wire, the greater will be its resistance. R is proportional to l. The greater its area of cross-section A, the smaller will be its resistance. R is inversely proportional to A. Combining these two statements into one equation gives

$$R \propto \frac{l}{A} \quad \text{and so} \quad R = \frac{\rho l}{A}$$

where ρ is a constant for the material of the wire and is called its **resistivity.**

Chapter Summary

- ✓ Charge = current × time. 1 coulomb is the charge that passes when there is a current of 1 ampere for 1 second
- ✓ The potential difference between two points is the quantity of energy transformed from electrical energy to other forms of energy in moving a unit positive charge between these two points. 1 volt is the potential difference when 1 joule of energy is transformed from the electrical energy of 1 coulomb of charge.

- ✓ Resistance is potential difference per unit current. 1 ohm is the resistance when a potential difference of 1 volt causes a current of 1 ampere.
- ✓ Resistivity ρ is a property of a material indicating how the shape of a material affects its resistance. It is defined from the equation $R = \rho l/A$ where R is the resistance of a material of length l and of area of cross section A.

Progress Check

11.1 Deduce all the "useful equations" listed on page 78, from the basic equations. These equations are:
$P = VI$, $P = I^2R$, $P = V^2/R$ and $W = VIt$, $W = I^2Rt$, $W = V^2t/R$. These equations link the six quantities: current I, potential difference V, resistance R, energy W, power P and time t.

11.2 An electric kettle operates on a potential difference of 240 V. It is marked 3000 W. Deduce
(a) the current,
(b) the resistance of the element when it is working,
(c) the time it takes to supply 6.0 MJ of energy.

11.3 A refrigerator for use in a caravan requires an input current of 8.0 A when working with a potential difference across it of 12 V. It is working continuously for 7 hours during a hot day. Deduce
(a) the power input to the refrigerator,
(b) the energy supplied to it during this time,
(c) the resistance of the refrigerator.

11.4 An X-ray tube works on an 80 kV supply and 1.5×10^{16} electrons pass through the tube every second for 3.0 s, when a photograph is being taken. The charge on one electron is -1.6×10^{-19} C. Deduce
(a) the total charge passing through the tube in the 3.0 s,
(b) the current in the tube,
(c) the power being provided to the electrons,
(d) the total energy of all the electrons,
(e) the resistance of the tube.

11.5 An electric motor in a train has a power input of 800 kW. It is supplied from a 25 kV supply. Deduce
(a) the current in the motor,
(b) the energy supplied during a 20 minute period.

11.6 Figure 11.7 shows how the current through a component varies with the potential difference across it.

What are the values of the resistance of the component when the potential difference across it is
(a) 4.0 V,
(b) 6.0 V,
(c) 0?

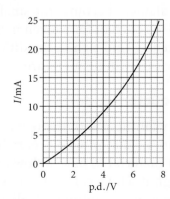

Figure 11.7

11.7 Figure 11.8 shows how the current through a different component varies with the potential difference across it.

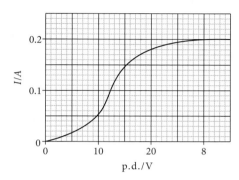

Figure 11.8

(a) At what two values of potential difference is the resistance 150 Ω?

(b) Deduce the minimum value of the resistance of the component.

(c) Sketch a graph to show how resistance varies with potential difference.

11.8 Show that the unit for resistivity is ohm metre, Ω m.

11.9 The resistivity of copper at 20 °C is 1.7×10^{-8} Ω m. What is the length of a piece of copper wire of diameter 1.2 mm that has a resistance of 2.0 Ω at this temperature? (Many mistakes made with questions like this are caused by confusing diameter and radius. If this is done then the area of cross section of the wire will be incorrect by a factor of four. Other common mistakes are with the conversion of 1.2 mm into 0.0012 m, or of forgetting to convert from millimetres altogether. Note that 1 square millimetre is 10^{-6} m^2 and not 10^{-3} m^2.)

11.10 An electromagnet is constructed with 2500 turns of copper wire of average length 45 mm. The wire used has a diameter of 0.122 mm. Calculate the resistance of the wire. The resistivity of copper at 20 °C is 1.70×10^{-8} Ω m. Suggest why the resistance of the electromagnet in use will be larger than the value you have calculated.

Direct Current (D.C.) Circuits

Introduction

Practical electrical circuits require more analysis than that given in Chapter 11. They are usually more complex than a supply of electrical power and a piece of electrical equipment.

Electrical power sources, for example, are not perfect. They always have some internal resistance and this must be considered. Circuit diagrams become more complex and conventional symbols are used for drawing them. Most of the ones used are given in Figure 12.1. The laws of conservation of charge and conservation of energy need to be applied to electrical circuits. These laws are called Kirchhoff's laws. (Yes, there is an 'hh' in the spelling of his name.)

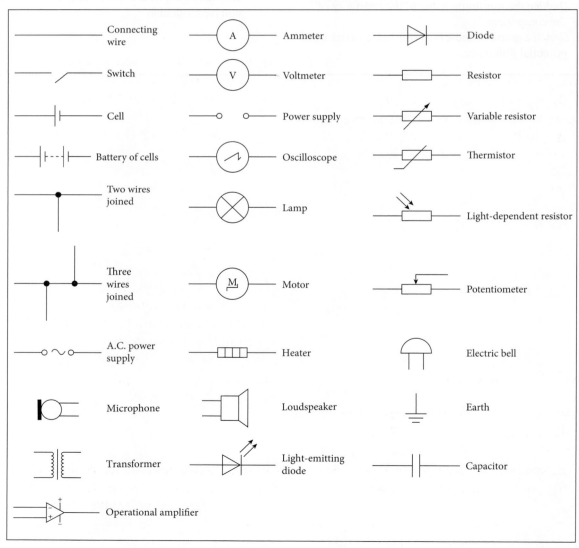

Figure 12.1 Conventional symbols used for drawing circuit diagrams

Electromotive force, e.m.f. and potential difference, p.d.

So far in this book only p.d. has been measured in volts. In fact, e.m.f. is another electrical quantity measured using the volt. The difference between these two terms is important. The energy transferred by a source in driving a unit charge round a complete circuit is referred to as its emf. The most important word here is 'source'. An e.m.f always applies to a source of electrical energy. A battery may have an e.m.f. of 9.0 V. The battery is supplying energy to the circuit. This battery is supplying 9.0 joules with each coulomb of charge. It is changing some of the chemical energy within the battery to electrical energy in the circuit. Potential difference (p.d.) arises when the supplied electrical energy is converted into other forms of energy.

Internal resistance

Any material has some electrical resistance and the chemicals in a battery are no exception. This resistance is called the internal resistance of the battery and is between the positive and negative terminals of the battery. For diagrammatic purposes however, the resistance is usually shown at the side of the battery symbol as illustrated in Figure 12.2.

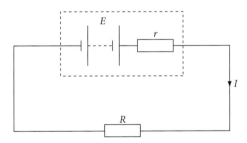

Figure 12.2

Here a battery of e.m.f. E and internal resistance r is connected to an external resistance R and the battery is causing a current I throughout the circuit. (Note that the symbol used for e.m.f. is E. This is one reason for using W for energy or work, rather than E.)

The total resistance in this circuit is $(R + r)$, so the current I will be given by $E/(R + r)$. This equation can be manipulated algebraically into several different forms:

$$I(R + r) = E \qquad E = IR + Ir \qquad (E - Ir) = IR$$

Example 1

A battery of e.m.f. 9.0 V has an internal resistance of 1.2 Ω. It is connected to a resistor of resistance 3.8 Ω. Calculate

(a) the current in the circuit,
(b) the p.d. across the 3.8 Ω resistor,
(c) the power supplied to the 3.8 Ω resistor,
(d) the power wasted heating the battery, and
(e) the efficiency of the distribution of power from the battery to the 3.8 Ω resistor.

Answers

(a) $9.0\,V/(1.2\,\Omega + 3.8\,\Omega) = 9.0\,V \div 5\,\Omega$
$$= 1.8\,A$$

(b) $V = IR = 1.8\,A \times 3.8\,\Omega = 6.8(4)\,V$

(c) $P = VI = 6.84\,V \times 1.8\,A = 12.3\,W$

(d) Total power provided by battery $= 9.0\,V \times 1.8\,A$
$$= 16.2\,W$$
So power wasted heating the battery $= 16.2\,W - 12.3\,W$
$$= 3.9\,W$$

(e) Efficiency of the distribution of power

$$= \frac{\text{power supplied to } R}{\text{power provided by battery}} = \frac{12.3\,W}{16.2\,W} = 0.76 \text{ or } 76\%$$

Teacher's Tip

With multistage questions such as this, it is bad practice to keep rounding up numbers to a set number of significant figures. Keep at least one extra significant figure, beyond what is strictly required to avoid a build up in uncertainty as you progress through the question. Restrict rounding up until the final stage.

Kirchhoff's laws

Kirchhoff's two laws of electricity are the basic electrical laws. They are electrical statements of two of the fundamental principles of physics namely, the principle of conservation of charge and the principle of conservation of energy.

Kirchhoff's first law

This law states that the current entering any junction is equal to the current leaving the junction.

This implies, for the circuit shown in Figure 12.3, if the currents in the left-hand branches are 6.3 A and 2.2 A, then the current I leaving the junction must be 8.5 A. Current cannot vanish or suddenly increase, no matter how complex a circuit is.

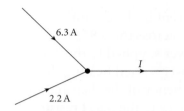

Figure 12.3

A battery supplying 2.46 A from one terminal must be receiving 2.46 A from the other terminal. Batteries do not make charge. Batteries pump charge round a circuit. Current cannot be lost because charge cannot be created or vanish.

Earth connections in circuits are often, mistakenly, thought to allow current to 'earth' and be lost. If there is a current in an earth connection then somewhere else in the same circuit there will be an exactly equal current from earth into the circuit.

Kirchhoff's second law

This law states that around any complete loop in a circuit, the sum of the potential differences is equal to the sum of the electromotive forces.

This is a rather more difficult concept, so it is worthwhile thinking about a corresponding mechanical situation. A man when hiking carries a rucksack that has a constant weight of 100 N. (He did not put his lunch in his rucksack.) He walks for 10 km going up and down many hills and ends up where he started from. During the hike the rucksack sometimes gains gravitational potential energy (G.P.E.) as he goes uphill and sometimes it loses G.P.E. when he goes downhill. However, since he has completed a loop around the countryside and is back where he started all the gains in G.P.E. exactly balance out all the losses in G.P.E.

In electrical terms, any charge moving around a complete circuit and returning to the point it started from will have gained electrical energy in a battery and lost electrical energy in resistors. It does not matter how many resistors or how many batteries are there. Conservation of energy will not allow a difference between the gains and losses of energy provided you start and finish at the same point. The law is equally true when the components are more sophisticated than just batteries and resistors.

Combination of resistors

Resistors in series

The diagram of Figure 12.4 shows a part of a circuit containing 3 resistors of resistances R_1, R_2 and R_3 connected to one another in series.

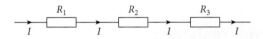

Figure 12.4

Using Kirchhoff's first law, the current in each resistor must be the same. No charge can be lost, so the last resistor has just as much current in it as the first.

Using the definition of resistance as V/I, we get $V = IR$ and so the potential difference across each resistor is given by

$$V_1 = IR_1, \quad V_2 = IR_2 \text{ and } V_3 = IR_3$$

Now using Kirchhoff's second law, we know that the potential difference V across all three resistors is given by

$$V = V_1 + V_2 + V_3 = I(R_1 + R_2 + R_3)$$

The total resistance R of the three resistors is given by

$$V/I = R = R_1 + R_2 + R_3$$

In other words, for resistors in series

- the current in each resistor is the same,
- the potential differences across each resistor are usually different, and
- the total resistance is the arithmetic sum of the individual resistances.

This means that the total resistance must be larger than the resistance of the resistor with the largest resistance.

Resistors in parallel

The diagram of Figure 12.5 shows a part of a circuit containing three resistors of resistances R_1, R_2 and R_3 connected to one another in parallel.

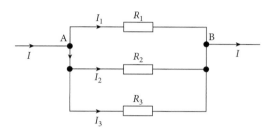

Figure 12.5

Using Kirchhoff's first law the total current I must split to cause currents I_1, I_2 and I_3 in the three resistors with $I = I_1 + I_2 + I_3$. So,

$$\frac{V}{R} = \frac{V_1}{R_1} + \frac{V_2}{R_2} + \frac{V_3}{R_3}$$

Now using Kirchhoff's second law, we know that the potential difference between points A and B has a certain value, so whether the current is present in R_1, R_2 or R_3 the potential difference must be the same for each route since all currents start at A and finish at B. In equation form this becomes $V = V_1 = V_2 = V_3$.

This gives,

$$\frac{V}{R} = \frac{V}{R_1} + \frac{V}{R_2} + \frac{V}{R_3}$$

and V cancels throughout to give

$$\frac{1}{R} = \frac{1}{R_1} + \frac{1}{R_2} + \frac{1}{R_3}$$

In other words, for resistors in parallel

- the current in each resistor is usually different,
- the potential differences across each resistor are the same, and
- the total resistance is found using the reciprocal equation above.

This means that the total resistance must be smaller than the resistance of the resistor with the smallest resistance.

Electrical circuits

Warning of common mistakes

The definitions, laws and principles described in Chapter 11 and up to this point in Chapter 12 enable the analysis of all standard D.C. circuits.

> **Teacher's Tip**
>
> Some mistakes are very common in calculations involving electrical circuits. Any careless mistake you might make will not be noticed unless you look critically at the answers you obtain.
>
> From a battery of AA cells expect currents in the range from a few milliamps to just over an ampere and potential differences up to 9 volts.
>
> From a car battery you might get tens of amperes for a few seconds and the potential difference will be 12 V.
>
> From a mains supply the current might be up to 30 amperes but mostly currents are in the range from a fraction of an ampere to 13 A. The potential difference will be either about 240 V or about 110 V depending on which country you live in. Only a power station will give currents of hundreds of amperes. Not only check that the answers are reasonable but also that you have used such terms as kΩ and mA correctly.

With resistors in series and in parallel make the checks described earlier. In series, the total resistance increases as more resistors are added; in parallel, the resistance decreases as more resistors are added. Also with resistors it is frequently found that the final $1/R$ term is quoted as the total resistance. If $1/R = 0.025$, this cannot be a sensible value for the resistance itself. $R = 1/0.025 = 40\,\Omega$.

One useful technique with parallel resistors, but only when two resistors are used, is to make use of the following equation.

$$\frac{1}{R} = \frac{1}{R_1} + \frac{1}{R_2} = \frac{R_2 + R_1}{R_1 R_2}$$

so $$R = \frac{R_1 R_2}{R_1 + R_2} = \frac{\text{product of } R_1 \text{ and } R_2}{\text{sum of } R_1 \text{ and } R_2}$$

For example, with a resistor of resistance $8\,\Omega$ in parallel with one of $2\,\Omega$, the total resistance is $(8 \times 2)/(8 + 2) = 16/10 = 1.6\,\Omega$. By similar working, or by common sense, the total resistance of two equal resistors in parallel is equal to half the resistance of one of them, i.e two $3000\,\Omega$ resistors in parallel have a total resistance of $1500\,\Omega$. This must be the case since the second resistor takes as much current as the first and doubling the current halves the resistance.

Sample circuits

A circuit containing both series and parallel connections is shown in Figure 12.6.

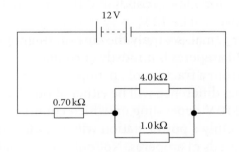

Figure 12.6

The resistance of $4.0\,\text{k}\Omega$ and $1.0\,\text{k}\Omega$ in parallel
$= (4.0 \times 1.0)/(5.0) = 0.80\,\text{k}\Omega$
Total resistance of the circuit
$= 0.80\,\text{k}\Omega + 0.70\,\text{k}\Omega = 1.5\,\text{k}\Omega$
Total current from battery
$= V/R = 12\,\text{V}/1.5\,\text{k}\Omega = 8.0\,\text{mA}$
Potential difference (p.d.) across $0.70\,\text{k}\Omega$
$= IR = 0.0080\,\text{A} \times 700\,\Omega = 5.6\,\text{V}$
Therefore p.d. across both parallel resistors
$= 12.0\,\text{V} - 5.6\,\text{V} = 6.4\,\text{V}$
giving the current in the $4.0\,\text{k}\Omega$ resistor
$= 6.4\,\text{V}/4.0\,\text{k}\Omega = 1.6\,\text{mA}$
and the current in the $1.0\,\text{k}\Omega$ resistor
$= 6.4\,\text{V}/1.0\,\text{k}\Omega = 6.4\,\text{mA}$

These two currents can be added to get a current of $8.0\,\text{mA}$ in the $0.70\,\text{kW}$ resistor.
Powers in each can be found using, power $= I^2 R$
Power in the $0.70\,\text{k}\Omega$ resistor $= 45\,\text{mW}$,
in the $4.0\,\text{k}\Omega$ resistor $= 10\,\text{mW}$ and
in the $1.0\,\text{k}\Omega$ resistor $= 41\,\text{mW}$.
The power from the battery
$= V \times I = 12\,\text{V} \times 0.008\,\text{A} = 0.096\,\text{W} = 96\,\text{mW}$

The effect of a voltmeter being used

A voltmeter reading up to $6\,\text{V}$ has a resistance of $50\,\text{k}\Omega$. Deduce the p.d. across the $20\,\text{k}\Omega$ resistor in the circuit of Figure 12.7 (a) when the voltmeter is not in place and (b) when the voltmeter is in place.

- When the voltmeter is not in place the reading is two-thirds of the total $= 4.0\,\text{V}$. (There is the same current in both resistors, therefore the p.d. across the $20\,\text{k}\Omega$ resistor is twice that across the $10\,\text{k}\Omega$ resistor.)

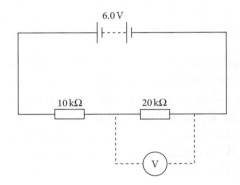

Figure 12.7

- When the voltmeter is in place, the resistance of it is in parallel with the $20\,\text{k}\Omega$ resistor. This gives a resistance of $(20 \times 50)/(20 + 50) = 1000/70 = 14.3\,\text{k}\Omega$. Therefore, reading on voltmeter

$$= \frac{14.3}{14.3 + 10} \times 6.0\,\text{V} = 3.5\,\text{V}$$

To be accurate, voltmeters must have a resistance that is high in comparison with the other resistors in the circuit. Many modern digital voltmeters have very high resistance, of the order of megaohms.

Example 2

An ammeter has a resistance of 0.50 Ω. Deduce the current in the circuit of Figure 12.8 (a) before an ammeter is introduced and (b) after it is introduced.

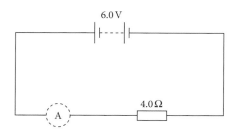

Figure 12.8

Answers

(a) Before the ammeter is introduced the current is 6.0 V/4.0 Ω = 1.5 A

(b) After the ammeter is put in position the current = 6.0 V/(4.0 + 0.5) Ω = 1.33 A.

The ammeter is correctly reading the current but this is not what the current was before the measurement is taken. For an ammeter to have little effect on a current it must have a very low resistance.

The potential divider circuit

A potential divider is used when a variable potential difference is required. The circuit uses a variable resistance that has three connections to it. One of these connections is to a sliding contact on a resistor and the other two are to the ends of the resistor. A photograph of one typical potential divider is shown in Figure 12.9. The construction of a smaller and different type of potential divider is shown in Figure 12.10(a).

Figure 12.9 Photograph of a potential divider

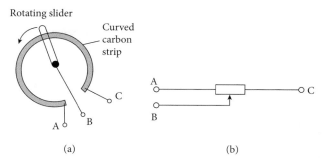

Figure 12.10 (a) Construction of a potential divider (b) Symbol of a potential divider

A potential divider circuit can provide any required potential difference between zero and the supply potential difference. Essentially it splits its input into two parts. If terminals A and C are connected across a 12 V battery, then the p.d. across the carbon strip is 12 V. When the slider is turned anticlockwise to be near to A, then the p.d. from A to B is small and the p.d. from B to C is large. By rotating the slider clockwise from that position, the p.d. from A to B will increase from zero up to near 12 V as the p.d. from B to C decreases from near 12 V down to near zero. The full 12 V always exists across the whole carbon resistor but the slider enables any fraction of 12 V to be supplied to any part of a circuit.

There is a problem with potential dividers when high power circuits are used. The problem is that there is a large amount of wasted power in the carbon strip so the overall efficiency is low. You may have noticed that on an electric cooker, if you have one at home, the hotplates come on and go off frequently when less than full heating is required. It is more efficient to have the hotplates on fully rather than at half power. Cookers do not have potential divider circuits. If half power is required it is done by having alternately 20 seconds, say, of full power followed by 20 seconds of zero power.

The potentiometer

The potentiometer is an instrument capable of comparing potential differences (p.d.s) to a high degree of accuracy. Making use of standard cells, which can have their e.m.f.s known to six significant figures, it can measure the e.m.f. of a supply to the same high accuracy.

The principle the potentiometer uses is that if two cells of equal e.m.f. are connected to oppose one another, then there will be zero current.

To start, all that is required is a well-charged battery and a piece of uniform resistance wire held firmly on top of a metre rule, as shown in Figure 12.11.

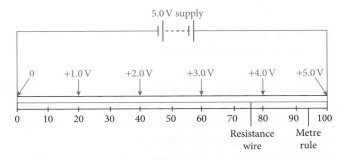

Figure 12.11

With 5.00 V across the 100 cm of wire, there will be a 1.00 V drop in potential across every 20 cm length from one end to the other. The values this gives are printed on the diagram though actual values are not important in practice. What is important is that they stay constant while the experiment proceeds.

A standard cell, of say 2.04 V is then connected through a sensitive, centre reading ammeter, called a galvanometer, between the zero of the ruler and a point 40.8 cm along the ruler, as shown in Figure 12.12.

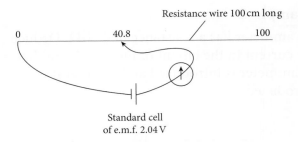

Figure 12.12

At this point only, the cell is trying to push electrons one way through the galvanometer and the p.d. across the wire is trying to push them in the opposite direction. The result is zero current. A method, such as this, is called a **null method**. Zero current is the requirement for calibrating the instrument.

This is the preliminary part of the experiment. To measure any other e.m.f., you repeat the process. If you find that with the new e.m.f. the point at which there is zero current is at 31.8 cm then the measured e.m.f. (x) of this cell is given by

$$\frac{2.04\,\text{V}}{40.8\,\text{cm}} = \frac{2.00\,\text{V}}{40.0\,\text{cm}} = \frac{x}{31.7\,\text{cm}}$$

$$x = \frac{31.7\,\text{cm} \times 2.00\,\text{V}}{40\,\text{cm}} = 1.59\,\text{V}$$

One real advantage of this comparison method is that the e.m.f. of the cell is the p.d. across its terminals when it is not supplying current, and that is exactly what is happening here. The internal resistance of the cell is not affecting the result at all.

Chapter Summary

✓ Kirchhoff's first law: the total current arriving at a junction in any circuit is always equal to the total current leaving the junction.

✓ Kirchhoff's second law: around any complete loop in a circuit the sum of the potential differences is equal to the sum of the electromotive forces.

✓ Resistors in series. Total resistance
$$R = R_1 + R_2 + R_3 + \dots$$

✓ Resistors in parallel. Total resistance R given by
$$\frac{1}{R} = \frac{1}{R_1} + \frac{1}{R_2} + \frac{1}{R_3} + \dots$$

✓ All sources of electrical power have some resistance r within them. When connected to an external resistance R, the total circuit resistance is $(R + r)$. The relationship between the current I and the emf E of the supply will be $E = IR + Ir$.

Progress Check

12.1 Calculate the total resistance of the following arrangements.
  (a) 480 kΩ, 680 kΩ and 1.20 MΩ all in series.
  (b) 60 Ω in parallel with 120 Ω.
  (c) 4.0 kΩ, 12 kΩ and 16 kΩ all in parallel.
  (d) 4.0 kΩ in series with 12 kΩ and one 16 kΩ resistor in parallel with both.
  (e) 4.0 kΩ in series with a parallel arrangement of a 12 kΩ and a 6 kΩ in parallel.
  (f) 40 1.0 MΩ resistors all in parallel.

12.2 Deduce each of the unknown currents in the circuit of Figure 12.13.

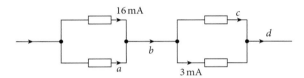

Figure 12.13

12.3 A network cube is constructed of 12 equal resistors as shown in Figure 12.14.

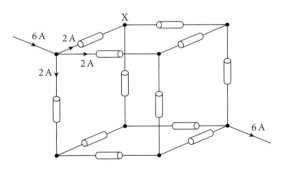

Figure 12.14

(a) There is a current of 6 A entering the cube network at one corner at one corner and divides equally as shown. How does the current divide at point X?
(b) On a copy of the diagram show the current in the various parts of the cube until 6 A emerges at the bottom right corner.
(c) The p.d across the cube is 25 V. Deduce the resistance of each resistor.

12.4 (a) Complete the following table for the circuit shown in Figure 12.15. The circuit is switched on for 200 s.

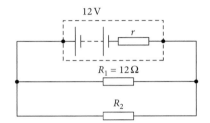

Figure 12.15

(b) What is the meaning of the symbol inside the dotted line?
(c) Explain what ratio of e.m.f. to current would be present in the box outlined with a solid rectangle.

	p.d. / V	current /A	resistance /Ω	charge /C	power /W	energy /J
battery	12			480		
internal resistance r						
resistance R_1			12			
resistance R_2		1.6				

12.5 (a) Draw a circuit diagram for a potentiometer circuit used for comparing e.m.f.s.

(b) A potentiometer is calibrated using a standard cell with e.m.f. 1.019 V. The balance point using this cell is 70.7 cm. Using a source with an unknown e.m.f. V, a balance point of 94.6 was obtained. Calculate V.

(c) Explain the effect on the result if the current from the driver cell decreases during the course of the experiment.

12.6 A torch battery that is almost 'dead' has an e.m.f. of 4.5 V and an internal resistance of 2.7 Ω. It is connected to a bulb with a resistance of 1.3 Ω.

Calculate the power being supplied to the bulb and compare this power with the power the bulb would have received when the battery was new and the internal resistance was only 0.3 Ω.

12.7 Explain why long mains extension leads are always sold with warnings

(a) not to be used for power over 2 kW when coiled up.

(b) the voltage supplied when using this lead may be lower than that required for certain pieces of equipment.

Examination Questions VI

1. (a) Define *potential difference* (p.d.).   [1]

(b) A power supply of e.m.f. 240 V and zero internal resistance is connected to a heater as shown in Figure 1.

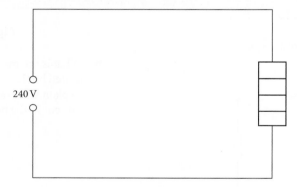

240 V

Figure 1

The wires used to connect the heater to the power supply each have length 75 m. The wires have a cross-sectional area 2.5 mm² and resistivity 18 nΩ m. The heater has a constant resistance of 38 Ω.

(i) Show that the resistance of each wire is 0.54 Ω.   [3]

(ii) Calculate the current in the wires, in A.   [3]

(iii) Calculate the power loss in the wires, in W.   [3]

(c) The wires to the heater are replaced by wires of the same length and material but having a cross-sectional area of 0.50 mm². Without further calculation, state and explain the effect on the power loss in the wires.   [2]

(Cambridge International AS and A Level Physics 9702 Paper 21 Question 6 October/November 2013)

2. An electric shower unit is to be fitted in a house. The shower is rated as 10.5 kW, 230 V. The shower unit is connected to the 230 V mains supply by a cable of length 16 m, as shown in Figure 2.

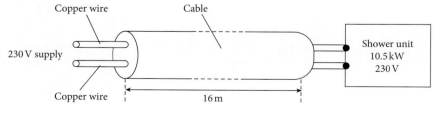

Copper wire   Cable

230 V supply

Shower unit
10.5 kW
230 V

Copper wire   16 m

Figure 2

(a) Show that, for normal operation of the shower unit, the current is approximately 46 A.   [2]

(b) The resistance of the two wires in the cable causes the potential difference across the shower unit to be reduced.
The potential difference across the shower unit must not be less than 225 V.
The wires in the cable are made of copper of resistivity $1.8 \times 10^{-8}\,\Omega$m.
Assuming that the current in the wires is 46 A, calculate
(i) the maximum resistance of the cable in Ω,   [3]
(ii) the minimum area of cross-section of each wire in the cable, in m^2.   [3]

(c) Connecting the shower unit to the mains supply by means of a cable having wires with too small a cross-sectional
area would significantly reduce the power output of the shower unit.
(i) Assuming that the shower is operating at 210 V, rather than 230 V, and that its resistance is unchanged,
determine the ratio

$$\frac{\text{power dissipated by shower unit at 210V}}{\text{power dissipated by shower unit at 230V}}$$

[2]
(ii) Suggest and explain one further disadvantage of using wires of small cross-sectional area in the cable.   [2]

(Cambridge International AS and A Level Physics 9702 Paper 02 Question 6 October/November 2007)

3. (a) A lamp is rated as 12V, 36W.
(i) Calculate the resistance of the lamp at its working temperature in Ω.   [2]
(ii) On the axes of Figure 3, sketch a graph to show the current-voltage (I–V) characteristic of the lamp. Mark an
appropriate scale for current on the y-axis.

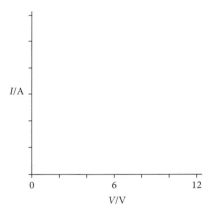

Figure 3

(b) Some heaters are each labelled 230V, 1.0 kW. The heaters have constant resistance.   [3]

Determine the total power dissipation for the heaters, in kW, connected as shown in each of the diagrams
shown below.

(i)

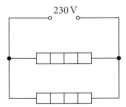

[1]

(ii)

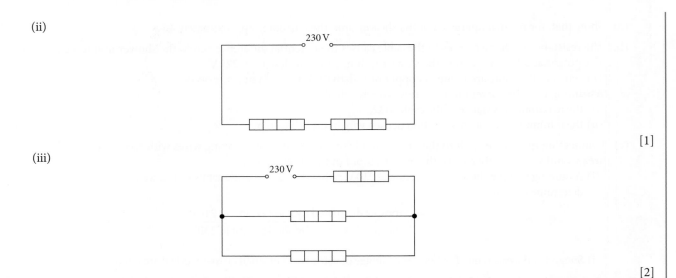

[1]

(iii)

[2]

(Cambridge International AS and A Level Physics 9702 Paper 21 Question 6 October/November 2010)

4. (a) (i) State Kirchhoff's second law. [1]
(ii) Kirchhoff's second law is linked to the conservation of a certain quantity. State this quantity. [1]

(b) The circuit shown in Figure 4 is used to compare potential differences.

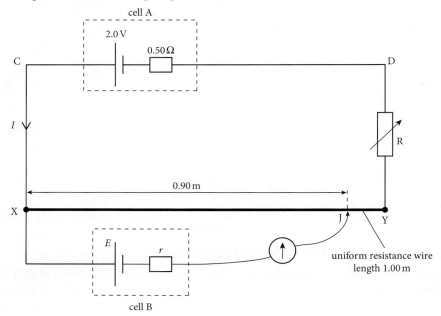

Figure 4

The uniform resistance wire XY has length 1.00 m and resistance 4.0 Ω. Cell A has e.m.f. 2.0 V and internal resistance 0.50 Ω. The current in cell A is I. Cell B has e.m.f. E and internal resistance r.

The current in cell B is made zero when the movable connection J is adjusted so that the length of XJ is 0.90 m. The variable resistor R has resistance 2.5 Ω.

(i) Apply Kirchhoff's second law to the circuit CXYDC to determine the current I, in A. [2]
(ii) Calculate the potential difference, in V, across the length of wire XJ. [2]
(iii) Use your answer in (ii) to state the value of E, in V. [1]
(iv) State why the value of the internal resistance of cell B is not required for the determination of E. [1]

(Cambridge International AS and A Level Physics 9702 Paper 21 Question 5 May/June 2012)

Nuclear Physics: Part A 13

Introduction

Until 1897 the atom was regarded as the smallest particle of any element. The hydrogen atom, as the smallest atom, was hence the smallest possible particle. Its mass was known reasonably accurately as 1.67×10^{-27} kg and from electrolysis experiments it was found that the H$^+$ ion had a charge to mass ratio of 9.6×10^7 coulombs per kilogram.

In 1897, J.J. Thomson found from experiments with high voltages on low-pressure gases that some particles existed with a charge to mass ratio 1840 times greater than that of the hydrogen ion. He soon showed that this was a particle with a charge equal and opposite to that on the hydrogen ion and so its mass needed to be 1/1840th of the hydrogen ion. He, thus, discovered the electron. He also found that electrons were present in all atoms. The search was then on for other particles smaller than an atom. This search is still going on.

Structure of the atom

Discovery of the nucleus of atoms

During the 1890s some other important discoveries were made. Roentgen discovered X-rays and Becquerel discovered radioactivity. Madame Curie did many experiments on radioactivity and had determined the mass, charge and speed of alpha particles, although she did not know their composition. Rutherford suggested to two of his students, Geiger and Marsden, that they should use alpha particles to bombard atoms just to see what happens. To reduce the likely number of multiple collisions, Geiger and Marsden used very thin sheets of gold foil as the target for the alpha particles. The experiment was carried out in a vacuum with the apparatus shown in Figure 13.1.

As expected these high energy particles in large numbers just passed straight through this very thin gold layer. This was not surprising since they were

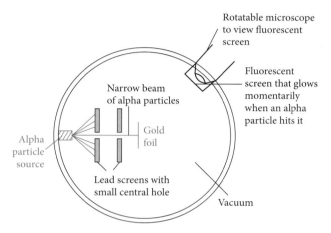

Figure 13.1

travelling with a speed about one tenth of the speed of light, and the gold foil was only about a thousandth of a millimetre thick. They did notice some stray alpha particles emerging at strange angles but at first thought that this was due to experimental error. Further analysis, however, showed that it was not an experimental error at all but a genuine deflection caused by a gold atom as shown in Figure 13.2.

When the numerical size of the electrical force necessary for these deflections was calculated it was found to be so large that the distance between the charge on the alpha particle and the charge on the gold atom had to be about 1/100 000 of the diameter of the atom. In other words, an atom must have all of its positive charge and most of its mass concentrated at its centre, it must have a nucleus. Experiments later confirmed that the ratio

$$\frac{\text{diameter of atom}}{\text{diameter of nucleus}} \text{ is of the order of } 10^5.$$

This makes the density of the nucleus about 10^{15} times the density of matter on a large scale.

This suggested a structure for atoms. For example, a hydrogen atom has a single proton as its nucleus

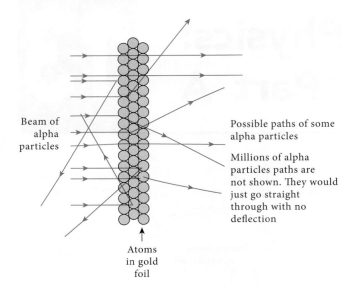

Beam of alpha particles

Possible paths of some alpha particles

Millions of alpha particles paths are not shown. They would just go straight through with no deflection

Atoms in gold foil

Figure 13.2

and an electron orbiting this nucleus. The proton contains nearly all the mass and is positively charged. The electron has a much smaller mass and is negatively charged. For atoms of other elements, the situation is more complicated. For example, helium has two protons in its nucleus and two electrons in orbit around the nucleus. The scientists discovered a problem: helium atoms have four times the mass of a hydrogen atom, not two times. Various suggestions were put forward to explain this, but it took another 20 years before Chadwick discovered the neutron. Neutrons have approximately the same mass as protons but they are uncharged. The helium atom contains two protons and usually two neutrons in its nucleus with two orbiting electrons.

The two positively charged protons are very close to one another in the nucleus , which means there is another problem. They repel one another with enormous electrostatic force. So what holds them together? It cannot be gravitational force because that force is too weak by a factor of over 10^{40}. There must be some force operating within the nucleus that is not any of the usual forces. This force is called the **nuclear force** and is in some way associated with neutrons. No element other than hydrogen exists without one or more neutrons in its nucleus, so neutrons do provide some sort of nuclear glue.

Isotopes

The number of neutrons in the nucleus of most elements is not fixed. For example, in an oxygen

atom, the number of both protons and electrons is 8. The 8 protons determine the atom to be oxygen. The number of neutrons in a stable oxygen atom, for example, can be 8 or 9 or 10. This makes some oxygen atoms more massive than other oxygen atoms. In oxygen, the proportion of uncharged atoms

- with 8 protons, 8 neutrons and 8 electrons is 99.759%,
- with 8 protons, 9 neutrons and 8 electrons is 0. 037%,
- with 8 protons, 10 neutrons and 8 electrons is 0.204%.

These three different forms of atoms are three isotopes of oxygen.

Isotopes are atoms with the same number of protons but with different numbers of neutrons in their nucleus.

Definitions and data

The number of protons in the nucleus of an atom determines the atom. This number is called the **proton number**. It used to be called the atomic number.

In an uncharged atom, the number of electrons is equal to the proton number.

An **ion** is an atom (or group of atoms) where the number of electrons is different from the proton number. Some ions are negative when they have more electrons than protons; some are positive when they have fewer electrons than protons.

The number of protons plus the number of neutrons in a nucleus is called the **nucleon number**. Both protons and neutrons are called **nucleons** as they are nuclear particles.

A **nuclide** is one particular atomic structure. This term is sometimes useful in sentences such as 'the carbon-12 nuclide and the carbon-13 nuclide are isotopes'.

Teacher's Tip
Be careful with the spelling of words beginning with an N. (There really are too many of them in nuclear physics.) Anything that has no charge is neutral – like a neutron. Anything to do with the centre of an atom is nuclear – like nuclide, nucleus and nuclear.

The full symbols used for nuclei are constructed in the way shown in Figure 13.3.

$$^{15}_{7}\text{N}$$

Figure 13.3

This symbol means that a nitrogen nucleus contains 7 protons and 15 nucleons, i.e. 7 protons and 8 neutrons.

Abbreviated table of data

It is useful to know some of the more obvious data from the table so that you are able to give examples. In Table 13.1, the mass of an atom is given in terms of the unified mass unit u. You may notice that a carbon-12 atom has a mass of 12 u exactly. This is because the **atomic mass unit is defined as**

one-twelfth of the mass of the carbon-12 atom. It is much more convenient to use u as the unit of mass for atoms because otherwise the masses in kilograms would be very clumsy. For example, the mass of the carbon-12 atom in kilograms is 1.9925×10^{-26} kg. This makes the conversion factor from units of u to units of kilograms as $1.000\,\text{u} = 1.6604 \times 10^{-27}$ kg.

Nuclear reactions

There is a wide range of different types of nuclear reaction. Radioactivity is one of them. Radioactivity was discovered by Becquerel because certain elements, of which uranium is the most common in the Earth's crust, have been undergoing decay ever since the Earth was formed, and are still decaying today. This should give you some idea of how very large is the

Table 13.1

Element	Symbol	Proton number	Nucleon number	No. of protons	No. of neutrons	No. of electrons	% of isotope	Mass/u
hydrogen	$^{1}_{1}\text{H}$	1	1	1	0	1	99.985	1.00783
deuterium	$^{2}_{1}\text{D}$	1	2	1	1	1	0.015	2.01410
tritium	$^{3}_{1}\text{T}$	1	3	1	2	1	trace	3.01605
helium	$^{3}_{2}\text{He}$	2	3	2	1	2	1.4×10^{-4}	3.01603
	$^{4}_{2}\text{He}$	2	4	2	2	2	100	4.00260
lithium	$^{6}_{3}\text{Li}$	3	6	3	3	3	7.42	6.01513
	$^{7}_{3}\text{Li}$	3	7	3	4	3	92.58	7.01600
carbon	$^{12}_{6}\text{C}$	6	12	6	6	6	98.89	12 exact
	$^{13}_{6}\text{C}$	6	13	6	7	6	1.11	13.00335
nitrogen	$^{14}_{7}\text{N}$	7	14	7	7	7	99.63	14.00307
	$^{15}_{7}\text{N}$	7	15	7	8	7	0,37	15.00011
oxygen	$^{16}_{8}\text{O}$	8	16	8	8	8	99.759	15.99492
	$^{17}_{8}\text{O}$	8	17	8	9	8	0.037	16.99913
	$^{18}_{8}\text{O}$	8	18	8	10	8	0.204	17.99916
lead	$^{204}_{82}\text{Pb}$	82	204	82	122	82	1.5	203.973
	$^{206}_{82}\text{Pb}$	82	206	82	124	82	23.6	205.974
	$^{207}_{82}\text{Pb}$	82	207	82	125	82	22.6	206.976
	$^{208}_{82}\text{Pb}$	82	208	82	126	82	52.3	207.977
uranium	$^{235}_{92}\text{U}$	92	235	92	143	92	0.72	235.044
	$^{238}_{92}\text{U}$	92	238	92	146	92	99.28	238.051

number of atoms in a kilogram of any substance. Thousands of atoms can decay from a kilogram of uranium every second for five billion years and there are still many left to decay during the next few billion years.

This decay from uranium can be expressed in this equation.

$$^{238}_{92}U \rightarrow \, ^{4}_{2}He + \, ^{234}_{90}Th + energy$$

The uranium nucleus consists of 92 protons and 146 neutrons. What causes it to emit an alpha particle is not known. The alpha particle is a helium nucleus with 2 protons and 2 neutrons and it is ejected at high speed leaving behind a thorium nucleus of 90 protons and 144 neutrons. Conservation laws apply to this process:

1. The sums of the proton numbers on both sides of the equation are equal $(92 = 2 + 90)$,
2. the sums of the nucleon numbers on both sides of the equation are equal $(238 = 4 + 234)$,
3. the mass-energy totals on both sides of the equation are equal.

The first two of these conservation laws are clear from the equation. More detail about mass-energy will be given later in this book. At present you need to be aware that there is an equivalence between mass and energy $(E = mc^2)$ and if all mass and energy is added together then there is equality between the two sides of the equation. In practice, the kinetic energy of the alpha particle is possible because the mass of the alpha particle plus the mass of the thorium nucleus is not quite equal to the mass of the uranium nucleus.

Once formed, the thorium-234 nucleus is itself radioactive. It decays by this process.

$$^{234}_{90}Th \rightarrow \, ^{0}_{-1}\beta + \, ^{234}_{91}Pa + energy$$

The beta particle has a charge of −1 and negligible mass. It is an electron that comes from the nucleus by a reaction that changes a neutron into an electron and a proton. Note that proton number, nucleon number and mass-energy are conserved in the equation. Note also that this was

why Becquerel was able to identify two types of radiation from uranium. He also found a third type of radiation, gamma rays, that are now known to be electromagnetic radiation of very high frequencies.

Other nuclear reactions can be caused by firing particles at different materials. For example, when alpha particles travel through air an occasional collision takes place between the alpha particles and a nitrogen nucleus. The collision causes a nuclear reaction of which the equation is

$$^{14}_{7}N + \, ^{4}_{2}He + energy = \, ^{17}_{8}O + \, ^{1}_{1}H$$

This equation provided the first evidence that it was possible to change elements into different elements. (This was called the transmutation of elements, something that alchemists had been trying to do for centuries in their search for making gold.) Here all it changes nitrogen into oxygen – one atom at a time.

Neutrons hitting uranium-235 can cause this reaction.

$$^{235}_{92}U + \, ^{1}_{0}n \rightarrow \, ^{236}_{92}U \rightarrow \, ^{90}_{38}Sr + \, ^{143}_{54}Xe + 3\, ^{1}_{0}n + energy$$

This is called a fission reaction. More neutrons are created than start the reaction so a chain reaction is possible. It can release energy explosively in a nuclear bomb. It is the reaction used in nuclear power stations where the excess neutrons are carefully controlled.

Experiments with radioactive materials

Becquerel first detected radioactivity using photographic film. The film became darkened in the presence of uranium salts. Later cloud chambers were used. These enabled tracks of individual particles, particularly alpha particles, to be seen. When an alpha particle travels through air it causes a large amount of ionisation of the air. If the air is moist then condensation of the vapour takes place on the ionisation and the track can be seen. A photograph of alpha particle tracks is shown in Figure 13.4.

Figure 13.4

Figure 13.6

The same principle is now used in bubble chambers where high energy particles are passed into liquid hydrogen. The energy provided by the particle is sufficient to cause hydrogen along the path of the particle to vaporise. This is shown in Figure 13.5. The complex nature of the photograph not only shows how many particles can be produced in a nuclear reaction but also that the particles must have been travelling in a magnetic field in order to be moved in circles of decreasing radius. In school laboratories Geiger tubes or solid state detectors can be used to detect radioactivity. These are connected to counters that can record either the rate at which nuclear reactions are taking place or the total number of reactions. A typical set up is shown in Figure 13.6. The counters usually have built in loudspeakers that give a click when a count takes place.

The radioactive events which give rise to the individual counts take place at *random*. It is impossible to predict when a count will occur; there may be pauses, there may be a sudden rush of counts. No one knows when any particular atom is going to decay. A nucleus of a uranium atom may have existed on the Earth for almost five billion years without changing at all – and then decay while you are carrying out an experiment with it.

Figure 13.5

Decay of a nucleus is not only random it is also *spontaneous*. This means that there is nothing that can be done to affect the rate of decay by a particular radioactive source. Scientists have tried many different things to get a source to decay at a different rate.

- Raising or lowering the temperature makes no difference.
- Raising or lowering the pressure makes no difference.
- Chemical combination makes no difference.
- Electric or magnetic field strength makes no difference.

This is not really surprising because all of these processes affect atoms whereas what is needed is something to affect a nucleus. The energy associated with atoms is usually of the order of a few electron-volts. (1 electron-volt = 1.60×10^{-19} J.) The energy associated with the nucleus is of the order of a few million electron-volts.

Properties of alpha (α), beta (β^-) and gamma (γ) radiations

These radiations have been mentioned several times in this chapter. Table 13.2 summarises their properties.

They were the first radioactive radiations to be discovered and although since then hundreds of different radiations have been discovered, most of these are only seen in very high energy nuclear reactions. The Large Hadron Collider at CERN is revealing more nuclear particles.

Table 13.2

	Symbol	Typical speed	Charge	Mass /u	Ionising power arbitrary units	Penetrating power	Effect of fields	
							electric	magnetic
alpha	α	a tenth the speed of light, $c/10$	$+2e$	4	10 000	a few cm of air	little curvature	circles of large radius
beta	β^-	almost the speed of light, $0.99c$	$-e$	1/1840	100	3 mm aluminium	large curvature opposite to alpha	circles of small radius
gamma	γ	the speed of light, c	zero	zero	1	several cm of lead	none	none

Antiparticles

In 1932 a particle with similar properties to an electron was found to have a positive charge. It is called a positron and has been given the symbol β^+ in contrast to β^- for an electron. This was the first particle of antimatter to be discovered but since then corresponding antimatter particles have been found for all particles. When an electron combines with a positron they can annihilate one another to produce gamma radiation only.

One aspect of the decay given in Table 13.2 is that when a beta particle is emitted, another particle is also emitted. This particle is called a neutrino. A neutrino has no charge and negligible mass. It barely reacts with any other particle but there are vast numbers of neutrinos passing through you every second as a result of nuclear reactions on the Sun and every other star. There are also antineutrinos. In β^- decay one of the neutrons (n) in the nucleus of the decaying element changes to a proton (p), an electron (e) and a particle called an electron-antineutrino ($\overline{v}_e$). The equation is

$$n = p + e^- + \overline{v}_e$$

Fundamental Particles

During the last 120 years many experiments have been performed to establish the nature of matter. The discovery of radioactivity in 1896 and the electron in 1897 was followed by Geiger and Marsden's experiment in 1911 establishing the presence of the nucleus, containing protons, in all atoms. Neutrons were not discovered until the 1930s. Even at that time other subatomic particles were being suggested.

The methods used in research on fundamental particles are varied. The earliest experiments used the fact that emissions of radioactivity caused photographic film to darken. This was later improved by using large cubes of emulsion floated to great heights under balloons to investigate highly energetic particles from the Sun. Mesons were discovered this way. Energetic particles can cause a vapour to condense to form a liquid, and this effect is frequently used in modern particle detector experiments. Bubble chambers use this method in getting liquid hydrogen to vaporise along the path of a particle. By carrying out an experiment in a magnetic field, the charge on any particle can be determined. A photograph showing the detail that can be obtained is given in Figure 13.5.

All the recent experiments have established that protons and neutrons are not fundamental particles. They contain *quarks*.

The (relatively) massive particles: protons, neutrons and mesons are collectively called hadrons. Table 13.3 shows some of the physical properties of three types of quark, the up, down and strange quarks. The Baryon number is a property assigned to quarks to assist in explaining how different numbers of quarks 'add up' to make particles such as protons and neutrons. Strangeness is another such property, which helps to explain the existence of other more unusual particles.

Table 13.3

Quark	Up	Down	Strange
Symbol	u	d	s
Charge	$+\frac{2}{3}e$	$-\frac{1}{3}e$	$-\frac{1}{3}e$
Baryon number	$\frac{1}{3}$	$\frac{1}{3}$	$\frac{1}{3}$
Strangeness	0	0	−1

Each of these quarks has a corresponding antiparticle $\bar{u}$, $\bar{d}$ and $\bar{s}$.

The quark arrangement of four hadrons is shown in Figure 13.7.

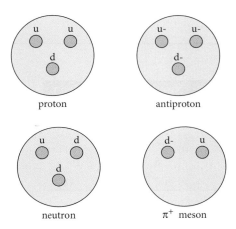

proton

antiproton

neutron

π^+ meson

Figure 13.7

All protons have baryon number $\frac{1}{3} + \frac{1}{3} + \frac{1}{3} = 1$ and charge $\frac{2}{3}e + \frac{2}{3}e - \frac{1}{3}e = e$

Mesons have two quarks in their structure.

Beta decay

In all the physics you have studied so far the forces between objects have been the (very weak) gravitational force and the much stronger electric and magnetic forces. Within the nucleus, these forces cannot explain how protons are held tightly together despite the electrical repulsion due to their charge. Physicists discovered a force called the 'strong nuclear force' that overcomes the electrical repulsion at very short range. However, this force alone cannot account for beta decay. There is a weak interaction between quarks that gives rise to both β^- and β^+ decay. The following two equations show an example of each decay.

$$^{14}_{6}C \rightarrow {}^{14}_{7}N + {}^{0}_{-1}e + {}^{0}_{0}\bar{\nu} \quad (\beta^- \text{ decay})$$
$$^{16}_{8}O \rightarrow {}^{16}_{7}N + {}^{0}_{+1}e + {}^{0}_{0}\nu \quad (\beta^+ \text{ decay})$$

The electrons and neutrinos in these equations are fundamental particles with zero or very little mass. These types of fundamental particles are called **leptons**.

Chapter Summary

✓   The experiment of firing α-particles at gold foil and finding that some of them bounced backwards led to the conclusion that all atoms had a positively charged nucleus of very small diameter. The electrons necessary to make the atom neutral overall were initially thought to be in orbit around the nucleus.

✓   Later, neutrons were discovered and these provide a way of holding the protons together within the nucleus.

✓   The proton number of an atom is the number of protons in its nucleus. This determines what element it is. In a neutral atom this will equal the number of electrons in the atom.

✓   The nucleon number of any atom is the number of protons plus the number of neutrons. The number of neutrons in an atom of an element can vary, giving rise to isotopes of different mass for most elements.

✓   α-particles consist of two protons and two neutrons.

✓   β⁻-particles are electrons.

✓   γ-rays are high frequency electromagnetic radiation.

✓   β⁻-particles are electrons, β⁺-particles are positrons.

✓   γ-rays are high frequency electromagnetic radiation.

✓   Protons and neutrons each contain 3 quarks.

✓   The weak interaction between quarks is responsible for β decay.

Progress Check

13.1 In the table, which line contains two isotopes?

	Number of protons	Number of neutrons	Nucleon number	Number of protons	Number of neutrons	Nucleon number
A	8	8	16	8	9	17
B	8	9	17	9	8	17
C	7	9	16	8	8	16
D	7	8	15	8	7	15

13.2 A mass of 1u is equal to 1.660×10^{-27} kg. Calculate the mass of a carbon-13 atom.

13.3 A good breath will result in you inhaling around 0.2 g of oxygen. How many atoms of oxygen will be inhaled?

13.4 Write equations to show the following nuclear reactions:

(a) Two hydrogen-2 nuclei fusing to form a neutron and a helium nucleus.

(b) A helium-4 nucleus (an alpha particle) colliding with a nitrogen nucleus to form an oxygen nucleus and another particle.

(c) A neutron colliding with a boron-10 nucleus to produce both a lithium nucleus and a helium nucleus.

1. (a) An electric field is set up between two parallel metal plates in a vacuum. The deflection of α-particles as they pass between the plates is shown in Figure 1.

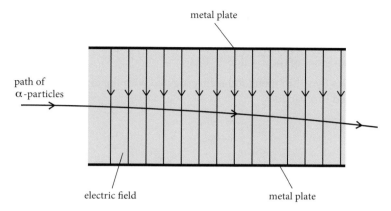

metal plate

path of
α-particles

electric field   metal plate

Figure 1

The electric field strength between the plates is reduced. The α-particles are replaced by β-particles. The deflection of β-particles is shown in Figure 2.

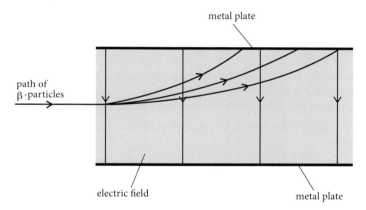

metal plate

path of
β-particles

electric field   metal plate

Figure 2

(i) State one similarity of the electric fields shown in FIgure 1 and Figure 2. [1]

(ii) The electric field strength in Figure 2 is less than that in Figure 1. State two methods of reducing this electric field strength. [2]

(iii) By reference to the properties of α-particles and β-particles, suggest three reasons for the differences in the deflections shown in Figure 1 and Figure 2. [3]

(b) A source of α-particles is uranium-238. The nuclear reaction for the emission of α-particles is represented by

$$^{238}_{92}U \rightarrow {}^{W}_{X}Q + {}^{Y}_{Z}\alpha.$$

State the values of W, X, Y and Z. [2]

(c) A source of β-particles is phosphorus-32. The nuclear reaction for the emission of β-particles is represented by

$$^{32}_{15}P \rightarrow ^{A}_{B}R + ^{C}_{D}\beta.$$

State the values of A, B, C and D. [1]

**(Cambridge International AS and A Level Physics 9702
Paper 21 Question 7 October/November 2013)**

2. (a) Describe the structure of an atom of the nuclide $^{235}_{92}U$. [2]

(b) The deflection of α-particles by a thin metal foil is investigated with the arrangement shown in Figure 3. All the apparatus is enclosed in a vacuum.

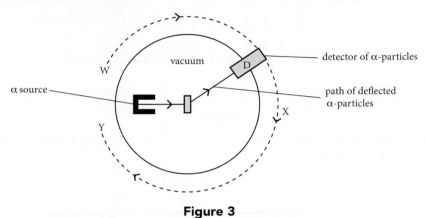

Figure 3

The detector of α-particles, D, is moved around the path labelled WXY.
(i) Explain why the apparatus is enclosed in a vacuum. [1]
(ii) State and explain the readings detected by D when it is moved along WXY. [3]

(c) A beam of α-particles produces a current of 1.5 pA. Calculate the number of α-particles per second passing a point in the beam. [3]

**(Cambridge International AS and A Level Physics 9702
Paper 21 Question 6 October/November 2012)**

Physical Quantities, Units and Measurement Techniques

This chapter is short because it adds some extra A-level detail to the work covered for AS-level in Chapters 1 and 2.

Amount of substance

Those of you who are studying both chemistry and physics will no doubt be very familiar with this concept. In the early 19th century, Avogadro investigated the chemical combination of gases. Avogadro found that when gases combined with one another they combined in small whole number volumes. For example, under the same conditions of temperature and pressure, two volumes of hydrogen combined with one volume of oxygen to form two volumes of steam. Avogadro deduced that on a small scale it must mean that two molecules of hydrogen were combining with one molecule of oxygen to produce two molecules of steam. Avogadro had little idea about the actual size of these molecules but that did not alter his belief that molecules did exist. We now know that in a particular reaction, perhaps 1.084×10^{23} molecules of hydrogen would combine with 0.542×10^{23} molecules of oxygen to form 1.084×10^{23} molecules of steam, but numbers such as this are inconvenient to use and lose the simple clarity of the two volumes, one volume, two volumes relationship.

Avogadro was at an advantage using gases because, as he also stated, equal volumes of gases at the same temperature and pressure contain the same number of molecules. This is not true for liquids and solids. The reason why solids and liquids behave differently from gases is that whereas in solids and liquids the molecules are tightly packed together, in a gas the volume occupied is often a thousand times greater than the volume of the molecules themselves. More details will be given about this in Chapter 17.

In order to avoid the problems of considering large numbers of molecules it was decided to have a standard **amount of substance**. This is now one of the SI base units. Amount of substance is measured in **moles,** for which the abbreviation is **mol.**

As usual with the base units the choice of numerical size of the unit is based partly on historical values and partly on practicalities. A large number was required and the value now chosen is called the **Avogadro constant.**

The Avogadro constant, symbol N_A, is the number of atoms in 12 grams (0.012 kg) of the nuclide carbon-12. Its value can be measured very precisely and is $6.022\ 141\ 8 \times 10^{23}$. You will be unlikely to need this number of significant figures and its value to three significant figures usually will be stated in questions you are given or on a data sheet.

Teacher's Tip

12 grams of carbon-12 contain a mole of atoms but be careful to get the mass you are considering in the correct unit. 12 kilograms of carbon-12 atoms will obviously contain 1000 moles of atoms. Errors of a factor of 1000 are common when answering questions using moles.

One mole is the amount of any substance that contains a number of particles equal to the Avogadro constant.

This means that the Avogadro constant can be written as $6.022 \times 10^{23}\ \text{mol}^{-1}$.

It also means that the earlier awkward large number equation for the formation of steam can be replaced by the much simpler molar equation

1.80 mol of hydrogen + 0.90 mol oxygen
$$\rightarrow 1.80\,\text{mol steam}$$

Experimental techniques

See Chapter 24 for details of measuring magnetic flux density using a Hall probe.

Motion in a Circle

Angular measure

The division of a right angle into 90° and a revolution into 360° is a very old measurement linked to the rotation of the Earth and time. It is an arbitrary definition that in several situations is not very convenient. You will find it necessary to be able to use a different system of angular measure in which the basic unit of angle is called the **radian**. Figure 15.1 shows how a radian is defined.

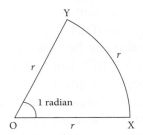

Figure 15.1

A point O is at the centre of a circle of radius r. A compass drawing the circle moves from X to a point Y after it has drawn an arc of length r. The angle YOX is then defined as one **radian** and the abbreviation is 'rad'. An angle measured in radians is the distance along the arc of a circle divided by the radius of the circle.

$$\text{angle } \theta = \frac{\text{arc length}}{\text{radius of circle}}$$

This means that if a complete circle is drawn, then the length of the arc is $2\pi r$ and the angle for one complete revolution will be $2\pi r/r = 2\pi$, as shown in Figure 15.2.

Note that from the definition of an angle, the equation of which gives a length divided by another length, the angle measured in radians has no units. It is convention, however, to always write 'rad' after an angle measurement.

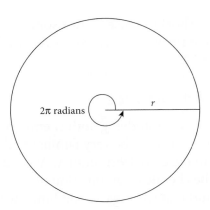

Figure 15.2

Angular velocity

The Earth rotates about its axis and during one day it completes one revolution, so it has an angular displacement of 2π rad. It is logical from this statement to define that **angular velocity** is the angular displacement per unit time.

The symbol used for angular velocity is ω, the Greek lower case letter omega.

The angular velocity of the Earth on its axis is therefore

$$\frac{2\pi \,\text{rad}}{(60 \times 60 \times 24)\text{s}} = 7.272 \times 10^{-5} \text{ rad s}^{-1}$$

The relationship between angular velocity ω and speed v

An object travelling with a constant speed v around the circumference of a circle of radius r, will travel a distance $x = vt$ in time t.

The angle moved through in this time is $\theta = x/r = vt/r$

This gives the angular velocity

$$\omega = \theta/t = vt/rt = v/r \quad \text{or} \quad v = r\omega$$

Small angle approximations for angles

Radian measure is particularly useful when considering small angles. Figure 15.3 shows a small angle θ and a line of length OA at which an arc of arc length AC is drawn.

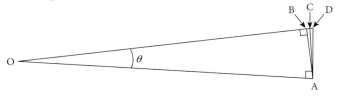

Figure 15.3

Two triangles are superimposed on the diagram, $\triangle$OAB with a right angle at B and $\triangle$OAD with a right angle at A. From $\angle$OAB,

$$\sin \theta = \frac{AB}{OA} \text{ and from } \triangle OAD \tan \theta = \frac{AD}{OA}$$

$$\text{and } \theta \text{ in radians} = \frac{AC}{OA}.$$

Notice that as θ gets smaller and smaller, the three lines AB, AC and AD get closer and closer together, and as they do this they get nearer and nearer to becoming the same length. This means that as θ gets smaller $\sin \theta$, $\tan \theta$ and θ itself approach equality, as shown in the following table.

θ rad	$\sin \theta$	$\tan \theta$	$\theta/°$
0.5000	0.4794	0.5463	28.65
0.2000	0.1986	0.2027	11.46
0.1000	0.0998	0.1003	5.73
0.0800	0.0799	0.0802	4.58
0.0100	0.0100	0.0100	0.57

Circular motion

Circular motion is very common. There are the obvious examples such as the movement of the hands of a clock, a roundabout on a playground, a CD or DVD in a CD player or computer, the London Eye big wheel, etc. In most machines some parts rotate; a drill, the gearwheels in the gear-box of a car, the wheels of a car, the fan in a cooling system and an electrical generator are some examples. Then there are situations involving orbits; the movement of planets and moons, the movement of electrons around nuclei, the movement of protons in the Large Hadron Collider at CERN. In many cases, a complete circle may not be achieved but for part of a circle the same criterion is valid as for a complete circle. Examples are an aircraft changing course, a motorcyclist negotiating a bend and even an animal moving to escape from a predator.

This topic will be different from the mechanics you have done earlier. There you were considering acceleration in a straight line as a result of change in velocity, where the two velocities were in the same direction. In this section, the velocities are not in the same direction but Newton's laws still hold in exactly the same way as before. The problem arises in deducing the direction of the acceleration.

Acceleration at constant speed

This heading may seem at first sight to be a contradiction in terms. It is not. The following example will show you why it is not. Once you have understood the concept of acceleration at constant speed, the rest of this chapter should be easier to understand. The example will be followed with the generalisation of the idea in algebraic terms.

Example 1

An aircraft has to be kept in a holding circle for a time before there is a space available for landing. It is travelling in a horizontal circle of radius 6000 m with a constant speed of 120 m s^{-1}. Calculate

(a) the time to complete one circle, this is a rotation of 2π radians,
(b) the short time taken for the angular movement to be 0.01 radians,
(c) the distance moved in this time,
(d) the change in velocity in the short time calculated in (b),
(e) the magnitude of the acceleration,
(f) the direction of the acceleration.

Answer
(a) Circumference/speed for one orbit
    $= (2\pi \times 6000)/120 = 314.16\,s$

(b) Time for 1 radian $= 314.16\,s/2\pi = 50.0\,s$
    Therefore time for 1/100 radian $= 50.0/100$
    $= 0.500\,s$

(c) $120\,m\,s^{-1} \times 0.500\,s = 60.0\,m$

(d) This is an important question. Figure 15.4 shows the original velocity at $120\,\mathrm{m\,s^{-1}}$ and the new velocity, also at $120\,\mathrm{m\,s^{-1}}$ in a direction that is at an angle of 0.01 radians to the original velocity. The speed is the same only the direction is slightly different.

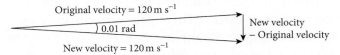

Figure 15.4

The change in velocity is required. Subtraction of vectors was explained in Chapter 1 where it was pointed out that it can be done by establishing the vector that needs to be added to the original vector in order to get the final vector. In this case it is the small vector labelled 'new velocity – original velocity'. The magnitude of this velocity, using the small angle approximation explained earlier in this chapter, equals $v\theta$.

$$v\theta = 120\,\mathrm{m\,s^{-1}} \times 0.01\,\mathrm{rad} = 1.2\,\mathrm{m\,s^{-1}}$$

(e) magnitude of acceleration

$$= \frac{\text{change in velocity}}{\text{time}} = \frac{1.2\,\mathrm{m\,s^{-1}}}{0.500\,\mathrm{s}} = 2.4\,\mathrm{m\,s^{-2}}t$$

(f) The change in velocity is given by the small arrow in Figure 15.4 and is effectively at right angles to both velocity vectors. It is inwards towards the centre of the circular path.

Acceleration in circular motion at constant speed

Consider an object moving in a circle of radius r at a constant speed v.

Figure 15.5(a) shows the object when its initial velocity is v_i and after it has travelled round in the circle by a very small angle θ, its final velocity v_f.

The distance the object has travelled $= r\theta$

This distance travelled is also vt where t is the time taken to get from the initial to the final position.

Figure 15.5(b) shows the vector triangle to find the change in the velocity of the object Δv which is $\Delta v = v\theta$ by use of the small angle approximation.

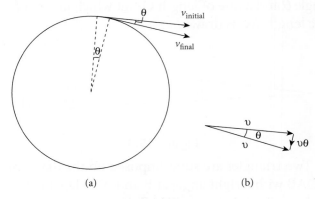

(a)   (b)

Figure 15.5

Combining the above equations for distance travelled, we get $t = r\theta/v$ and

$$\text{acceleration} = \frac{\text{change in velocity}}{\text{time}} = \frac{\Delta v}{t} = \frac{v\theta}{r\theta/v} = \frac{v^2}{r}$$

Note that θ cancels out in this analysis so it could have been vanishingly small, making the small angle approximation perfect.

By substituting the expression of angular velocity $\omega = v/r$ in the above equation, we can get another expression for the acceleration of an object travelling with constant speed in a circle as

$$\text{acceleration} = \frac{v^2}{r} = r\omega^2$$

This acceleration is directed towards the centre of the circular path and is called the **centripetal acceleration.**

The force required for a centripetal acceleration

This part of the chapter is straightforward. Just apply Newton's second law of motion, $F = ma$. As the force and the acceleration are vectors, they must be in the same direction. The force will be the **resultant** force on the object and it is called the **centripetal force**. Note carefully that it is a resultant force. It is the sum of all the forces acting on the body. For example, consider the aircraft travelling horizontally in its holding circle in the example given on the previous page. Figure 15.6 shows a free-body force diagram for the aircraft. The aircraft has a mass of 1.80×10^5 kg, so its weight is 1.76×10^6 N.

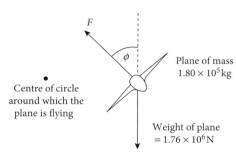

Figure 15.6

The aircraft is only touching one thing – the air around it. Apart from the engine forces acting forwards and equal drag forces acting backwards if the aircraft has constant speed, the only two forces acting on the aircraft are the gravitational force on the aircraft (its weight) and the force that air exerts on the aircraft. The wings of the aircraft cannot be horizontal when the aircraft is turning. This means that the force F the air exerts on the aircraft is at an angle ϕ to the vertical, as shown.

For horizontal flight the resultant upward force must be zero, so

$$F \cos \phi = 1.76 \times 10^6 \, \text{N} \qquad \textbf{Equation I}$$

For acceleration of 2.4 m s⁻², the horizontal component of F is given by

$$F \sin \phi = ma = 1.80 \times 10^5 \times 2.4 = 432\,000 \, \text{N}$$
$$\textbf{Equation II}$$

Dividing Equation II by Equation I, we get

$$\tan \phi = 432\,000 / 1.76 \times 10^6 = 0.245$$

and ϕ is therefore 13.8°.

F is, therefore, $1.76 \times 10^6 / \cos 13.8° = 1.81 \times 10^6$ N.

Note that in this case, the resultant force on the aircraft is the horizontal component of the lift, 4.32×10^5 N, and this would be called the centripetal force. This resultant centripetal force F is given by

$$F = mr\omega^2 \text{ or } F = \frac{mv^2}{r}.$$

Teacher's Tip

Mistakes on circular motion are often caused by people putting in a centripetal force as well as the forces actually acting. Avoid this problem by concentrating on actual forces. Weight is one obvious force to go on a force diagram and so is any contact force. For example, consider yourself sitting in the aircraft travelling in the horizontal circle described above. You have your weight acting vertically downwards and the force your seat exerts on you. This would be a force acting directly towards the ceiling of the cabin. It would not be vertical. If you look out of the windows you will see on one side the ground and on the other side the sky. NO OTHER FORCES ACT ON YOU so do not put any other forces on your diagram. The resultant of these two forces is what is causing you to rotate in a horizontal circle with the aircraft itself.

Chapter Summary

✓ Angular velocity $\omega = 2\pi$/time for one revolution, $\omega = 2\pi/T$.
✓ For an object travelling in a circle of radius r with constant angular velocity ω the speed v of the object is given by $v = r\omega$.

✓ The centripetal acceleration a of an object travelling at constant speed v in a circle of radius r is given by
$a = \dfrac{v^2}{r} = r\omega^2$, where ω is the angular velocity.
✓ The resultant centripetal force F is given by $F = mr\omega^2$
or $F = \dfrac{mv^2}{r}$.

Progress Check

15.1 Convert
  (a) a right angle into radians,
  (b) 45° into radians,
  (c) 0.001° into radians,
  (d) 3 radians into degrees,
  (e) π radians into degrees.

15.2 Calculate the angular velocity of
  (a) an electric drill making 2750 revolutions per minute,
  (b) a food mixer making one revolution in 0.32 s,
  (c) the Moon making one revolution of the Earth in 27 days and 8 hours,
  (d) a roundabout making a revolution in 13.5 s.

15.3 (a) Calculate the angular velocity of an object travelling along a circular path of radius 6.4 m with a speed of 3.8 m s⁻¹.
  (b) Calculate the radius of the circular path of an object that has an angular velocity of 4.5 rad s⁻¹ and a constant speed of 27 m s⁻¹.
  (c) Calculate the speed of the International Space Station that has an angular velocity of 1.16×10^{-3} rad s⁻¹ and is in a circular orbit of radius 7200 km.

15.4 Calculate the magnitude of the acceleration of each of the objects in question **15.3.**

15.5 A ball of mass 2.0 kg is rotating in a horizontal circle of radius 0.24 m. This arrangement, known as a conical pendulum, is shown in Figure 15.7.

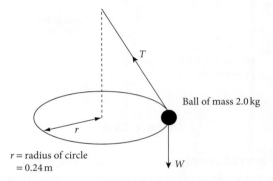

r = radius of circle
  = 0.24 m

Figure 15.7

The length of the string supporting the ball is 1.6 m. Calculate the tension in the string, the magnitude of the acceleration of the ball, and its angular velocity.

Gravitational Field

Introduction

We all live in a gravitational field. In fact we all can observe the effects of three gravitational fields. There is the gravitational field of the Earth itself, that is by far the largest gravitational field at the surface of the Earth but there are also the gravitational fields of the Moon and the Sun.

Gravitational field strength

Although gravitational field acts on mass, the human body has no gravitational sensor and so it cannot be felt. What we certainly do notice is its effect on mass. It causes acceleration of free fall. It was mentioned in Chapter 4 that the alternative ways of defining g either as the acceleration of free fall or the gravitational force per unit mass gives $g = 9.81\,\mathrm{m\,s^{-2}}$ or $g = 9.81\,\mathrm{N\,kg^{-1}}$ and that this is little more than using the equation from Newton's second law as either

$$F = mg \quad \text{OR} \quad g = \frac{F}{m}$$

Gravitational field strength, however, uses the second equation.

Gravitational field strength is the force per unit mass. It is a vector so its direction needs to be given.

For the Earth, the gravitational field strength has the value $9.8\,\mathrm{N\,kg^{-1}}$ to two significant figures. There are small variations in its value on Earth because the Earth is not quite a sphere and also its density is not constant. In places where there are large deposits of heavy metal compounds, the value of 'g' is larger. Also, the gravitational field strength of the Earth is not usually identical to the acceleration of free fall. This is because of the rotation of the Earth. Part of the gravitational force on an object is used to cause the object's rotation once per day and the rest of the force causes its free fall acceleration towards the ground.

Figure 16.1 is a two-dimensional diagram of the Earth's gravitational field.

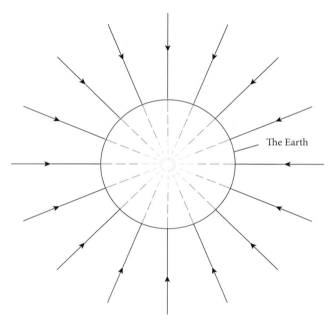

Figure 16.1 Earth's gravitational field

The field is greatest at the Earth's surface and gradually fades out until it becomes zero at the centre of the Earth. One useful fact about this field is that, at and beyond the Earth's surface, the gravitational field strength has the same value as it would have if all the mass of the Earth were concentrated at a point at its centre.

For any point outside a uniform sphere, the mass of the sphere may be considered to be a point mass at its centre.

Newton's law of gravitation

After Newton had stated his three laws of motion, he began to apply them to situations he was familiar with. He deduced the following facts:

- the value of the acceleration due to gravity, g
- the radius of the Earth, r
- the distance between the centre of the Earth and the centre of the Moon, R
- the centripetal acceleration of the Moon, a.

When he compared distances and accelerations he found, in round figures, that

$$R = 60r \quad \text{and} \quad a = \frac{g}{3600}$$

He deduced that it could not be a coincidence that 3600 is 60^2. He realised that gravity, the force causing objects to fall on the Earth, is the same type of force that keeps the Moon in orbit round the Earth. It is apparent that the gravitational field decreases with the square of the distance. That is, when 60 times further away the gravitational field is smaller by a factor of 3600. Newton then summarised his findings in a universal law of gravitation now known as Newton's law of gravitation. Expressed in equation form, this is

$$F = \frac{Gm_1m_2}{r^2}$$

where F is the force of attraction between two point masses m_1 and m_2 when placed at a distance r apart. G is a constant known as the **universal constant of gravitation**. Its value is $6.673 \times 10^{-11}\,\text{N}\,\text{m}^2\,\text{kg}^{-2}$. Gravitational force is always an attractive force. No gravitational force of repulsion has ever been detected, even between matter and antimatter. (Antimatter existed at the time of the Big Bang. When antimatter meets matter both are annihilated to give energy. Luckily there is very, very little antimatter about now!)

The relationship between g and G

The gravitational field strength g at a point is defined as the gravitational force per unit mass at that point. Figure 16.2 shows a point mass M at a distance r from a mass of one kilogram.

The force on the one kilogram mass is given by

$$F = \frac{Gm_1m_2}{r^2} = \frac{GM \times 1}{r^2} = \frac{GM}{r^2}$$

The gravitational force per unit mass is g, so the equation relating g to G is

$$g = \frac{GM}{r^2}$$

Gravitational potential

From time to time people worry about terrible disasters. One particular disaster that affected the Earth around 60 million years ago wiped out the dinosaurs. This may have been caused by a collision between the Earth and some large object from space. On 15 February 2013, an asteroid of mass 130 000 tonnes passed within 32 000 km of the Earth travelling with speed 29 000 km h⁻¹. At this distance it was close enough to hit a communications satellite. Certainly some collisions between asteroids of masses of a few thousand tonnes are well known because of the craters they have left behind. The damage that could be caused by such objects is considerable and depends on the kinetic energy of the object. Gravitational potential is a quantity that enables this to be calculated.

An object out in space that happens to be on course for the Earth has only a small force accelerating it towards the Earth, but as it gently falls towards the Earth the force gets marginally larger. This carries on with the force increasing the nearer it gets. During the last few hours of its approach, when it is still outside of any real atmosphere its speed will increase very rapidly. Only in the last few seconds will the atmosphere have much influence on it. It is like a ball falling down a slope of the shape shown in Figure 16.3(a). In three dimensions it is falling into a gravitational well as shown in Figure 16.3(b).

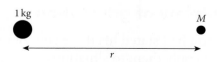

Figure 16.2

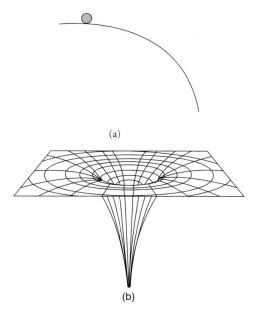

(a)

(b)

Figure 16.3

For the sake of calculation, the zero baseline of a quantity, called gravitational potential is taken to be on the flat portion of the gravitational well. That is when the distance from the mass, in this case the Earth, is very large.

The gravitational potential at a point is the work done in bringing a unit mass from infinity to that point.

This does have the effect of making all the values for gravitational potential negative. The equation for gravitational potential ϕ is

$$\phi = -\frac{GM}{r}$$

You do not need to know how to prove this equation and it usually would be given to you in questions or on a data and formulae sheet. You do need to know what it means and be able to use it.

Example 3

Calculate the potential energy (PE) lost by a meteorite of mass 200 grams when it falls from a height of 2000 km above the Earth's surface to 200 km above the Earth's surface. The radius of the Earth is 6.4×10^6 m and its mass is 6.0×10^{24} kg.

Answer Note that with these distances it is not possible to use PE = mgh because g is varying.

At 2000 km above the surface of the Earth the distance r from the centre of the Earth is given by

$$r = (6.4 + 2.0) \times 10^6 \, \text{m}$$

$$= 8.4 \times 10^6 \, \text{m}$$

At 200 km above the surface of the Earth the new value of the distance from the centre of the Earth r' is given by

$$r' = (6.4 + 0.2) \times 10^6 \, \text{m}$$

$$= 6.6 \times 10^6 \, \text{m}$$

This gives the potential at 2000 km

$$= -6.7 \times 10^{-11} \times 6.0 \times 10^{24}/8.4 \times 10^6$$

$$= -4.8 \times 10^7 \, \text{J kg}^{-1} \text{ and}$$

the potential at 200 km

$$= -6.7 \times 10^{-11} \times 6.0 \times 10^{24}/6.6 \times 10^6$$

$$= -6.1 \times 10^7 \, \text{J kg}^{-1}$$

The change in potential = $-1.3 \times 10^7 \, \text{J kg}^{-1}$

For the meteorite of mass 0.20 kg the loss in potential energy is, therefore,

$$1.3 \times 10^7 \, \text{J kg}^{-1} \times 0.20 \, \text{kg} = 2.6 \times 10^6 \, \text{J}.$$

This will be the increase in the kinetic energy of the meteorite, since the atmosphere is very thin at high altitudes and air resistance will not affect the meteorite significantly.

Space travel

Problems like the one in the paragraph above are rather artificial and do not have much practical application. However, gravitational potential is of considerable practical importance when used in relation to space travel. For any distant space travel, a rocket must be able to get out of the Earth's gravitational well, but there is not much point in escaping if the velocity of the rocket is then so slow that it would take centuries to get anywhere. To put some values on this we need to calculate the gain in gravitational potential from the bottom of the well

to infinity. This is $+GM/r - 0$ where r is the radius of the Earth and the zero because $GM/\infty =$ zero. Therefore the gain in potential
$= 6.7 \times 10^{-11} \times 6.0 \times 10^{24}/6.4 \times 10^{6} = 6.3 \times 10^{7}\,\mathrm{J\,kg^{-1}}$

If all this gain in potential comes from the initial kinetic energy of the rocket then

$$\frac{1}{2}mv^2 = 6.3 \times 10^7 \quad \mathrm{J\,kg^{-1}} \times m$$

m cancels, so the result is true for any size of rocket.

This gives $v = \sqrt{(2 \times 6.3 \times 10^7)} = 11\,200\,\mathrm{m\,s^{-1}}$

If a rocket is fired from the Earth's surface and in a matter of a few minutes reaches a speed of $11.2\,\mathrm{km\,s^{-1}}$ before its engines are switched off, it will be able to use its kinetic energy to escape from the Earth. This is called the **escape velocity** of the Earth. Unfortunately it escapes with zero kinetic energy eventually, so in practice it needs more energy to start with or extra boosts later on its journey. This large speed is one of the main reasons for the large costs involved with space travel. There is another problem with this high value of speed. A capsule returning from the Moon, for example, would gain the same amount of kinetic energy. Slowing it down is difficult. First, friction with the atmosphere is used to slow the capsule down, but this causes the temperature of the capsule to rise. Lower down in the atmosphere, the air is dense enough for parachutes to slow the capsule even more. Question 16.6 asks you to repeat this calculation but with a requirement that the rocket should be travelling at $5.0\,\mathrm{km\,s^{-1}}$ after leaving the Earth's gravitational well. Much of this escape velocity calculation can save a lot of time in answering Question 16.6.

Circular orbits

Most moons and planets have orbits that are nearly circular. Venus and Neptune have very nearly exactly circular orbits. Only Mercury and Pluto (a dwarf planet) have orbits that are considerably elliptical. One of the early studies of planetary orbits was carried out by Kepler in about the year 1600. He found that the orbital period of a planet squared was proportional to its distance from the Sun cubed. Newton applied his laws of motion and his

universal law of gravitation to show why this was so. This was his deduction.

Figure 16.4 shows a planet of mass m in a circular orbit of radius r around the Sun of mass M. The period of the planet is T.

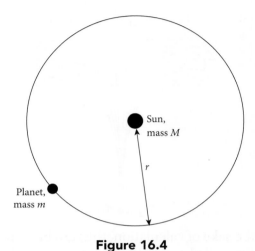

Figure 16.4

Gravitational force on planet $= \dfrac{GmM}{r^2}$

For circular motion, the centripetal force
$=$ mass of planet $\times$ acceleration of planet

$$= m \times \frac{v^2}{r} = mr\omega^2$$

where for the planet $\omega = \dfrac{2\pi}{T}$

Equating the above two equations of force, we get

$$\frac{GmM}{r^2} = mr\left(\frac{2\pi}{T}\right)^2 \text{ and } m \text{ cancels giving}$$

$$\frac{GM}{r^2} = \frac{4\pi^2 r}{T^2} \text{ and by rearranging}$$

$$T^2 = \frac{4\pi^2}{GM}r^3$$

Geostationary satellites

A satellite travelling from west to east and directly over the equator can, provided its distance from the

Earth is correct, rotate with the Earth once per day. To an observer on the ground, with a good telescope for viewing, this satellite remains at a fixed position in the sky. It seems stationary.

The theory for a satellite moving around the Earth is identical to that for a planet around the Sun. This enables the radius of the orbit of a geostationary satellite to be calculated.

$T = 24 \text{ hours} = 86\,400 \text{ s}$

$M = \text{mass of Earth} = 5.98 \times 10^{24} \text{ kg}$

$G = 6.67 \times 10^{-11} \text{ N m}^2 \text{ kg}^{-2}$

$r^3 = \dfrac{GMT^2}{4\pi^2} = \dfrac{6.67 \times 10^{-11} \times 5.98 \times 10^{24} \times 86\,400^2}{4\pi^2}$

$= 7.54 \times 10^{22}$

$r = 4.23 \times 10^7 \text{ m} = 42\,300 \text{ km}$

At this distance from the Earth, the value of the Earth's gravitational field strength is given by the inverse square law as

$$9.81 \times \left(\frac{6370}{42\,300}\right)^2 = 0.222 \text{ N kg}^{-1}$$

Chapter Summary

✓ Gravitational field strength g is force per unit mass

$$g = \frac{Gm}{r^2}$$

On the surface of the Earth it has the value 9.8 N kg^{-1}.

✓ Gravitational potential in the field of a point mass

$$\phi = -\frac{Gm}{r}$$

✓ Newton's universal law of gravitation can be summarised by the equation

$$F = \frac{Gm_1m_2}{r^2}$$

where F is the gravitational force of attraction between two bodies of masses m_1 and m_2 separated by a distance r. G is the universal constant of gravitation and has the value $6.67 \times 10^{-11} \text{ N m}^2 \text{ kg}^{-2}$.

✓ A planet orbiting at a radius r from a Sun of mass M takes a time T to complete one orbit. The relationship between these quantities is

$$T^2 = \frac{4\pi^2}{GM}r^3$$

Progress Check

16.1 (a) Draw a diagram showing the gravitational field between the pair of binary stars drawn in Figure 16.5.

Figure 16.5

(b) How would your diagram change if the star on the left was 20 times more massive than the star on the right?

16.2 The radius of the Earth is 6370 km and g at its surface is 9.83 N kg^{-1}. Calculate the value of the acceleration due to gravity
(a) at a distance of 12 740 km from the centre of the Earth,
(b) at a height of 500 km above the Earth's surface.

16.3 The distance from the centre of the Earth to the centre of the Moon is 3.844×10^8 m. The radius of the Earth is 6.371×10^6 m. Assuming that Moon travels on a circular path, calculate
(a) the centripetal acceleration of the Moon,
(b) the angular velocity of the Moon,
(c) the period of the Moon's rotation around the Earth.

16.4 Calculate the gravitational field strength at the surface of Jupiter. Jupiter has a radius of 7.14×10^7 m and a mass of 1.90×10^{27} kg.

16.5 Show that on a trip to the Moon, astronauts pass a point where the gravitational field strength of the Earth–Moon system is zero at a distance when the astronauts have travelled 90% of the distance to the Moon.

Mass of Earth = 5.98×10^{24} kg,
Mass of Moon = 7.35×10^{22} kg.

16.6 Using data from the text on space travel, calculate the speed required shortly after the launch of a rocket to be travelling at 5.0 km s^{-1} when far out in space.

16.7 The distance of the Earth from the Sun is 1.50×10^{11} m. Use the value of G and the period of rotation of the Earth around the Sun to calculate the mass of the Sun.

16.8 Explain why a geostationary satellite
(a) has to move from west to east,
(b) must be directly over the equator,
(c) can have its rocket motors switched off.

Explain also how a satellite with a period of one day would appear to move to an observer on the ground if it was travelling with the centre of its path at the centre of the Earth but was not travelling along the Equator.

16.9 Calculate, from $g = 9.83$ N kg^{-1} and the radius of the Earth = 6.371×10^6 m, the period of a satellite in a circular orbit around the Earth, and hence its speed, when it is at an altitude of 500 km.

Examination Questions VIII

1. (a) Define *gravitational potential* at a point. [1]

(b) The gravitational potential ϕ at distance r from point mass M is given by the expression

$$\phi = -\frac{Gm}{r}$$

where G is the gravitational constant.

Explain the significance of the negative sign in this expression. [2]

(c) A spherical planet may be assumed to be an isolated point mass with its mass concentrated at its centre. A small mass m is moving near to, and normal to, the surface of the planet. The mass moves away from the planet through a short distance h.

State and explain why the change in gravitational potential energy ΔE_p of the mass is given by the expression

$$\Delta E_\mathrm{p} = mgh$$

where g is the acceleration of free fall. [4]

(d) The planet in (c) has mass M and diameter 6.8×10^3 km. The product GM for this planet is 4.3×10^{13} N m^2 kg^{-1}.

A rock, initially at rest a long distance from the planet, accelerates towards the planet. Assuming that the planet has negligible atmosphere, calculate the speed of the rock, in m s^{-1} as it hits the surface of the planet. [3]

(Cambridge International AS and A Level Physics 9702 Paper 41 Question 1 May/June 2012)

2. (a)   (i) Define the *radian*.   [2]

(ii) A small mass is attached to a string. The mass is rotating about a fixed point P at constant speed, as shown in Figure 1.

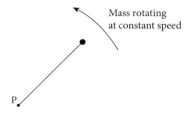

Mass rotating
at constant speed

P

Figure 1

Explain what is meant by the *angular* speed about point P of the mass.   [2]

(b) A horizontal flat plate is free to rotate about a vertical axis through its centre, as shown in Figure 2.

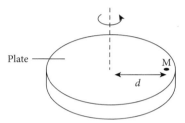

Plate

M

d

Figure 2

A small mass M is placed on the plate, a distance d from the axis of rotation. The speed of rotation of the plate is gradually increased from zero until the mass is seen to slide off the plate.

The maximum frictional force F between the plate and the mass is given by the expression

$$F = 0.72\,W,$$

where W is the weight of the mass M.

The distance d is 35 cm.

Determine the maximum number of revolutions of the plate per minute for the mass M to remain on the plate. Explain your working.   [5]

(c) The plate in (b) is covered, when stationary, with mud.

Suggest and explain whether mud near the edge of the plate or near the centre will first leave the plate as the angular speed of the plate is slowly increased.   [2]

**(Cambridge International AS and A Level Physics 9702
Paper 04 Question 1 May/June 2008)**

3. (a) State what is meant by a *gravitational field*.   [2]

(b) In the Solar System, the planets may be assumed to be in circular orbits about the Sun. Data for the radii of the orbits of the Earth and Jupiter about the Sun are given in Figure 3.

	radius of orbit / km
Earth	1.50×10^8
Jupiter	7.78×10^8

Figure 3

(i) State Newton's law of gravitation.   [3]

   (ii) Use Newton's law to determine the ratio   [3]

$$\frac{\text{gravitational field strength due to the Sun at orbit of Earth}}{\text{gravitational field strength due to the Sun at orbit of Jupiter}}.$$

(c) The orbital period of the Earth about the Sun is T.
   (i) Use ideas about circular motion to show that the mass M of the Sun is given by

$$M = \frac{4\pi^2 R^3}{GT^2}$$

   where R is the radius of the Earth's orbit about the Sun and G is the gravitational constant.

   Explain your working.   [3]
   (ii) The orbital period T of the Earth about the Sun is 3.16×10^7 s.
   The radius of the Earth's orbit is given in Figure 3.
   Use the expression in (i) to determine the mass of the Sun, in kg.   [2]
   (Cambridge International AS and A Level Physics 9702 Paper 41 Question 1 May/June 2013)

4. (a) State Newton's law of gravitation.   [2]

(b) The Earth may be considered to be a uniform sphere of radius R equal to

6.4×10^6 m. A satellite is in a geostationary orbit.
   (i) Describe what is meant by a *geostationary orbit*.   [3]
   (ii) Show that the radius x of the geostationary orbit is given by the expression

$$gR^2 = x^3 \omega^2$$

   where g is the acceleration of free fall at the Earth's surface and ω is the angular speed of the satellite about the centre of the Earth.   [3]
   (iii) Determine the radius x, in m, of the geostationary orbit.   [3]
   (Cambridge International AS and A Level Physics 9702 Paper 41 Question 1 October/November 2009)

5. (a) A moon is in a circular orbit of radius r about a planet. The angular speed of the moon in its orbit is ω. The planet and its moon may be considered to be point masses that are isolated in space.

Show that r and ω are related by the expression

$$r^3 \omega^2 = \text{constant}.$$

Explain your working.   [3]

(b) Phobos and Deimos are moons that are in circular orbits about the planet Mars. Data for Phobos and Deimos are shown in Figure 4.

moon	radius of orbit /m	period of rotation about Mars /hours
Phobos	9.39×10^6	7.65
Deimos	1.99×10^7	

Figure 4

  (i) Use data from Figure 4 to determine
    1. the mass of Mars, in kg,   [3]
    2. the period of Deimos in its orbit about Mars, in hours.   [3]
  (ii) The period of rotation of Mars about its axis is 24.6 hours.
    Deimos is in an equatorial orbit, orbiting in the same direction as the spin of Mars about its axis.
    Use your answer in **(i)** to comment on the orbit of Deimos.   [1]
    (Cambridge International AS and A Level Physics 9702 Paper 41 Question 1 October/November 2011)

Ideal Gases

Introduction

It was mentioned in Chapter 14 that many different gases have very similar properties. The reason for this is that intermolecular attractions are far smaller for gases than for either solids or liquids. The density of both solids and liquids is almost completely independent of the pressure. The molecules in solids and liquids are packed tightly together, so any reduction in volume due to pressure is mostly dependent on reducing the size of the molecules themselves. In a gas, the situation is completely different. Thinking about some numerical values can explain why this is so.

The density of water at $0\,°C$ and standard atmospheric pressure is $999.87\,kg\,m^{-3}$.

The density of water vapour at $0\,°C$ and standard atmospheric pressure is $0.800\,kg\,m^{-3}$.

In other words, each molecule in the vapour has 1250 times more space (volume) to move about in than a corresponding molecule in the liquid. It is not therefore surprising that water vapour can easily be compressed into a smaller volume. Note that 1250 times more space does not mean that the molecules are 1250 times further apart. The cube root of 1250 is needed to work out the distance. The molecules in water vapour are 10.8 times further apart than molecules in the liquid.

The equation of state for an ideal gas

The molecules in gases occupy a space far larger than the volume of the molecules themselves. Also the molecules in a gas are in a state of perpetual motion with their kinetic energy dependent on the temperature. This results in several common features of different gases. One of these features was mentioned when considering the mole in Chapter 14, namely that equal volumes of all gases at the same temperature and pressure contain the same number of molecules. Gradually, during the 17th

and 18th centuries, as different people did different experiments on gases, a whole series of gas laws were introduced. These are now all incorporated into the idea of an ideal gas whose behaviour is expressed by the **equation of state for an ideal gas**.

The equation is $pV = nRT$,

where p is the pressure of the gas, V its volume, n the amount of gas, T the temperature of the gas and R is the universal molar gas constant.

Experiments to determine the value of the universal gas constant measure p in pascals, V in m^3, n in moles and T in kelvin. The experiments are done using gases at low pressure since gases approach ideal behaviour as their pressure is reduced.

The value obtained for R is $8.314\,J\,K^{-1}\,mol^{-1}$.

Direct evidence for the movement of molecules is provided by an experiment that demonstrates Brownian motion. When smoke particles are viewed through a microscope it can be seen that, besides any large-scale movement they have, they also have a small, jerky, irregular but continuous movement. This can only be explained by the smoke particles being bombarded unevenly on all sides by air molecules that are too small to be visible. The just-visible smoke particles could have a mass of a fraction of a picogram ($10^{-15}\,kg$). This is around a hundred million times the mass of an air molecule, but given that the air molecules travel at around $500\,m\,s^{-1}$, their momentum is sufficient to cause the slight jerkiness of the smoke particle.

Example 1

An oxygen cylinder for use in hospitals contains oxygen at a pressure of $1.4 \times 10^7\,Pa$ when full. The internal volume of the cylinder is $0.038\,m^3$ and it is at a temperature of $24\,°C$. Calculate

(a) the volume of oxygen that can be supplied to a patient at $24\,°C$ and normal air pressure of $1.1 \times 10^5\,Pa$,

(b) the length of time the cylinder can be used with the patient who requires 0.85 litres of oxygen every 10 seconds, and

(c) the number of oxygen molecules in the full cylinder.

Answer   (a) Using $pV = nRT$, we get
$$1.4 \times 10^7\,\text{Pa} \times 0.038\,\text{m}^3 = nRT$$

Now the pressure and the volume change but n, R and T do not change, so equating pV initially with $p'V'$ when all the oxygen has been released gives,

$$1.4 \times 10^7\,\text{Pa} \times 0.038\,\text{m}^3 = 1.1 \times 10^5\,\text{Pa} \times V$$

This gives the required volume
$$= 1.4 \times 10^7\,\text{Pa} \times 0.038\,\text{m}^3/1.1 \times 10^5\,\text{Pa} = 4.84\,\text{m}^3$$

(b) Now, $1\,\text{m}^3 = 1000$ litres, so 4840 litres of oxygen is available.

The patient requires $0.85 \times 6 = 5.1$ litres per minute, so the cylinder will last for $4840/5.1 = 950$ minutes or just under 16 hours.

(c) Now putting all the values available for completion of the ideal gas equation, we get

$$1.4 \times 10^7\,\text{Pa} \times 0.038\,\text{m}^3 = n \times 8.31 \times (273 + 24)\,\text{K}$$

$$n = \frac{1.4 \times 10^7 \times 0.038}{8.31 \times 297} = 216\,\text{mol}$$

Since 1 mole contains the Avogadro number of molecules, $6.02 \times 10^{23}\,\text{mol}^{-1}$, the number of oxygen molecules in the full cylinder

$$= 216\,\text{mol} \times 6.02 \times 10^{23}\,\text{mol}^{-1} = 1.30 \times 10^{26}.$$

Teacher's Tip

1.   Units can be a problem in this type of question, so do not ignore them. It is always necessary to take care with the units used but is particularly important when there are two different units being used for the same quantity. This frequently happens with temperature when sometimes Celsius and Kelvin temperatures may be used. Here the problem is that litres and cubic metres are being used together. Once you are aware of the problem still be careful to get the conversion factor the right way round. There are 1000 litres in a cubic metre – NOT 1 litre in $1000\,\text{m}^3$! Looking to see whether an answer makes

sense should ensure you do not make that sort of mistake. If an answer seems to be wrong by a factor of a million, it is almost certainly wrong. It helps to keep units in equations in order to have a check. Working in numbers by themselves takes reality out of a problem.

2.   The oxygen in this question is being treated as an ideal gas even though the pressure is high initially. This would mean that answers are unlikely to be accurate to more than 2 sig. figs.

Standard temperature and pressure, S.T.P.

You may encounter this term when answering questions. The temperature will be 0 °C and that needs to be converted to 273.16 K; the pressure will be 1 atmosphere. This was stated in Chapter 5 to be the pressure of a 76 cm column of mercury and its pressure is 1.014×10^5 Pa.

The kinetic theory of gases

This theory takes the concept of an ideal gas one stage further. The basic assumptions of the ideal gas are:

- Any gas consists of a large number of molecules in rapid, random motion.
- Collisions between molecules and between molecules and the container are elastic.
- There are no intermolecular attractive forces.
- Intermolecular repulsive forces only act for a short time during collisions between molecules.
- The volume of the molecules themselves is negligible compared to the volume of the container.

Consider a situation where there is one molecule of mass m in a cubical container of side l, and the molecule is travelling with a speed u parallel to one of the sides, as shown in Figure 17.1.

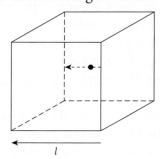

Figure 17.1

The time to cross from one wall to the other $= l/u$

The time between collisions with the left-hand wall $= 2l/u$

The number of collisions per unit time with this wall $= u/2l$

The change in the momentum of the molecule each time it hits the wall $= 2mu$

The rate of change of momentum at the wall $= 2mu \times u/2l = mu^2/l$

If there were N molecules travelling in this way then the rate of change of momentum of them all would be

$$\frac{mu_1^2}{l} + \frac{mu_2^2}{l} + \frac{mu_3^2}{l} + \frac{mu_4^2}{l} + \frac{mu_5^2}{l} + ... + \frac{mu_N^2}{l}$$

where u_1 is the speed of the first molecule, u_2 is the speed of the second molecule, etc.

Since force is the rate of change of momentum, the force F exerted on the wall is given by

$$F = \frac{m}{l}\left(u_1^2 + u_2^2 + u_3^2 + u_4^2 + u_5^2 + ... + u_N^2\right)$$

If the average value of all the u^2 terms is $<u^2>$, this expression becomes

$$F = \frac{m}{l} \times N<u^2>$$

The pressure on the wall is given by

$$p = \frac{F}{A} = \frac{F}{l^2} = \frac{m}{l^3} \times N<u^2>$$

Since l^3 is the volume V of the gas, we get

$$pV = Nm<u^2>$$

However, the molecules do not just travel in one dimension.

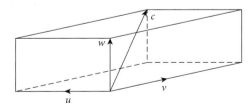

Figure 17.2

For one molecule moving with speed c, we can use Pythagoras' theorem in three dimensions as shown in Figure 17.2 to get

$$u^2 + v^2 + w^2 = c^2$$

and extending this to millions of molecules

$$<u^2> + <v^2> + <w^2> = <c^2>$$

For the entire number of molecules the mean square speed must be the same in all directions so $<u^2> = <v^2> = <w^2>$ giving

$$3<u^2> = <c^2> \quad \text{or} \quad <u^2> = \frac{1}{3}<c^2>$$

This finally gives the relationship

$$pV = \frac{1}{3}Nm<c^2>$$

This equation can be written in terms of the gas density ρ giving

$$p = \frac{1}{3}\rho<c^2>$$

The Boltzmann constant, k

Boltzmann was particularly interested in the behaviour of individual molecules rather than in their behaviour as a group of molecules. He studied molecules statistically, for example in terms of the percentages of molecules that happened to be travelling at ten times the average speed. To do this, he was interested in the average increase in the kinetic energy of a single molecule for each degree rise in temperature. The universal gas constant is related to the average increase in the kinetic energy of a mole of molecules for each degree rise in temperature.

The Boltzmann constant is defined by the equation

$$k = \frac{\text{universal gas constant}}{\text{Avogadro constant}} = \frac{R}{N_A}$$

The numerical value of the Boltzmann constant is $1.38 \times 10^{-23}\,\text{J K}^{-1}$.

This now means that we have two equations for the product of p and V, namely

$$pV = nRT = nT \times kN_A \quad \text{and} \quad pV = \frac{1}{3}Nm<c^2>$$

The number of moles (n) $\times$ the number of molecules in one mole (N_A) $=$ the total number of molecules (N). Equating and simplifying the right-hand sides of the above two equations gives

$$kT = \frac{1}{3}m<c^2>$$

The average kinetic energy of a single molecule is given by

$$E_k = \frac{1}{2}m<c^2> = \frac{3}{2}kT$$

This equation tells you that the average kinetic energy of a molecule is directly proportional to T, the absolute temperature in kelvin.

Chapter Summary

✓ The equation of state for an ideal gas is $pV = nRT$, where p is the pressure of the gas, V is its volume, n is the amount of gas (the number of moles), T is the temperature of the gas and R is the universal molar gas constant having the value $8.31\,\mathrm{J\,K^{-1}\,mol^{-1}}$.

✓ Standard temperature and pressure (STP) is 273 K and standard atmospheric pressure $1.014 \times 10^5\,\mathrm{Pa}$.

✓ The kinetic theory of gases gives the product of the pressure p and the volume V of an ideal gas in terms of the number of molecules N of the gas, the mass m of a molecule of the gas and the mean square speed $<c^2>$ of all its molecules

$$pV = \frac{1}{3}Nm<c^2>$$

✓ Boltzmann's constant is used when considering gases at a molecular level. The Boltzmann constant k is defined as

$$k = \frac{\text{universal gas constant}}{\text{Avogadro constant}} = \frac{R}{N_A}$$

$$= \frac{8.31\,\mathrm{J\ K^{-1}\,mol^{-1}}}{6.02 \times 10^{23}\,\mathrm{mol^{-1}}}$$

$$= 1.38 \times 10^{-23}\,\mathrm{J\,K^{-1}}$$

This gives the average kinetic energy E_k of a single molecule at temperature T as

$$E_k = \frac{3}{2}kT$$

Progress Check

17.1 Show that the unit of the universal gas constant is $\mathrm{J\,K^{-1}\,mol^{-1}}$.

17.2 A scuba diver has a cylinder of compressed air of internal volume $0.015\,\mathrm{m^3}$. It contains air at a pressure of $8.3 \times 10^7\,\mathrm{Pa}$ and a temperature of 290 K.
(a) Calculate the volume of air in use when at a pressure of $2.0 \times 10^5\,\mathrm{Pa}$ and temperature 300 K.
(b) The diver breathes a litre of air every 6.0 s. Calculate the time for which the cylinder can supply this rate of use.

17.3 (a) Calculate the volume occupied by one mole of helium at S.T.P.
(b) The volume of a helium atom is about $3 \times 10^{-30}\,\mathrm{m^3}$. What fraction of the volume in (a) is actually occupied by the atoms?

17.4 (a) Calculate the average kinetic energy of an oxygen molecule at a temperature of $20\,^\circ\mathrm{C}$. How does this compare with the average kinetic energy of a hydrogen molecule at the same temperature?
(b) What is the ratio of average speed of a hydrogen molecule to average speed of an oxygen molecule at the same temperature? [**Given:** The mass of a hydrogen molecule is 2 u and the mass of an oxygen molecule is 32 u.]

17.5 A hot air balloon has a volume of $2500\,\mathrm{m^3}$ and the fabric and the passengers have mass of 800 kg. It is taking-off when the air around the balloon has a temperature of $10\,^\circ\mathrm{C}$ and a density of $1.29\,\mathrm{kg\,m^{-3}}$. Calculate the minimum temperature of the air inside the balloon for take off. Note that the pressure inside and outside the balloon must be equal, since the balloon is open at the bottom.

Temperature

18

Introduction

Accurate measurement of temperature is still a difficult exercise. While time and distance can be measured to nine or ten significant figures, temperature is often restricted to only six or seven significant figures at best. Everyone has a feel for what is meant by *temperature* but putting that feel into a definition is difficult. In practice, your sense of temperature is very unreliable for two reasons. The first is that how hot (or cold) something seems depends on what you have just been doing. If you come into a house after being outside in the cold, the house will seem warm. Another person may have had a warm bath and then the same house feels cold. The second problem is that two objects at the same temperature can often feel as if they are at different temperatures. In an oven, a hot tray made of metal, a good conductor of heat, will seem very much hotter than the air in the oven. Both are at the same temperature but the flow of thermal energy from the metal is far greater than the flow from the air.

One separate but important point for someone studying physics is not to confuse the word *heat* with the word *temperature*. **Temperature is measured in degrees Celsius but heat, now usually referred to as thermal energy, is a form of energy and will, therefore, be measured in joules**.

Thermal equilibrium

Assume that the temperature of an oven is kept at exactly the required temperature when some food is placed in it for cooking. The food starts to heat up and provided the cooking time is long, the food will reach the same temperature as the oven. The oven and the food are then said to be in thermal equilibrium with one another. The same thermal equilibrium happens some time after a potato is put in a saucepan of boiling water. At the time of thermal equilibrium the temperatures of the two objects are identical. Temperature is the property of a body that determines which way the net energy flow between two bodies will take place. **Thermal energy is transferred from a region of higher temperature to a region of lower temperature**. For example, there is a net flow of thermal energy from the Sun to the Earth. This is because the temperature of the Sun is higher than the temperature of the Earth.

Measurement of temperature

In theory, any physical property that varies with temperature may be used for the measurement of temperature. The following properties are used in practice, some of them you will be very familiar with and others may surprise you.

- The volume of a liquid.
- The volume of a gas at constant pressure.
- The pressure of a gas at constant volume.
- The length of a piece of metal.
- The resistance of a wire.
- The e.m.f. produced by a thermocouple.
- The colour of the light from an object.

The variety of different shapes and sizes of thermometers is large. All thermometers need to be calibrated, that is, have a scale put on them. To do this accurately requires the use of a constant-volume gas thermometer and is a very lengthy process. Once it has been done, however, the values for the scale can be transferred to other thermometers. Figure 18.1 shows a traditional mercury in glass thermometer.

Figure 18.1 A traditional mercury in glass thermometer

Figure 18.2 shows a bimetallic strip thermometer.

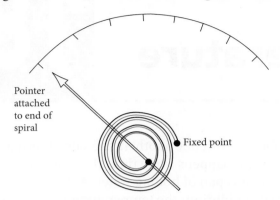

Figure 18.2 A bimetallic strip thermometer

In this type of thermometer, strips of two metals that expand at different rates are bonded to one another. On heating, the bimetallic strip bends. In the figure, the spiral has been formed at a low temperature and as the temperature rises, the metal shown coloured expands faster than the metal shown black. This opens the spiral and the pointer moves to the right.

Figure 18.3 shows the basic circuit of a thermocouple thermometer.

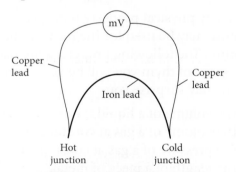

Figure 18.3 Basic circuit of a thermocouple thermometer

In this thermometer, a small e.m.f. is generated when two metal wires are joined and the junctions between the metals are at different temperatures. This enables thermocouple thermometers to be used in electronic thermometers.

The potential divider in use

In the following circuits the division of potential is not done manually by moving a slider along a resistor, but by changing the ratio of resistances themselves.

Temperature control

Temperature control can be provided by a potential divider circuit containing a **thermistor**. This is shown in Figure 18.4 and the output will be connected to an electronic circuit that will switch a heater on or off.

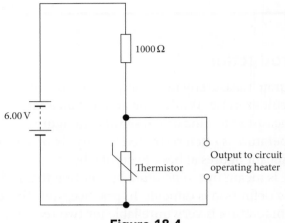

Figure 18.4

The resistance of the thermistor at 0 °C is 2500 Ω and at 50 °C is 100 Ω.

At 50 °C, therefore, the total resistance is 1100 Ω, the current is 6 V/1100 Ω = 0.0055 A and the p.d. across the thermistor is 0.0055 A × 100 Ω = 0.55 V.

This p.d. is insufficient to trigger the circuit switching the heater on.

A very useful method for working with potential divider circuits is to use proportion – with care. In this case the thermistor has a resistance of 100 Ω out of a total of 1100 Ω in the circuit. It will, therefore, 100/1100 of the supply p.d. since the current in both is the same.

$$\frac{100}{1100} \times 6\,\text{V} = \frac{6}{11}\,\text{V} = 0.55\,\text{V}$$

This means that there will be 5.45 V across the fixed resistor. Using the same method for the thermistor at 0 °C gives

$$\text{output} = \frac{2500\,\Omega}{3500\,\Omega} \times 6.0\,\text{V} = 0.71 \times 6\,\text{V} = 4.3\,\text{V}$$

This must be arranged to be sufficient to trigger the switch to operate the heater.

If a circuit is required to turn on air conditioning when the temperature gets too high then the same basic circuit can be used but with the two components swapped over. The values may need altering and it is usual to replace the fixed resistor with an adjustable one so that there is some control over the temperature at which the air conditioning is switched on.

Lighting control

The same method is used here as for temperature control. The thermistor is replaced by a light-dependent resistor (LDR) as shown in Figure 18.5.

Example 1

A circuit designer uses an operating switch that requires 5 V to turn on a light and has the information given on Figure 18.5 and needs to purchase a suitable LDR. What characteristics must the LDR have?

Answer When it is getting dark and the light needs to come on, there must be a p.d. of 1.0 V across the 4000 Ω resistor so that there is 5.0 V across the LDR.

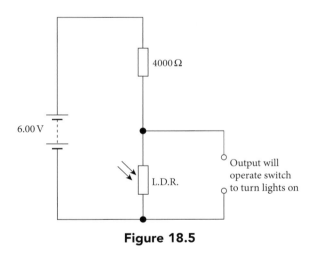

Figure 18.5

With 1.0 V across 4000 Ω there will be 5.0 V across 20 000 Ω, since they have the same current in each. This must be the resistance of the LDR when in dim light. In daylight the resistance of the LDR will be much less and the light will not come on.

The thermistor

A thermistor uses a small piece of a solid state semiconductor material. As the temperature of this material increases, its resistance decreases, as shown in Figure 18.6(a). This is defined as a negative temperature coefficient (NTC) thermistor. Typical values for resistance are a few hundred

ohms when cold and a few ohms when hot. The symbol for a thermistor is shown in Figure 18.6(b).

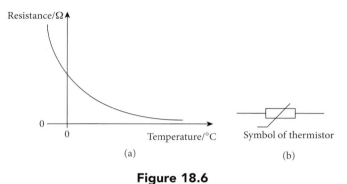

Figure 18.6

Most thermistors are NTC thermistors, but positive temperature coefficient (PTC) thermistors are available. Many thermometers use thermistors with a small battery providing not only the current through the thermistor but also powering a digital temperature display.

Figure 18.7 is a photograph of part of the sky. Some of the stars emit intense blue/white light. These are very hot stars. Rigel, for example is at a temperature of over 20 000 K. Betelgeuse is a red giant star. It is much cooler, and therefore redder than Rigel. You will be familiar with the change in colour of a piece of metal from deep red, to red, to orange, to yellow, to white as it is heated. The temperature of a filament bulb is usually about 2500 K; the temperature of the Sun's surface is about 5800 K. Instruments called pyrometers can deduce the temperature of a body from the colour of the light it radiates.

Figure 18.7 Part of the sky

Table 18.1

Thermometer	Property varying with temperature	Temperature range/K	Advantages	Disadvantages
Mercury in glass	volume of a liquid	234–630	direct reading, easy to use	mercury is poisonous
Constant volume gas thermometer	pressure of a gas	3–1800	very accurate	awkward to use, very slow response
Resistance thermometer	resistance of a metal	10–2000	wide range	can be too slow for rapid temperature changes
Thermocouple	e.m.f. generated	20–1800	wide range, quick response, useful in electronic measuring instruments	not very accurate, can be misleading by having one value of e.m.f. for two different temperatures
Thermistor	resistance of semiconductor material	200–600	wide range, quick response, used in electrical control circuits	need for an electrical circuit

The calibration of thermometers can be a lengthy process if high accuracy is required but for normal laboratory use many thermometers are calibrated by relying on certain well-known standard temperatures, such as the melting point of ice at standard pressure. For best accuracy, the pressure of a gas at constant volume is used, with the gas itself at low pressure.

Table 18.1 gives some of the advantages and disadvantages of thermometers. The table should be treated only as a guide, since there are thousands of different thermometers manufactured by different manufacturers and there are a lot of specialist thermometers on the market, each with their own advantages.

Temperature scales

For a long time, temperature was defined in terms of melting and boiling points of water in particular and the centigrade unit of temperature became used as a result of this definition. Problems arose when a theoretical value of absolute temperature became required with the development of the science of thermodynamics. As a result of this, a new definition

of temperature was required. This absolute scale does not depend on the properties of any particular substance. It is a thermodynamic scale based on the concept of absolute zero. In an ideal world everyone would use the absolute scale of temperature and people would make such comments as "Isn't it cold today with the temperature down as low as 270 kelvin?" In practice it was agreed in 1947 that it would be impossible to persuade people to use such a scale and so a new scale of temperature was introduced. It is the Celsius scale of temperature and it is an absolute thermodynamic scale but adjusted to make it look like the old centigrade scale. The numerical values on the Celsius scale are the same as the old centigrade scale as long as very high accuracy is not required.

A temperature in Celsius is the absolute temperature minus 273.15.

$$\text{or } \theta/°C = T/K - 273.15 \text{ exactly.}$$

With absolute zero fixing the lowest temperature for the thermodynamic scale there was a need to have some other fixed point in order to set the size of one degree. The temperature chosen was the so-called **triple point** of water. This is the temperature at which ice, water and water vapour co-exist (in the absence of air). By choosing this temperature as 273.16 K, the size of one degree is almost identical to the size of the old centigrade degree. The discrepancy between 273.15 and 273.16 is because the triple point temperature of water is one hundredth of a degree higher than the ice point.

Teacher's Tip

Be careful when subtracting temperatures. A temperature change from 6 °C to 80 °C is obviously 74 °C. This could have been written 353 K − 279 K = 74 K. The temperature interval between two temperatures must be the same whether the Celsius scale or the Kelvin scale are used. You must not add on 273 when considering temperature intervals.

Chapter Summary

✓ Thermal energy is transferred from a region of higher temperature to a region of lower temperature.

✓ The thermodynamic scale of temperature uses two fixed points. One is 0 K at absolute zero and the other is 273.16 K at the triple point of water.

✓ The Celsius scale of temperature is based on the thermodynamic scale. It is defined by the equation $\theta/°C = T/K − 273.15$ exactly.
(This is not a mistake. It makes the temperature of the triple point of water just 0.01 K higher than the ice point.)

Progress Check

18.1 Convert the following Celsius temperatures to kelvin.
(a) 0 °C   (b) 37.4 °C   (c) 100 °C
(d) 440 °C   (e) −80 °C   (f) −273.15 °C
(g) 5600 °C

18.2 Convert the following kelvin temperatures to Celsius.
(a) 0 K   (b) 220 K
(c) 280 K   (d) 450 K

18.3 Temperatures at the centre of stars are very large. Explain why it is unnecessary to know whether kelvin or Celsius temperatures are used in these cases.

18.4 Make estimates of the following temperatures, using the Celsius scale. The temperature of
(a) dry ice,
(b) body temperature,
(c) hot water for a shower,
(d) hot water in a room radiator
(e) hot water in a pressure cooker,
(f) a hot oven cooking a cake,
(g) a red hot ring on an electric stove,
(h) a filament in a lamp.

Thermal Properties of Materials 19

Specific heat capacity

The kinetic theory showed that the average kinetic energy of a molecule is proportional to the absolute temperature. This implies the well-appreciated fact that to raise the temperature of any substance it is necessary to supply some energy to it. Heating a kettle of water for a hot drink involves supplying energy to the water, and eventually paying for that energy. The amount of energy required for any substance can be found by using its specific heat capacity. **Specific heat capacity** of a substance is the energy required per unit mass per unit rise in temperature. In equation form, this becomes

$$c = \frac{Q}{m\Delta T}$$

where c is the specific heat capacity, Q the energy supplied, m the mass and ΔT the rise in temperature. Using SI units, the unit for c will be $J\,kg^{-1}\,K^{-1}$.

Some numerical values for the specific heat capacity of different substances are given in Table 19.1. Note that a change in state of a substance, say from ice to water, changes the specific heat capacity.

Table 19.1	
Substance	**Specific heat capacity/$J\,kg^{-1}\,K^{-1}$**
Water	4190
Ice	2100
Mercury	140
Aluminium	913
Copper	385
Iron	106
Concrete	3350

The following example shows how a rough estimate of the specific heat capacity of water can be measured. The same basic principles can be applied to a more accurate determination of heat losses, for example by insulating the container well.

Example 1

A kettle contains 1450 g of water at a temperature of 15 °C. The kettle has an electrical power of 3000 W. After the kettle has been switched on for 160 s the temperature of the water has reached 88 °C.

(a) Calculate a value for the specific heat capacity of water.
(b) Explain why the answer given is likely to be higher than the true value
(c) List ways in which the experiment could be improved.

Answer

(a) Energy supplied to water
   = $3000\,J\,s^{-1} \times 160\,s = 480\,000\,J$
   Mass of water = 1.450 kg
   Temperature rise = $(88 - 15)\,°C = 73\,K$

[Note that if you convert temperatures to kelvin you get $361 - 288 = 73$. This is the same as in Celsius because a temperature *difference* in kelvin is exactly the same as a temperature difference in Celsius.]

$$c = \frac{Q}{mT} = \frac{480\,000\,J}{1.45\,kg \times 73\,K} = 4534\,J\,kg^{-1}\,K^{-1}$$

(b) Some of the 480 000 J supplied by the kettle does not go into heating the water. The amount of energy supplied to the water will be lower than 480 000 J making the actual value lower.

(c) The kettle needs to be well lagged to reduce heat losses.

The kettle, the thermometer and the heater itself need energy to be heated. These items need to be taken into account in the calculation. The kettle should be marked 3000 W when used at a particular voltage. The mains voltage needs to be known and adjustments made if the voltage is not the stated value.

Figure 19.1

Figure 19.2

Figure 19.3

Change of state

Everyone is aware of the following:

- Water on a wet road evaporates to leave the road surface dry.
- Water evaporating on your hands makes them feel cold.
- Ice cubes taken out of a fridge melt to form water.
- A boiling kettle produces steam (Figure 19.1).
- On a very cold morning, frost forms on the ground from water vapour in the atmosphere (Figure 19.2).
- Snow on high mountains will melt in warm weather to form water for rivers (Figure 19.3).

All of these common experiences involve a change of state, even if people would not use this term.

The three common states of matter are solid, liquid and gas. There is a fourth state of matter that will not concern you at this stage. It is called **plasma** and happens at very high temperatures when atoms move so fast that the atoms lose most of the electrons normally attached to them. The nuclei of the atoms move in a sea of electrons.

All of the changes listed above concern the three states of water, namely ice, water and steam but change of state can take place with most substances, although there is a real possibility with many substances that a chemical reaction will take place before a change of state occurs. For instance, heating paper until it melts is impossible under normal circumstances, but heating solder will cause melting.

Melting

Melting involves a change of state from a solid to a liquid. The reverse process is called freezing (or solidification). The melting point of ice is the same as the freezing point of water and is 0 °C. Note that at standard pressure, both ice and water can exist at 0 °C. Melting normally results in only a small change in the total volume of the substance. The mean separation of molecules in a liquid is usually very similar to the mean separation in a solid. The change from ice to water is unusual in the sense that molecules are more tightly packed in water than they are in ice. This is why ice floats on water, as shown by the photograph of a floating iceberg in Figure 19.4. The iceberg looks huge. What you see though is only a small fraction of its total volume. The volume beneath the surface of the sea is over 11 times more than the volume above the surface. This is why captains of ships keep well clear of icebergs.

The kinetic theory shows that the kinetic energy of molecules is directly proportional to the absolute

Iceberg, Disko Bay, Greenland

Figure 19.4

temperature. The mean kinetic energy of molecules in ice at $0\,°C$ is, therefore, equal to the mean kinetic energy of molecules in water at $0\,°C$. Melting does not involve a rise in temperature, even though energy needs to be supplied to ice to turn it into water. This energy is called the **latent heat of fusion** and it is used to alter the potential energy of the molecules not their kinetic energy. Similarly, water molecules lose potential energy when the arrangement of the molecules changes from a random pattern to a rigid, crystalline pattern as the water freezes. This is **not** gravitational potential energy but elastic potential energy of the molecules.

The **specific latent heat of fusion** is the energy required to change unit mass of a solid to a liquid at the same temperature. The following example shows how the latent heat of fusion of water can be measured.

Example 2

480 g of water at a temperature of $43\,°C$ is placed in a well lagged can. Ice cubes at $0\,°C$ and of total mass 136 g are added to the water. By the time all the ice has melted, the final temperature of water is $16\,°C$. The specific heat capacity of water is $4200\,\mathrm{J\,kg^{-1}\,K^{-1}}$. Calculate the specific latent heat of fusion of water.

Answer   Heat lost by warm water
$= 0.480\,\mathrm{kg} \times 4200\,\mathrm{J\,kg^{-1}\,K^{-1}} \times (43-16)\,\mathrm{K} = 54\,400\,\mathrm{J}$

Heat gained by the ice $= 0.136\,\mathrm{kg} \times L$, where L is the specific latent heat of fusion of water.

Heat gained by water formed when the ice melts
$= 0.136\,\mathrm{kg} \times 4200\,\mathrm{J\,kg^{-1}\,K^{-1}} \times 16\,\mathrm{K} = 9140\,\mathrm{J}$

So, $54\,400 = 0.136\,L + 9140$

$0.136\,L = 45\,260$ and $L = 333\,000\,\mathrm{J\,kg^{-1}}$

Boiling and evaporation

A change of state from a liquid to a gas always requires a greater input of energy than the change from a solid to a liquid. This is because the molecules in a vapour or a gas are separated by a much greater distance than in a liquid and so the molecules need to gain a large amount of potential energy. As was the case with melting, boiling does not imply a rise in temperature. In water at $100\,°C$ and steam at $100\,°C$ the kinetic energy of the molecules is the same.

For evaporation to take place some of the molecules on the surface of the liquid escape. This will be the molecules that happen to be travelling upwards

considerably faster than the average molecular speed. The net result of this is that the average speed of the molecules remaining in the liquid is reduced. Evaporation therefore leads to a cooling effect. It is the large increase in the potential energy of the molecules in steam that is responsible for the large value of the specific latent heat of vaporisation.

Oddly, steam is invisible; and in steam turbines in a power station, for example, the steam circulating through them is dry. What you see coming out of the spout of a kettle is water droplets formed when the steam meets the relatively cold air. Water vapour too is invisible. There is a lot of water vapour in the room you are sitting in but you cannot see it. When water vapour rises through the atmosphere it cools and eventually cools sufficiently to turn back into water droplets. The water droplets are clouds. Clouds are wet because they are water and not water vapour. The droplets may fall as rain when they are large enough but most droplets are so small that their terminal velocity is low and upward air currents are often much faster than the droplets' terminal velocity.

To determine the latent heat of vaporisation of water at $100\,°C$, a continuous flow method can be used. The apparatus is shown in Figure 19.5.

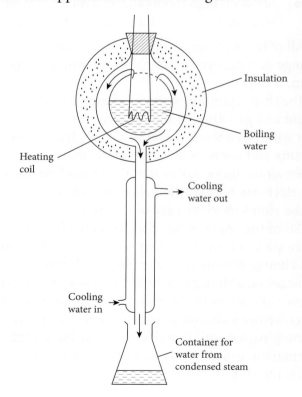

Figure 19.5

It consists of a double-walled glass container with a heater. The power P supplied to the heater is the voltage V across it multiplied by the current I. A few minutes after the water starts to boil, steam will condense in the condenser and is collected in a flask. The mass m of water collected in time t is measured.

This gives the total energy supplied to produce steam = VIt

Since the mass of steam produced = m,

the specific latent heat of vaporisation $L_v = \dfrac{VIt}{m}$.

Teacher's Tip

Be careful with calculations involving change of state. If you have a numerical problem involving ice being changed into steam you may have four stages to consider.
1. Heating the ice from below $0\,°C$ up to $0\,°C$. Use $mc_{ice}\Delta T$
2. Melting the ice. Use mL_{fusion}
3. Heating the water from $0\,°C$ to $100\,°C$. Use $mc_{water} \times 100$
4. Changing the water into steam. Use $mL_{vaporisation}$

Internal energy

Often, when considering the energy of gases, it is the total energy all the molecules possess rather than the energy of individual molecules that is needed. The total energy comprises all the random kinetic energies of all the molecules and all their potential energies. The total kinetic energy of all the molecules is the sum of all the individual kinetic energies of each molecule. The total potential energy of the molecules is a consequence of the intermolecular forces. It will be zero if the gas is ideal and this will also apply for a real gas if the pressure is low. If the pressure is high in a real gas, intermolecular forces will become important and, for example, when the volume of the gas decreases and the molecules are forced closer together, work will need to be done on the gas molecules. This will increase their potential energy. The sum of all these random energies is called the **internal energy** of the gas. Internal energy is dependent on factors such as the pressure, the volume, the temperature, the mass

and the type of gas. These factors determine the **state of the gas**. Once the state of a gas is known, its internal energy can be worked out. There are additional factors that do not affect the state of a gas or its internal energy. One is the previous history of the gas, that is the sequence of events prior to the time when its state is being determined. Another is the speed of travel of the gas. For example, if the air in an aircraft is at a pressure of 0.9 atmospheres, a temperature of $300\,K$ and has a volume of $350\,m^3$, the internal energy has exactly the same value whether the aircraft is stationary on the runway or travelling at an altitude of $10\,000\,m$ at a speed of $250\,m\,s^{-1}$. The aircraft's speed over the ground does not affect its random kinetic energy at all and its altitude does not affect its random potential energy.

In Chapter 17, the average kinetic energy E_k of a single molecule in an ideal gas was found to be given by

$$E_k = \frac{3}{2}kT$$

where k is the Boltzmann constant and T is the kelvin temperature.

This enables the total internal kinetic energy of a sample of an ideal gas to be found provided the number of molecules can be determined. For n moles of a gas, the number of molecules N will be nN_A, where N_A is the Avogadro constant. This gives

$$E = \frac{3}{2}nN_A kT = \frac{3}{2}nRT$$

This equation gives the internal energy for any sample of an ideal gas, since an ideal gas has zero potential energy.

Teacher's Tip

Do be particularly careful with all the N terms in equations such as this. The number of moles n, may well be a small number, typically anything from 0.01 to 100. The number of molecules N will always be large, about 10 to the power of 24. N_A is something special, it is a constant, the Avogadro constant, so it will always be $6.02 \times 10^{23}\,mol^{-1}$.

The first law of thermodynamics

This law is one of the important laws of physics. It relates any change in the internal energy of any system to the amount of work done on the system and the heating of the system. A formal statement of the first law is as follows.

The increase in the internal energy of a system is equal to the work done on the system plus the heating of the system.

It is important to get the signs correct with this law so an equation form is useful.

Increase in internal energy	=	the heating of the system	+	the work done on the system
ΔU	=	w	+	q

Teacher's Tip

You are strongly advised to keep this equation in this form always. One reason for doing this is that the internal energy of an ideal gas is fixed by its temperature. The other two terms are not so restricted. The other reason is that mistakes can so easily be made with signs when one term, say the work done, is rewritten 'work done by the system'. If 200 J of work is done BY the system', simply enter the work done ON the system as −200 J.

An indication of the importance of the first law can be seen from the following example question that you should work through. Much of the information required has already been worked out for you.

Example 3

In a petrol engine, a fixed mass of gas undergoes four stages of a cycle called an Otto cycle. The sequence of events is shown in Figure 19.6 and a graph showing how the pressure varies with the volume is shown in Figure 19.7.

- A → B: The petrol vapour/air mixture is compressed.
- B → C: The mixture is ignited by a spark. The pressure and temperature rise almost instantly.
- C → D: The high pressure forces the piston down. Temperature and pressure fall.
- D → A: This is a complicated procedure in which waste gases are ejected and some fresh petrol/air mixture is introduced to get to the starting point again.

Throughout this exercise, the gas in the engine is considered to be ideal and so are several of the stages. A real engine will be less efficient than this example gives.

Data:

Maximum volume for gas in the cylinder = $450 \, cm^3$
$= 4.5 \times 10^{-4} \, m^3$

Minimum volume for gas in the cylinder = $50 \, cm^3$
$= 0.5 \times 10^{-4} \, m^3$

Starting temperature of petrol/air mixture = $300 \, K$
Starting volume of petrol/air mixture = $4.5 \times 10^{-4} \, m^3$
Starting pressure of petrol/air mixture = $1.0 \times 10^5 \, Pa$

Task 1. Show that the amount of gas in the engine at the start is 0.018 mol.

The following table summarises the pressure and volume of the gas at points A, B, C and D. These points are shown on the graph. The values for the temperature at each point can be found from knowing that pV/T is constant.

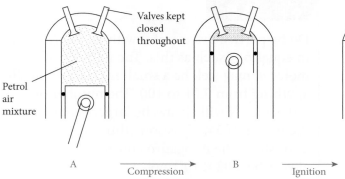
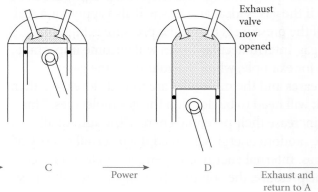

A   Compression   B   Ignition   C   Power   D   Exhaust and return to A

Figure 19.6

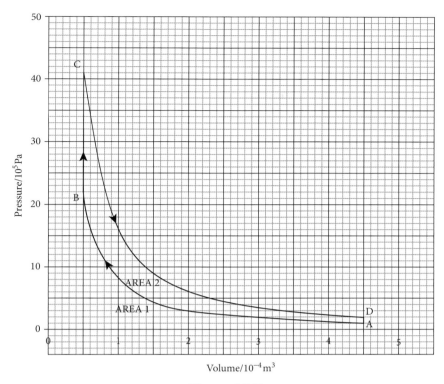

Figure 19.7

	Pressure/ 10^5 Pa	Volume/ 10^{-4} m^3	Temperature/K
A	1.00	4.50	300
B	21.7	0.50	722
C	41.0	0.50	1370
D	1.89	4.50	567

Task 2. Show that PV/T is constant for all these points. What is the value of this constant? Watch out for powers of 10.

From Chapter 6 you may remember that the area beneath a graph of pressure against volume gives the work done. In stage A → B, the area required is Area 1 and is the work done on the petrol/air mixture.

Task 3. How much work is represented by one small square on the graph?

Task 4. Deduce the work done on the petrol/air mixture in stage A → B.

Task 5. Which two stages result in zero work being done on the petrol/air mixture?

These last three tasks enable three values to be inserted into a copy of the following table for work done on the gas. The fourth value is the work done by

the gas in stage C → D. Its numerical value is 300 J. This is entered as −300 J. The minus sign indicates work done **by** the gas as the heading is 'work done **on** the gas'.

Before the table can be completed details are required of the heating that takes place. Stages A → B and C → D are a pure compression and pure expansion respectively, within which no heating occurs. Stage B → C provides energy by burning a quantity of petrol, so here heating does take place and its numerical value depends on the supply of petrol. The figure used for exercise has enough fuel for the temperature to rise to 1370 °C. To do this, 240 J must be supplied by the burning petrol.

This gives all the values for completion of the table.

Stage	Work done on gas/J	Heat supplied to gas/J	Internal energy increase/J
A → B	160	0	
B → C	0	240	
C → D	−300	0	
D → A	0		

Task 6. Complete the table.

Although you now have enough information to complete the table, there is one important factor that you need to use. It is that the internal energy of a gas depends only on its state and not on its past history. Therefore, since the graph starts and finishes at the same point, with the same values of p, V and T, any gain in internal energy is balanced by a corresponding loss of internal energy, whatever happens between D → A.

Task 7. Show that the heating of the gas in stage D → A is actually a loss of 100 J, so must be entered into the table as −100 J.

The reason why analysis such as this is so important commercially is that it places the efficiency of vehicle engines on a sound scientific basis. This calculation not only provides numerical values for efficiency but also points in directions to improve efficiency. For example, when the temperature of the gas after ignition is raised,

the efficiency increases. Unfortunately, too high a temperature might melt the engine, so cooling becomes necessary and this uses energy.

Task 8. What is the efficiency of this engine?

Answer this question by putting in the following values.

Energy supplied in one cycle by burning petrol = … J

Net work done by the gas in one cycle = … J

Energy lost heating exhaust gases in one cycle = … J

(Some of this energy may used to heat the passengers in the car)

The resulting figure should be 58%. Remember though that the exercise has assumed the gas behaves as an ideal gas and also that ideal circumstances have been met. However the exercise does show that no engine working on this cycle between these two temperatures can ever be more than 58% efficient. In practice, car petrol engines are around 40% efficient when working at optimum speed.

Chapter Summary

✓   The energy Q required to raise the temperature of m kilograms of a substance of specific heat c by ΔT degrees is given by $Q = mc\Delta T$.

✓   The energy Q required to change the state of m kilograms of a substance of latent heat L (of either fusion or evaporation) is given by $Q = mL$.

✓   The internal energy of a gas is the sum of all the internal kinetic and potential energies of its molecules.

✓   The first law of thermodynamics: The increase in the internal energy of a system is equal to the sum of the work done on the system and the heating of the system.

Increase in internal energy	=	the heating of the system	+	the work done on the system
ΔU	=	w	+	q

Progress Check

19.1 (a) In order to heat up 6.0 kg of cold water at 10 °C, 2.0 kilogram of water at 95 °C is added to the water. Calculate the final temperature of the water, assuming no heat losses.

   (b) A 1500 W electric heater is used to produce the same temperature rise in the 6.0 kg of water as in (a). How long does this take?

   [**Given:** Specific heat capacity of water = 4200 J kg^{-1} K^{-1}]

19.2 Ice cubes of total mass 150 gm are placed in a vacuum flask holding 350 gm of water at a temperature of 80 °C. Assuming the vacuum flask loses no heat and has negligible heat capacity, what will be the final temperature of the water after all the ice has melted?

   [**Given:** Specific heat capacity of water = 4200 J kg^{-1} K^{-1} and specific latent heat of ice = 330 J kg^{-1}]

19.3 Many thermometers are used for control in situations where the response to temperatures being too high or too low can be fed to a computer that is programmed to take appropriate action. The following examples give some idea of the range of uses. In each case state what is required and suggest a suitable thermometer to use.

   (a) An overheating car engine
   (b) A thermostat to protect against frost on a central heating system for a house
   (c) A deep freeze
   (d) A fire alarm in an office block
   (e) An electric kettle
   (f) A refrigerated lorry carrying perishable goods
   (g) A meteorologist forecasting the weather
   (h) Keeping plants in a greenhouse in-between an upper and a lower temperature

Examination Questions IX

1. (a) The kinetic theory of gases is based on some simplifying assumptions. The molecules of the gas are assumed to behave as hard elastic identical spheres. State the assumption about ideal gas molecules based on
    (i) the nature of their movement,   [1]
    (ii) their volume.   [2]

   (b) A cube of volume V contains N molecules of an ideal gas. Each molecule has a component c_X of velocity normal to one side S of the cube, as shown in Figure 1.

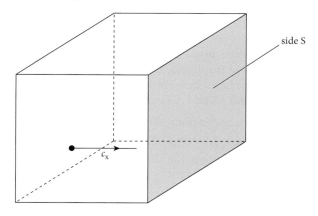

side S

c_X

Figure 1

The pressure p of the gas due to the component c_X of velocity is given by the expression

$$pV = Nmc_X{}^2$$

where m is the mass of a molecule.

Explain how the expression leads to the relation

$$pV = \frac{1}{3}Nm<c^2>$$

where $<c^2>$ is the mean square speed of the molecules.   [3]

   (c) The molecules of an ideal gas have a root-mean-square (r.m.s.) speed of $520\,\text{m s}^{-1}$ at a temperature of $27\,°\text{C}$.

   Calculate the r.m.s. speed, in m s^{-1} of the molecules at a temperature of $100\,°\text{C}$.   [3]

   (Cambridge International AS and A Level Physics 9702 Paper 41 Question 2 May/June 2012)

2. (a) Define *specific latent heat of fusion*.   [2]

   (b) Some crushed ice at $0\,°\text{C}$ is placed in a funnel together with an electric heater, as shown in Figure 2.

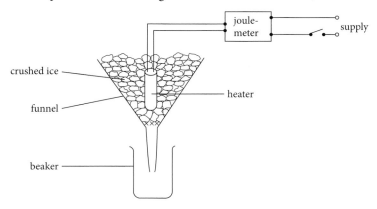

joule-meter

supply

crushed ice

heater

funnel

beaker

Figure 2

The mass of water collected in the beaker in a measured interval of time is determined with the heater switched off. The mass is then found with the heater switched on. The energy supplied to the heater is also measured.

For both measurements of the mass, water is not collected until melting occurs at a constant rate.

The data shown in Table 1 are obtained.

Table 1

	mass of water/g	energy supplied to heater/J	time interval/min
heater switched off	16.6	0	10.0
heater switched on	64.7	18 000	5.0

   (i) State why the mass of water is determined with the heater switched off. [1]
   (ii) Suggest how it can be determined that the ice is melting at a constant rate. [1]
   (iii) Calculate a value for the specific latent heat of fusion of ice, in kJ kg^{-1}. [3]

(Cambridge International AS and A Level Physics 9702 Paper 04 Question 2 October/November 2008)

3. A student suggests that, when an ideal gas is heated from 100 °C to 200 °C, the internal energy of the gas is doubled.

(a)   (i) State what is meant by *internal energy*. [2]
    (ii) By reference to one of the assumptions of the kinetic theory of gases and your answer in (i), deduce what is meant by the internal energy of an ideal gas. [3]

(b) State and explain whether the student's suggestion is correct. [2]

(Cambridge International AS and A Level Physics 9702 Paper 42 Question 2 October/November 2012)

4. (a) State what is meant by an *ideal gas*. [3]

(b) Two cylinders A and B are connected by a tube of negligible volume, as shown in Figure 3.

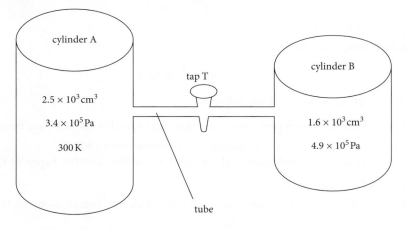

cylinder A

tap T

cylinder B

2.5×10^3 cm^3

3.4×10^5 Pa

300 K

1.6×10^3 cm^3

4.9×10^5 Pa

tube

Figure 3

Initially, tap T is closed. The cylinders contain an ideal gas at different pressures.
  (i) Cylinder A has a constant volume of 2.5×10^3 cm^3 and contains gas at pressure 3.4×10^5 Pa and temperature 300 K. Show that cylinder A contains 0.34 mol of gas. [1]
  (ii) Cylinder B has a constant volume of 1.6×10^3 cm^3 and contains 0.20 mol of gas. When tap T is opened, the pressure of the gas in both cylinders is 3.9×10^5 Pa. No thermal energy enters or leaves the gas. Determine the final temperature of the gas, in K. [2]

(c) By reference to work done and change in internal energy, suggest why the temperature of the gas in cylinder A has changed. [3]

(Cambridge International AS and A Level Physics 9702 Paper 41 Question 2 May/June 2013)

5. The product of the pressure p and the volume V of an ideal gas is given by the expression

$$pV = \frac{1}{3}Nm<c^2>$$

where m is the mass of one molecule of the gas.

(a) State the meaning of the symbol
   (i) N,   [1]
   (ii) $<c^2>$.   [1]

(b) The product pV is also given by the expression

$$pV = NkT.$$

Deduce an expression, in terms of the Boltzmann constant k and the thermodynamic temperature T, for the mean kinetic energy of a molecule of the ideal gas.   [2]

(c) A cylinder contains 1.0 mol of an ideal gas.
   (i) The volume of the cylinder is constant.
       Calculate the energy, in J, required to raise the temperature of the gas by 1.0 kelvin.   [2]
   (ii) The volume of the cylinder is now allowed to increase so that the gas remains at constant pressure when it is heated.
       Explain whether the energy required to raise the temperature of the gas by 1.0 kelvin is now different from your answer in (i).   [2]

(Cambridge International AS and A Level Physics 9702 Paper 42 Question 2 October/November 2013)

Oscillations 20

Introduction

In Chapter 8, considering waves, it was pointed out that water waves are just one type of wave and that there are many other waves of considerable importance. The same comment can be made about oscillations. A swinging pendulum oscillates in a clock making a swing to the right in one second and a swing to the left in one second. This gives the complete oscillation a period of two seconds, if the clock is accurate. This is rather slow and inaccurate when compared with today's atomic clocks. A photograph of an atomic clock is shown in Figure 20.1.

Figure 20.1 An atomic clock

Atomic clocks agree with one another to within a billionth of a second in a day. That is an uncertainty of 1 part in 10^{14}. Satellite navigation systems depend on atomic clocks to find your position on the Earth to the nearest metre and the wobble of the Earth from day to day and year to year can be measured.

Patterns of oscillation

There is a multitude of different ways in which objects can oscillate. Some of these are shown as examples in Figures 20.2(a) to (f) where graphs of displacement against time are plotted. The time scales on the x-axes are not the same.

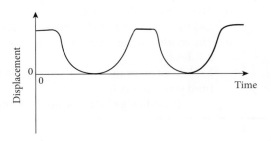

(a) Someone on a skateboard ramp

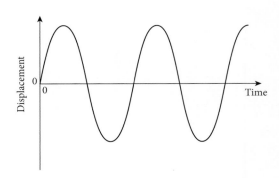

(b) The small displacements of a pendulum

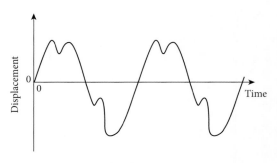

(c) The reed in a clarinet

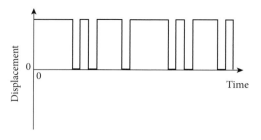

(d) Electrons running a computer program

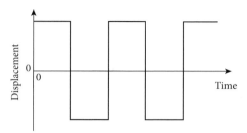

(e) A slider moving to-and-fro on an air track

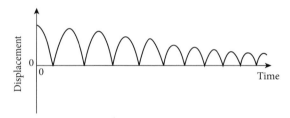

(f) A table tennis ball bouncing on a table

Figure 20.2

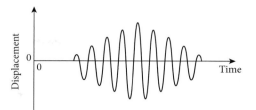

(a) Pattern of sound produced by a horn while playing a note

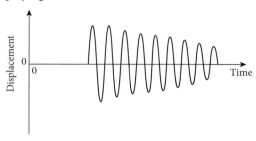

(b) Pattern of sound produced by a piano playing the same note

Figure 20.3

Graphs such as these are usually obtained electronically. Motion or position sensors connected to a computer will be able to give graphical outputs of position against time for comparatively slow oscillations. For faster oscillations, an oscilloscope can be used. A microphone connected to the input of an oscilloscope could be used to display the sound pattern from a clarinet, for example. Some adjustment of the gain and the speed of the time-base may be necessary. An interesting point about oscillation from musical instruments is that the while the pattern of the sound waves from individual instruments affects the quality of the note being played, so does the overall pattern of the shape of the sound level. Figure 20.3(a) shows the pattern of sound from a horn, where the volume of sound increases and decreases relatively slowly while Figure 20.3(b) shows the pattern produced by a piano when playing the same note.

The piano is a percussion instrument in which the strings are struck by a hammer. The volume of sound is suddenly loud and then decays away. A musician can tell the difference in sound from different instruments even when they are playing notes of the same pitch (frequency).

Wave terminology

Much of the terminology of oscillations is the same as that for wave theory. You have already learnt about the following terms.

- The **displacement** (x) in an oscillation is the distance from the mean position. It is a vector quantity and may be positive or negative.
- The **amplitude** (x_0) of an oscillation is the maximum value of the displacement.
- The **period** (T) of an oscillation is the time taken for one complete oscillation.
- The **frequency** (f) of an oscillation is the number of oscillations per unit time. It is the reciprocal of the period. In SI units, frequency is measured in Hertz (Hz). 50 Hz means 50 oscillations per second. The period of this oscillation will be 1/50 second or 0.020 s.

Angular frequency (ω)

Angular velocity (ω) measured in radians per second, is used frequently when considering circular motion. The corresponding term for oscillation is called angular frequency and ω is still the symbol used. The reason that the same term can be used for an oscillation is because the purest form of oscillation has a direct link with circular motion.

In Figure 20.4, a rod of length r is shown in position OB. It started from position OA and is rotating with uniform angular velocity ω about point O. A graph is drawn of the height h of the end of the rod above its starting level. The value of h is given by $h = r\sin\theta$ where θ is the angle between the rod and its starting position as shown.

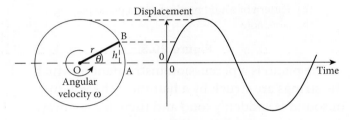

Figure 20.4

This graph shows the pure form of oscillation. It is a sine wave pattern and is called simple harmonic motion (SHM). '*Simple*' because it has a sine wave pattern and '*harmonic*' because of its connection with pure musical sounds. For the rotation of the rod, the angle θ will be given by $\theta = \omega t$ so the equation of the graph will be

$$h = r\sin\omega t$$

In practice, for oscillations ω is often just called 'omega' rather than angular frequency.

The definition of simple harmonic motion (SHM)

Simple harmonic motion takes place when an object has an acceleration that is directed towards a fixed point and is proportional to the displacement from the point. A graph of acceleration against displacement is, therefore, a straight line as shown in Figure 20.5.

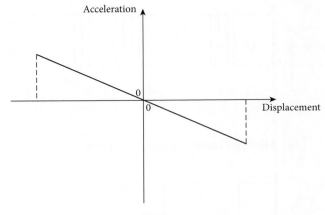

Figure 20.5

It shows that when the displacement is positive, e.g. to the right, then the acceleration is negative, to the left. When the object moves to the left, the acceleration is positive. A force is acting that produces an acceleration towards the rest position.

The equation that states the definition is

$$a = -\omega^2 x$$

where a is the acceleration, x is the displacement and ω, as you might have guessed, is the angular frequency. The minus sign shows that a and x are in opposite directions and ω^2 is used to ensure that the constant is always positive.

Calculus is required to show that the sine wave pattern of motion is a solution to the equation $a = -\omega^2 x$, but you do not need to remember the derivation. If you have not studied calculus, just miss out the next paragraph, but do remember the final line.

This sequence just shows that an oscillation with displacement showing a sine wave pattern (sinusoidal) does have an acceleration as given by the SHM definition. Given that $x = x_0 \sin \omega t$ where x is the displacement and x_0 is the maximum displacement, we get

$$v = \frac{\mathrm{d}x}{\mathrm{d}t} = \frac{\mathrm{d}}{\mathrm{d}t}(x_0 \sin\omega t) = x_0 \omega \cos\omega t = v_0 \cos\omega t$$

since the maximum value of v is $x_0 \omega$

this gives $a = \dfrac{dv}{dt} = \dfrac{d}{dt}(x_0 \omega \cos\omega t)$

$$= -x_0 \omega^2 \sin\omega t = -\omega^2 x$$

So, $x = x_0 \sin\omega t$ is a solution of the equation $a = -\omega^2 x$.

These equations give x, v and a in terms of time, t and a in terms of displacement x. To find v in terms of x we can use the fact that $\sin^2 \omega t + \cos^2 \omega t = 1$. This gives

$$\left(\frac{x}{x_0}\right)^2 + \left(\frac{v}{x_0 \omega}\right)^2 = 1 \text{ which can be rearranged to give}$$

$$v^2 = x_0^2 \omega^2 - x^2 \omega^2 \text{ and hence}$$

$$v = \pm \omega \sqrt{\left(x_0^2 - x^2\right)}$$

Teacher's Tip

Do note that $\sqrt{(10^2 - 4^2)}$ is NOT $\sqrt{100} - \sqrt{16} = 6$.

It is $\sqrt{(100 - 16)} = \sqrt{84} = 9.165$.

Example 1

A mass of 1.2 kg suspended on the end of a spring, undergoes SHM with a period of 0.36 s and amplitude 0.28 m.

(a) Plot graphs to show how the velocity and the kinetic energy of the mass vary with displacement.
(b) Comment on how the potential energy of the system changes during a cycle.

Answer (a) The value of ω is given by $\omega = 2\pi/T$ $= 2\pi/0.36 = 17.45$ rad s^{-1}. The table is based on the equations:

$$v = \pm \omega \sqrt{\left(x_0^2 - x^2\right)} \quad \text{and} \quad E_k = \tfrac{1}{2}mv^2$$

x/m	$0.28^2 - x^2/\text{m}^2$	v/m s^{-1}	E_k/J
0	0.0784	±4.89	14.3
0.05	0.0759	±4.81	13.9
0.10	0.0684	±4.56	12.5
0.15	0.0559	±4.13	10.2
0.20	0.0384	±3.42	7.02
0.25	0.0159	±2.20	2.90
0.27	0.0055	±1.29	1.00
0.28	0	0	0
−0.05	0.0759	±4.81	13.9

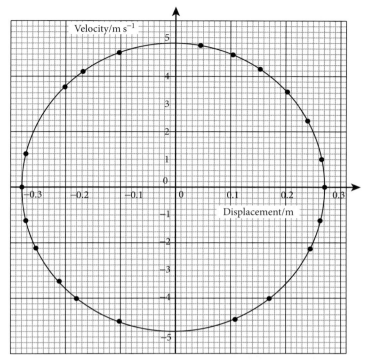

(a)

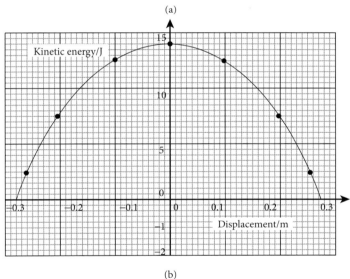

(b)

Figure 20.6

The two graphs are plotted in Figures 20.6(a) and (b).

You should notice from the table that both positive and negative values of displacement give the same value for v and that v can be either negative or positive, obviously whether the mass is rising or falling. The kinetic energy, however, can only be positive, because it depends on v^2 and it is a scalar quantity. The shape of the velocity-displacement graph is an ellipse; the kinetic energy-displacement graph is a parabola.

(b) The total energy of the system will be constant because this is assumed to be perfect SHM and, therefore, there is no change in the amplitude of the oscillation over time. The assumption is, therefore, that resistive effects, due to air resistance for example, are zero.

Any loss of kinetic energy must result in a gain of potential energy. When the mass is rising, it gains gravitational potential energy but the spring loses elastic potential energy at the same time. When the mass is falling the mass loses gravitational potential energy and the spring gains elastic potential energy. The **total** potential energy-displacement graph will be a parabola upside down to the kinetic energy-displacement graph. The two graphs are often drawn in the way shown in Figure 20.7 but this depends on arbitrarily making the zero of potential energy at displacement zero.

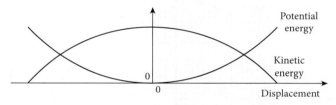

Figure 20.7

Damped oscillations

Simple harmonic motion makes the assumption that the amplitude of the oscillation is constant. While this is possible, with electrical oscillations for example, in practice it can only be achieved by drip feeding energy into the system. A clock or a watch maintains a constant period and amplitude by energy being fed into the oscillating system from a falling weight or a spring, or a battery. Figure 20.8 shows an old clock with heavy weights that needed to be lifted up every week. As they fell back down they transferred energy to the clock to keep it going.

In the absence of this supply of energy the amplitude of any oscillation will decrease. An oscillation with a decreasing amplitude is said to be **damped**.

Figure 20.8

Teacher's Tip

It helps to check details about SHM (simple harmonic motion) if you know what to expect. This table outlines what to expect at the top, bottom and middle of the oscillation of a mass bouncing up and down on the end of a spring. It can be applied to most SHM.

	displacement	speed	acceleration	kinetic energy	potential energy
top	positive	zero	negative	zero	maximum gravitational
middle	zero	maximum	zero	maximum	reference zero
bottom	negative	zero	positive	zero	maximum elastic

Damping can be light or heavy. It can be so heavy that oscillation does not take place at all. Figure 20.9 shows a series of oscillations with different degrees of damping.

The damping becomes progressively heavier through the series. The first example could be the oscillation of a pendulum bob in air. This might swing for a few hundred times before it stops. The last one might be the same pendulum bob but simply falling to the vertical when immersed in thick oil. Note that these are free oscillations. The object starts with displacement and will always finish, given time, at zero displacement.

How much damping should be provided for different practical problems is a real concern for designers of cars, for example. When a car runs over a sudden change in level of the road surface,

it would be very uncomfortable for the passengers in the car were the car not to have any springing; but if the springing causes the passengers to bounce many times that will also be unpleasant. Designers usually aim for a situation called **critical damping** in which a complete oscillation does not occur and the passengers are brought back to equilibrium reasonably quickly. This is illustrated by the series of graphs of Figure 20.10.

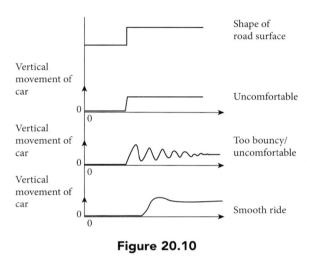

Figure 20.10

Forced oscillations and resonance

Situations often arise where unwanted oscillations can be created. You have probably been in a bus when it starts to shake as a result of the engine speed matching the natural frequency of oscillation of the frame of the bus. It would be very frightening if the same thing happened when travelling by aircraft. Almost everything will rattle at some frequency if there is something else driving it at just the right frequency. Opera singers might sometimes cause a wine glass to break! Good designers try to eliminate unwanted oscillations, noises and rattles. Manufacturers of expensive cars spend much time and money to obtain a quiet ride for their customers.

Whenever forced oscillations are being considered there must be a driving oscillation and a system undergoing the forced oscillation. A simple but effective illustration of forced oscillations is shown in Figure 20.11(a). It is an arrangement of pendulums

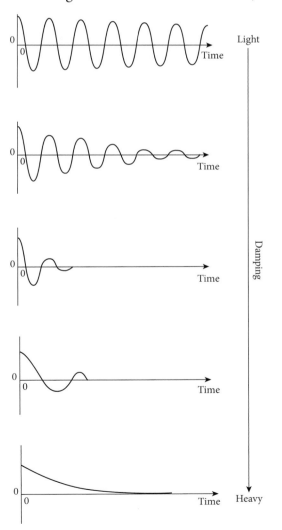

Figure 20.9

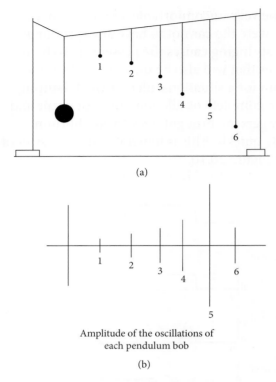

(a)

(b)

Amplitude of the oscillations of
each pendulum bob

Figure 20.11

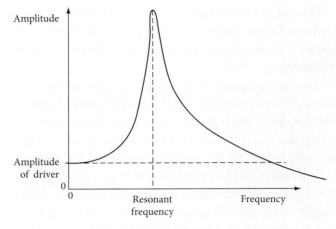

Figure 20.12

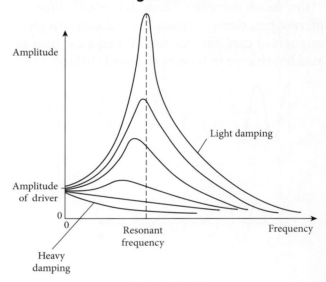

Figure 20.13

of different lengths called **Barton's pendulums**. One of the pendulums is more massive than the rest of the pendulums and this acts as the driver. The other pendulums are caused to oscillate and the pendulum of natural frequency closest to the frequency of the driver frequency has the greatest amplitude. It is said to **resonate.**

Figure 20.11(b) shows how the range of displacements of oscillation varies with the length of the pendulums.

When a freely supported single oscillator is made to oscillate by a driver of varying frequency, a graph can be drawn of the amplitude of the forced oscillation against frequency of the driver. The result is a graph of the shape shown in Figure 20.12.

Large resonant oscillations such as this can be dangerous. If pilots are subjected to frequencies around 35 Hz, physiological tests show that their eyeballs vibrate alarmingly in their sockets causing impaired vision. Oscillations such as this can be avoided either by preventing the oscillations altogether or by damping them. Even sitting on a cushioned seat reduces the amplitude of the oscillation. Figure 20.13 shows, in general, how

damping has two main effects on the amplitude of the driven oscillator. It reduces the amplitude of the oscillation, especially the resonant oscillation, and it reduces the frequency at which maximum amplitude is produced. The diagram also shows that with heavy damping high frequency oscillations become almost impossible.

However, resonance is made use of in other circumstances. Electrical circuits can be made to resonate. The production of high frequency radio signals at broadcasting stations enables the transmission of signals at pre-determined frequencies. When you want to listen to a radio, or watch a television programme, the action of tuning into a station is a process of altering a circuit in your radio so that it resonates at the frequency of the incoming radio waves. If you move along a frequency band near the required frequency, and plot a graph of the loudness of the signal you receive will get a graph of the same shape as Figure 20.12, only it will probably be much higher and sharper.

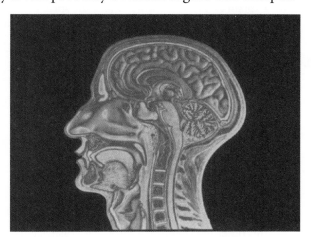

Figure 20.14

One prime example of the use of resonance is an MRI scan. A photograph of the head of a person is shown in Figure 20.14. The detail in the image is extraordinary.

MRI stands for Magnetic Resonance Imaging. In these systems the objects undergoing resonant oscillations are the nuclei of hydrogen atoms in water. They are made to resonate by short pulses of radio waves in very strong magnetic fields. How quickly the oscillation dies away depends on the nature of the tissue that oscillates, and provides information that a computer uses to produce the images.

Chapter Summary

✓ Angular frequency ω corresponds with angular velocity in circular motion. In circular motion the angular velocity, $\omega = 2\pi/T$. In simple harmonic motion one cycle of the motion is the period T and the angular frequency is also defined by $\omega = 2\pi/T$

✓ Simple harmonic motion occurs when the acceleration is proportional to the displacement and in the opposite direction to the displacement. The defining equation is

$$a = -\omega^2 x$$

$x = x_0 \sin \omega t$ is a solution of the equation $a = -\omega^2 x$

✓ Several equations can be deduced from this defining equation. Once the displacement has been found, equations for the velocity follow.

$$v = x_0 \omega \cos \omega t = v_0 \cos \omega t$$

since the maximum value of v is $x_0 \omega$.

$$v = \pm \omega \sqrt{\left(x_0^2 - x^2 \right)}$$

✓ Forced oscillations occur when a driving system causes another system to oscillate. Resonance will occur when the frequency of the driver system equals the natural frequency of the driven system.

✓ The effect of friction or air resistance on a mechanical oscillating system results in a loss of energy in the system. The effect is called damping and it reduces the amplitude of the oscillation. In electrical systems, it is electrical resistance in the circuit that causes the same reduction in amplitude.

Progress Check

20.1 (a) Convert a right angle into radian measure.

(b) (i)   A fairground ride completes 8 rotations in 26.3 s. Calculate its angular speed in radians per second. Give your answer to the correct number of significant figures.

(ii) Calculate the linear speed of a rider who is sitting at a distance of 4.5 m from the axis of rotation.

(c) One cycle of a simple harmonic oscillation, its period, takes 0.0743 s. Calculate the value of the angular frequency, ω.

20.2 A mass of 4.57 kg is suspended from a spring of spring constant 3.28 kN m^{-1}. Calculate the frequency of the oscillation after the mass is lifted a little from its equilibrium position and then released.

20.3 (a) One of the springs in the suspension system of a car supports a weight of 2500 N. Under this condition the spring is compressed by a distance of 0.087 m. After travelling over a bump in the road, the spring is compressed further by 0.020 m. Calculate

(i) the period of the subsequent oscillation that takes place,

(ii) the maximum vertical velocity of the part of the car the spring is attached to.

(b) Explain two features which make the spring system unacceptable in this simple form and describe how, in practice, the spring system can be improved.

20.4 A mass of 2.00 kg is undergoing SHM in a vertical plane. Its gravitational potential energy increases by 1.18 J between the bottom and the top of the oscillation. The kinetic energy of the object at the equilibrium position is 0.24 J.

(a) Sketch energy–displacement graphs, on the same axes, showing how the gravitational potential energy and the kinetic energy change during one cycle of the oscillation.

(b) Explain how there must be some other type of energy involved: add a third graph showing how this other type of energy varies with displacement.

20.5 Describe **two** situations where resonant frequencies can be destructive and **two** situations where resonant frequency oscillations are made use of. (One of the useful applications might well be employed in a device in your kitchen at home.)

Examination Questions X

1. (a)   State Newton's law of gravitation.   [2]

(b) A satellite of mass m is in a circular orbit of radius r about a planet of mass M.

For this planet, the product GM is 4.00×10^{14} N m^2 kg^{-1}, where G is the gravitational constant.

The planet may be assumed to be isolated in space.

(i) By considering the gravitational force on the satellite and the centripetal force, show that the kinetic energy E_K of the satellite is given by the expression

$$E_K = \frac{GMm}{2}$$

[2]

(ii) The satellite has mass 620 kg and is initially in a circular orbit of radius 7.34×10^6 m, as illustrated in Figure 1.

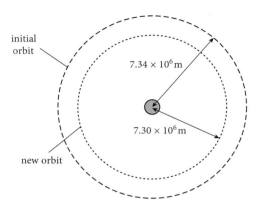

initial
orbit

7.34×10^6 m

7.30×10^6 m

new orbit

Figure 1 (not to scale)

Resistive forces cause the satellite to move into a new orbit of radius 7.30×10^6 m.
Determine, for the satellite, the change in
1. kinetic energy, in J,   [2]
2. gravitational potential energy, in J.   [2]
(iii) Use your answers in (ii) to explain whether the linear speed of the satellite increases, decreases or remains
unchanged when the radius of the orbit decreases.   [2]

(Cambridge International AS and A Level Physics 9702 Paper 42 Question 1 October/November 2012)

2. A ball is held between two fixed points A and B by means of two stretched springs, as shown in Figure 2.

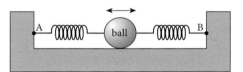

A   ball   B

Figure 2

The ball is free to oscillate along the straight line AB. The springs remain stretched and the motion of the ball is
simple harmonic.
The variation with time t of the displacement x of the ball from its equilibrium position is shown in Figure 3.

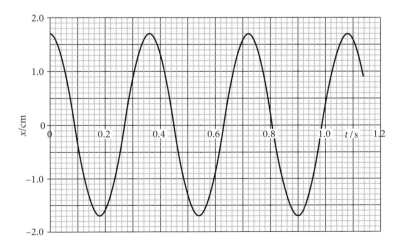

Figure 3

(a) (i) Use Figure 3 to determine, for the oscillations of the ball,
     1. the amplitude, in cm,   [1]
     2. the frequency, in Hz.   [2]
    (ii) Show that the maximum acceleration of the ball is 5.2 m s^{-2}.   [2]

(b) Use your answers in **(a)** to plot, on the axes of Figure 4, the variation with displacement x of the acceleration a of the ball.   [2]

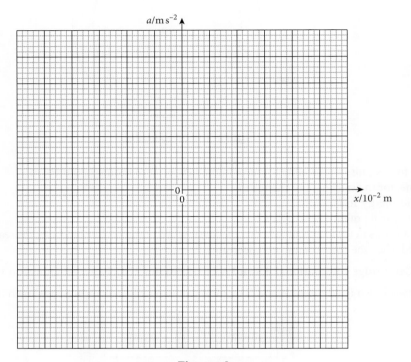

Figure 4

(c) Calculate the displacement of the ball, in cm, at which its kinetic energy is equal to one half of the maximum kinetic energy.   [3]

(Cambridge International AS and A Level Physics 9702 Paper 41 Question 3 May/June 2013)

3. A metal ball is suspended from a fixed point by means of a string, as illustrated in Figure 5.

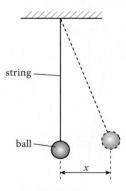

Figure 5

The ball is given a small displacement and then released. The variation with time t of the displacement x of the ball is shown in Figure 6.

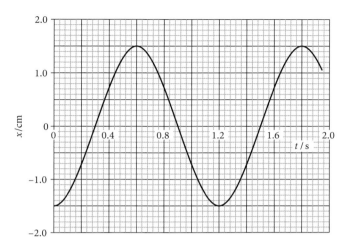

Figure 6

(a) (i) State two times, in s, at which the speed of the ball is a maximum.   [1]
    (ii) Show that the maximum speed of the ball is approximately $0.08 \, \text{m s}^{-1}$.   [2]

(b) The variation with displacement x of the potential energy E_p of the oscillations of the ball is shown in Figure 7.

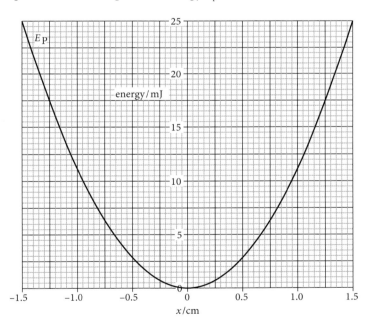

Figure 7

   (i) On the axes of Figure 7, sketch a graph to show the variation with displacement x of the kinetic
      energy of the ball.   [2]
  (ii) The amplitude of the oscillations reduces over a long period of time.
      After many oscillations, the amplitude of the oscillations is $0.60 \, \text{cm}$.
      Use Figure 7 to determine the total energy, in J, of the oscillations of the ball for oscillations of
      amplitude $0.60 \, \text{cm}$. Explain your working.   [2]

(Cambridge International AS and A Level Physics 9702 Paper 42 Question 3 October/November 2013)

4. A bar magnet is suspended from the free end of a helical spring, as illustrated in Figure 8.

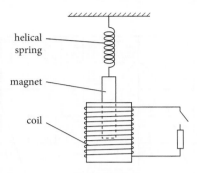

helical — spring

magnet —

coil —

Figure 8

One pole of the magnet is situated in a coil of wire. The coil is connected in series with a switch and a resistor. The switch is open.

The magnet is displaced vertically and then released. As the magnet passes through its rest position, a timer is started. The variation with time t of the vertical displacement y of the magnet from its rest position is shown in Figure 9.

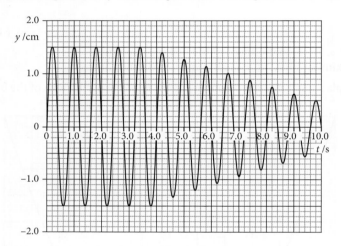

Figure 9

At time $t = 4.0\,\text{s}$, the switch is closed.

(a) Use Figure 9 to

   (i) state the evidence for the magnet to be undergoing free oscillations during the period $t = 0$ to $t = 4.0\,\text{s}$, [1]

   (ii) state, with a reason, whether the damping after time $t = 4.0\,\text{s}$ is light, critical or heavy, [2]

   (iii) determine the natural frequency of vibration of the magnet on the spring, in Hz. [2]

(b) (i) State Faraday's law of electromagnetic induction. [2]

   (ii) Explain why, after time $t = 4.0\,\text{s}$, the amplitude of vibration of the magnet is seen to decrease. [4]

(Cambridge International AS and A Level Physics 9702 Paper 41 Question 3 October/November 2011)

Ultrasound 21

The piezo-electric transducer

Certain crystals (lead zirconate titanate, for example) produce a small potential difference across two of their faces when they are squeezed, as shown in Figure 21.1.

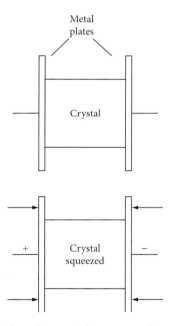

Figure 21.1 When the crystal is squeezed, a potential difference is formed across it.

The voltage is very small but it does respond very quickly to changes in the forces applied. So much so, that crystals of this type can be used in microphones where the passage of the sound wave past the crystal acts to vary the force on the crystal. This causes a small, varying potential difference across the crystal, which can be amplified. The crystal used in this way is called a **piezo-electric transducer**.

The process can be reversed. When a varying potential difference is applied to the crystal it causes the crystal to vibrate.

This process is used in producing very high frequency sound waves that are inaudible to a human ear. These waves are called **ultrasound**. The frequency of the potential difference applied to the crystal will be of the order of megahertz (MHz).

In practice, a single crystal can be used both to produce and to receive ultrasound. The structure of an ultrasound transducer that generates and receives ultrasound is shown in Figure 21.2.

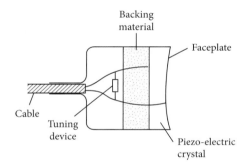

Figure 21.2 The structure of an ultrasound transducer. It acts as both a transmitter and a receiver of ultrasound.

Electrical signals can be supplied from the cable to the crystal or taken from the crystal through the cable to an amplifier. Adjusting the value of the resistor gives optimum sensitivity to the crystal.

Ultrasound scanning

A practical use of ultrasound is to obtain images of a baby in the womb. One advantage of ultrasound scanning is that no radiation dose is used. Other advantages include its simplicity and that it is possible to obtain moving images, of the blood flow through a baby's heart, for example.

The description of ultrasound scanning that follows is for a so-called A-scan. This gives an elementary view of the reflection of a pulse of ultrasound on an oscilloscope, as shown in Figure 21.3. To get a two-dimensional picture, a B-scan, as shown in Figure 21.4, it is necessary to use an array of piezo-electric transducers sending out fan-shaped ultrasound signals and to use a computer to decode the reflected echoes.

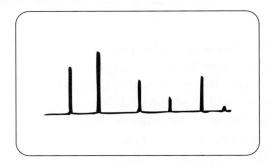

Figure 21.3 Reflected pulses of ultrasound using an A-scan.

The principle of ultrasound scanning depends on ultrasound being reflected at a boundary between two different materials. Many reflections are required from different boundaries so an important factor for any boundary is the ratio between the fraction of the ultrasound that is reflected and the fraction transmitted. To determine this ratio a term called the **specific acoustic impedance** is used.

Specific acoustic impedance = density of material × speed of sound in the material

In symbol form this is $Z = \rho c$

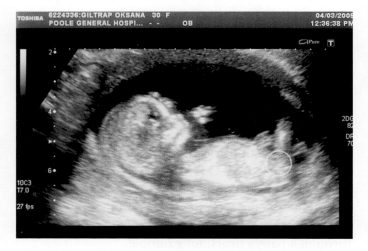

Figure 21.4 An ultrasound scan of a baby in the womb.

Table 21.1 lists values of these three quantities for some different materials.

Table 21.1

Material	$c/$ m s^{-1}	$\rho/$ kg m^{-3}	$Z/$ kg m^{-2} s^{-1}
air	340	1.3	440
bone	3500	1600	5.6×10^6
muscle	1600	1000	1.6×10^6
soft tissue	1500	1000	1.5×10^6
fat	1400	1000	1.4×10^6
blood	1600	1000	1.6×10^6
skin	1600	1000	1.6×10^6

The equation relating the ratio of intensity reflected I_r to incident intensity I_o for ultrasound leaving a material of acoustic impedance Z_1 and entering another material of acoustic impedance Z_2 is

$$\frac{I_r}{I_o} = \left(\frac{Z_2 - Z_1}{Z_2 + Z_1}\right)^2$$

This ratio is called the **intensity reflection coefficient**.

Example 1

Calculate the fraction of ultrasound reflected when ultrasound passes from air into skin.

Answer

$$\frac{I_r}{I_o} = \left(\frac{Z_2 - Z_1}{Z_2 + Z_1}\right)^2 = \left(\frac{1.6 \times 10^6 - 440}{1.6 \times 10^6 + 440}\right)^2 = \left(\frac{1599\,566}{1600\,440}\right)^2 = 0.9989$$

This means that any ultrasound in the air is almost totally reflected by skin. It explains why a gel needs to be used between any ultrasound source and the skin in order to get the ultrasound into anyone's body.

To see how the intensity of an image on the screen of an A-type scan can be related to the thickness and intensity reflection coefficient of the materials, work through the following exercise.

A pulse of ultrasound of intensity I after entering a fat layer 20 mm thick carries on through a 30 mm thick layer of muscle and a 25 mm thick bone. At each boundary some of the ultrasound is reflected and some continues. The absorption of the ultrasound by each layer is assumed to be zero here.

Three paths are considered:

- through just the fat before being reflected back through the fat,
- through fat and muscle before being reflected back through fat, and
- through fat, muscle and bone before being reflected.

The **reflection coefficients** when calculated using the data from the table above are:

fat to muscle = muscle to fat = 0.0044
muscle to bone = bone to muscle = 0.31

Times for passage of pulses
fat only: $2 \times 0.020/1400 = 28.6\,\mu s$
fat and muscle:
$2 \times 0.030/1600 + 28.6\,\mu s = 66.1\,\mu s$
fat, muscle and bone:
$2 \times 0.025/3500 + 66.1\,\mu s = 80.4\,\mu s$

Intensity is shown in Figure 21.5. Note that the reflected intensity, for example at the far side of the bone is 31% of the 69% arriving at that boundary. The amount reflected at the fat-muscle boundary is almost negligible.

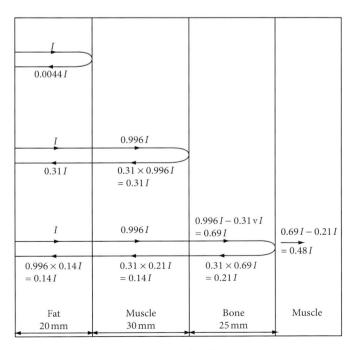

Figure 21.5

Figure 21.6 shows the appearance of an oscilloscope screen that receives the three reflected pulses.

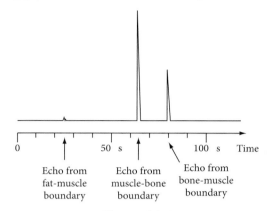

Figure 21.6

Note that after a suitable time has elapsed for all the reflected echoes to return, another pulse of ultrasound will be transmitted. Note also that if pulses are too long, echoes will be returning while the next pulse is being sent. This will have the effect of causing the scan to miss some detail.

Absorption coefficients

In the previous exercise it was convenient to assume that the ultrasound intensity remained constant within one type of material. In practice this is not the case. Even with a parallel beam every material does absorb energy and, therefore, the intensity falls off with distance. This is called **attenuation**. For a point source of ultrasound there will also be a fall off of intensity that follows an inverse square law.

The equation relating I, the intensity for a parallel-sided beam at a distance x from a point where the intensity is I_o is

$$I = I_o\, e^{-\mu x}$$

μ is called the linear absorption coefficient. As with all exponential decreases it is possible to use half-distance values. The intensity of gamma radiation through lead reduces to half its value in about 0.7 cm. For concrete the value will be higher, around 4 cm. Exact figures cannot be given for gamma radiation or for ultrasound because the wavelength of the radiation also affects the attenuation.

Example 2

A parallel ultrasound beam travels through flesh with a linear absorption coefficient of $100\,\text{m}^{-1}$. (A parallel beam is sometimes called a collimated beam.) The initial power of the beam is $84\,\text{W}$. Calculate the power of the beam after it has travelled $0.047\,\text{m}$ through the flesh.

Answer We know, $I = I_o e^{-\mu x}$ where $I_o = 8.4\,\text{W}$, $\mu = 86\,\text{m}^{-1}$ and $x = 0.047\,\text{m}$.

Take natural logs to get
$$\ln I = \ln 8.4 - \mu x$$
This gives $\ln I = 2.128 - (86 \times 0.047)$
$$= 2.128 - 4.042 = -1.914$$
Use the e^x button to get the antilog of -1.914 and this gives $I = 0.15\,\text{W}$

Chapter Summary

✓ Ultrasound scanning technique does not involve the use of radiation dose; instead it depends upon the ultrasound being reflected at a boundary between two different materials. It is possible to obtain the moving images of the blood or liquid inside patients.

✓ A parallel beam of ultrasound is attenuated as it passes through matter. The intensity I after passing through a distance x is given by

$$I = I_o e^{-\mu x}$$

where I_o is the initial intensity and μ is the linear absorption coefficient.

Progress Check

21.1 Using data from Table 21.1, calculate the fraction of ultrasound that is reflected when it meets a boundary between
(a) muscle and blood,
(b) fat to bone.

21.2 A parallel ultrasound wave travelling through flesh is reduced to half its intensity in a distance of $0.87\,\text{cm}$. An ultrasound wave of initial intensity $630\,\text{W}\,\text{m}^{-2}$ passes through flesh a distance of $9.7\,\text{cm}$. What will be the final intensity of the ultrasound wave?

21.3 The power of a collimated beam of ultrasound is $75\,\text{W}$ before it enters a person's body and its power after travelling through a thickness of flesh is $0.58\,\text{W}$. The linear absorption coefficient of flesh in this case is $100\,\text{m}^{-1}$. Calculate the thickness of flesh through which the ultrasound has passed.

Communicating Information 22

The principles of modulation

Introduction

Long ago getting information from one place to another used to be a very slow process. Now all communication systems travel at the speed of light but in various different ways. Radio waves are one obvious method but electric currents in wires and co-axial cables are still used to a considerable extent. Ground-based and satellite-based microwave links together with optic fibre links have become increasingly important. Many of these systems are combined with one another for transmission. The information transmitted may be digital or analogue and may be changed from one form to another during transmission.

Signal modulation

If you connect a microphone to an oscilloscope and speak into the microphone, you will see the pattern of the variation of air pressure caused by speaking. A graph of this variation of pressure is shown in a simplified pattern in Figure 22.1.

The microphone has converted the change in pressure to an electrical **signal**. This particular signal is called an audio signal. It will have frequencies within it of anything from 20 to 20 000 Hz. Early telephone systems used audio signals and amplified them, often many times, before they reached their destinations.

Now, audio signals, whether produced using a telephone or from a broadcasting station, are used to modulate radio waves. The effect of **amplitude modulation (AM)** on a radio wave is shown in Figure 22.2. The frequency of the carrier wave will normally be very much greater than that shown in the diagram.

Another form of modulation is **frequency modulation (FM)**. In this case it is not the amplitude of the carrier wave that changes but the frequency. This is shown in Figure 22.3. The frequency of the carrier wave is again much higher in practice than can conveniently be shown in a diagram.

Bandwidth

A radio carrier wave of frequency f_c that is amplitude modulated by a single audio frequency f_a can be

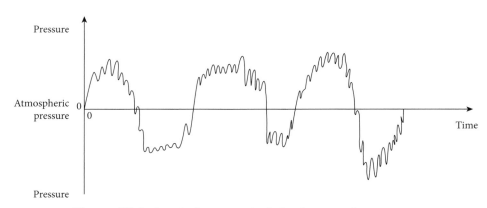

Figure 22.1 A typical pressure variation in a sound wave.

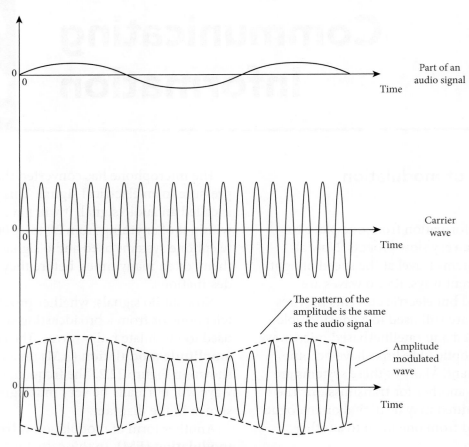

Figure 22.2 An amplitude modulated (AM) wave.

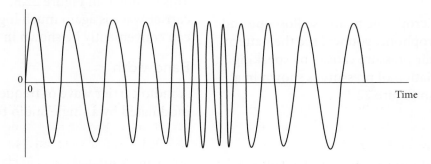

Figure 22.3 A frequency modulated (FM) wave.

analysed into three separate frequencies. These are f_c, the carrier frequency, and $f_c - f_a$ and $f_c + f_a$, which are called the sideband frequencies. This means that if waves of these three frequencies were added together the resultant wave would be a wave of the form shown in Figure 22.4(a). The amplitude of these three waves is shown in Figure 22.4(b). The depth of modulation is controlled by the

amplitude of the $f_c - f_a$ and $f_c + f_a$ frequencies. Figures 22.5(a) and (b) show the corresponding graphs for a small amount of modulation.

To put some numbers on this, if a radio carrier wave of frequency 600 000 Hz is modulated by an audio wave of frequency 5000 Hz, the modulated radio wave has frequencies of 595 000 Hz, 600 000 Hz and 605 000 Hz. Any transmission

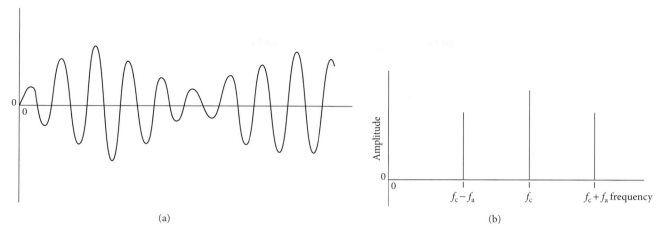

Figure 22.4 A high degree of modulation (a) requires large sideband amplitudes (b).

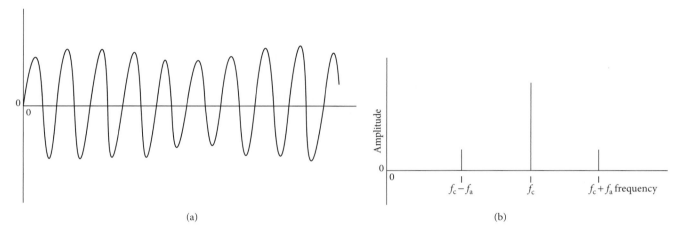

Figure 22.5 A low degree of modulation (a) requires small sideband amplitude (b).

or amplifying system must be able to cope with all these frequencies. In practice, a radio wave modulated by an audio wave will have to cope with any frequencies in the audio range from 30 to 20 000 Hz. This means that a band of frequencies is required from 580 000 Hz up to 620 000 Hz. The bandwidth will be 40 000 Hz; a lower sideband of 20 000 Hz and an upper sideband of 20 000 Hz. Two radio stations broadcasting in the same area must have their frequencies separated by a frequency equal to the bandwidth. You must have experienced a situation when the radio station you want to listen to is picking up another broadcast that you do not want. There is always great pressure on the authorities when they

are allocating radio frequencies. Note that the frequencies used here would normally be written as 600 kHz, 580 kHz, and so on. MHz and GHz are units used for 10^6 and 10^9 Hz respectively.

Comparison between amplitude modulation (AM) and frequency modulation (FM)

The main advantage of FM over AM is the absence of interference. Most unwanted electromagnetic radiation, called noise, affects the amplitude of any transmission. An AM receiver picks up noise. An FM transmission has a constant amplitude and since the amplitude is not the feature carrying the audio signal, noise is not detected.

Table 22.1

Classification		Frequency	Wavelength	Some uses
infra-low	ILF	$300 \rightarrow 3000\,\text{Hz}$	$1000 \rightarrow 100\,\text{km}$	telephone
very low	VLF	$3 \rightarrow 30\,\text{kHz}$	$100 \rightarrow 10\,\text{km}$	navigation
low	LF	$30 \rightarrow 300\,\text{kHz}$	$10 \rightarrow 1\,\text{km}$	AM radio broadcasting
medium	MF	$300 \rightarrow 3000\,\text{kHz}$	$1000 \rightarrow 100\,\text{m}$	AM radio broadcasting
high	HF	$3 \rightarrow 30\,\text{MHz}$	$100 \rightarrow 10\,\text{m}$	amateur radio, ship communication
very high	VHF	$30 \rightarrow 300\,\text{MHz}$	$10 \rightarrow 1\,\text{m}$	FM radio broadcasting, TV broadcasting
ultra-high	UHF	$300 \rightarrow 3000\,\text{MHz}$	$100 \rightarrow 10\,\text{cm}$	TV broadcasting, mobile phones
super-high	SHF	$3 \rightarrow 30\,\text{GHz}$	$10 \rightarrow 1\,\text{cm}$	microwave links, satellite communication

Frequency modulation does require a larger bandwidth than amplitude modulation but it does usually have a considerably higher carrier frequency than amplitude modulation. The reason for this is largely historical. Amplitude modulation was the only type of modulation used for public service broadcasting in the early days of radio. With a bandwidth of 40 kHz, only 120 broadcasts are possible using carrier frequencies between 200 kHz and 5000 kHz. Using carrier frequencies between 2 MHz and 50 MHz there would be 1200 possible transmitting frequencies with a 40 kHz bandwidth, so even with their greater bandwidth more FM stations are possible.

Another matter for consideration is the possible range of any transmitter. Radio waves with frequencies around 200 kHz are able to be picked up at great distances from the transmitter. It is, therefore, not possible for two radio transmitting stations to use this frequency if they are only 1000 km apart because many receivers in between them would pick up both transmissions. With its higher transmitting frequency, however, FM has a much more limited range. This makes it possible for two transmitters to use the same frequency, perhaps when only 400 km apart. Sometimes broadcasters have to advise listeners or viewers that the interference they are experiencing is due to unusual weather conditions over which they have no control, such as electrically charged clouds in lightning storms.

Frequencies and wavelengths used in telecommunications

Table 22.1 shows the ranges of frequencies used for different types of communication. Gradually, over the years the frequencies used have increased. Note that for all radio waves and microwaves frequency × wavelength = c, the speed of light = $3.00 \times 10^8\,\text{m s}^{-1}$.

Digital information

Sound and vision are essentially analogue information, yet we now live in a world of rapidly increasing digital information. The advent of the ability of electronic circuits to process digital information at very high speeds has led to this surge in the use of digital equipment. It is also much easier to store digital rather than analogue information. Another crucial reason for the choice of digital rather than analogue information is that any noise on analogue is difficult to remove but with digital information, noise removal is easy. This is illustrated in Figure 22.6.

It is possible to preserve perfectly a digital signal even if a large amount of noise has been accumulated during transmission.

Sampling rates

Transmitting speech or music digitally must be preceded by converting an analogue signal into a

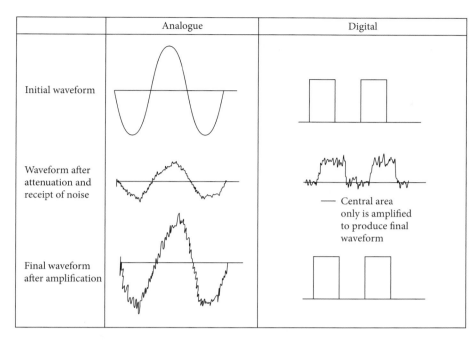

Figure 22.6 Noise is much more easily removed from a digital signal than from an analogue wave.

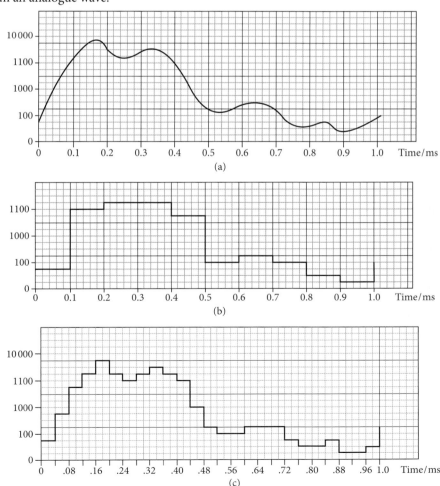

Figure 22.7 Digitising wave (a) using coarse sampling in (b) and in finer sampling in (c).

digital signal. This is done using an electronic circuit called an **analogue to digital converter (ADC)**. On reception the signal needs to be changed back into an analogue signal for use with a loudspeaker. The circuit for doing this is called a **digital to analogue converter (DAC)**. In both of these cases there will be some loss of detail. It is important that the loss of detail is minimal. This can be achieved by adjusting the sampling rate, as illustrated by the following example.

Example 1

A sound wave of period 1.0 millisecond has the shape shown in Figure 22.7(a). The scale on the y-axis is using binary notation (100 = 4, 1000 = 8, 1100 = 12 and 10 000 = 16). Show the pattern produced when the wave is sampled

(a)   every 0.10 ms, (a rate of 10 kHz) and

(b)   every 0.04 ms, (a rate of 25 kHz).

Answer The answer is shown in Figures 22.7(b) and (c). The faster sampling process keeps more closely to the original pattern than the slower, but there is still an appreciable difference between the original and the digital copy. Once these digital signals are put through a DAC the original pattern will show some distortion from the original. Clearly, if the sampling rate is increased then the final analogue signal will be closer to the original analogue signal. This does mean that more digital data has to be transmitted. These graphs have a digital low value of zero and a high value of 15. Each byte of information can be transmitted with 4 bits. When converted into digital values, 0 becomes 0000, 1 becomes 0001, 4 becomes 0100, 8 becomes 1000, and so on. The 10 kHz pattern is 3,12,13,13,11,4,5,4,2,1. It will be sent with the 3 first, so you have to read it backwards, starting from the right-hand side of the page, i.e.

last 1000 0100 0010 1010 0010 1101 1011 1011 0011 1100 first

Reading backwards 3, which in digital is 0011, is transmitted as 1100. (If you want to see them as digital numbers – turn the book upside down and that will reverse them for you.)

Modes of communication

Whether communication is analogue or digital, the aim of any communication system is to get information from one place to another. Obviously there are likely to be differences between a local radio station communicating with its audience on an island where the furthest distance is only a few kilometres and the United States Government communicating with the Government of France half a world away.

The following ways by which communication takes place are all in regular use. Some of the uses are given in the list:

- copper wires, e.g. the telephone line into your house,
- radio waves, e.g. from a transmitter to an aerial in a radio,
- co-axial cable, e.g. the TV signal from an aerial on the roof to a TV set,
- microwaves, e.g. from transmitter to a receiver with millions of emails,
- optic fibres, e.g. very pure, very thin glass fibres under the sea connecting continents and carrying vast amounts of information,
- satellites, e.g. providing digital information for sat-nav systems.

This list has been arranged in approximate chronological order of invention. Early electrical communication was by telephone using wire connections: radio came shortly afterwards.

Now satellite communication is widespread for television as well as for sat-navs, though many television signals, telephone conversations and business messages are carried by optic fibres. Optic fibres are cheaper to install.

When watching an interview on television between someone in a studio and a reporter in a remote place, it is possible to tell whether a satellite communications system is being used or an optic fibre or landline. If there is a gap in time between a question being asked and the response by the reporter, then a satellite system is being used. The gap is the time taken for the signal to be beamed to the satellite and then beamed back to Earth.

In general, as you move down this list, the sophistication of each system results in greater capacity and speed of information transfer, but there are problems with any system and choice of system depends on individual requirements and the amount of investment from companies in the telecommunications business.

One additional advantage of digital transmission is security. Signals can be encrypted before transmission so that anyone not intended to receive the signal gets a meaningless mass of ones (1) and zeroes (0). The intended receiver will have a decoder that is able to change the coded message back into readable information.

This system is used by pay TV companies. Once a person has paid a subscription to the company their television will need a decoder in it that enables them to view the programmes they have paid for.

Attenuation

Before considering these systems in more detail it is necessary to understand the term **attenuation**. When a light ray passes along an optic fibre it is totally internally reflected thousands of times. During this time, it will pass through kilometres of glass and the power of the light beam decreases. The power falls off logarithmically so if P_{in} is the power at the start and P_{out} is the power at the end then the attenuation of the signal is $\log (P_{out}/P_{in})$.

In practice, just to make the numbers larger, a factor of 10 is included in this expression and the value is then said to be measured in decibels. This gives

$$\text{attenuation} = 10 \log \frac{P_{out}}{P_{in}}$$

Anything measured in decibels is a ratio, so it is not meaningful to talk about "a signal of strength 50 dB". A comment such as this will only be sensible provided a reference strength is being compared with it. One way of doing this is by referring to the power loss per unit distance. For example, a cable can be quoted as having an attenuation of 5.0 dB km^{-1}. This means that over a distance of 4 km the power loss will be 20 dB. The ratio of the power at the beginning of the 4 km will be 100 times the power at the end. [-20 dB = 10 log (ratio of powers). This gives a ratio of 10^2.]

(Attenuation is basically exactly the same problem as with the absorption of X-rays or ultrasound but for historical reasons it is considered somewhat differently in telecommunications.)

Example 2

A signal is sent into an optic fibre with a power of 800 mW. It suffers an attenuation of 25 decibels (-25 dB) in passing along the fibre. Calculate the power emerging from the fibre.

Answer Putting the figures into the equation gives

$$-25 = 10 \log \frac{P_{out}}{800 \text{ mW}}$$

$$\text{so} \quad -25 = \log \frac{P_{out}}{800 \text{ mW}}$$

Now take antilogs to get

$$0.003\,16 = 10 \log \frac{P_{out}}{800 \text{ mW}} \quad \text{and } P_{out} = 2.5 \text{ mW}$$

Be careful to get the signs correct when using this equation. When the signal's power is falling, its decibel level goes down. In this example the power, therefore, has a drop of 25 dB and this is reflected in the -25 term entered into the equation.

One other point is about the use of a calculator in these expressions.

Note that $1000 = 10^3$ and therefore $\log_{10} 1000 = 3$.

This is taking logs of the equation. If you start with the equation $\log_{10} 1000 = 3$ and want to get back to the first equation you have to reverse the process, i.e. take antilogs. On a calculator this means using the *shift* key before using the *log* key. It is usually marked 10^x on calculators.

Comparison of channels of communication

The telephone system in many countries uses almost exclusively copper wire pairs near domestic telephones. In most cases the wires have been installed for many years and the cost would be very large if all of them were to be replaced with optic fibres, but over the next few decades this will probably happen. The reason that copper wires still work well is that the signals are suitable for the transmission of speech. Many computer internet connections make use of the same wires. These connections are comparatively slow by internet standards due to the limitations of wire pairs, where the attenuation is large and there is crosstalk between one pair of wires and an adjacent pair. This comes about because the magnetic field around one pair of wires inevitably passes the adjacent wires and can set up a small e.m.f. in the adjacent wires. Not only does this increase the attenuation but it also means that the system is less secure. Phone tapping is a well-known method of getting information that ought to be secret.

Some of these drawbacks can be overcome by the use of co-axial (co-ax) cable, where the conductor is surrounded by a braiding of copper, as shown in Figure 22.8.

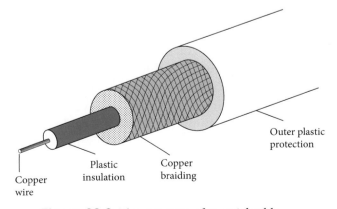

Figure 22.8 The structure of co-axial cable.

Crosstalk is avoided with co-ax and the attenuation is far less. With the higher frequencies used for television signals, co-ax is generally used for connection between the aerial and the television. Co-ax is also normally used between dish aerials receiving signals from satellites and televisions.

Once lots of telephone signals are collected together at an exchange, however there is now less likelihood of the signals being sent nationally or internationally using copper wires. The under sea cables laid across the oceans in the twentieth century are still used in some cases and while some international telecommunication is done by digitising phone calls and sending them by satellite, most are now sent using very thin, very pure under ocean optic fibres. Even the microwave system set up in the 1960s and 1970s is rather outdated compared with satellite and optic fibre communication systems.

If a signal is to be sent a large distance by cable or optic fibre it is necessary to ensure that the signal itself is considerably larger than any unwanted noise. The signal to noise ratio for digital signals needs to be kept above 30 dB and for analogue signals above 40 dB. The reason for the difference is that noise on a digital signal can be removed whereas noise on an analogue signal cannot, as explained earlier. Noise tends to be constant in an optic fibre but signal strength will gradually decrease. Eventually a point is reached where the signal strength is getting too low. There will then be a need to regenerate the signal and increase its power.

The glass from which optic fibres are manufactured is so pure that signals sent along optic fibres can travel up to 200 km without requiring regeneration but clearly, a cable crossing the Pacific Ocean will require regeneration and amplification of the signal several times. This does involve the cost of incorporating the equipment when the cable is laid and providing power for it. The equipment needs to be very reliable as lifting a cable from the bottom of the Pacific Ocean to make a repair would be a very expensive exercise.

Typical values of the distance between regeneration stations for different channels of communication are as follows.

telephone cables	5 km
co-axial cable	10 km
microwave links	40 km
optic fibres	80 km

Satellite communication

People are starting to get worried about the number of telecommunications satellites in orbit around the Earth and the danger that exists in any collision between them. The reason that there are so many satellites is, of course, because the demand for them has increased significantly during the last 30 years. Before satellites became available, global telecommunications depended either on telephone links or on the unreliable reflection of radio waves by the ionosphere, a charged layer in the high atmosphere. The reason for the rapid increase in demand for satellites becomes apparent when you walk along a street and see the number of satellite dishes on houses, together with the number of different television programmes available at any one time. Then, additionally, you have the large increase in internet use, with much of the information available on the internet being used in all countries of the world. Add to this the number of international emails being sent and telephone calls being made, the weather satellites, the financial information, the global positioning system and you may get some idea of the amount of international information being transmitted. We live in a global village, as far as communication is concerned.

Satellite orbits

A geostationary satellite rotates with the same angular velocity as the Earth. When such a satellite is placed directly over the Equator and is rotating with the Earth from west to east it appears to stay in the same position. A transmitting or receiving dish on the Earth, once set up correctly, will always be pointing at the satellite. For this orbit the satellite needs to be travelling in a circle at a distance of 42 200 km from the centre of the Earth. A telecommunications company using just a few geostationary satellites is able to receive and send signals from or to the entire surface of the Earth from this position.

Geostationary satellites are expensive to launch because of their distance from the Earth and their transmitting power needs to be higher for the same reason. For some purposes satellites are put into low polar orbits. These will move across the surface of the Earth so they need to be tracked but they get greater resolution, when they are used for taking photographs (for spying, for weather forecasting and for mapping.) A network of such satellites is used for global positioning systems, using which it is now possible to know your position on the Earth's surface to better than the nearest metre. In the past it was difficult to know whether sea levels were rising due to global warming. Now, satellite measurements on the surface of the sea, even with waves, can determine the height of the sea to the nearest centimetre.

For all communications satellites there must be an uplink from the ground as well as a downlink back from the satellite to the Earth. As shown in Figure 22.9 these signals may start and finish at different places, making global microwave linking possible. For television transmission the downlink will spread its power over a large area.

The satellite receives a weak signal from a dish transmitting aerial on the Earth, amplifies it and also changes its frequency. This is necessary because if the two frequencies were the same there would be a danger of the receiver picking up positive feedback from its own transmitted signal. Typical frequencies and bandwidths available to a satellite are

Uplink frequency	15 GHz
Downlink frequency	12 GHz
Bandwidth	0.5 GHz

A bandwidth of 0.5 GHz might look small, but it is 500 000 000 Hz and so if a TV station needs a bandwidth of 25 MHz it does mean that 20 stations can be accommodated.

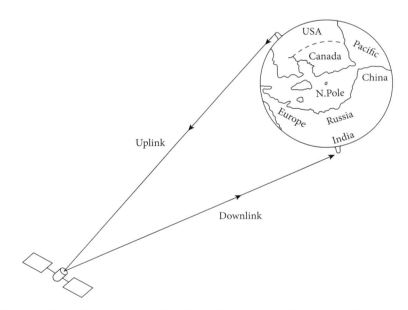

Figure 22.9 The coverage of the Earth from a geostationary satellite.

Chapter Summary

- ✓ Amplitude modulation (AM) and frequency modulation (FM) are the two forms of modulation, which uses high frequency signals.
- ✓ Transferring of speech or sound is done by converting an analogue signal into a digital signal by using an electronic circuit.
- ✓ International telecommunication falls into two main categories. Most international telephone and computer information is sent using optic fibres. Television reporting can also be done this way if the reporter is in an accessible place. Television signals to dish aerials on houses are first sent out to a satellite and then re-transmitted back to Earth.
- ✓ The satellite receives a weak signal from a dish transmitting aerial on the Earth, amplifies it and also changes its frequency.

Progress Check

22.1 Give the range of frequencies that needs to be transmitted for each of the following modulated waves.
   (a) A carrier wave of frequency 200 kHz modulated by an audio wave of frequency 8000 Hz.
   (b) A carrier wave of frequency 1.6 MHz modulated by audio waves of all frequencies up to 20 kHz.
   (c) A carrier wave of frequency 20 MHz frequency modulated and requiring a bandwidth of 40 kHz.

22.2 What is the ratio of power of signal to power of noise for a signal to noise ratio of 30 dB?

22.3 (a) An optic-fibre cable has an attenuation of 0.17 dB per kilometre. A signal of power of 54 mW is injected into the cable at the transmitting end and at the receiving end the power must be at least 30 μW. Calculate the maximum length of the cable.
   (b) For clarity the so-called signal to noise ratio must be at least 23 dB. What is the maximum acceptable noise power in the optic-fibre cable being considered?

22.4 A geostationary satellite transmits television signals with a power of 300 W to an area of the Earth of radius 1000 km.
   (a) Estimate the power received by a television dish aerial of area 0.10 m^2.
   (b) Calculate the ratio of the power received by a single dish to the total power transmitted in dB.

22.5 A signal has a power of 4.2 W when it is sent along a cable which has a length of 200 km and an attenuation of 5.0 dB km^{-1}. The cable has a constant noise power of 3.5 μW. The signal to noise ratio must not be allowed to fall below 30 dB. Deduce
   (a) the maximum distance between regenerator units and, hence
   (b) how many regeneration units will be necessary along the whole length of the cable?

Examination Questions XI

1. (a) State what is meant by *acoustic impedance*. [1]

(b) Explain why acoustic impedance is important when considering reflection of ultrasound at the boundary between two media. [2]

(c) Explain the principles behind the use of ultrasound to obtain diagnostic information about structures within the body. [5]

(Cambridge International AS and A Level Physics 9702 Paper 04 Question 9 October/November 2007)

2. (a) Optic fibre transmission has, in some instances, replaced transmission using co-axial cables and wire pairs. Optic fibres have negligible cross-talk and are less noisy than co-axial cables. Explain what is meant by

(i) cross-talk, [2]

(ii) noise. [2]

(b) An optic fibre has a signal attenuation of $0.20\,\text{dB km}^{-1}$.

The input signal to the optic fibre has a power of 26 mW. The receiver at the output of the fibre has a noise power of $6.5\,\mu\text{W}$.

Calculate the maximum uninterrupted length of optic fibre, in km, given that the signal-to-noise ratio at the receiver must not be less than 30 dB. [5]

(Cambridge International AS and A Level Physics 9702 Paper 04 Question 5 May/June 2008)

3. (a) Outline the principles of the use of a geostationary satellite for communication on Earth. [4]

(b) Polar-orbiting satellites are also used for communication on Earth.
State and explain one advantage and one disadvantage of polar-orbiting satellites as compared with geostationary satellites. [4]

(Cambridge International AS and A Level Physics 9702 Paper 04 Question 12 October/November 2010)

Electric Fields: Part B 23

Introduction

In Chapter 10, where electric fields were introduced, any quantitative work was done assuming that the electric field was uniform. This will not be the case for many important situations. The electric field around ions, for example, will be complex but will determine the shape and structure of molecules and crystals. On a large scale, the electric field of a charged sphere will not be uniform; it must have spherical symmetry. Although few people realise it, the Earth has an electric field and that too cannot possibly be uniform.

In order to analyse fields of different shapes, first it is necessary to examine the force acting between two point charges. For any point outside a conducting sphere, the charge on the sphere may be considered to act as a point charge at the centre of the sphere.

Coulomb (1736–1806) was the first person to carry out quantitative measurements of electrical repulsion. He performed many very accurate and sensitive experiments on an instrument called a **torsion balance** that he designed himself. Instead of a balance that usually measures vertical forces Coulomb's balance caused rotation when electric charges were brought close to one another. A diagram of Coulomb's balance is shown in Figure 23.1.

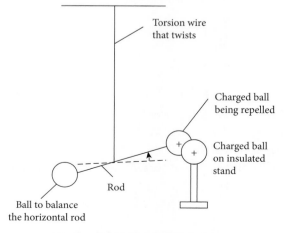

Figure 23.1 Coulomb's balance

Coulomb's law

When two point charges Q_1 and Q_2 are separated by a distance r in free space, the force F acting between them is

- proportional to Q_1 and Q_2 and
- inversely proportional to r^2.

Put into an equation this becomes

$$\text{Force} = k\frac{Q_1 Q_2}{r^2} \text{ where } k \text{ is a constant.}$$

In SI units, the numerical value of k is 8.988×10^9 $\text{N m}^2\text{C}^{-2}$. For largely historical reasons, the constant, when using SI units, is not normally written as k but as $1/4\pi\varepsilon_0$. It still has to have the same numerical value so this makes $1/4\pi\varepsilon_0 = 8.988 \times 10^9\,\text{N m}^2\text{C}^{-2}$ and therefore

$$\varepsilon_0 = \frac{1}{4\pi k} = \frac{1}{4\pi \times 8.988 \times 10^9\,\text{N m}^2\,\text{C}^{-2}}$$
$$= 8.854 \times 10^{-12}\,\text{C}^2\,\text{m}^{-2}\,\text{N}^{-1}.$$

This is all rather artificial but the equation you will need to be able to use is

$$\text{Force} = \frac{Q_1 Q_2}{4\pi\varepsilon_0 r^2} \text{ where } \varepsilon_0 = 8.854 \times 10^{-12}\,\text{F m}^{-1}$$

F m^{-1} is identical to $\text{C}^2\,\text{m}^{-2}\,\text{N}^{-1}$. F is the farad, a unit of capacitance. It is charge per unit potential difference, or C V^{-1}.

The electric field strength at a distance r from a point charge

Electric field strength E at a point is defined as the force per unit positive charge at the point. E will be a vector. This situation is shown in Figure 23.2 where a point charge $+q$ is shown with its electric field around it. The field will be three-dimensional.

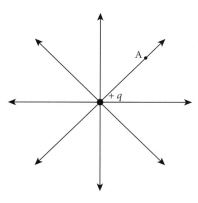

Figure 23.2

When the value of the field is required at A, a point at a distance r from the point charge, we imagine a positive charge of 1 coulomb to be placed at A and calculate the value of the force on it using Coulomb's law. This gives

$$F = \frac{Q_1 Q_2}{4\pi\varepsilon_0 r^2} = \frac{q \times 1}{4\pi\varepsilon_0 r^2} \text{ and hence}$$

$$E = \frac{q}{4\pi\varepsilon_0 r^2}$$

Example 1

Two singly charged ions, one positive and one negative are separated by a distance of 0.50 nm. Calculate the electric field at P a distance of 0.30 nm from one of the ions and 0.40 nm from the other, as shown in Figure 23.3(a).

Answer

$$\text{Field due to positive ion } = \frac{q}{4\pi\varepsilon_0 r^2}$$

$$= E_{\mathrm{p}} = \frac{1.6 \times 10^{-19}}{4\pi\varepsilon_0 (0.30 \times 10^{-9})^2}$$

$$= 1.6 \times 10^{10} \text{ V m}^{-1}$$

$$\text{Field due to negative ion } = \frac{q}{4\pi\varepsilon_0 r^2}$$

$$= E_{\mathrm{n}} = \frac{-1.6 \times 10^{-19}}{4\pi\varepsilon_0 (0.40 \times 10^{-9})^2}$$

$$= -0.90 \times 10^{10} \text{ V m}^{-1}$$

The signs here simply show that the field of the negative ion is directed to it whereas the field of the positive ion is directed away from it, as shown in Figure 23.3(b). Using Pythagoras' theorem for the total field gives $E_{\mathrm{t}} = 1.84 \times 10^{10}$ V m^{-1} in the direction shown.

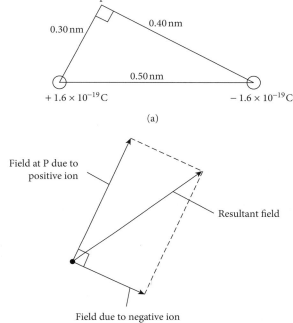

Figure 23.3

The analysis of the electric field in a three-dimensional crystal structure can be very complex but gives understanding about the structure of matter – and computers can be programmed to do the complex mathematics.

Electrical potential

Comparison between electric fields and gravitational fields

Just like it is useful to have quantities associated with force and with energy for gravitational fields, in the same way it is also useful to have these quantities for electrical fields.

In Chapter 6, gravitational field and potential energy were introduced. In Chapter 16, the relationship between gravitational field g and gravitational potential ϕ was established for fields around spherical objects. From Chapter 10, considering electric fields, the relationship between electrical potential V and electric field strength E was established for uniform fields. Table 23.1 shows the strong similarities between these terms as applied to uniform gravitational and electrical fields. For the electrical situation charge replaces mass but apart from this the only changes are the different symbols for fields, potentials and distances.

Table 23.1

	General – applied per unit	Specific – applied for an actual quantity
Gravitational	**Field** $= g$ force per unit mass	**Force** $= mg$ force on a mass m
	Potential $\phi = gh$ energy gain per unit mass	**Energy** $= mgh$ energy for moving mass m a distance h against the field
Electrical	**Field** $= E$ force per unit charge	**Force** $= EQ$ force on a charge Q
	Potential $V = Ex$ energy gain per unit charge	**Energy** $= EQx$ energy for moving charge Q a distance x against the field

The definition of electrical potential

With such a close relationship between electrical field theory and gravitational field theory, it should not come as a surprise to you that electrical potential at a distance r from a point charge Q is defined in a similar way as gravitational potential was defined in Chapter 16. This involves the zero of electrical potential being taken when r is infinity. In other words, the electrical potential is zero at a point which is at a great distance from the charge.

Electrical potential V at a point is the work done in bringing unit positive charge from infinity to the point.

One difference between the gravitational situation and the electrical situation is that, in the gravitational system the potential is always negative.

For the electrical situation, since charge may be positive or negative, the work done in bringing a unit positive charge towards Q will be positive, but negative in bringing a negative charge towards Q.

The equation for electrical potential is

$$V = \frac{Q}{4\pi\varepsilon_0 r}$$

If you want to know where this equation comes from and if you are studying calculus, it is found by integrating the force $\times$ the distance from infinity to r as follows.

$$V = -\int_{\infty}^{r} F \, dx = -\int_{\infty}^{r} \frac{Q}{4\pi\varepsilon_0 x^2} \, dx$$

In Chapter 10 it was shown that in a uniform electric field the potential gradient equalled the electrical field strength. The numerical values of the potential gradient and the electric field strength are indeed equal to one another, but the positive direction of the electric field strength will be in the direction of decreasing potential. It is therefore useful to remind yourself of this fact by using the equation for electric field strength in the form $E = \Delta V / \Delta d$.

Example 2

An electric field is used in the cathode ray tube of an oscilloscope to focus a beam of electrons on a spot on the screen. (This is also done in X-ray tubes, photomultiplier tubes and large oscilloscopes, but in these cases magnetic fields are used as well.) Two (or more) cylinders are used, through which the electrons pass. Figure 23.4 is a diagram of the arrangement in which the first cylinder is kept at 0 V and the second cylinder is at 1000 V. The purple lines on the diagram show the electric field inside the cylinders. The dotted lines are equipotential lines every 100 V from 100 V to 900 V. Note that equipotential lines always cut field lines at right angles.

(a) Calculate the increase in the kinetic energy of an electron in passing through the system.
(b) Explain why electrons travelling along the axis of the cylinders are not deflected.
(c) Explain how electrons travelling off the axis can be brought to a focus.

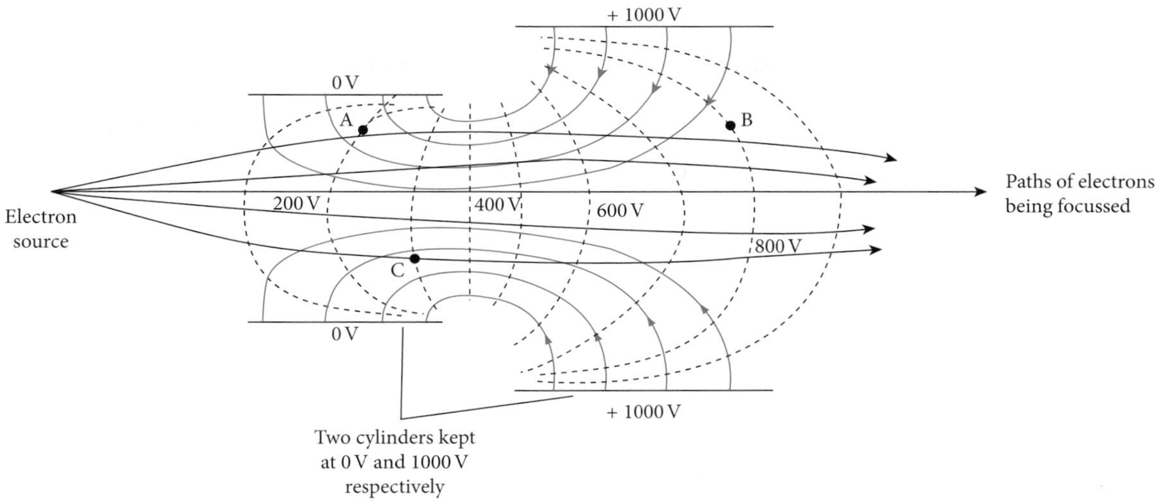

+ 1000 V

0 V

A

B

200 V   400 V   600 V

Electron
source

800 V

Paths of electrons
being focussed

C

0 V

+ 1000 V

Two cylinders kept
at 0 V and 1000 V
respectively

Figure 23.4

(d) Calculate how much work is done on an electron in moving it from point A to point B.

Answer (a) The gain in potential of an electron is 1000 V, that is 1000 joules per coulomb. The charge on an electron is 1.6×10^{-19} C so the gain in energy is 1.6×10^{-16} J.

(b) An electron moving along the axis of the cylinders always crosses lines of equipotential at right angles. This means that the force on the electron will be forward with no component up or down. It will accelerate in a horizontal direction. (It is negative so it will accelerate in a direction opposite to the field direction.)

(c) An electron travelling off axis and downward, at C for example, will have a resultant force in the opposite direction to the field. It has components in the direction of travel, which will speed it up, but also at right angles to this, upwards. This will give it acceleration upwards and adjustment of the field can control where it, and similar electrons, will be brought to a focus. Note that these electrons will all gain the same amount of kinetic energy as the ones that pass along the axis, because they all have a gain of 1000 V potential difference.

(d) The potential at A is 200 V and at B is 800 V. The work done W is, therefore, given by $W = QV = 1.6 \times 10^{-19}$ C $\times$ 600 V $= 9.6 \times 10^{-17}$ J.

Chapter Summary

✓ The force F between two charges Q_1 and Q_2 separated by a distance r is given by Coulomb's law.

$$F = \frac{Q_1 Q_2}{4\pi\varepsilon_0 r^2} \text{ where } \varepsilon_0 = 8.854 \times 10^{-12} \text{ F m}^{-1}$$

✓ The electric field strength at a distance r from a charge Q:

$$E = \frac{Q}{4\pi\varepsilon_0 r^2}$$

✓ The electric potential at a distance r from a charge Q:

$$V = \frac{Q}{4\pi\varepsilon_0 r}$$

Progress Check

23.1 Show that the unit $F\,m^{-1}$ is the same as $C^2\,m^{-2}\,N^{-1}$.

23.2 Two parallel plates are separated by a distance of 0.005 m. One of the plates has a potential of zero and the other a potential difference of +400 V.
(a) Calculate the value of the electric field between the plates, ignoring any edge effect.
(b) Draw a diagram, using a large scale, showing the field near the centre of the plates and on the diagram show, in a different colour, lines of equal potential. (Lines of equal potential are always at right angles to field. The same is true with contour lines on a map. Contour lines connect places of equal gravitational potential: gravitational field causes water to flow at right angles to contour lines.)

23.3 Draw electrical field diagrams for the following situations.
(a) A positively charged sphere placed near an uncharged metal plate.

(b) A large positively charged sphere near a small charged sphere carrying an equal charge.
(c) Three small spheres placed at the corners of an equilateral triangle. Two of the spheres have the same positive charge and the third sphere has a negative charge of equal magnitude to the other two spheres.

23.4 (a) An electron circulates around a proton in a hydrogen atom at a distance of 5.3×10^{-11} m from the proton. Calculate the electrical potential of the electron.
(b) Another electron rotates at a distance of 5.4×10^{-10} m from the proton. Calculate its electrical potential and hence the potential energy it loses when it moves in to the state of lower potential as calculated in (a). (Regard both the proton and the electron as being point charges.)

Capacitance 24

Introduction

There are many electrical circuits where it is essential to store electrical energy. Note that batteries do not store charge. They use chemical energy to push electrons around a circuit. A **capacitor** is a device that stores energy in an electric field.

A capacitor consists of a pair of parallel plates with an insulator, called a dielectric, between them. In use a capacitor might have a charge of + 2.7 millicoulombs (mC) on one plate and normally therefore a charge of −2.7 mC on the other plate. Under these circumstances the charge on the capacitor is said to be 2.7 mC. Note that the total charge is always zero but the use of the energy stored by this arrangement can provide a current as the capacitor discharges. Figure 24.1(a) shows a possible arrangement and (b) gives the circuit symbol for a capacitor.

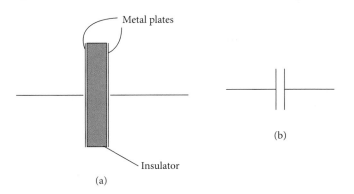

(a)

(b)

Figure 24.1

For a given potential difference between the plates, the closer they are together, the greater the charge on the capacitor. This is because the force between positive and negative charges increases as they are moved closer together. Some very good dielectrics can be manufactured with thickness of only 0.01 mm and these give capacitors with very high capacitance.

The definition of capacitance

As might be expected from the introduction, capacitance links charge with potential difference. It is found experimentally that the charge on a capacitor is proportional to the potential difference across it so the ratio of charge to potential difference is constant.

Capacitance C is defined as the charge Q per unit potential difference V.

$$C = \frac{Q}{V}$$

The SI unit of capacitance is the farad (F). One farad is one coulomb per volt.

Most capacitors have capacitance considerably less than a farad.

$$1\,\mu F = 10^{-6}\,F$$
$$1\,pF = 10^{-12}\,F$$

Example 1

A 22 μF capacitor is connected across a 12 V battery. Calculate the charge on the capacitor.

Answer

$$\text{Since } C = Q/V, \; Q = CV = 22 \times 10^{-6}\,F \times 12\,V$$
$$= 2.64 \times 10^{-4}\,C = 264\,\mu C$$

Capacitors in series and in parallel

Capacitors in parallel

The circuit shown in Figure 24.2 shows the 22 μF capacitor from the example in a circuit with two other capacitors connected in parallel with it. One of these is a 150 μF capacitor and the other a 10 μF capacitor. These two capacitors will also charge from

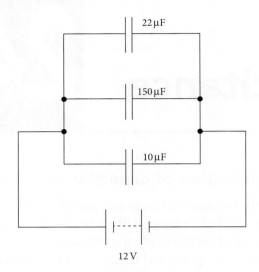

Figure 24.2

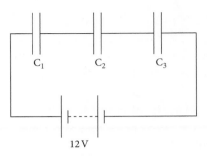

Figure 24.3

the battery. The charge on the 150 μF capacitor will be $150\,\mu\text{F} \times 12\text{ V} = 1800\,\mu\text{C}$ and the charge on the $10\,\mu\text{F}$ capacitor will be $10\,\mu\text{F} \times 12\text{ V} = 120\,\mu\text{C}$. The total charge supplied by the battery will be

$$264\,\mu\text{C} + 1800\,\mu\text{C} + 120\,\mu\text{C} = 2184\,\mu\text{C}.$$

The capacitance of the complete circuit is, therefore, $2184\,\mu\text{C}/12\text{ V} = 182\,\mu\text{F}$. This is the sum of $22\,\mu\text{F} + 150\,\mu\text{F} + 10\,\mu\text{F}$. In other words, for capacitors in *parallel* the total capacitance is the sum of the individual capacitances.

A formal proof of this would label the three capacitors with capacitances of C_1, C_2 and C_3.

The charge on each capacitor would be Q_1, Q_2, and Q_3 with

$$Q_1 = C_1V, Q_2 = C_2V \text{ and } Q_3 = C_3V.$$

This gives a total charge Q supplied as
$$Q = C_1V + C_2V + C_3V = (C_1 + C_2 + C_3)V.$$

So the total capacitance
$C = Q/C = (C_1 + C_2 + C_3)V/V = C_1 + C_2 + C_3.$
For capacitors in parallel $C = C_1 + C_2 + C_3 + \ldots\ldots$

Capacitors in series

Capacitors in series are harder to understand than capacitors in parallel. Look at the circuit in Figure 24.3.

Only the left-hand plate of C_1 and the right-hand plate of C_3 are connected to the battery. C_2 has no connections to the battery at all: it has insulators between it and the battery. The right-hand plate of C_1 and the left-hand plate of C_2 must have zero total charge on them. This can be achieved by one plate having positive charge and the other plate having an equal and opposite charge. This is what happens. As soon as the connection is made, some electrons move to the right-hand plate of C_3, making it negative. Immediately electrons in atoms on the left-hand plate of C_3 are repelled leaving it positively charged and the right-hand plate of C_2 becomes negatively charged. This continues through the three capacitors and electrons will leave the left-hand plate of C_1 to complete the circuit to the supply. The situation once charged is as shown in Figure 24.4.

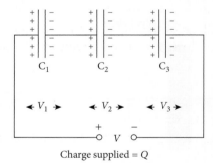

Charge supplied = Q

Figure 24.4

For any number of capacitors in series, therefore, we have the curious situation in which every capacitor has the same charge and that is equal to the charge the battery has supplied. This is a good example of conservation of charge in action. It must be that in a series string of eight capacitors, all eight capacitors, whatever their capacitance, will have the same charge.

Now we are in a position to calculate the total capacitance of a number of capacitors in series. The three capacitors of capacitance C_1, C_2 and C_3 are in series with a supply of potential difference V.

Assuming the charge from the supply is Q then the charge on each capacitor is also Q, as explained above. This gives the potential differences across each capacitor as

$$V_1 = \frac{Q}{C_1}; \quad V_2 = \frac{Q}{C_2}; \quad V_3 = \frac{Q}{C_3}$$

The total potential difference across all three capacitors

$$= V = V_1 + V_2 + V_3$$

So $\quad V = \dfrac{Q}{C_1} + \dfrac{Q}{C_2} + \dfrac{Q}{C_3} = Q\left(\dfrac{1}{C_1} + \dfrac{1}{C_2} + \dfrac{1}{C_3}\right)$

But $Q/V = C$, the total capacitance of the circuit, so $V/Q = 1/C$ giving

$$\frac{1}{C} = \frac{1}{C_1} + \frac{1}{C_2} + \frac{1}{C_3} \quad \text{for capacitors in series.}$$

Teacher's Tip

1. The pattern of these equations for capacitors is the opposite way round from those for resistors. For capacitors in parallel, the addition of the capacitor values is used; for capacitors in series the reciprocal equation is used.
2. Putting capacitors in parallel increases the total capacitance; putting them in series decreases the total capacitance.
3. When using the reciprocal equation, many mistakes are made through carelessness. Working that is done correctly until the final stage is spoilt if the final value is given as, say 0.01 μF when it should be given as 100 μF. The sum of the reciprocals gives $1/C$ and not C.
4. It is often useful with capacitor problems to work in volts, microcoulombs and microfarads. It avoids too many 10^x terms. These can be awkward if you have, for example, capacitors of 5×10^{-5} F, 1×10^{-4} F and 2×10^{-3} F. It is usually easier to write 50 μF, 100 μF and 2000 μF.

Example 2

Figure 24.5(a) shows a combination of capacitors of capacitances 2.0 μF, 5.0 μF and 3.0 μF connected to a 240 V supply. Calculate the charge and the p.d. for each capacitor.

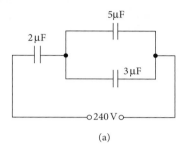

(a)

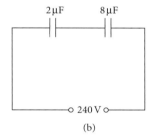

(b)

Figure 24.5

Answer

Start by drawing Figure 24.5(b). That is by recognising that two capacitors of capacitances 5.0 μF and 3.0 μF in parallel are equivalent to a single capacitor of capacitance 8.0 μF.

The reciprocal formula can now be used to find the total circuit capacitance.

$$\frac{1}{C} = \frac{1}{2} + \frac{1}{8} = \frac{4+1}{8} = \frac{5}{8} \quad \text{so} \quad C = \frac{8}{5} = 1.6 \text{ μF}$$

The supply, therefore, provides a charge given by $Q = CV = 1.6\,\text{μF} \times 240\,\text{V} = 384\,\text{μC}$ and this is the charge on both the 2 μF and the 8 μF capacitors. The p.d across the 2 μF capacitor is, therefore, given by $Q/C = 384\,\text{μC}/2\,\text{μF} = 192$ V. With this p.d. across the 2 μF capacitor there must be $(240 - 192)\text{V} = 48$ V across the 8 μF capacitor.

Going back to circuit in Figure 24.5(a) at this stage gives a charge
   on the 5 μF capacitor of 5 μF × 48 V = 240 μC and
   on the 3 μF capacitor of 3 μF × 48 V = 144 μC.

A check now is to see that 144 μC + 240 μC = 384 μC, which equals the charge on the 2 μF capacitor, as it must be. The final figures are summarised in Table 24.1. The whole problem could have been done within a table.

Table 24.1

Capacitance/ μF	Potential difference/V	Charge/ μC	Energy/ μJ
2.0	192	384	
5.0	48	240	
3.0	48	144	
whole circuit 1.6	240	384	

The last column is deliberately left blank so that after the next section of the chapter on energy stored in a capacitor, the column can be filled.

The energy stored in a charged capacitor

When a capacitor is charged by gradually increasing the potential difference across it, the charge is always proportional to the potential difference, as shown in Figure 24.6.

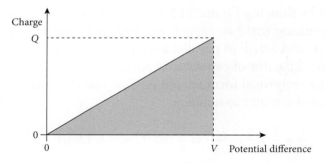

Figure 24.6

The energy stored by the capacitor will be the area under the graph, namely $\frac{1}{2}QV$. In terms of C and V this becomes $\frac{1}{2}CV^2$ and in terms of C and Q this becomes $\frac{1}{2}Q^2/C$. You might have expected the energy stored to have been simply QV, because Q is measured in coulombs and V in joules per coulomb. The $\frac{1}{2}$ appears in much the same way as with the stretching of a spring. The energy stored there is $\frac{1}{2}Fx$ because you can start stretching the spring with a much smaller force than F, the final force. With a capacitor the first charge put on the plates can be done with a small potential difference and as the charge increases so the potential difference needs to rise to its final value V. If a capacitor is charged by suddenly applying the full voltage, then a spark often occurs and this wastes energy in the form of heat (and sound).

The energies can now be put in the earlier table.

Capacitance/ μF	Potential difference/V	Charge/ μC	Energy/ μJ
2.0	192	384	36 900
5.0	48	240	5760
3.0	48	144	3460
whole circuit 1.6	240	384	46 100

Chapter Summary

✓ Capacitance C is defined as the charge Q per unit potential difference V.
$$C = Q/V$$

✓ Capacitors in parallel: $C_{total} = C_1 + C_2 + C_3 + ...$
It is not like resistors in parallel.

✓ Capacitors in series are added in the way resistors in parallel are added:
$$\frac{1}{C} = \frac{1}{C_1} + \frac{1}{C_2} + \frac{1}{C_2} + ...$$

✓ The energy stored in a capacitor
$$= \frac{1}{2}QV = \frac{1}{2}CV^2 = \frac{1}{2}Q^2/C$$

Progress Check

24.1 Calculate the resultant capacity of
  (a) two $10\,\mu F$ capacitors in series,
  (b) two $10\,\mu F$ capacitors in parallel,
  (c) a $10\,\mu F$, $20\,\mu F$ and $50\,\mu F$ capacitor all in series,
  (d) a $20\,\mu F$ capacitor in series with a $30\,\mu F$ capacitor and these two capacitors having a $40\,\mu F$ capacitor in parallel with them.

24.2 Complete the following statement with the words *parallel* and *series*.
  (i) To increase the total capacitance, capacitors must be placed in _____
  (ii) To decrease the total capacitance, capacitors must be placed in _____

24.3 Calculate the charge on a $5000\,\mu F$ capacitor when there is a p.d. of 200 V across it.

24.4 Having as many $1000\,pF$ capacitors as you need, explain how to make a capacitor of capacitance $0.0062\,\mu F$.

24.5 A $1000\,\mu F$ capacitor is to be used to store 3.0 J of energy. Calculate the potential difference required across it and the charge on it.

24.6 A capacitor used in a smoothing circuit has a potential difference across it that falls from 20.50 V to 20.10 V in 0.020 s. Assuming that the current from the capacitor during this time has a constant value of 0.56 mA, deduce the value of the capacitor.

Sensing Devices 25

Sensing devices

Any sensing device is a piece of equipment that enables some physical phenomena to be monitored. Long ago before the computer was invented, there were devices such as rain gauges to measure rainfall, thermometers to measure temperature, seismometers to measure earthquake activity, anemometers to measure wind speed, altimeters to measure altitude and hundreds of other instruments. All of these physical phenomena still need to be monitored today, but the output from the sensor now needs to be suitable to provide a computer input. The output, therefore, needs to be an electrical potential difference, a voltage. In this chapter, a sensing device will be considered as something that, with a suitable electronic circuit, can provide a voltage output for connection to the input of a computer.

The light-dependent resistor

A light-dependent resistor, an LDR, is basically a piece of semiconductor material, such as silicon. When light falls on the silicon, electrons within it are able to flow and hence its resistance decreases. The graph, Figure 25.1 shows this effect.

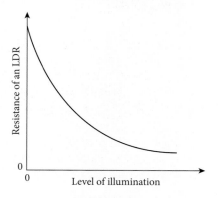

Figure 25.1

The resistance might fall from hundreds of kilo ohms in the dark to a hundred ohms in a strong light.

In order to obtain an electrical output for a computer input, a potential divider circuit such as the one shown in Figure 25.2 is used. Using this circuit, the output will be high when the LDR is illuminated and low when it is in the dark.

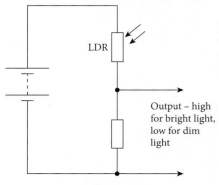

Figure 25.2

Example 1

An LDR has a resistance of $100\,k\Omega$ in the dark and $200\,\Omega$ in the light. It is connected as shown in Figure 25.3 in series with a resistor of resistance $7800\,\Omega$.

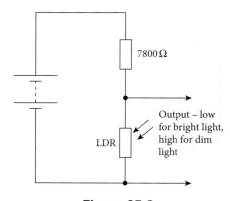

Figure 25.3

What will be the output in the light and in the dark?

Answer

In the light, the total resistance is $8000\,\Omega$ so the current is $\dfrac{12}{8000} = 0.0015$ A.

This gives a low output of $200 \times 0.0015 = 0.30$ V. In the dark the total resistance is $107\,800\,\Omega$, the current is 1.11×10^{-4} A and the output is 11.1 V. This example shows that reversing the positions of the resistor and the LDR reverses the behaviour of the LDR, to give a high output when in the dark.

The negative temperature coefficient thermistor

A negative temperature coefficient (NTC) thermistor, is a thermistor that has a high resistance when cold and a low resistance when hot. The graph, Figure 25.4 shows this effect.

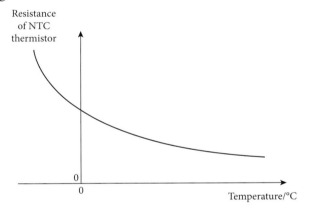

Figure 25.4

The resistance might fall from hundreds of kilo ohms when cold to a hundred ohms when hot. In order to obtain an electrical output for a computer input, a potential divider circuit, similar to the one for an LDR, is used. It is shown in Figure 25.5. Using this circuit, the output will be high when the NTC is cold and low when it is hot.

It is possible to buy positive temperature coefficient thermistors, but they are less commonly used. What might the graph of resistance against temperature look like for such a thermistor?

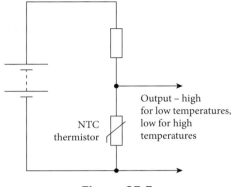

Figure 25.5

The piezo-electric transducer

The piezo-electric transducer is a device that can be used to measure pressure. Details of its use were given in Chapter 21 on ultrasound, where it is pointed out that crystals of lead zirconate titanate can be used in microphones. The passage of a sound wave past the crystal causes rapid variation in the forces applied to the crystal, and the consequent variation in voltage can be amplified and used to provide an electrical input to an amplifier.

Strain gauges

A strain gauge is basically a metal wire. When a force is applied to it its length increases by a small amount. Apart from simply measuring forces it is a useful device for monitoring small movements. When a prototype aircraft is undergoing initial tests, its wings and fuselage can be almost covered in strain gauges.

Figure 25.6 A worker is installing a strain gauge on a bridge to measure how much a part of the bridge is distorted when a load is put on it.

The strain gauges will be firmly attached to the aircraft and when, under stress, a part of the aircraft stretches, the strain gauge is stretched with it. All the strain gauges will be connected to many circuits that will measure the resistance of every strain gauge.

The principle of the strain gauge is easy to understand. A small length of wire has a particular resistance. When it is stretched, its length increases and its area of cross-section decreases. Both of these effects cause an increase in the wire's resistance. Provided the wire does not go past its elastic limit, the stretching can be repeated many times. The structural metals used in aircraft in the past have been known to suffer fatigue after many journeys. This results in fracture of some metals at below normal stresses. Fatigue has caused aircraft to crash. Now, all aircraft are tested to determine how many take-offs and landings they are allowed before fatigue becomes a hazard.

Example 3

A piece of nichrome wire of length 60 mm and radius 0.076 mm has a resistance of $3.6\,\Omega$. What will be its resistance when it is stretched by a distance of 2 mm?

Answer The mass, density and the resistivity of the wire do not change when it is stretched so its volume is unchanged. This gives

volume $= l \times \pi r^2 = 60 \times \pi \times (0.076)^2 = 62 \times \pi \times r_n^{\,2}$
where r_n is the new radius.

This gives $r_n = 0.07476$ mm so

$$\text{resistivity} = \frac{RA}{l} = \frac{3.6 \times \pi \times 0.076^2}{60}$$

$$= \frac{R \times \pi \times 0.07476^2}{62}$$

giving $R = 3.84\,\Omega$.

A change in resistance from $3.6(0)\,\Omega$ to $3.8(4)\,\Omega$ is easily detected by an electrical measurement. This example illustrates several important points.

- With any problem it is vital to think about the units being used in the calculation, yet here millimetres have been used as the unit of length rather than metres, that would be the SI unit normally used for a resistivity problem.
- This is a comparison problem. We are comparing a new resistance with an original resistance. In this type of problem it is not necessary to use the basic unit because essentially we simply want to know how many times larger one resistance is compared with the other. 6 metres is three times larger than 2 metres, as 6000 mm is three times larger than 2000 mm.
- It is possible to take an even more radical approach to this problem. It needs care but can be very helpful and quick if you know what you are doing. It is as follows.

A 3.3% (2 mm in 60 mm) increase in the length implies a 3.3% decrease in the area of cross section.

Since $R = \rho l/A$ this means a 6.6% increase in resistance from $3.6(0)\,\Omega$ to $3.8(4)\,\Omega$. Note that a 3.3% decrease in A, on the bottom of the expression, results in a 3.3% increase in R.

Chapter Summary

- ✓ A light-dependent resistor (LDR) has high resistance in the dark and low resistance in the light.
- ✓ A negative temperature coefficient (NTC) thermistor has high resistance when cold and low resistance when hot.

- ✓ A piezo-electric transducer produces a potential difference across opposite faces when squeezed.
- ✓ A strain gauge has increased resistance when stretched.

Progress Check

25.1 A piece of copper wire of diameter 0.315 mm and length 250 mm has resistance 0.0553 Ω. It is then subjected to a stretching force that increases its length by 2.0 mm. Assuming that the volume of the wire is unchanged, calculate the new resistance of the wire.

25.2 A wire in a strain gauge has its length increased by 0.80%.
  (a) Show that this means that the area of cross section of the wire decreases by 0.80%, assuming that the density of the metal of the wire remains unaltered.
  (b) Deduce the percentage increase in the resistance of the strain gauge wire.
  (Did you notice the connection between questions 1 and 2?)

25.3 A light-dependent resistor has a resistance of 220 kΩ when it is in the dark and 2400 Ω when illuminated strongly. Draw a circuit diagram to show it correctly connected to a 12.0 V battery of internal resistance of 16 Ω, and an output connected across a resistor of resistance 10 kΩ.
  Calculate the output voltage when the LDR is
  (a) in the dark,
  (b) illuminated strongly.

25.4 A positive temperature coefficient thermistor has a resistance of 4.0 kΩ at 300 K and a resistance of 25 kΩ at 600 K. It is connected in a circuit like the one shown in Figure 25.5 in which the supply e.m.f. is 12.0 V and the resistor has a value of 10 kΩ.
  What will be the output when the PTC thermistor is at a temperature of
  (a) 300 K and
  (b) 600 K?

Electronics 26

The operational amplifier (op-amp)

The op-amp is the basic building block of many control systems. The voltage output of circuits such as those shown in Figures 25.2 and 25.5 are frequently connected to, or incorporated into, the input of an op-amp: the output from the op-amp controls the switches required. In many control systems multiple op-amps and switches are required. For example, a set of traffic lights at a crossroads might have 40 lights to be controlled from timers, vehicle sensors, pedestrian switches and sequence patterns.

The op-amp is an amplifier with two inputs, an inverting input and a non-inverting input. The circuit symbol for an op-amp is shown in Figure 26.1 together with the function of the five connections to it.

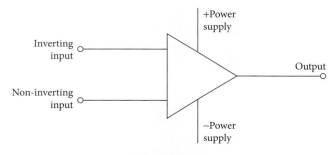

Figure 26.1

The two power supplies to an op-amp are usually balanced + and −, e.g. + 15 V and − 15 V. On circuit diagrams the power supplies are often omitted.

The properties of an op-amp

An *ideal* op-amp has the following properties.

- **An infinite input resistance**. This means that when it is connected to any circuit, no current will be drawn from the circuit.
- **A zero output resistance**. This means that the current it supplies will be determined

by the resistance of the device to which its output terminal is connected and the supply voltage of the circuit.

- **An infinite gain**. The gain is the ratio of the output voltage to the difference between the two input voltages.

A real op-amp comes very close to an ideal op-amp. While its input resistance is not infinite, it does have a resistance of the order of megaohms so currents to the input are very small. The gain is not infinite in a real op-amp but can be as high as 200 000. In practical circuits, this is usually far too high and steps have to be taken to reduce its value, as the following circuits illustrate.

The op-amp as a comparator

When an op-amp is used as a comparator it is said to be in open-loop mode and the gain provided does have the high value referred to above. This is called the open-loop gain A_{ol}. A comparator compares the voltage on its two inputs. If the voltage is V_1 on the inverting input and the voltage is V_2 on the non-inverting input then the output V_{out} is given by

$$V_{out} = A_{ol}(V_2 - V_1).$$

This means that if the voltage V_1 on the inverting input is greater than the voltage V_2 on the non-inverting input, then the output is negative and nearly equal to the −15 V of the supply. If V_2 is greater than V_1, then the output is positive and nearly equal to the +15 V of the supply.

As a comparator, in this mode the gain is so large that it is almost impossible to obtain any voltage in between +15 V and −15 V.

A comparator circuit is shown in Figure 26.2.

This circuit will switch off a light-emitting diode (LED) when the temperature of a thermistor gets high enough. Consider V_2, the non-inverting input, to have a fixed value. At low temperatures the resistance of the thermistor is high, and therefore V_1, the inverting input, is low and lower than V_2. Under these circumstances the output is high, there will be a current in the light-emitting diode (LED) and it will light up. When the temperature of the thermistor rises so that V_1 is higher than V_2, there is no current in the LED and it will go off. The value of V_2 can be adjusted so that the temperature at which the LED goes off can be changed.

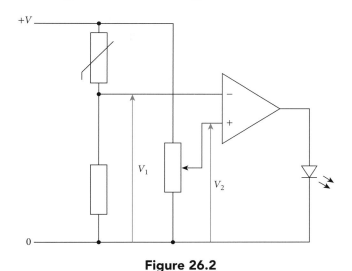

Figure 26.2

Adjusting the gain of an op-amp

Using an op-amp in a comparator circuit effectively means that the output will either be approaching +15 V or −15 V. In order to get a gradual change between these two values instead of a sudden jump it is necessary to use feedback. This can be done by making use of the circuit shown in Figure 26.3, in which a feedback resistor R_f is connected from the output to the inverting input.

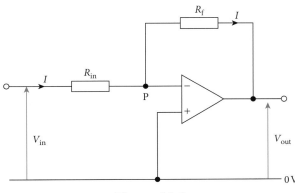

Figure 26.3

Since in this circuit the non-inverting input is 0 V, it follows that the inverting input must also be very close to zero. This is because, from the basic equation at the top of the previous column $(V_2 - V_1) = V_{out} / $ (a very large number) ≈ 0. For this reason point P on Figure 26.3 is said to be a **virtual earth**. Not only is this point at zero potential but virtually no current enters the op-amp past P because one of the properties of an ideal op-amp is that it has infinite input resistance and real op-amps get very near to this ideal. So, any current from the input must go from P and through the feedback resistor to the output.

$$I = \frac{V_{in}}{R_{in}} = \frac{-V_{out}}{R_f}$$

giving the gain on this closed loop, $A_{cl} = \dfrac{-V_{out}}{V_{in}} = \dfrac{-R_f}{R_{in}}$

This enables the gain in an inverting amplifier to be calculated.

The minus sign here reminds you that the input is to the inverting input, so the output will always have the opposite sign to the input.

The non-inverting amplifier

The same principles are used with this amplifier circuit, shown in Figure 26.4.

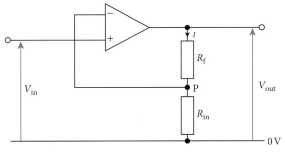

Figure 26.4

Since the inverting input has an almost infinite resistance, no current is in the wire to this input from point P. Therefore the current I is the same through R_f and R_{in}. As before $V_2 - V_1 \approx 0$ so the voltage at the inverting input $= V_{in}$, and this is the same as the voltage at P. The gain, therefore, can be found as before.

$$I = \frac{V_{in}}{R_{in}} = \frac{V_{out}}{R_f + R_{in}}$$

giving the gain on this closed loop,

$$A_{c1} = \frac{V_{out}}{V_{in}} = \frac{R_f + R_{in}}{R_{in}} = 1 + \frac{R_f}{R_{in}}$$

A slightly different equation and no minus sign this time because the input is to the non-inverting input.

Output devices

The output from an op-amp circuit can simply be monitored by a calibrated digital or analogue voltmeter or milliammeter, but often a simple switch will be used. Controls on such systems as a washing machine monitor the time for the different stages of the wash, the temperature and the speed control on the drum. This will be done using a series of relays. In Chapter 27, a relay is described as a device that acts as an electromagnetic switch (see Figure 27.5).

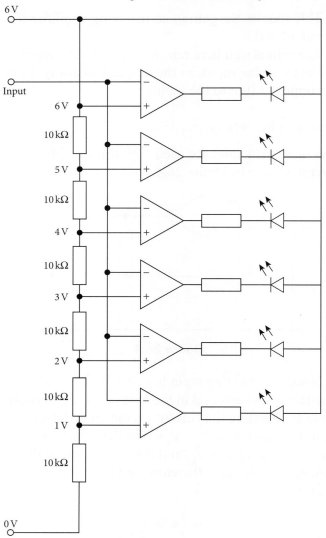

Figure 26.5

It enables a small current to switch a large current off or on. Such a device is often used on the output of an op-amp circuit. Relays can be purchased with multiple contacts. The lever that moves in the relay could, for example, turn three circuits on and two circuits off when actuated by a current of just a few milliamps passing through its coil.

Another way the output from an op-amp can be used is to operate a sequence of lights. One practical use of this is familiar on many audio systems to give an indication of volume. Figure 26.5 shows a circuit for such a system, using six op-amp circuits as comparators.

The same audio signal is applied to all six inverting inputs of the op-amps. The non-inverting inputs to the op-amps gradually increase from 1 V to 6 V using a chain of six 10 kΩ resistors. When the signal input reaches just over 1 volt the output from the bottom op-amp switches its output from positive to negative. A current is set up in the bottom LED which therefore lights up. The other op-amps remain with positive outputs and so will not be illuminated. Only when the input reaches just over 6 V will all LEDs light up.

Calibration of an op-amp

Often when an output from an op-amp is provided it is necessary to have some way of knowing how the potential difference (voltage) across the output is related to the input potential difference.

The output from an op-amp will always be a voltage. That voltage may be representative of many different physical quantities. Op-amp circuits may be using a variety of information from digital or analogue sources. For example, if the sensor being used is a thermistor, then the electric output voltage will depend on the resistance of the thermistor. It will though, also depend on the values of the input resistor and the feedback resistor. Knowing the output voltage will be insufficient to determine the temperature of the thermistor. At some stage a calibration exercise needs to be carried out to relate output with temperature. This can be done using the circuit drawn in Figure 26.6 in which the thermistor is connected in a series circuit with a standard resistor and the 6V supply. The junction between these components is connected to the inverting input of the op-amp.

The non-inverting input is earthed. An accurate voltmeter is connected on the output. When the thermistor is placed in a beaker of water together with an accurate thermometer, the water can be stirred to ensure it is all at the same temperature and a series of

readings can be taken of the thermistor temperature and corresponding voltmeter readings, enabling a calibration curve to be drawn, such as the one shown in Figure 26.7.

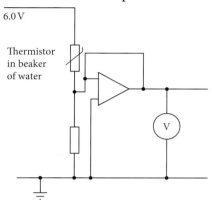

Figure 26.6

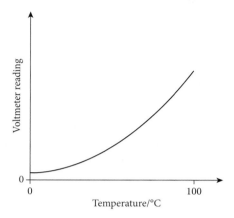

Figure 26.7

Chapter Summary

✓ The op-amp is an amplifier with two inputs and, therefore, serves as building block of many control systems. An op-amp used as a comparator is said to be in open-loop mode and the open-loop gain A_{ol}.

✓ A relay is a device which acts as an electromagnetic switch and enables a small current to switch a large current off or on.

✓ Gain provided by inverting amplifier =

$$\frac{-V_{out}}{V_{in}} = \frac{-R_f}{R_{in}}$$

✓ Gain provided by non-inverting amplifier =

$$\frac{V_{out}}{V_{in}} = 1 + \frac{R_f}{R_{in}}$$

Progress Check

26.1 A comparator circuit, as shown in Figure 26.2, uses a value of $V = 12\,V$ with the op-amp having a gain of 10 000. Show that with $V_2 = 8.0\,V$ the output will switch from positive to negative between 7.999 V and 8.001 V.

26.2 Draw a circuit diagram to show an op-amp comparator circuit acting as a sensor to control a relay that can switch on the heating in a greenhouse when the temperature falls to a predetermined value.

26.3 Deduce the output voltage of the circuits shown in Figures 26.8 and 26.9.

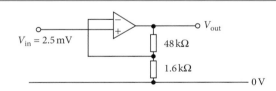

Figure 26.9

26.4 Sketch a drawing of a relay where the contacts switch two separate circuits on and one circuit off when sufficient current passes through the coil of the relay to move a lever.

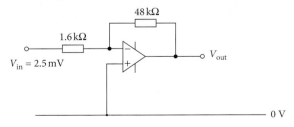

Figure 26.8

Magnetic Fields 27

Introduction

You have been aware of magnets and magnetism from a very early age. Magnets are used in lots of toys and the fun of playing with them stems from the fact that they can both attract and repel one another. You might have noted that certain metals are attracted to magnets and that most other materials are non-magnetic, i.e. magnets do not attract them. In fact, all materials are magnetic but most materials are so weakly attracted that the force of attraction is not noticed. Iron is very strongly magnetic, whereas stainless steel is usually non-magnetic. Cobalt and nickel are two other elements that are strongly magnetic. Ceramic magnets are now used in many devices as are magnetic sheets of a rubber like material that can be cut with scissors.

Concept of a magnetic field

You have probably spread iron filings on a piece of paper on top of a magnet and seen a pattern like the one shown in Figure 27.1.

The pattern shows a region of influence of the magnet that gets weaker as the distance from the magnet increases. This region of influence is called **magnetic field**. You will be aware that the Earth too has a magnetic field and that the field can be used for navigation. A suspended magnet will align itself with the Earth's magnetic field. The end pointing approximately north is called the north pole. The angle between true north and magnetic north varies from place to place on the Earth's surface and ships have charts that give this information. Global Positioning Satellites, GPS, give a ship's position more accurately than a compass, but most ships still have a compass on the bridge in case of breakdown of GPS. A ship's compass is shown in Figure 27.2.

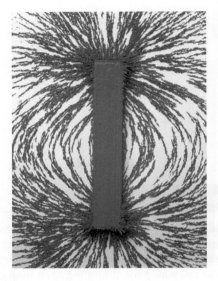

Figure 27.1 Photograph of iron filings on top of a magnet

Figure 27.2 Photograph of a ship's compass

It is clear from Figure 27.1 that the magnetic field is strongest near the ends of the magnet. The direction of the field is arbitrarily taken to be from north to south. Figures 27.3(a) and (b) show the

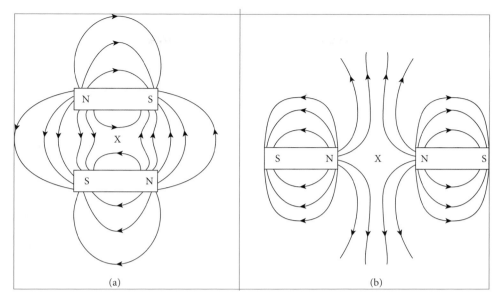

(a)   (b)

Figure 27.3

shape of the magnetic field around combinations of magnets. Where the field is strongest, the lines are closer together. The fact that the field has strength and a direction tells you that magnetic field is a vector. To obtain magnetic field diagrams such as those in Figures 27.3(a) and (b), it is necessary at each point to add the field from each magnet vectorially.

Making magnets

Many of the magnets discussed so far in this chapter are permanent magnets. That means they always have a magnetic field around them, and if they are not abused by knocking them, they will retain their magnetism for many years. To make a permanent magnet, it is necessary to use a coil of wire wrapped around a metallic core and then pass a large electric current through the coil. This is shown in Figure 27.4.

Provided there are enough turns of wire in the coil and the current is large enough, the metal inside

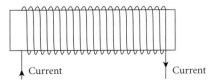

Current   Current

Figure 27.4 Making a permanent magnet

the coil will be magnetised. Certain cobalt steel materials will retain their magnetism even when the current is switched off.

If the material in the core is just iron then the magnetism will not be retained and the magnet is then called an **electromagnet**. Electromagnets are very useful, and not just for lifting scrap iron in a scrapyard. Many pieces of electronic equipment such as thermostats, televisions, CD and DVD players and computers contain relays. These are small electromagnetic switching devices that were mentioned in the previous chapter. Figure 27.5 shows the structure of a relay.

The relay consists of an iron core on which is wound sometimes thousands of turns of very fine insulated wire connected to terminals A and B. A current, that can be as small as a few milliamps, when passed through the coil will magnetise the core and the core attracts a small piece of iron mounted on a springy piece of steel. In doing this contact is made between terminals C and D and this acts as a switch to turn on a current that may be many amperes. For example, in a thermostat circuit, a fall in temperature may generate an output of 3 mA to the relay. The relay may switch on a heater connected to the mains and the current through the heater may be 10 A. When the current through the coil is switched off, the current between C and D will be switched off.

The click you often hear when you switch on electronic equipment is often the control relays operating. These will control items such as the disc eject motor on a DVD player or computer.

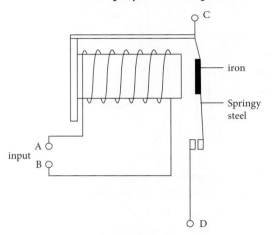

Figure 27.5

Magnetic flux density

Experimentally it is found that when a wire carrying an electric current is placed in a magnetic field, a force is exerted on the wire. It is this force that is used to drive all electric motors. The magnitude of the force increases as the current increases and is also proportional to the length of the wire. It varies with the angle between the direction of the current and the direction of the field. The force has its maximum value when the field is at right angles to the current and falls to zero when the field and the current are in the same direction. Putting all of this information into mathematical terms gives

force $F \propto$ length of wire l

$\propto$ current I

$\propto$ sine of angle between current and field θ

$\propto$ strength of field B

and hence $F = BIl \sin \theta$.

Notice that the proportional sign has suddenly changed to an equals sign. This is because an experiment is not possible to show proportion between F and B until we know how to define B. The strength of the magnetic field is given the name **magnetic flux density** and the above equation is used in the definition. By definition, the force is proportional to the magnetic flux density.

The formal definition of magnetic flux density is: **magnetic flux is the force acting per unit current in a wire of unit length which is at right angles to the field.**

$$B = \frac{F}{Il \sin 90°} = \frac{F}{Il}$$

The unit of magnetic flux density is, therefore, $N\,A^{-1}\,m^{-1}$ and this unit is called the tesla (T). One tesla is the magnetic flux density in a region when a wire of 1 metre length, carrying a current of 1 ampere experiences a force of 1 newton when placed at right angles to the field.

There is a further consideration about magnetic flux density and the force on a current carrying wire when placed in the field. This concerns the direction of the force. Figure 27.6 shows the direction in which a force acts on a wire placed between the poles of a magnet.

The field, the current and the direction of the force are all at right angles to one another. If you hold your left hand so that the seCond finger points in the direction of the **C**urrent and the **F**irst finger in the direction of the **F**ield, then the thu**M**b will be pointing in the direction of the force, the direction of **M**otion. This is known as **Fleming's left-hand motor rule**.

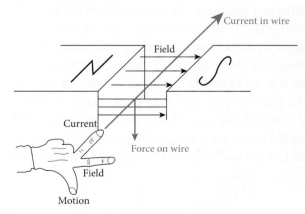

Figure 27.6

The current balance

A current balance is an accurate scientific instrument for measuring magnetic flux density. It depends directly on the use of the defining equation for magnetic flux density, namely $B = F/Il$. A diagram of a simple current balance is shown in Figure 27.7 with (a) a view from the top and (b) a view from the side.

The theory for calculating the magnetic flux density starts by using the principle of moments, $Wx = Fy$.

$$\text{Then since } B = \frac{F}{Il}, \text{ we get } B = \frac{Wx}{yIl}$$

All these quantities are measurable and so B can be found.

The instrument consists of a U-shaped piece of wire balanced on two knife-edges P and Q. A measured current I passes into the U-shaped wire at Q, moves around to P where it leaves the balance. The only place where this current is in a direction at right-angles to the magnetic field is over the RS part of the wire of length l. The U-shaped wire is carefully balanced before the current passes through RS and is re-balanced by a weight W after switching on the current I.

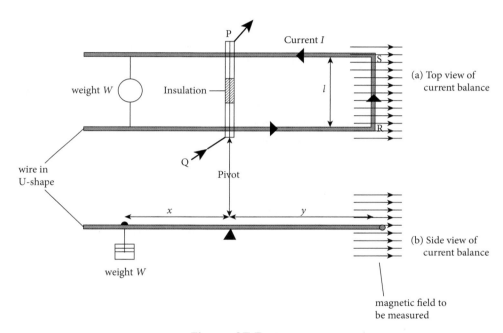

Figure 27.7

The force on a charge q moving with velocity v in a magnetic field

Since current is the rate of flow of charge, the equation $F = BIl$ can be rewritten as

$$F = \frac{Bql}{t}$$

where q is the charge flowing for a time t. However l/t is the speed v of the charge and so $F = Bqv$. If the movement is not at right angles to the field, then a $\sin\theta$ term is required giving the force on a charge moving in a magnetic field to be

$$F = Bqv\sin\theta.$$

The direction of the force is given in the same way as for a current, by Fleming's left-hand rule, but be careful, if the particle is an electron, it has a negative charge and so the direction of the current is in the opposite direction to the direction of the electron's velocity.

Example 1

A beam of electrons generated with speed $1.44 \times 10^8\,\text{m s}^{-1}$ in a magnetic field of flux density $0.0087\,\text{T}$ is travelling at right angles to the field, as shown in Figure 27.8.

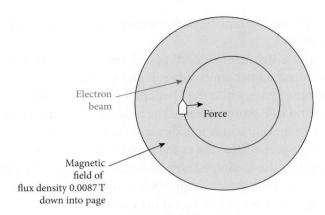

Figure 27.8

(a) Deduce the radius of the path that the beam will follow.
(b) Describe qualitatively the alteration to the path if the angle of emission of the electrons is tilted slightly downwards, that is into the paper a little in the figure.

[Given: Charge on electron = 1.60×10^{-19} C; mass of electron = 9.11×10^{-31} kg]

Answer (a) The force on an individual electron will be given by

force = $Bqv \sin \theta$
  = $0.0087 \times 1.6 \times 10^{-19} \times 1.44 \times 10^{8} \times \sin 90°$
  = 2.00×10^{-13} N to the right and at right angles to the electron velocity

[Fleming's left-hand rule has your first finger pointing into the page, your second finger pointing towards you (current is towards the bottom of the page as the negative electrons are travelling towards the top of the page) and your thumb pointing to the right.]

This is the situation for circular motion as, when the direction of the electron changes, the direction of the force will change so that it is still at right angles to the motion.

The radius of the motion is given by using

$$F = m \frac{v^2}{r}$$

so $$r = \frac{mv^2}{F} = \frac{9.11 \times 10^{-31} \times \left(1.44 \times 10^{8}\right)^2}{2.00 \times 10^{-13}}$$

$$= 0.094 \, \text{m}$$

(b) When the initial velocity has a component down into the page the magnetic field will not cause any force in the downward direction. So while the path of the electrons will continue to be circular they will all have a downward velocity into the page. This will result in the electrons following a helical path, as shown in Figure 27.9.

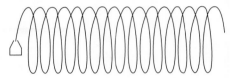

Figure 27.9 View of path of electrons from the side

As a footnote to this example, notice that the force is never in the direction of travel and so the speed of electrons remains constant as they go round in the circle or the helix. This property of charges keeping a constant speed when deflected in a magnetic field is made use of in cyclotrons where charged particles can be accelerated across a gap between two semicircular enclosures but within the enclosures they travel at constant speed. This is shown in Figure 27.10.

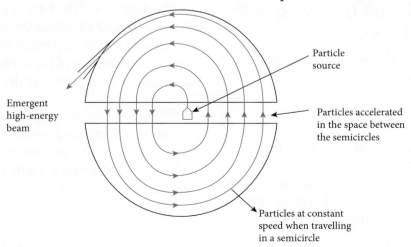

Figure 27.10

Particles coming into the Earth's high atmosphere near the Earth's magnetic poles also follow a helical or spiral path and lose energy in the process of colliding with gas atoms. This results in the Aurora Borealis or Northern Lights in the northern hemisphere.

Magnetic field patterns of electric currents in wires and forces on the wires

Figure 27.11 shows the pattern of the magnetic field around a wire carrying a current upwards out of the page. In Figure 27.11 the current is represented by a dot within the wire. A current downwards into the page is represented by a cross within the wire.

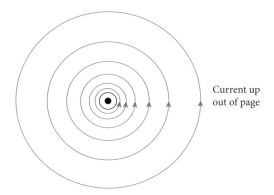

Current up
out of page

Figure 27.11

The field is strongest near the wire, shown by field lines close together, and getting weaker further from the wire. If this wire is placed into the uniform field between the poles of a permanent magnet, then Figure 27.12(a) shows the two fields superimposed and you will notice that the north pole of the magnet is being pushed downwards by the field of the wire as the direction of all the arrows is the direction in which a north pole will move. The south pole, therefore, is also being pushed downwards. If the wire is pushing the magnet downwards then the magnet is pushing the wire upwards. If you check, this confirms Fleming's left-hand rule. The combined field of the magnet and the current in the wire is shown in Figure 27.12(b).

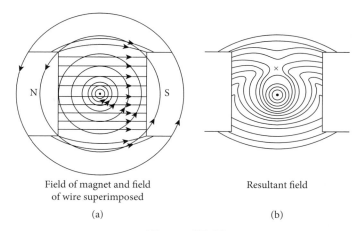

Field of magnet and field
of wire superimposed

Resultant field

(a)

(b)

Figure 27.12

With the concentration of lines below the wire and the neutral point where there is zero field the force is upwards from strong field to weak field. This is always the case. It is as if field lines behave like rubber. This is sometimes called a **catapult field**.

Figure 27.13 shows the field of equal currents in two parallel wires in the same direction.

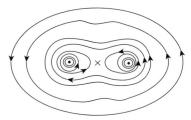

Figure 27.13

Here the field of the right-hand wire is anticlockwise and would, therefore, be down the page at the position of the left-hand wire. Combining this direction with the current up out of the page gives a force to the right when Fleming's left-hand rule is used. It again shows that wires tend to move towards neutral points and away from any region of strong magnetic field.

Figure 27.14 shows the field of equal currents in two parallel wires in opposite directions. This is also the cross-section of the pattern for a single loop of wire.

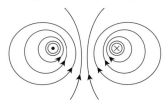

Figure 27.14

Figure 27.15 shows the field of a helical coil of wire, a solenoid.

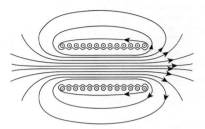

Figure 27.15

If an iron core is placed inside the solenoid the strength of the field is increased considerably. The core, known as a ferrous core, makes the solenoid an electromagnet.

The Hall probe

The fact that in a magnetic field there is a force on an electric current is made use of in a device called a **Hall probe**. It consists of a small (7 mm × 3 mm) strip of semiconductor material through which a current is passed and placed in a magnetic field B as shown in Figure 27.16(a). When the current is switched on the magnetic field causes a force on the moving charges within the semiconductor. This force moves them to the far side of the semiconductor and this immediately sets up an electric field across the strip, which then balances the effect of the magnetic field.

An electric field implies a potential difference (p.d.) across the strip. The value of this p.d. is called the **Hall potential difference V_H**.

Consider a charge $+q$ moving with velocity v from left to right along the length of the Hall probe.

Magnetic force on the charge $= Bqv$

Electric force due to electric field

$$E = qE = \frac{qV_H}{w} \text{ where } w \text{ is the width as}$$

shown on Figure 27.16(a).

This gives $\quad Bqv = \frac{qV_H}{w} \quad$ so $\quad V_H = Bvw.$

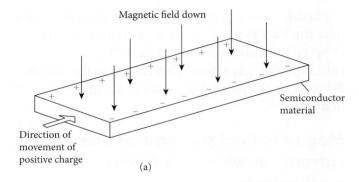

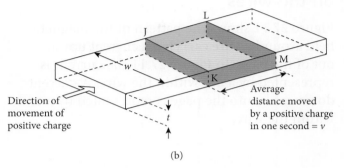

Figure 27.16

When the current through the strip is I it can be expressed in terms of the number of charged particles passing any point in the strip per second multiplied by the charge on each particle. This is shown in Figure 27.16(b). On average, all the charged particles move a distance v from WX to YZ in one second.

The number of charged particles in this volume is $vwt \times n$, where n is the number of charged particles per unit volume and t is the thickness of the strip.

The current I is therefore given by $I = nq \times vwt$

and $v = \dfrac{I}{nqwt}$ substituting into $V_H = Bvw$

gives $V_H = \dfrac{BIw}{nqwt} = \dfrac{BI}{ntq}$

Remember that q will be negative when the current is a flow of electrons.

A Hall probe can be used to measure magnetic flux density once it has been calibrated in a magnetic field of known flux density.

Velocity selection

An interesting situation arises if a beam of electrons is passed into a region in which there is an electric field, of field strength E and a magnetic field, of field strength B, at right angles to one another, as shown in Figure 27.17(a). Here the strengths of the two fields have been adjusted so that the force on an electron caused by the electric field is exactly equal and opposite to the force on it caused by the magnetic field.

This gives $Bev = Ee$

where e is the charge on an electron and v is its velocity.

This enables the speed of the electrons to be calculated as $v = E/B$.

If the electric field is then switched off, the electrons will travel in a circular path, as shown in Figure 27.17(b). For this situation the path will be a circular arc of radius r.

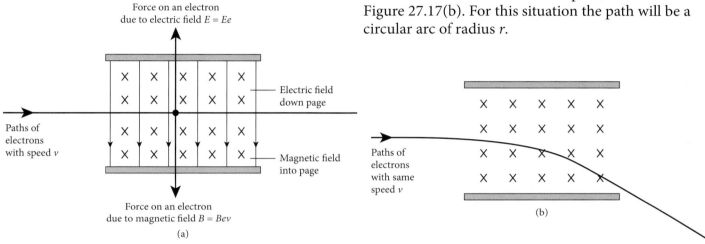

Figure 27.17

Teacher's Tip

A comparison between the effect on charges in electric and magnetic fields

	Electric field E	Magnetic field of flux density B
Force on charge $+Q$	EQ	$BQv\sin\theta$
Force on stationary charge	EQ	Zero
Direction of force	In direction of field	Given by Fleming's left-hand rule
Path followed by a moving charge	Parabola (a)	Arc of a circle (b) Field down into page
Energy gain by charge in passing across field	EQx where x is the distance moved in direction of field	Zero

Using force = mass × acceleration gives
force = $Bev = mv^2/r$.
Cancelling and rearranging gives $\dfrac{e}{m} = \dfrac{v}{Br}$

Using the value of v from the earlier calculation gives the value of e/m. The numerical value of e/m was historically important. When J.J. Thomson first found this value of e/m he realised that it was over 1800 times larger than the value of the charge-to-mass ratio for a hydrogen ion. This led directly to him announcing that a negative particle of much smaller mass than a hydrogen ion existed. This was the discovery of the electron.

Magnetic resonance imaging, MRI

Introduction

This technique can produce the most detailed images of organs, such as the brain, as shown in the photograph of Figure 27.18.

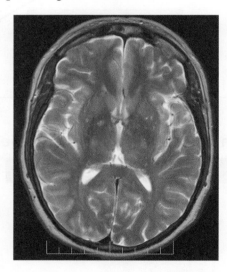

Figure 27.18 An image of the brain of a person, using an MRI scanning machine.

The system does not involve any radiation dose but it does take a longer time than a CT scan. During the time the image is being created the patient needs to keep still, so the technique is not suitable for use with young children.

As the name implies the system depends on resonance in a magnetic field. The object that does the resonating is the proton in a hydrogen atom and since all tissue in the body contains hydrogen atoms, magnetic resonance can occur throughout the body.

Precession of nuclei

All hydrogen protons spin. A spinning electrical charge produces a magnetic field along the axis of its spin. When an external magnetic field is applied to a large number of protons, most protons will spin so that their magnetic field axis is in the same direction as the external magnetic field, because this is a lower energy state. Only a small number of protons spin in the opposite direction, because this is a higher energy state.

The line up of the axes of the protons with the external magnetic field is not perfect, and any proton where the axis of rotation is different from the direction of the external field will have a torque on it. The effect of a torque on a spinning object is to make it precess. This is illustrated in Figure 27.19. (A toy gyroscope will precess in the same way and for the same reason if its axis is not vertical.)

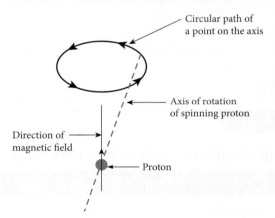

Figure 27.19 A precessing proton in a magnetic field is at the heart of all MRI scanners.

In the diagram, the axis of spin of the proton is at an angle to the vertical magnetic field. This angle remains constant as precession takes place. Any point on the axis rotates in a horizontal circle with an angular velocity ω. (See Page 104 for details of angular velocity.) This anngular velocity, in this situation, is usually called the angular frequesncy and given the name is the **Larmor frequency**. It is proportional to the magnetic flux density B. The constant of proportionality for a proton is known very accurately; to four significant figures it is 42.57 MHz T^{-1}. By using very strong magnetic fields, over 1 tesla, a Larmor frequency of the order of 40 MHz is possible. This is a radio frequency.

Nuclear resonance

The effect of applying, for a short time, a magnetic field that varies at the exact Larmor frequency causes a resonance effect in which the energy supplied to the protons causes them to flip into the higher energy state mentioned previously. They do not stay in the high-energy state however but relax back to their original low-energy state. In doing so, they emit radiation in the form of radio waves that can be detected by a radio receiver. The ability of this system to supply medical data depends on an average relaxation time of protons that varies with the chemical bonding between a proton and neighbouring atoms. A hydrogen proton in water has a relaxation time of about 2 seconds. In brain tissue the time is about 0.2 second and in a tumour the time might be 0.8 second. These differences can be converted by a computer into an image of the different materials in a body.

The MRI scanner

To make practical use of magnetic resonance involves a large and expensive piece of equipment. A scanner is shown in Figure 27.20.

The bulk of the scanner is necessary to provide a very accurately calibrated large strength magnetic field across the patient. To get the required field requires very large currents in solenoids. The currents are so large that a conventional system would be almost impossible, but the development of superconducting magnets has made it possible to

get the magnitude and the accuracy necessary. The coils of a superconducting electromagnet are kept at a temperature near to absolute zero, using liquid helium. At this temperature some materials have zero resistance. (Note: not *nearly* zero, but precisely zero.) When superconducting, currents of hundreds of amperes are possible with no heating effect.

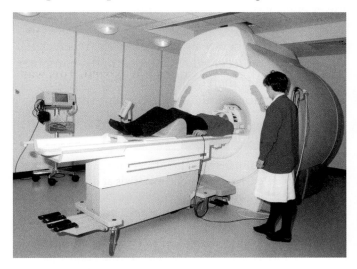

Figure 27.20 A patient undergoing an MRI scan.

Having provided this large, constant magnetic field, additional magnets are added in order to provide a magnetic field gradient. In the three-dimensional space inside a patient, the value of the magnetic flux density is known accurately at every point. The arrangement of the magnets is shown in Figure 27.21.

Figure 27.21 also shows the radio frequency coil that surrounds the patient. This coil is connected

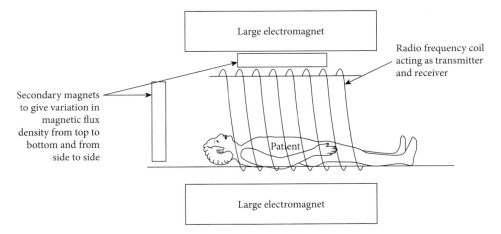

Figure 27.21 The arrangement of the magnets and transceiver coils for an MRI scanner.

to a generator/receiver. The generator gives a short pulse of radio waves at a particular Larmor frequency. Protons at points in the patient which have the magnetic field corresponding to this frequency may flip to their higher energy state. During the time before the next pulse of radio waves from the generator, most of these protons will flip back to the lower energy state, and emit radio waves as they do so. In its receiver mode, the coil will act as an aerial and send a radio frequency signal back to the receiver. All the information received will be sent to the computer.

The process is then continued using a slightly different Larmor frequency and other points will be examined. Gradually a photograph can be built up, but it is a relatively long process and the patient needs to stay still so that the pattern of the magnetic field can be associated with points inside his or her body. Fortunately, a doctor will usually have been able to instruct the scanner's technicians as to where in the body an image is required. Full body scans are seldom required. These would take hours.

The display provided by the computer is usually a slice through the patient. Colours can be artificially added so that, for example, short relaxation times could be shown blue and longer relaxation times could be shown red, and so on.

Chapter Summary

✓ Distinguish between permanent magnets that use, so called, hard magnetic materials and electromagnets, that use easily magnetised materials.
✓ Magnets capable of creating very strong and accurately calibrated magnetic fields are much in demand in modern industry today. The magnets at CERN, the European nuclear research centre near Geneva, have a ring of large magnets stretching 30 km. Some MRI (Magnetic resonance imagers) scanners for diagnosing and treating cancers are capable of producing magnetic fields of 4 tesla (over 10 000 times the strength of many ordinary magnets). These magnets cost hundreds of thousands of Euros.
✓ The force F on a wire of length L carrying a current I at an angle θ to the magnetic field, of field strength B, is given by $F = BIL \sin \theta$.

✓ The force F on a charge q travelling with speed v at an angle θ to the magnetic field, of field strength, B is given by $F = Bqv \sin \theta$.
✓ Fleming's left-hand motor rule: Second Finger: Current, First Finger: Field, Thumb: Motion.
✓ This can be used with the motion of charged particles but remember that if the particles are electrons, with a negative charge, the direction of the current will be in the opposite direction to the direction of movement of the particles.
✓ Magnetic Resonance Imaging (MRI) depends on resonance in a magnetic field. The resonating effect is produced by the proton in a hydrogen atom present in tissues of a living body.

Progress Check

27.1 Copy and complete the magnetic field pattern around the arrangements of magnets shown in Figures 27.22(a), (b) and (c).

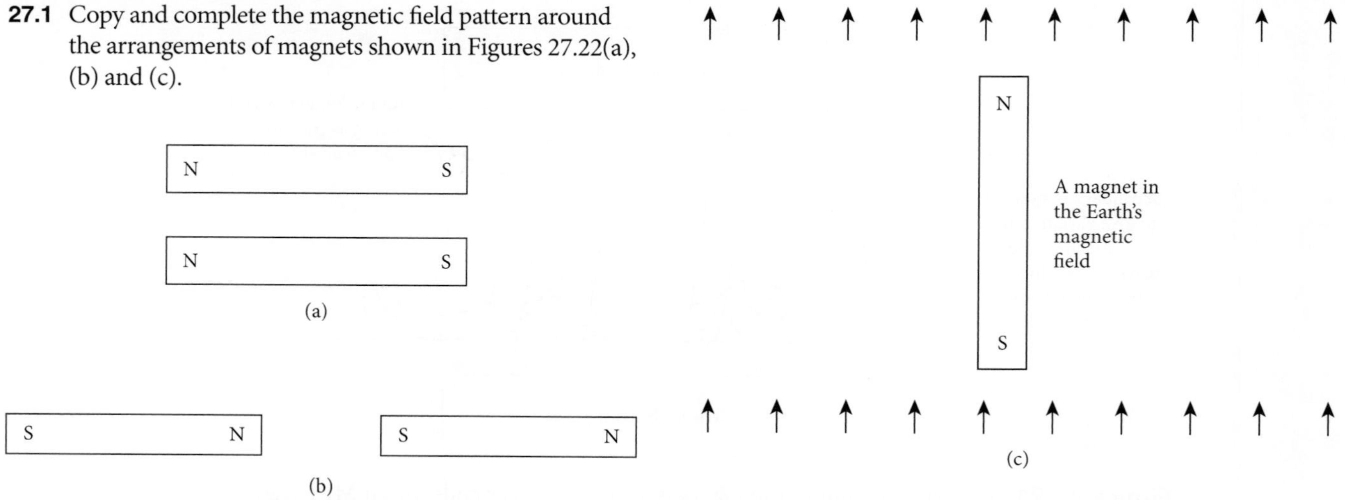

Figure 27.22

27.2 Draw a plan view of the magnetic field pattern around
  (a) parallel wires with equal currents in the same direction,
  (b) parallel wires with equal currents in opposite directions.

27.3 Copy and draw diagrams showing, in plan view, the magnetic field around the arrangement of wires shown in Figures 27.23 (a) and (b).

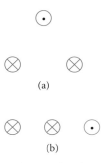

(a)

(b)

Figure 27.23

27.4 Explain why there must be a south pole at the Earth's magnetic north.

27.5 Draw a field diagram around a pair of parallel wires with equal currents in opposite directions placed between the poles of a permanent magnet. (This is the arrangement in electric motors; the parallel wires are then two sides of a rectangular coil.)

27.6 Calculate the force on a 20 cm length of wire placed at right-angles to a magnetic field of flux density 0.068 T when the wire carries a current of 18 A.

27.7 A square coil of 80 turns of wire and of side 35 cm is placed in a magnetic field of flux density 0.073 T at an angle of 40° to the field as shown in Figure 27.24.

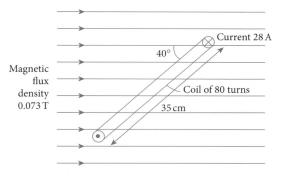

Figure 27.24

The current through the coil is 28 A. Calculate the torque on the coil.

27.8 A beam of electrons is passed into a magnetic field so that the direction of the beam is at right-angles to the direction of the field. The flux density of the field is 7.0 mT and the speed of the electrons is $9.7 \times 10^6\,\mathrm{m\,s^{-1}}$. Calculate the radius of the circle in which the electrons travel.

27.9 (a) Calculate the Larmor frequency of precession in an MRI scanner when the magnetic flux density at a point in the field is 1.374 T.
  (b) By how much will this frequency change at a slightly different point, in the field where the magnetic flux density is 1.380 T?
  (c) By considering the answer of (b), explain why
    (i) the magnetic flux density must be known so accurately at all points within the apparatus,
    (ii) the patient must remain still while a scan is being performed.

Electromagnetic Induction

28

Introduction

In 1820, Hans Oersted discovered that an electric current had a magnetic field associated with it. The current was supplied by a battery, because at that time it was the only way known for the production of an electric current. It took another 11 years before Faraday in 1831 not only used an electric current to produce motion in an electric motor but also found that an electric motor, when rotated manually backwards, produced an electric current. He had discovered electromagnetic induction. All the electrical energy supplied by power stations is now produced using electromagnetic induction.

Experiments on electromagnetic induction

The simplest experiment on electromagnetic induction is illustrated in Figure 28.1. It uses a strong permanent magnet, a sensitive meter, called a galvanometer, and a piece of wire connected to it.

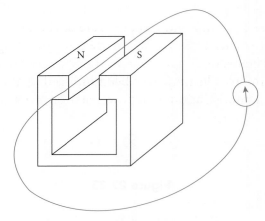

Figure 28.1

If the wire is moved downwards, so that it cuts through the magnetic field of the magnet, the needle of the galvanometer moves in one direction. When the wire is moved upwards, the needle moves in the opposite direction. If the wire is moved more rapidly, then the needle moves further, but for a shorter time. Figure 28.2 shows these results graphically.

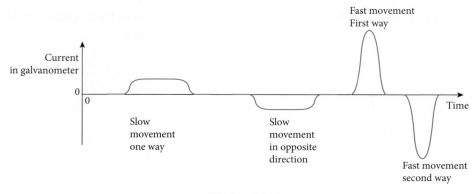

Figure 28.2

The current through the galvanometer will depend on the total circuit resistance but the electromotive force (e.m.f.) induced (or generated) is directly proportional to the rate at which magnetic flux is cut. Movement of the wire sideways produces no e.m.f. at all. Moving the magnet instead of the wire produces exactly the same effects, provided the wire is cutting through magnetic flux.

A single wire produces a very small effect. To increase the e.m.f. induced, the rate of change of flux needs to be increased. This can be done by using strong fields, rapid motion and thousands of wires. A few microvolts may have been induced by the above demonstration: in a power station, 6000 V is a common output e.m.f.

Definitions of terms used in electromagnetic induction

The term magnetic flux density B was introduced in Chapter 27. For electromagnetic induction, the total magnetic flux cut needs to be calculated.

Magnetic flux Φ is defined as the magnetic flux density multiplied by the area at right angles to the flux density.

$$\Phi = BA$$

If, in Figure 28.1, the magnetic flux density between the poles of the magnet had a constant value of 0.72 T and the area of the poles was $0.080\,\text{m} \times 0.050\,\text{m}$ ($8\,\text{cm} \times 5\,\text{cm}$), then the magnetic flux between the poles is

$$0.72\,\text{T} \times 0.080\,\text{m} \times 0.050\,\text{m} = 2.88 \times 10^{-3}\ \text{weber.}$$

The unit of magnetic flux is the **weber (Wb).** One weber is the flux of one tesla across an area of one square metre, $1\,\text{T}\,\text{m}^2$.

Another term sometimes used in electrical generators and transformers is **flux linkage.**

This is the magnetic flux multiplied by the number of turns of wire. For example, in a wire coil with n turns the flux linkage $= \Phi n$.

Faraday's law of electromagnetic induction

This law is a formal statement of the results of the experiment described above.

The e.m.f. induced by electromagnetic induction is proportional to the rate of change of magnetic flux.

$$E = -\frac{\text{Change in magnetic flux}}{\text{time}}$$

or in calculus terms

$$E = -\frac{\mathrm{d}\Phi}{\mathrm{d}t}$$

The reason for putting a minus sign in front of this term will be explained later in the chapter.

Example 1

A racing car has a sheet of metal of width 120 cm and 40 cm from front to back just in front of the front wheels, as shown in Figure 28.3. It is designed to push down on the front wheels so that they grip the track well. The car will reach speeds of $100\,\text{m}\,\text{s}^{-1}$ at times and will be travelling in some places through the Earth's vertical magnetic field of $55\,\mu\text{T}$. Check to see whether the generated e.m.f. might be capable of causing sparking.

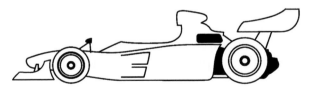

Figure 28.3

Answer The horizontal area swept out by the plate in one second will have a maximum possible value of $100\,\text{m} \times 1.20\,\text{m} = 120\,\text{m}^2$. (The front to back distance is irrelevant.)

Flux cut per second $= 55 \times 10^{-6}\,\text{T} \times 120\,\text{m}^2$ = e.m.f. generated $= 6.6\,\text{mV}$.

There is no danger of sparking with such a small e.m.f.

The a.c. generator, often called an alternator

An alternating current (a.c.) generator is an excellent example of the use of electromagnetic induction. A.c. generators produce almost all of the electrical power used world wide. In their simplest form they consist of a rectangular coil of many turns of wire rotating between the poles of a magnet as shown in Figure 28.4.

Each end of the coil is connected to slip rings that are connected to the circuit where the electrical power is required.

The coil is forced to rotate. For example, a car's alternator is driven by a belt directly from the engine.

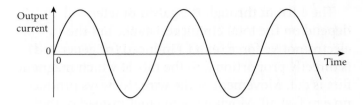

Figure 28.5

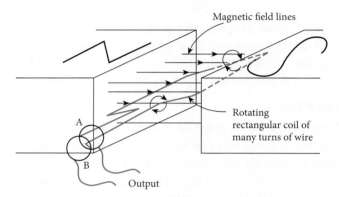

Figure 28.4

Look at the side of the coil connected to slip ring A in Figure 28.4. It is moving upwards and cutting magnetic flux so an e.m.f. is generated. The wire on the opposite side of the coil is moving downwards through the same field and it will generate an e.m.f. in the opposite direction. The two e.m.f.s will add to one another to provide a current through the slip rings. Half a cycle later the wire connected to slip ring A will be moving downwards so its e.m.f. will change direction, as will that connected to slip ring B. A graph of output current against time will therefore alternate, as shown in Figure 28.5.

Lenz's law

So far in this chapter nothing has been written about the actual direction in which an e.m.f. is induced. In the last paragraph it was simply stated that the direction reversed when the wire moved downwards rather than upwards. The direction of any induced current is, in fact, determined by the law of conservation of energy.

Consider the alternator in Figure 28.4. Its structure is very similar to the structure of an

electric motor. If an alternating current had been passed through the coil, with some control of its frequency, it would rotate as a motor. Now, if the current being generated by the alternator causes the coil to move itself as a motor, then we shall have perpetual motion and be able to withdraw power at the same time. This is where the principle of conservation of energy is being broken. It does not happen. In fact, any current induced by the rotation of the coil in an alternator **must** be in a direction to oppose motion, not to help motion. Mechanical power must be supplied to an alternator in order to get electrical power out. The more current the alternator is providing, the more mechanical power must be supplied to it.

This is **Lenz's law**. **It states that the direction of any induced current is such as to oppose the flux change that causes it.**

It is Lenz's law that causes the introduction of the minus sign in the Faraday law equation. The sign indicates that the induced e.m.f. causes opposition to any change in flux. For example, if an electromagnet, as described in Chapter 27, is being used and the current through its coil is increasing then the induced e.m.f. will oppose the current, slowing its rate of increase. When the electromagnet is switched off, the induced e.m.f. will change direction and will slow its rate of decrease.

As a result of Lenz's law, the law, governing directions of current, field and motion when considering induction become Fleming's **right**-hand law, in which the thumb, first finger and second finger are all held at right-angles to one another as was the case with the left-hand law. Fleming's right-hand law states:

If the direction of a magnetic field is represented by the first finger of the right hand and the direction of motion is represented by the thumb, then the direction of any induced current is represented by the second finger.

Example 2

A 12.0 V motor is connected into the circuit shown in Figure 28.6.

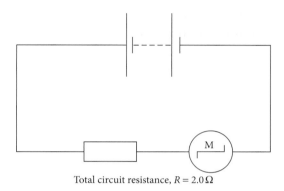

Total circuit resistance, $R = 2.0\,\Omega$

Figure 28.6

The 2.0 Ω resistor is the total resistance in the circuit. At different speeds of rotation the induced e.m.f. changes and this changes the current supplied by the battery. Several rows in the following table are completed showing how the output mechanical power of the motor varies as the current supplied changes. You are asked to work through the values given and to follow the pattern to complete the table.

Answer the following questions.

(a) Why would it be more sensible to run the motor with 4.0 V across the resistor R than with 8.0 V across this resistor?

(b) The induced e.m.f. is proportional to the speed of the motor. The top speed of the motor is 1150 revolutions per minute. What is the motor's speed when at its greatest output power?

(c) What will the power of 2.875 W be used for when the motor is running at its maximum speed?

> ### Teacher's Tip
>
> In the above exercise, the equation being used for potential differences and e.m.f.s is
>
> e.m.f. of battery = induced e.m.f. + p.d. across resistor
>
> The same equation could be written as
>
> e.m.f. of battery – induced e.m.f. = p.d. across resistor
>
> In this form you can see the minus sign from Lenz's law – but it does depend on which side of the equation you write it. You must be careful with signs when considering induced e.m.f. The principle of conservation of energy must be obeyed.

State of motor	p.d. across resistor R/V	Induced e.m.f. /V	Current/A	Power from battery/W	Power lost in resistor R/W	Power output of motor/W
Stopped	12	0	6.0	72	72	0
Top speed	0.5	11.5	0.25	3	0.125	2.875
	2.0					
	4.0					
Max. output power	6.0	6.0	3.0	36	18	18
	8.0					
	10.0	2.0	5.0	60	50	10

Chapter Summary

✓   Magnetic flux Φ is defined as the magnetic flux density multiplied by the area at right angles to the flux density.
    $\Phi = BA$
✓   Flux linkage $= \Phi n$, is a term used when a flux Φ passes through a coil of n turns.
✓   Faraday's law. The e.m.f. induced by electromagnetic induction is proportional to the rate of change of magnetic flux.

$$E = -\frac{\text{change in magnetic flux}}{\text{time}} \quad \text{or in calculus terms } E = -\frac{d\Phi}{dt}$$

✓   Lenz's law states that the direction of any induced current is such as to oppose the flux change that causes it.
✓   Fleming's right-hand law states that if the direction of a magnetic field is represented by the first finger of the right hand and the direction of motion is represented by the thumb, then the direction of any induced current is represented by the second finger. So it is 'use the left hand for motors and the right hand for induction'.

Progress Check

28.1 When the magnetic flux density has a constant value of 0.0076 T across an area 3 cm × 8 cm, what is the magnetic flux through the area? The unit of magnetic flux needs to be given.

28.2 An aircraft has a wingspan of 56 m and is travelling with a constant speed of 200 m s^{-1} (720 kph). The aircraft is at a place where the vertical component of the Earth's magnetic flux density is 2.3×10^{-5} T. Calculate the induced potential difference between the wingtips.

28.3 A rectangular coil in an electrical generator at a power station has an area of 15 m^2 and is kept at a rate of rotation of 50 revolutions per second. The magnetic flux density can be assumed to have a constant value of 0.079 T.

(a) At what position, relative to the direction of the magnetic field, is the coil when it is producing maximum e.m.f.?

(b) How much flux is cut by the coil during a half a revolution within which the flux is maximum, then zero, then maximum again but entering the opposite side of the coil?

(c) Deduce the average e.m.f. produced during this time.

(d) Deduce how many turns will be required for the generator to produce, on average, an output of around 11 000 V.

Alternating Currents 29

Introduction

Throughout the world the vast majority of electrical supply from power stations to homes and factories is alternating current. The reason for this is that alternating current is essential for the operation of transformers and transformers are necessary for changing voltages upwards or downwards without any moving parts. Transformers may work with well over 90% efficiency for 30 or more years with little requirement for maintenance. Alternating current can easily be converted into direct current when required.

Figure 28.5 in the previous chapter was a graph showing how the current varies in the simplest form of a.c. It is repeated here in Figure 29.1(a) with some extra detail added. It is a sinusoidal variation of the current with time. This means that the graph has the shape of a sine wave and follows an equation of the form $I = I_o \sin \omega t$, where ω is called the angular frequency. Beneath the current graph, in Figure 29.1(b) is the voltage graph, $V = V_o \sin \omega t$. For a resistive circuit the voltage is in phase with the current.

On both graphs the peak values are marked together with the so-called root mean square (r.m.s.) values. These will be explained shortly. The period

of the oscillation is T and the frequency f, as with simple harmonic motion, is $1/T$. Also, as with simple harmonic motion, $\omega = 2\pi f$. Mains frequency is often $50\,\text{Hz}$ giving $\omega = 2\pi \times 50 = 314.16\,\text{rad s}^{-1}$ and a period of $0.020\,\text{s}$.

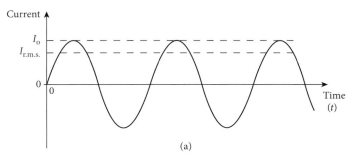

(a)

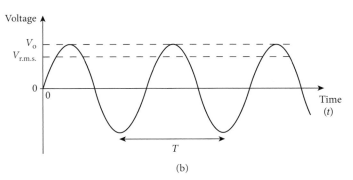

(b)

Figure 29.1

Power in an a.c. circuit

A characteristic of all a.c. circuits is that the average current is zero. The electrons in a wire carrying a.c. current just oscillate backwards and forwards. Their mean position does not change. This poses problems for deciding what the effective current is. There is no point in marking all electrical appliances used in the home as having a current of zero. To overcome this problem it is necessary to consider the power being supplied. This is shown graphically in Figure 29.2.

The variation of current with time is shown in black and the variation of power with time is shown

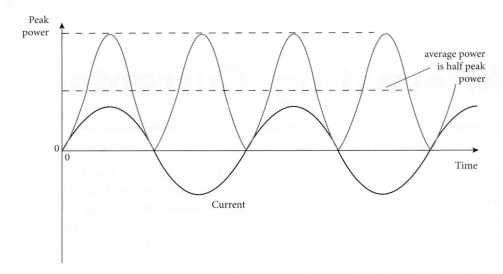

Figure 29.2

in purple. Since power P is given for resistive circuits at all times by $P = I^2R$, the power curve can never be negative. The power curve is also sinusoidal but with a frequency of twice the frequency of the current. In other words, maximum power is reached when the current is maximum positive and maximum negative. The average power is not zero. Because the power curve is sinusoidal the average power is half the peak power.

We, therefore, have the following equations.

$$V_{peak} \times I_{peak} = P_{peak} \quad \text{and}$$

$$\frac{1}{2} \times V_{peak} \times I_{peak} = \frac{1}{2} \times P_{peak} = P_{average}$$

$P_{average}$ is the quantity we want to be able to use readily from the voltage and the current but we must still keep the ratio of voltage to current the same. This can be achieved by splitting the factor of $\frac{1}{2}$ between the voltage and the current. This gives

$$\frac{V_{peak}}{\sqrt{2}} \times \frac{I_{peak}}{\sqrt{2}} = P_{average}$$

$\frac{V_{peak}}{\sqrt{2}}$ is known as the root mean square voltage, or $V_{r.m.s.}$

$\frac{I_{peak}}{\sqrt{2}}$ is known as the root mean square current, or $I_{r.m.s.}$

Although this seems complicated when met for the first time, it has the effect of making most a.c. calculations exactly the same as calculations for d.c. as is shown by the following example.

Example 1

An electric cooker is marked 200 V, 50 Hz a.c. maximum current 30.0 A. What are the average power and the peak power required by the unit when working with maximum current?

Answer The electrical information given with the cooker makes the assumption that d.c. rules will apply. No mention is made of r.m.s. values because these are the values always used. So to find the average power with maximum current we just need

$$P = V \times I = 200\,\text{V} \times 30\,\text{A} = 6000\,\text{W}.$$

In fact, during each cycle the power ranges from zero to 12 000 W, which is the peak power.

To sum up, for almost all the circuits you use the calculations which will be almost identical to d.c. calculations provided you use r.m.s. values. These will usually be the figures you are given.

The transformer

Transformers were mentioned in the introduction as a very efficient way of changing a.c. voltages up and down. A basic transformer consists of two coils of insulated wire wound on a laminated soft iron core. (Soft in this case means a material that can be easily magnetised and demagnetised.) The arrangement of primary and secondary coils in a transformer is shown in Figure 29.3.

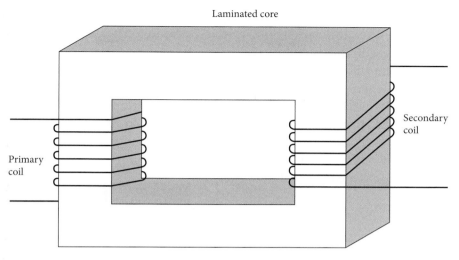

Laminated core

Secondary coil

Primary coil

Figure 29.3

The electrical symbol for a transformer is shown in Figure 29.4 and Figure 29.5 shows a variety of different transformers. Transformers can be as small as a centimetre across or as large as several metres in power stations and electrical sub-stations.

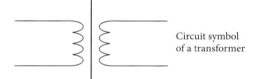

Circuit symbol of a transformer

Figure 29.4

One of the coils is connected to the supply of a.c. power and is called the primary coil; the other coil is called the secondary and is connected to the electrical device in use. A transformer used to increase the voltage is called a step-up transformer; one that decreases the voltage is called a step-down transformer. A typical distribution system across a country could involve a power station generator supplying an a.c. voltage of 6000 V that can be stepped up first to 120 000 V and then to 480 000 V for long distance transmission. Then this voltage may be stepped down in stages to 32 000 V, 11 000 V and 230 V for domestic use. In a house transformer, such as those operating high intensity lights, the voltage may be further reduced to 12 V.

The theory of a transformer

The current in the primary coil magnetises the core: it produces magnetic flux in the core. Since the current

Figure 29.5 Different varieties of transformers

in the primary is a.c., the magnetic flux changes rapidly from one direction to the other and back again. This changing flux is also linking with the secondary coil and so, by Faraday's law there will be an a.c. voltage set up across each turn of the secondary coil. If a small output voltage V_S is required then the secondary coil will have few turns n_S, but if a large output voltage is required the secondary coil will have a large number of turns. For a transformer working at maximum efficiency, the turns ratio equals the ratio of the voltages.

$$\text{i.e. turns ratio} = \frac{n_S}{n_P} = \frac{V_S}{V_P}$$

It may seem as though the rise in voltage is breaking the principle of conservation of energy. As you should expect, this is not the case. If the voltage output is 100 times the voltage input, then the output current will be, at maximum, only one hundredth of the input current, since the power output $V_S I_S$ can, at most, only be equal to the power input $V_P I_P$. Overall, therefore, the equation above can be extended for an ideal transformer to

$$\frac{n_S}{n_P} = \frac{V_S}{V_P} = \frac{I_P}{I_S}$$

The following example makes use of the above equations but it also shows the necessity of using transformers in electrical power distribution systems.

Example 2

A power station supplies a small town with 2.0 MW of electrical power.

In case A, it does not use transformers and the people in the town use a high (and dangerous)

supply at 1000 V. The two cables from the power station to the town are thick copper with a small total resistance of only 1.0 Ω.

In case B, it does use a transformer so it generates power to provide the (ideal) transformer with 10 000 V and the transformer reduces this to 250 V for the town.

The two circuits are drawn in Figures 29.6(a) and (b) Compare the efficiency of the two systems.

Answer Given in table.

	System A	System B
Power supplied	2 MW = 2 000 000 W	2 000 000 W
r.m.s voltage to town	1000 V	250 V
r.m.s current to town	2000 A	8000 A
Turns ratio of transformer $= V_s / V_P$	not applicable	250/10 000 = 1/40
r.m.s. current from power station	2000 A	= 8000 ÷ 40 = 200 A
Voltage drop along 1 Ω cables	2000 V	200 V
Supply voltage needed at power station	3000 V	10 200 V
Power station output power	3000 V × 2000 A = 6.00 MW	10 200 V × 200 A = 2.04 MW
System efficiency = power to town/ power from power station	2.00 MW / 6.00 MW $= \frac{1}{3} = 33\%$	2.00 MW / 2.04 MW = 0.98 = 98%

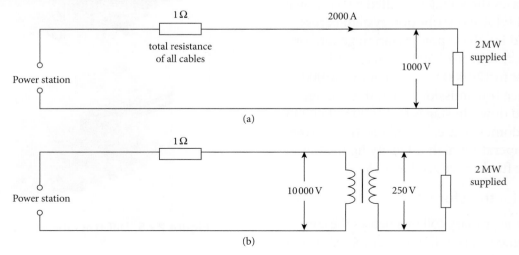

Figure 29.6

The large difference between the two efficiencies indicates clearly that the current must be kept as low as possible when transmitting electrical energy. This necessitates the use of high voltage and transformers.

Transformer losses

As stated earlier the transformer is a very efficient device. This is partly because there are no moving parts and so no wind or friction losses occur. However, with large transformers handling many megawatts of power, even a 2% loss of power does cause a considerable heating effect. For this reason cooling of large transformers can be necessary. Many transformers have external metal attachments to conduct heat away to the atmosphere and others have their coils in oil that can circulate and lose heat by convection.

The losses from a transformer are as follows.

1. Resistive losses (I^2R) from the resistance of the wires.
2. Flux losses when magnetic flux from the primary coil does not completely link the secondary. This is usually small as in most transformers the secondary coil is wound on top of the primary coil.
3. Hysteresis losses. These occur because the core is magnetised and remagnetised in the opposite direction 100 times per second. Each cycle does involve some loss of energy. The coil will heat up, but the loss is reduced by using special, so-called 'soft' iron.
4. Eddy current losses. Large swirling currents will be generated in a solid core and these will heat the resistance of the core. Eddy losses are reduced by not having solid cores. Transformer cores are sometimes made out of hundreds of separate sheet iron laminations pressed together with a thin insulation between them. This reduces the eddy currents to a very small value.

Teacher's Tip

Overhead and underground supply cables

When new power lines are planned across the countryside, some people near the routes argue that the cables should be buried. This does make any project more expensive. The very large increase is for both obvious and hidden costs. The following are some of the reasons. Individual projects may have costs peculiar to that project, crossing rivers, special viewpoints, mountains, etc.

Obvious costs

- Digging deep enough trenches for the cables not to be disturbed is expensive.
- Avoiding built up areas so that less disruption is caused by digging.
- Crossing streams and roads is more difficult for underground cables.
- Bypassing woods may be difficult; going through them is more difficult.
- More time will be taken and there will be more disruption during construction.

Hidden costs – these are the main cause of the large difference in price.

Insulation problems. When suspended in the air, the air is the insulator, apart from at the pylon where glass insulators are used. Underground there has to be an insulator capable of insulating to maybe 400 000 V. This will have to be a thick special plastic.

Cable protection. Tree roots, rats and burrowing animals may cause damage to the cable so the cable has to be armoured with steel casing. It also has to be totally waterproof, with no possibility of leaking as wet soil around the cable would conduct well with high voltage. None of this matters when suspended in air where bare aluminium wire is used. Raindrops always have air gaps between them so there is almost no chance of a current sparking to the ground. In a strong storm there is the occasional spark from a cable to the towers of an overhead system but this does not cause damage or danger for people on the ground. Birds can land on it and no shock is possible since there is no route any current can pass through the bird.

Heating problems. Up in the air, the air cools the cable so no cooling system is required. Underground the heat generated by the current is considerable and could easily melt the cable at times of high demand. This is the worst problem of all. A cooling system must be provided which necessitates oil being pumped through the cable all the time. Pumping stations have to be built to receive the heated oil, cool it and pump it back to the cable. An underground cable may well have a total area of cross section of $150\,cm^2$ compared with a corresponding cable in an overhead system of $5\,cm^2$.

A.C. current problems. There are large problems with putting a.c. cables in sea water. Being a conductor means that the live and neutral cables are effectively very close to one another. Electrically they are separated just by the insulation around the cables. This insulation acts as the insulation in a capacitor and a.c. can pass through a capacitor. A.C. that starts off on its passage through the cables simply does not get to its destination. The answer is to convert the a.c. to d.c., transmit it as d.c. and then convert it back to a.c. after passing through the sea. This is also a very expensive and inefficient process.

Rectification

Rectification is the process by which an alternating current is changed to a direct current. Quite often there is no need for the current to be a constant direct current, it just needs to be a current in which the average flow of electrons is one way only.

Half-wave rectification

When a diode is included in a circuit with an a.c. supply, it has the effect of allowing the current in the circuit to be in one direction only. This is shown in the graph of Figure 29.7.

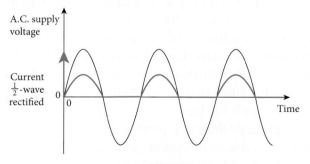

Figure 29.7

The current is in one direction for half a cycle and is zero for the other half. The circuit is said to be a half-wave rectifier circuit.

Full-wave rectification

In order to rectify both halves of the cycle it is necessary to use four diodes in a circuit called a bridge rectifier. The circuit is drawn in Figure 29.8.

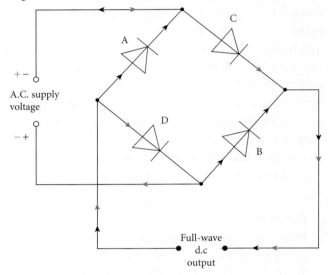

Figure 29.8

You need to follow the arrows on the figure. When the a.c. supply is as shown in black the current is through diodes A and B. When the a.c. supply changes direction, the current path shown in purple is through diodes C and D. In both cases, the current from the output is in the same direction on both halves of the cycle, giving a full-wave rectification graph as shown in Figure 29.9.

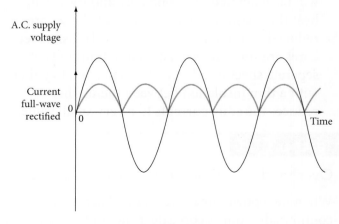

Figure 29.9

Smoothing the output from a rectifier circuit

Sometimes a smooth d.c. current is required from a rectifier circuit. A capacitor in the circuit can perform this function. It can be charged up when the supply voltage is high and provide the current by discharging when the current is too small (or zero). Figure 29.10 shows a half-wave rectifier circuit using a diode connected between the supply and the load resistor R, with a capacitor C placed in parallel with the resistor.

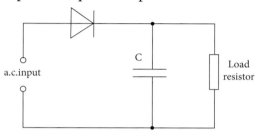

Figure 29.10

Figure 29.11 shows how both the p.d. of the supply (the purple curve that touches the 'time' axis) and the p.d. across the load resistor (the black curve that does not touch the 'time' axis) vary with time.

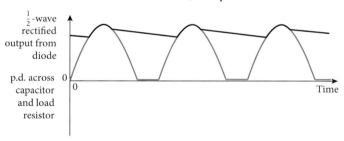

Figure 29.11

The following example shows how to calculate the value of the capacitor, once certain operational details have been given. You need to be able to do this for yourself, so it is important to work through this example.

Example 3

A half-wave rectified 50 Hz a.c. supply has a peak value of just over 80 V. It is used to supply a $800\,\Omega$ resistor with a current of 50 mA and a p.d. that needs to be kept between 76 V and 80 V. Calculate the capacitance of a suitable capacitor that can be placed in parallel with the resistor.

Answer The situation is similar to that shown in Figure 29.10.

The time for one cycle of a 50 hertz supply is 0.020 s. (1 Hz is 1 cycle per second.)
The capacitor needs to be able to supply a current of 0.050 A for this time.
The charge from the capacitor is given by

$$\Delta Q = I \times \Delta t = 0.050\,\text{A} \times 0.020\,\text{s} = 0.0010\,\text{C}$$

Read 'Δ' as 'the change in'.
The fall in voltage across the capacitor is 4 V maximum.

$$\text{So } C = \frac{\Delta Q}{\Delta V} = \frac{0.0010\,\text{C}}{4\,\text{V}} = 0.00025\,\text{F} = 250\,\mu\text{F}$$

Teacher's Tip

Be careful always with the symbol C. Here the first C is italic and is the symbol used for capacitance. The second C is roman and is, therefore, a unit. The unit of charge is the coulomb.

Chapter Summary

✓   To make many calculations with a.c. seem the same as with d.c. the most frequently used terms for voltage and current are the root mean square voltage and the root mean square current.

$\dfrac{V_{\text{peak}}}{\sqrt{2}}$ is known as the root mean square voltage, or $V_{\text{r.m.s}}$

$\dfrac{I_{\text{peak}}}{\sqrt{2}}$ is known as the root mean square current, or $I_{\text{r.m.s}}$

✓   The turns ratio in an ideal transformer is related to the currents and voltages in the primary and secondary coils by the following equations:

$$\text{Turns ratio} = \frac{n_{\text{S}}}{n_{\text{P}}} = \frac{V_{\text{S}}}{V_{\text{P}}} = \frac{I_{\text{P}}}{I_{\text{S}}}$$

✓   Rectification of a.c. means having the current in one direction only. This is done by incorporating diodes into the circuit.

29.1 An electric heater is supplied from a 230 V r.m.s. mains provider. The heater has a resistance of 26.4 Ω when at its working temperature.

Calculate
(a) the maximum voltage supplied to the heater,
(b) the maximum power supplied to the heater,
(c) the average power supplied to the heater,
(d) the energy supplied by the heater when switched on for 2 hours.

29.2 (a) A light bulb that uses a filament is marked 230 V 60 W. These will be r.m.s. values. Draw three labelled sketch graphs on the same time axis showing how the current, the potential difference and the power vary with time. Mark on the vertical axis the maximum value for each of these quantities.
(b) Explain two reasons why the light bulb does not appear to vary in brightness when run on alternating current.

29.3 A transformer using a 50 Hz, 110 V r.m.s. mains is used to provide a 15.0 V d.c. supply for an op-amp circuit. This p.d. must not fall below 14.9 V.
(a) Draw a circuit diagram of the arrangement. Show the transformer with the mains input terminals together with, a single (ideal) diode, a capacitor and the supply terminals for the op-amp all connected correctly to the secondary windings.
(b) Calculate the turns ratio for the transformer, assuming a 15 V peak output is required.
(c) Explain why the capacitor can be used to keep the input to the op-amp circuit almost constant.
(d) Deduce the value of the capacitor required if it has to supply the op-amp with 0.50 μA of current for the period of time between adjacent peaks of the output from the transformer.

29.4 A 50 m long extension lead has a resistance of 0.750 Ω in its live cable and another 0.750 Ω in its neutral cable. It is used to supply power to an electric heater in a greenhouse. The heater is marked "2000 W, 250 V".
(a) Calculate the resistance of the heater. Assume this stays constant.
(b) What will be the current when the extension lead from the 250 V supply is used?
(c) Deduce the total power taken from the 250 V supply, when using the extension lead and the power being supplied to the heater.

29.5 (a) A town requiring 100 000 W from a 250 V supply is connected to a power station by cables having a total resistance of 0.40 Ω.

Calculate:
(i) the current supplied to the town,
(ii) the potential difference across the cables,
(iii) the required output e.m.f. from the power station,
(iv) the efficiency of the system, that is the ratio of the power station to the town to the power from the power station.
(b) The efficiency of the system in (a) is far too low. To correct this, transformers are used at the power station and in the town so that the transmission is done at high voltage and low current, as shown in Figure 29.12.

The supply to the town is still 400 A at 250 V but the transformer at the town uses a supply at 10 000 V.

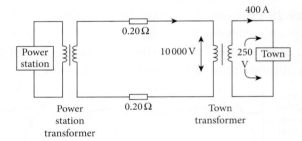

Figure 29.12

Calculate:
(i) the current required as input to the town transformer to give a power of 100 000 W,
(ii) the total potential difference across the two cables,
(iii) the required output e.m.f. from the power station's transformer,
(iv) the efficiency of this system.
(c) All countries use the system with transformers because transformers themselves are very efficient, have no moving parts and so require minimal maintenance. Suggest the only alternative to the transformer system that would keep the resistance of the cables low enough to be able to use low voltage supply.

Examination Questions XII

1. (a) State one function of capacitors in simple circuits.   [1]

(b) A capacitor is charged to a potential difference of 15 V and then connected in series with a switch, a resistor of resistance 12 kΩ and a sensitive ammeter, as shown in Figure 1.

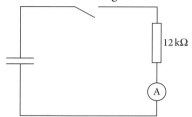

Figure 1

The switch is closed and the variation with time t of the current I in the circuit is shown in Figure 2.

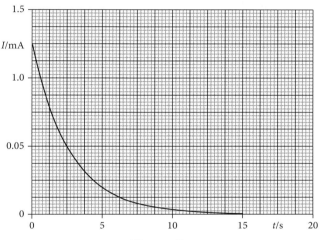

Figure 2

(i) State the relation between the current in a circuit and the charge that passes a point in the circuit.   [1]

(ii) The area below the graph line of Figure 2 represents charge.
Use Figure 2 to determine the initial charge stored in the capacitor in µC.   [4]

(iii) Initially, the potential difference across the capacitor was 15 V.
Calculate the capacitance of the capacitor in µF.   [2]

(c) The capacitor in **(b)** discharges one half of its initial energy. Calculate the new potential difference, in V, across the capacitor.   [3]

(Cambridge International AS and A Level Physics 9702 Paper 04 Question 5 October/November 2007)

2. (a) Define *electric potential* at a point.   [2]

(b) Two isolated point charges A and B are separated by a distance of 30.0 cm, as shown in Figure 3.

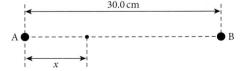

Figure 3

The charge at A is $+3.6 \times 10^{-9}$ C.
The variation with distance x from A along AB of the potential V is shown in Figure 4.

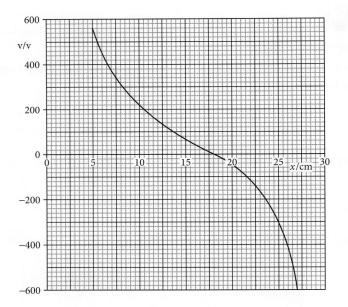

Figure 4

    (i) State the value of x, in cm, at which the potential is zero. [1]
    (ii) Use your answer in **(i)** to determine the charge at B, in C. [3]
  (c) A small test charge is now moved along the line AB in **(b)** from $x = 5.0$ cm to $x = 27$ cm. State and explain the value of x at which the force on the test charge will be maximum. [3]

        (Cambridge International AS and A Level Physics 9702 Paper 04 Question 4 May/June 2008)

3. (a) (i) Define *capacitance*. [1]
      (ii) A capacitor is made of two metal plates, insulated from one another, as shown in Figure 5.

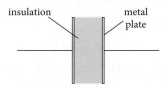

Figure 5

    Explain why the capacitor is said to store energy but not charge. [4]

  (b) Three uncharged capacitors X, Y and Z, each of capacitance 12 μF, are connected as shown in Figure 6.

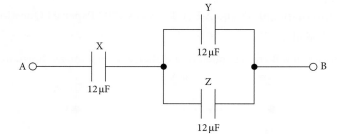

Figure 6

A potential difference of 9.0 V is applied between points A and B.
  (i) Calculate the combined capacitance of the capacitors X, Y and Z in μF. [2]

(ii) Explain why, when the potential difference of 9.0 V is applied, the charge on one plate of capacitor X is 72 μC. [2]
(iii) Determine
1. the potential difference across, in V, capacitor X, [1]
2. the charge on one plate of capacitor Y in μC. [2]

(Cambridge International AS and A Level Physics 9702 Paper 42 Question 5 October/November 2012)

4. A simple iron-cored transformer is illustrated in Figure 7.

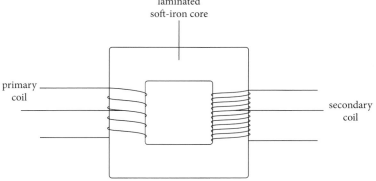

Figure 7

(a) Suggest why the core is
(i) a continuous loop, [1]
(ii) laminated. [2]

(b) (i) State Faraday's law of electromagnetic induction. [2]
(ii) Use Faraday's law to explain the operation of the transformer. [3]

(c) State two advantages of the use of alternating voltages for the transmission and use of electrical energy. [2]

(Cambridge International AS and A Level Physics 9702 Paper 04 Question 6 October/November 2008)

5. (a) Define *electric potential* at a point. [2]

(b) An α-particle is emitted from a radioactive source with kinetic energy of 4.8 MeV. The α-particle travels in a vacuum directly towards a gold ($^{197}_{79}$Au) nucleus, as illustrated in Figure 8.

Figure 8

The α-particle and the gold nucleus may be considered to be point charges in an isolated system.
(i) Explain why, as the α-particle approaches the gold nucleus, it comes to rest. [2]
(ii) For the closest approach of the α-particle to the gold nucleus determine
1. their separation, in m, [3]
2. the magnitude of the force, in N, on the α-particle. [2]

(Cambridge International AS and A Level Physics 9702 Paper 41 Question 5 October/November 2009)

6. (a) State Lenz's law. [2]

(b) A simple transformer with a soft-iron core is illustrated in Figure 9.

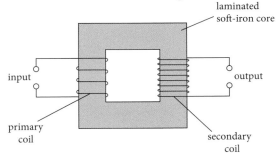

Figure 9

  (i) Explain why the core is
      1. made of iron,   [1]
      2. laminated.   [2]
  (ii) An e.m.f. is induced in the secondary coil of the transformer. Explain how a current in
       the primary coil gives rise to this induced e.m.f.   [4]
      (Cambridge International AS and A Level Physics 9702 Paper 42 Question 7 October/November 2012)

7. A sinusoidal alternating voltage supply is connected to a bridge rectifier consisting of four ideal diodes. The output of the
rectifier is connected to a resistor R and a capacitor C as shown in Figure 10.

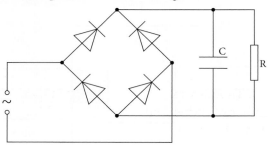

Figure 10

The function of C is to provide some smoothing to the potential difference across R. The variation with time t of the potential
difference V across the resistor R is shown in Figure 11.

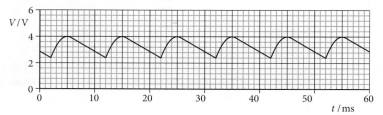

Figure 11

(a) Use Figure 11 to determine, for the alternating supply,
    (i) the peak voltage, in V,   [1]
    (ii) the root-mean-square (r.m.s.) voltage, in V,   [1]
    (iii) the frequency, in Hz. Show your working.   [2]

(b) The capacitor C has capacitance 5.0 μF. For a single discharge of the capacitor through the
    resistor R, use Figure 11 to
    (i) determine the change in potential difference, in V,   [1]
    (ii) determine the change in charge, in C, on each plate of the capacitor,   [2]
    (iii) show that the average current in the resistor is 1.1×10^{-3} A.   [2]

(c) Use Figure 11 and the value of the current given in (b)(iii) to estimate the resistance
    of resistor R.   [2]
    (Cambridge International AS and A Level Physics 9702 Paper 41 Question 6 May/June 2012)

Quantum Physics 30

Introduction

The development of quantum physics started with the Greek philosophers around 400 BC with the first ideas of matter being quantised. Then it was suggested that matter is a large number of individual atoms that cannot be further divided. The word 'atom' comes from the Greek word '*atomos*'. By the end of the nineteenth century, it was clear that charge also was quantised. It is not possible, on a *very* small scale, to have any charge required; it must be the charge of a whole number of elementary charges.

At the beginning of the twentieth century, scientists such as Einstein wondered about energy being quantised. If that was the case then wave energy, of light in particular, would be possible only in small packets of energy. The photoelectric effect was studied by Einstein and his researches revealed these packets of light energy, now called **photons**. Einstein received the Nobel Prize for his researches on the photoelectric effect.

The energy of a photon E is proportional to the frequency f of the wave, $E = hf$, where h is a constant called the **Planck constant**. It has the numerical value of 6.626×10^{-34} J s.

The photoelectric effect

The photoelectric effect, as its name implies, is the production of electricity from light. When light falls on some metals, electrons are emitted. When visible light is used then only metals such as sodium and potassium cause the emission, but if ultra-violet radiation is used then metals such as zinc and copper will emit electrons. Figure 30.1 shows a piece of apparatus that can be used to obtain quantitative data about this phenomenon.

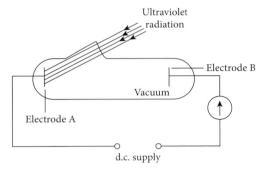

Figure 30.1

A glass tube is fitted with two electrodes A and B and evacuated. The metal under test is electrode A and it is illuminated with ultra-violet radiation. A variable d.c. supply is connected between electrodes A and B together with a very sensitive galvanometer. Currents of the order of nanoamperes, 10^{-9} A, need to be measured. It is found that, provided electrode B is kept positive, all the electrons emitted from electrode A are collected and the current is constant. When the p.d. across the electrodes is reduced the current drops, but even when the p.d. is zero there is still a photoelectric effect causing a current. It requires electrode B to be made negative with respect to electrode A, before that all the electrons are prevented from arriving at electrode B. This stopping potential difference is called the **stopping voltage**. This is shown in the sketch graph of Figure 30.2.

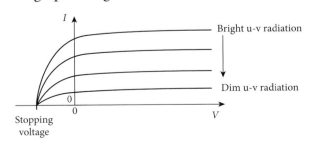

Figure 30.2

Figure 30.2 also shows the effect of reducing the intensity of the ultra-violet. The pattern of the graphs remains the same as the intensity is reduced but with smaller currents. The photoelectric current is proportional to the intensity. However, using the wave theory, as the intensity falls the wave energy falls so it would be expected, in dim radiation, that the stopping potential would also fall. This does not happen. Even in very dim ultra-violet, the electrons are still emitted with as much energy as they were with intense ultra-violet. The wave theory of light cannot explain this. It was this experiment that led Einstein to suggest that energy of light is quantised in packets of light called **photons**. This experiment implies that every individual photon of the ultra-violet radiation that is absorbed is absorbed completely by one electron. The radiation behaves not as a wave but as a stream of particles, called photons.

A separate experiment, using radiation of different frequencies f, can measure how the stopping voltage for a particular metal varies with the frequency. The result of this experiment is shown in Figure 30.3. It shows that there is a frequency, called the **threshold frequency f_0**, below which photoelectrons will not be emitted from that metal.

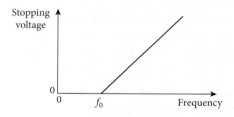

Figure 30.3

The minimum photon energy necessary to cause photoelectrons is called the **work function ϕ**. This is given by hf_0.

At the level of an electron being emitted we can apply the principle of conservation of energy to get,

Energy of arriving photon = Work function + maximum kinetic energy of emitted electron.

In symbols this becomes,

$$hf = \phi + \frac{1}{2}m_e v^2_{max}$$

where m_e is the mass of an electron and v_{max} its maximum velocity.

It is the electrons with maximum velocity that are stopped by the stopping voltage V_s,

$$\text{so} \quad \frac{1}{2}m_e v^2_{max} = eV_s$$

where e is the magnitude of the charge on an electron.

The equation can be written in different ways, e.g.

$$hf = hf_0 + \frac{1}{2}m_e v^2_{max} \quad \text{or} \quad hf = \phi + eV_s$$

You are less likely to make a mistake with this if you think of the energies involved.

One final point — the theory keeps stating the *maximum* kinetic energy of the photoelectrons. This implies that some electrons are emitted with less energy than this maximum. This is true because some of the emitted electrons lose energy within the metal of the electrode after they have been ejected from atoms a few atomic diameters below the surface.

Teacher's Tip

Powers of 10 can be a problem when considering the photoelectric effect. You are less likely to make a mistake with this if you think of the energies involved. If you use joules as the unit of energy you will be considering all three terms in one of the equations above with energies of the order of 10^{-19} J. It is often useful to work in energy units of electron-volts (1.6×10^{-19} J). In these units the numbers will be a few electron volts so powers of 10 are less of a problem. If you ever get to the stage where you have a calculation to do like $(2.6 \times 10^{-19} + 2.3)$, you have made a mistake with units.

The Planck constant, h

The graph in Figure 30.3 has the stopping voltage V_s on the y-axis and frequency on the x-axis. Putting the above equation $hf = \phi + eV_s$ into the form of $y = mx + c$, it becomes a graph of

$$V_s = \frac{h}{e}f - \frac{\phi}{e}$$

From the equation you will notice that the gradient of the graph is h/e.

Figure 30.4 is drawn to scale and shows that different metals have different threshold frequencies but that all the graphs have the same gradient.

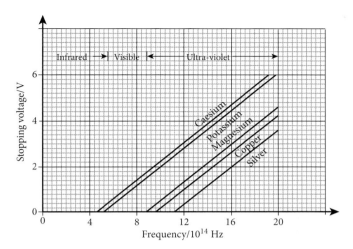

Figure 30.4

Note that, of the metals on the graph, only caesium and potassium will give any photoelectrons in the visible range of the electromagnetic spectrum.

Wave-particle duality

The above section on the photoelectric effect emphasises the fact that photons behave like particles. However, light definitely behaves as a wave when experiments are done on diffraction. We are faced with the necessity that all the range of the electromagnetic spectrum has dual wave and particle properties. The long wavelength end of the spectrum, the radio waves, exhibit very little particle property. The short wavelength end of the spectrum, the X-rays and the gamma rays exhibit many more particle-like properties, when a photon of gamma rays is emitted from a radioactive material for example.

Louis de Broglie (pronounced de Broy) wondered whether, since waves can exhibit particle like properties, can particles exhibit wave like properties? He carried out experiments on electrons that had been accelerated in a vacuum and directed at a thin screen of tiny graphite particles, as shown in Figure 30.5.

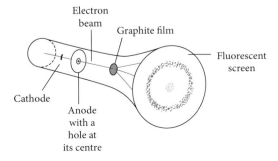

Figure 30.5

The graphite particles act like a diffraction grating, but in two planes rather than the usual one plane for an optical diffraction grating. The effect of the graphite on the electrons is shown on a fluorescent screen. Figure 30.5 clearly indicates that some of the electrons cause a central bright patch and that there is a first order diffraction pattern surrounding this. A second order can be seen if the speed of the electrons is increased, indicating that moving electrons do have a wave nature and their wavelength decreases as their speed increases. It is found that the wavelength λ of particles of mass m travelling with speed v is given by the equation

$$\lambda = \frac{h}{mv} = \frac{h}{p}$$

where h is the Planck constant and p represents the momentum mv.

Example 1

What is the wavelength of (a) an electron travelling at $6.3 \times 10^7 \, \mathrm{m \, s^{-1}}$ and (b) a proton travelling at the same speed?

Answer Using the equation above gives

(a) $\lambda = \dfrac{6.63 \times 10^{-34}}{9.1 \times 10^{-31} \times 6.3 \times 10^7} = 1.2 \times 10^{-11} \, \mathrm{m}$

This wavelength is comparable to the wavelength of X-rays.

(b) $\lambda = \dfrac{6.63 \times 10^{-34}}{1.62 \times 10^{-27} \times 6.3 \times 10^7} = 6.5 \times 10^{-15} \, \mathrm{m}$

This wavelength is comparable to the wavelength of high energy gamma rays.

The wave like properties at such a high frequency would be very difficult to detect.

Spectra

Early in the twentieth century Bohr suggested that the wave behaviour of electrons was responsible for spectra. He imagined that the electron wave around a proton in a hydrogen atom was a stationary wave pattern of the electron. The circumference of the orbit needed to be a whole number of waves. This was the start of a whole branch of science called wave mechanics. Bohr's theory works quite well for hydrogen but it fails to give results which agree with experiments as soon as more electrons are present in an atom. However, in all atoms, any electrons in stable orbits must have certain exact energies. This is one more example of quantisation. Atoms can move from low energy to high energy by gaining exactly the correct amount of energy, or can lose the right amount of energy by the reverse process of emitting a photon.

Figure 30.6 is a diagram of the energy levels possible in a hydrogen atom.

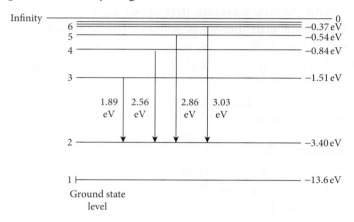

Figure 30.6

The energy levels are given in electron-volts. The energy of a free electron separated from the atom is taken to have zero energy, so all the electrons within the atom have negative energies, with those nearest to the proton having least energy. At the top of the diagram, the energy levels get closer together. There are an infinite number of levels in this part of the pattern. In a stable hydrogen atom the single electron will occupy the ground state at −13.6 eV.

When some hydrogen gas is contained in a glass tube at low pressure and a high voltage is placed across it, it emits light. (The same process is used in fluorescent tubes and sodium street lights.) The light from the hydrogen gas can be analysed using a diffraction grating mounted on an instrument called a spectrometer and certain definite wavelengths are found, as illustrated in Figure 30.7. There are other lines in both the infra-red and the ultra-violet ranges, but these are not visible to the human eye. A spectrum like this is called a **line emission spectrum**.

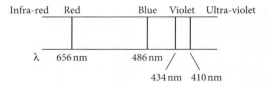

Figure 30.7

The wavelengths can be compared with the energy level values on the diagram by using the relationship for the energy of a photon as given earlier in the chapter when considering the photoelectric effect, namely $E = hf$.

These values are tabulated below.

Wavelength $\lambda / \cdot 10^{-7}$ m	Frequency $f = c/\lambda$ Hz	Photon energy/J	Photon energy/eV
656	4.57×10^{14}	3.03×10^{-19}	1.89
486	6.17×10^{14}	4.09×10^{-19}	2.56
434	6.91×10^{14}	4.58×10^{-19}	2.86
410	7.32×10^{14}	4.85×10^{-19}	3.03

When the energies of the emitted photons are compared with the energy level chart, you will see that this series of wavelengths correspond to electrons always falling from higher levels to level 2. This series of wavelengths is called the **Balmer series**. There are other series falling to the ground state, level 1, level 3 and level 4. An energy loss to the ground state will produce short wavelength ultra-violet radiation: drops to levels 3 and 4 produce infra-red radiation. The loss of energy of an electron from high state x to a lower state y is always equal to the energy of the photon, hf. Put into an equation this becomes

$$E_x - E_y = hf$$

Band theory

Spectra become rather more complicated when considering solids rather than gases. In a molecule of a gas, the energies of the electrons have quite specific values. In a solid, ranges of energy are possible and other ranges are not. The permitted ranges of energy are called energy bands, and those not permitted are called forbidden bands as shown in Figure 30.8. The upper bands are normally filled by the outer electrons of an atom. These are the valence electrons and the highest band containing electrons is called the **valence band**.

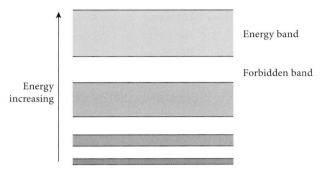

Figure 30.8

There is a difference between the upper energy bands of a conductor, an insulator and a semiconductor. This is shown in Figure 30.9.

In a **conductor** the valence band is only partially full, so when an electron is placed in an electric field, it can absorb small amounts of energy from the field and move to a slightly higher level. This happens when it is conducting. In an **insulator** the valence band is full and is separated from the next band, called the conduction band, by a large energy gap. This makes conduction virtually impossible.

In a pure **semiconductor** (called an intrinsic semiconductor) the valence band is full, but the energy gap between the valence band and the conduction band is small. It is possible for electrons near the top of the valence band to acquire energy and move to the conduction band.

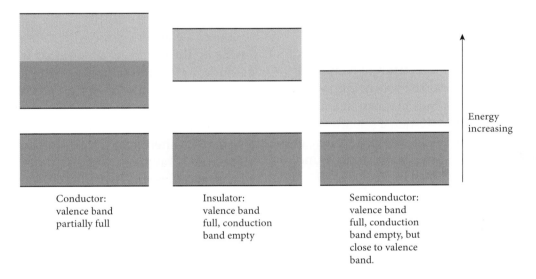

Figure 30.9

Variation of resistance with temperature

The resistance of metals increases slightly with temperature. This is because of an increase in the rate of collision between conduction electrons and the atoms of the crystal lattice (metals are crystalline).

However, intrinsic conductors show a large fall in resistance when the temperature is increased. This is because, with a rise in temperature, more electrons acquire sufficient energy to move from the valence band to the conduction band. This effect is much greater than the rate of collision effect. Thermistors are made of intrinsic semiconductor material and their resistance might fall from several hundreds

of ohms to a few tens of ohms over a temperature range from 200 °C to 20 °C, for example.

Variation of resistance with intensity of light

A light-dependent resistor (LDR) functions in a similar way. When an LDR is illuminated, the energy of the photons can enable electrons to move from the valence band to the conduction band. As the intensity of illumination increases, so more electrons reach the conduction band and the resistance of this intrinsic semiconductor device might decrease from a few kilo ohms in the dark to less than a hundred ohms in sunlight.

Absorption spectra

The reverse situation from that just described for emission spectra can be seen in the spectrum of the Sun. As the Sun is a hot body with a mixture of many different hot gases, liquids and solids, it emits all frequencies and therefore a continuous spectrum stretching across the whole range from infra-red to ultra violet and visible to the naked eye from deep red to deep violet. When this spectrum is observed, it is found to be crossed by hundreds of lines that are darker than the background. These dark lines are called an absorption spectrum. They are the reverse process to an emission spectrum. Light from the Sun has to pass through its own atmosphere, which is much cooler than its surface. Some gas atoms in the atmosphere absorb photons that happen to fit their energy pattern, so less of that particular energy arrives at the Earth.

One particularly interesting absorption spectral pattern in the Sun's spectrum is that which corresponds to the emission spectrum of helium. It is interesting because that was the way helium was discovered. 'Helium' means 'Sun' element. It was discovered on the Sun first and then a scientist found it, as a small percentage of the Earth's atmosphere and since, it has been found in some deep underground caves in greater concentrations.

The production and use of X-rays

Introduction

When Röntgen discovered X-rays in 1895 he immediately realised their importance in medical diagnosis. The X-ray of his wife's hand clearly showing the bones was the first medical X-ray ever taken. It has been followed by untold millions of X-rays since that time. Until X-rays were available to surgeons they often had impossible tasks, particularly in war time. They might have been able to see a wound where a bullet had entered someone's body, but that was not necessarily where the bullet was lodged. A surgeon cannot dig around inside someone hoping to come across a bullet.

They simply had to guess where it was, and often they were wrong. X-rays made this sort of diagnosis straightforward because it is a form of remote sensing. It was non-invasive.

The production of X-rays

X-rays are high energy electromagnetic waves. Their frequency is higher than that of ultra-violet radiation and has the same frequency as that of some gamma (γ) rays. The difference between X-rays and gamma rays is that X-rays are generated when electrons lose energy whereas gamma rays are generated from the nucleus of an atom when it undergoes radioactive decay.

In order to produce X-rays it is necessary to use a stream of high energy electrons and allow them to strike a metal target. A modern X-ray tube is illustrated in Figure 30.10.

It uses a glass envelope with a very high vacuum inside it. The electrons are emitted from a heated cathode, in just the same way that electrons are emitted from a cathode in the cathode ray tube of an oscilloscope. These electrons are then accelerated by a very high voltage. An oscilloscope might use a potential difference of 1500 V to accelerate its electrons. X-ray tubes will often use 100 times this potential difference. A dentist's X-ray tube typically will use a p.d. of 85 kV. A tube producing hard (that is energetic) X-rays might have a p.d. of a million or more volts.

The electrons are focussed by the shape of the cathode on to the metal anode to give nearly a point source of X-rays. The power of the emitted X-rays is often only about 1% of the power of the accelerated electrons, so the anode would melt with the power supplied by the electrons were it not cooled with a coolant passing through a tube inside the anode.

The **intensity** of an X-ray beam is the total power per unit area. This is determined by the power supplied to the electrons. The **hardness** of the beam is controlled by the p.d. between the anode and the cathode.

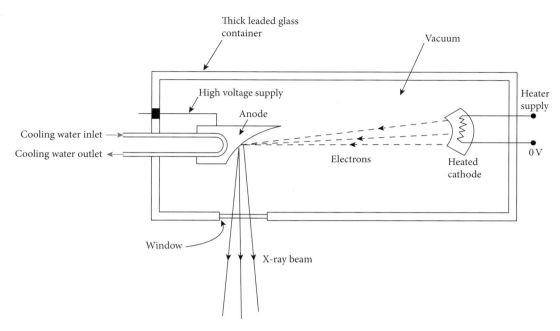

Figure 30.10 A modern X-ray tube

The use of X-rays

The advantage of using a point source of X-rays is that a sharp shadow is produced. In the same way that light from a fluorescent tube produces a very fuzzy shadow, but light from a lamp with a small filament produces a sharp shadow. This is illustrated for X-rays in Figure 30.11 in which (a) shows the shadow from a point source and (b) from an extended source.

If an extended source were used then small detail on the photographic film can easily be lost altogether. An X-ray image of this type is not really a photograph at all. It is just a shadow.

Another problem with X-rays used this way is contrast. When an X-ray passes through any material its intensity decreases as a result of absorption. The beam is said to be attenuated. The intensity I of an X-ray beam is the power per unit area and is given by the equation

$$I = I_0 e^{-\mu x}$$

where I_0 is the initial intensity, e indicates an exponential function, μ is called the attenuation coefficient and x is the thickness of the material. An example in the use of this equation is given in Chapter 21. The value of μ does depend on the voltage used in generating the X-rays. A typical value for bone is $600\,\text{m}^{-1}$.

Unfortunately the corresponding values of μ for different organs of the body, such as kidneys, liver, heart are all about $100\,\text{m}^{-1}$ so there is no way that a shadow image can distinguish between different soft tissue unless some contrast medium is used. A barium meal can be used to cause the intestines to absorb X-rays and hence make them appear white on the black X-ray photograph. Injections of iodine compounds into an artery can be used to enhance the image of other organs, such as the brain.

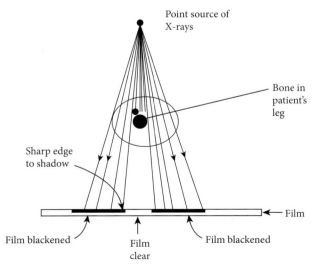

Figure 30.11 (a) A point source of X-rays produces a sharp X-ray image on film.

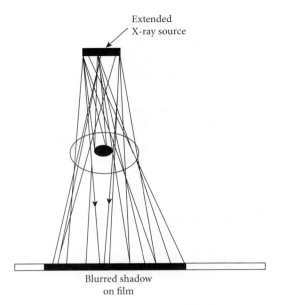

Figure 30.11 (b) An extended source of X-rays would give a blurred image.

X-rays, like all high energy radiation, are dangerous to living tissue. Carefully controlled doses of intense, hard X-rays are used for cancer treatment, and routine X-rays are carefully monitored to reduce radiation hazard. One way that this problem is minimised is by having more sensitive X-ray sensors.

Photographic film that is more sensitive means that the X-ray dose can be reduced. In hospital X-ray departments, there is now increasing use of a very sensitive fluorescent plate instead of film. This can be connected to a digital display. Another way of reducing exposure is by using various filters. A thin metal plate for the X-rays to travel through before entering the patient can, for example, absorb the low energy X-rays that would not have contributed to forming the image in any case because they would have been absorbed by the body.

Until the advent of linking up X-ray images with computers these shadow images were all that was available. Now there are a whole range of different approaches capable of producing images that are sharp, are in false colour, are of specific organs, and are able to compare two images and highlight any differences. One of these techniques is described in the next section.

Computed tomography (CT) scan

CT scans use X-rays to give outstanding images of any section through the body, as shown in Figure 30.12.

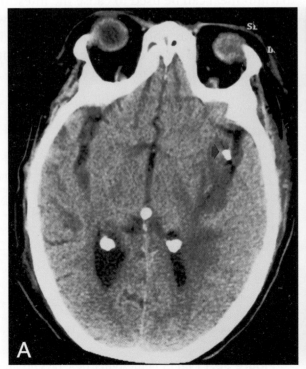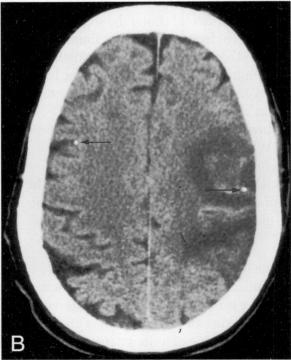

Figure 30.12 CT scans of the head of a patient.

To obtain such images a patient is placed in the centre of a stationary ring of 720 X-ray detectors, as shown in Figures 30.13 (a) and (b).

The X-rays themselves come from a point source in the X-ray tube and screening is used to give a thin fan-shaped beam. The X-ray tube rotates around the patient and after one complete revolution it moves approximately one centimetre along the patient. It will continue to rotate until the whole of the organ being examined has had X-rays passed through it. A complete scan of a head, for example, would take about 25 revolutions of the X-ray tube. As the X-rays are received by the detectors, data from them is passed to a computer for processing and then to give an image of a slice through the patient on a monitor. The image is a digital image and the doctor can adjust the magnification of the image produced. When too much magnification is asked for, the image will be seen to be digital.

The computer creates a three-dimensional image of any part of the body, involving a system using computed tomography or CT scanning. As the X-ray tube moves around the patient, the narrow beam of X-rays passes through the part of the patient being examined from different directions. Consider a patient with a brain injury. The affected part of the brain is a three-dimensional object and the doctor needs to know exactly the extent and type of damage to the brain. A CT scan uses a process in which the brain is divided into small imaginary cubes called voxels. A few of these voxels are illustrated in Fig. 30.13(c). As the narrow beam of X-rays goes round the patient it will meet, from different directions, every group of 8 voxels in a cube. Programs within the computer add all the X-rays transmitted through any one of the eight voxels, so that the screen image is built up using the density of each voxel. The doctor is able to choose to see any slice through the three-dimensional image held as data on the computer. Any colour required on the screen, to improve the image, has to be added artificially.

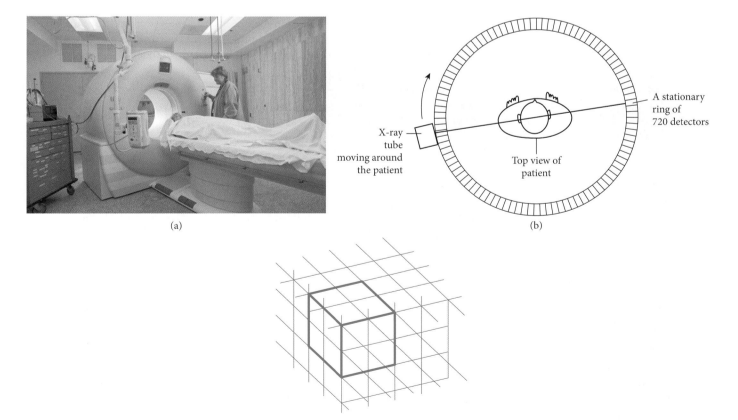

Figure 30.13 (a) A patient being given a CT scan (b) Top view of patient in a CT scanner (c) Representation of voxels in a cube

Chapter Summary

✓ Energy is quantised. The smallest packet of light energy is called a photon.

✓ A photon of frequency f has energy E given by $E = hf$ where h is called the Planck constant and has the value 6.626×10^{-34} J s.

✓ A photon of sufficient energy may liberate an electron from a metal. This energy, which is different for different metals, is called the work function of the metal.

✓ The threshold frequency, f_0, is the lowest frequency to cause an electron to be emitted. The energy ϕ of a photon of this frequency is hf_0. Putting all this together gives

$$hf = \phi + \frac{1}{2}m_e v^2_{max}$$

✓ The de Broglie equation for the wavelength λ of a particle of mass m travelling with speed v is $\lambda = h/mv$.

✓ The quantisation of energy results in electrons in an atom having certain exact energies. This causes line spectra.

✓ Band theory can be used to explain how thermistors and light-dependent resistors work.

✓ X-rays are highly energetic electromagnetic waves with frequency higher than that of ultra-violet radiation and possess the same frequency as possessed by gamma rays.

✓ The digital image obtained by CT scan is an image of slice through the patient on a monitor.

Progress Check

30.1 (a) Determine the energy of a photon of visible light with a wavelength of 550 nanometres. Quote your answer in both joules and electron volts.

   (b) Approximately how many photons are emitted per second by a lamp emitting 10 W of power at this wavelength?

30.2 (a) State what is meant by the term *threshold frequency* with respect to the photoelectric effect.

   (b) The threshold frequency for zinc is 1.01×10^{15} Hz. Explain why photoelectric emission is not possible for zinc illuminated, however brightly, with visible light.

   (c) The photoelectric effect is possible for zinc provided ultra-violet light is used. Explain why this is so, even if the light source is very dim.

   (d) Calculate the maximum possible speed of photoelectrons from a zinc surface when illuminated with ultra-violet light of frequency 1.83×10^{15} Hz.

30.3 Use Figure 30.4 to find

   (a) Planck constant h,

   (b) the stopping potential for magnesium at two different frequencies of UV radiation,

   (c) The work function of silver in eV and in J.

30.4 Calculate:

   (a) the speed of an electron after it has been accelerated in a vacuum by a potential difference of 50.0 kV,

   (b) the momentum of the electron after its acceleration,

   (c) the wavelength of this electron using the de Broglie relation.

30.5 Explain why a photograph of the spectrum of the Sun is crossed by many dark lines.

30.6 The energy levels for electrons in the hydrogen atom are given by the empirical equation

$$E_n = -\frac{13.6}{n^2} \text{ eV}$$

where n is a number of the energy level.

   For example, the lowest energy state, the ground state is level $n = 1$. In this state an electron has energy −13.6 electron volts compared with a free electron.

Tabulate the energy levels for $n = 2, 3, 4$ and 5 and then calculate

   (a) the energy released by an electron falling from level 5 to level 3,

   (b) the frequency of the light emitted by an electron falling from level 4 to level 2.

   (c) In what region of the electromagnetic spectrum would radiation be emitted by any electron falling to the ground state?

30.7 The following electrical supplies are available for production of X-rays from different X-ray tubes.

   A A p.d. of 160 kV between the cathode and the anode and a beam current of 4.3 mA.

   B A p.d. of 80 kV between the cathode and the anode and a beam current of 7.2 mA.

   C A p.d. of 120 kV between the cathode and the anode and a beam current of 6.8 mA.

   D A p.d. of 260 kV between the cathode and the anode and a beam current of 3.2 mA.

Explain which X-ray tube,

   (a) produces the hardest X-rays?

   (b) produces X-rays of the highest intensity?

   (c) might well be used in a dental surgery?

   (d) has a beam power of 688 W?

Nuclear Physics: Part B

Energy and mass

It was established at the end of the 19th century that the speed of light is constant. If you move away from a beam of light it approaches you at the same speed as it would if you were moving towards it. The speed of light does not depend on the speed of the light source or the speed of the observer. This means that nothing can ever overtake light.

This has important consequences. If a particle in an accelerator is travelling at near the speed of light and it is given some energy it goes faster, but the faster it goes the more difficult it is to make it go even faster, because it cannot ever go as fast as the speed of light. The fact that it is more and more difficult to accelerate as it nears the speed of light implies that its mass is increasing. The relationship between the extra mass and the extra energy has probably led to the best known and least understood equation of all time.

$$E = mc^2$$

where E is the energy equivalent of mass m and c is the velocity of light. This well-known equation is better written as $\Delta E = c^2 \Delta m$ where Δm is the increase in mass when an amount of energy ΔE is supplied.

Nuclear binding energy

Mass and energy considerations are essential when the mass of any nucleus is measured because the mass of a nucleus is not the sum of the masses of the protons and neutrons of which it is made. Take, for example a single nucleus of sulfur-32. This nucleus has an atomic number of 16 and, therefore, consists of

16 protons each of mass
1.00783 u, so total mass   = 16.12528 u,

16 neutrons each of
mass 1.00867 u, so total mass   = 16.13872 u

Mass of the individual particles
making up the nucleus   = 32.26400 u

Mass of the whole nucleus   = 31.96329 u

The difference between these two figures is called the nuclear **mass defect**. The mass of a whole nucleus is invariably less than the mass of the individual particles. For a single nucleus of sulfur-32 the mass defect is 0.30071 u.

Using the relationship between energy and mass, we can calculate the energy equivalent of this mass defect.

$$E = mc^2 = 0.30071 \, \text{u} \times 1.66043 \times 10^{-27} \, \text{kg u}^{-1}$$
$$\times \, (2.9979 \times 10^8 \, \text{m s}^{-1})^2$$
$$= 4.48748 \times 10^{-11} \, \text{J}.$$

This can be converted into electron volts by dividing it by 1.60219×10^{-19} to get

$$2.80084 \times 10^8 \, \text{eV} = 280.084 \, \text{MeV}.$$

This energy equivalent for any nucleus is called the nuclear **binding energy**.

The binding energy for the sulfur-32 nucleus is, therefore, 280 MeV to 3 significant figures. This is *not* the energy of the nucleus. It is the energy required to separate the nucleus into its constituent particles.

Teacher's Tip

This kind of calculation is full of opportunity for making careless mistakes. There are many different units involved and great care is needed to get things correct. There is usually no need to use as many significant figures as has been used here, but you do need to work with 5 significant figures when calculating mass defect, because the calculation involves subtracting two nearly equal numbers. Once you have the mass defect, 3 significant figures is usually enough.

In order to check the answers you get with these problems, it is worthwhile remembering the following fact.

$1.0000\,u = 1.66043 \times 10^{-27}\,kg$ so the mass of any atom will be very small.

$1.66043 \times 10^{-27}\,kg$ has an energy equivalence of

$E = mc^2 = 1.66043 \times 10^{-27} \times (2.9979 \times 10^8)^2$
$= 1.4923 \times 10^{-10}\,J$
$= 1.4923 \times 10^{-10} \div 1.6022 \times 10^{-19} = 9.3140 \times 10^8\,eV$

So **1.00 u is equivalent to 931 MeV** to 3 significant figures.

To sum up, you should expect masses in unified mass constant u, to be between 0.00055 u for an electron and 250 u for massive atoms, binding energies measured in MeV, to be between a few MeV up to several hundred MeV.

If you look critically at your own answers, including the units, you should spot your own mistakes. If you ignore answers such as *mass of nucleus = 235 kg* you will make significant mistakes!

Variation of binding energy with nucleon number

In general, as the nucleon number of a nucleus increases, the binding energy also increases. In order to obtain some idea of the stability of a nucleus, it is more useful to know the binding energy per nucleon.

$$\text{Binding energy per nucleon} = \frac{\text{binding energy of nucleus}}{\text{nucleon number}}$$
$$= \frac{E}{A}$$

For the sulfur nucleus described above, the binding energy per nucleon is

$$280\,MeV \div 32\,\text{nucleons} = 8.75\,MeV.$$

When a graph of energy per nucleon is plotted for all the different isotopes for all the elements it has the shape shown in Figure 31.1.

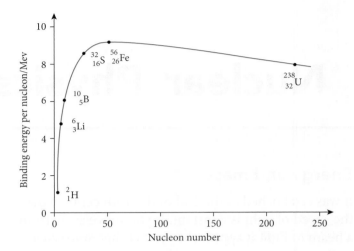

Figure 31.1

A few sample nucleons are named on the graph which shows that nuclei close to the iron nucleus Fe-56 are the most stable. That is, an iron-56 nucleus requires most energy to separate it into individual protons and neutrons. The graph also indicates that if a high nucleon number nucleus could be split into two smaller nuclei then energy would be released. This is **nuclear fission** and is the process used in all nuclear power stations. Energy would also be released if two small nuclei could be combined into a larger nucleus. This is the process of **nuclear fusion**. Nuclear fusion is the source of the Sun's almost inexhaustible supply of energy. It is the hope for the future in power stations on the Earth as no radioactive by-products are produced by it and the heavy hydrogen atoms, hydrogen-2, are in abundance even though they only make up 0.015% of all the hydrogen atoms in sea water. Unfortunately fusion only occurs at very high temperatures and at present only experimental fusion reactors exist. A new, large scale, fusion prototype plant is being built in France at a cost estimated to be $10 billion with cooperation from Europe, the USA, Russia, China, Japan and other countries. It should run for 35 years and will maintain a sustained fusion reaction by containing the hydrogen-2 nuclei at temperatures as high as 100 000 000 °C and held in strong magnetic fields since no solid substance could exist at that temperature.

Nuclear fission

Nuclear fission has been used in nuclear power stations since the 1950s. All of the commercial nuclear reactors depend on the use of uranium. Uranium has two relatively stable isotopes, uranium-235 and uranium-238. Uranium-235 will undergo fission if bombarded with slow neutrons. The nuclear reaction is as follows.

$$^{235}_{92}\text{U} + {}^{1}_{0}\text{n} \rightarrow {}^{236}_{92}\text{U} \rightarrow {}^{90}_{38}\text{Sr} + {}^{143}_{54}\text{Xe} + 3\,{}^{1}_{0}\text{n} + E$$

The energy E released in this reaction is about 200 MeV. This compares with just a few electron-volts from burning a single carbon atom in a coal-fired power station. The energy is released in a nuclear power station as gamma radiation and in the kinetic energy of the fission products, particularly the neutrons. The gamma radiation is absorbed by the materials of the reactor and its very thick concrete walls. In one type of reactor, the neutrons escape into a carbon moderator where their kinetic energy is lost. The Moderator's temperature would rise but circulating carbon dioxide gas extracts thermal energy and provides the power for the generating turbines. Some of these slow neutrons later re-enter the uranium fuel to maintain the chain reaction. Boron is an element that absorbs neutrons, so boron rods are placed in special channels in a reactor. By raising or lowering the rods, the energy output rate of the reactor can be controlled. In an emergency, all the boron rods will drop down in the channels and this will shut down the reactor.

Activity and half-life

As was explained in Chapter 14, radioactivity is spontaneous and random. Nothing associated with the atom affects it as it is essentially a nuclear phenomenon. If you place a piece of uranium in front of a Geiger counter, the uranium nuclei may have spent more than four billion years on the Earth totally unchanged, and then suddenly several of them will emit alpha particles. No one knows why or what causes the emission. The only way of understanding the mathematics of radioactivity is to use a statistical method. The one thing that is known is that the more uranium there is, the greater will be the number of emissions per unit time.

The number of decays per unit time is called the **activity A**. Activity is measured in becquerels, symbol Bq. One becquerel is one count per second.

For a radioactive substance containing N atoms, the activity A is proportional to N.

$$\text{i.e. } A \propto N \quad \text{so} \quad A = \lambda N$$

where λ is called the **decay constant**.

The decay constant is a probability. If it has a value of 1.0×10^{-6}, that is a millionth, it tells you that during the next second, one in every million nuclei will probably decay.

Using this definition enables a theoretical graph to be drawn plotting N against time as shown in Figure 31.2. As N decreases the gradient of the graph will also decrease; e.g. when N has fallen to half its original value, the gradient will be half its original value also.

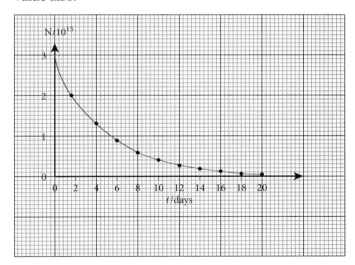

Figure 31.2

This graph is an exponential graph. The equation of the graph is of the form

$$x = x_0 e^{-\lambda t}$$

where x may be N or A or any fraction of A that is being detected by a measuring instrument. It, therefore, gives you three possible equations:

$$N = N_0 e^{-\lambda t}$$
$$A = A_0 e^{-\lambda t}$$

$C = C_0 e^{-\lambda t}$ where C is a count rate on an instrument.

The equation $x = x_0 e^{-\lambda t}$ may be given in the data on any exam paper so you need to be able to use a calculator correctly with the e^x button.

Example 1

A radioactive source has a decay constant of $3.87 \times 10^{-12}\,\text{s}^{-1}$ and an activity of 480 Bq. Determine the length of time it will take for the count to fall to 240 Bq.

Answer Use $A = A_0 e^{-\lambda t}$ and start by taking natural logarithms of the equation.

This gives $\ln A = \ln A_0 - \lambda t$ and hence
$\ln 240 = \ln 480 - 3.87 \times 10^{-12} \times t$
So, $5.4806 = 6.1738 - 3.87 \times 10^{-12} \times t$
Simplifying gives $\qquad 0.6932 = 3.87 \times 10^{-12} \times t$
and $\qquad t = 0.6932 \div 3.87 \times 10^{-12} = 1.79 \times 10^{11}\,\text{s}$

This works out to be 5670 years. It gives a good idea of just how many atoms there are in even a small amount of anything. This is a source providing between 480 and 240 decays per second and it can do this for 5670 years.

Half-life

The example just given has found the time it takes for a decay rate to fall from 480 Bq to 240 Bq. This is a reduction in activity by a factor of two. The calculation, in fact, has worked out the half-life of the substance.

Half-life ($t_{1/2}$) is the time taken for activity to fall to half its original value.

Working in half-lives the decay rate will fall in the following way:

Number of half-lives	0	1	2	3	4	5	6
Activity	A_0	$\frac{A_0}{2}$	$\frac{A_0}{4}$	$\frac{A_0}{8}$	$\frac{A_0}{16}$	$\frac{A_0}{32}$	$\frac{A_0}{64}$

For calculations involving anything other than whole numbers of half-lives the basic equation need to be used.

Since $A = A_0 e^{-\lambda t}$ and for one half-life $A = \frac{1}{2} A_0$

so $\frac{1}{2} = e^{-\lambda t}$ and by taking natural logs $\ln \frac{1}{2} = -\lambda t$

Since $\ln \frac{1}{2} = -0.693$ this gives the relationship between decay constant and half-life as

$$\lambda = \frac{0.693}{t_{\frac{1}{2}}}$$

This is another equation that you may need to use when answering questions.

Example 2

A radioactive source of cobalt-60 is used in a hospital for radiation treatment. It has a half-life of 5.3 years. The source, when first used at the hospital, requires that a patient is treated for 11 minutes. For how long can the source be used if the maximum time for treatment is not to exceed 20 minutes?

Answer For a half-life of 5.3 years the value of the decay constant λ

$$= 0.693/5.3 = 0.1308 \text{ year}^{-1}$$

(Note that this has not been converted to seconds. This is fine as long as all times are kept in years. If you have any doubt about this, conversion of every time into seconds is easy to do, it will give the same answer.)

If the same total dose is supplied in 11 minutes at the start and takes 20 minutes at the end of its use, then the activity must have fallen at the end to 11/20 of its initial value.

So if A_0 is the activity at the start then the activity A at the end is $0.55\,A_0$.

Substituting into the equation $A = A_0 e^{-\lambda t}$ gives

$0.55 = e^{-\lambda t}$ and hence
$\ln 0.55 = -0.1308 \times t = -0.5978$
and hence $t = 0.5978 \div 0.1308 = 4.57$ years.

In order to get as many patients treated in a day, hospitals that used this system often used to obtain new sources more quickly than this. The problem indicates one difficulty with radiation from a radioactive source. It is common now to use very high energy X-rays (at the same frequency as the previously used gamma rays) so that there is a constant, and more controllable, rate of irradiation.

Chapter Summary

✓ The difference in mass between the mass of an atom and the larger, total mass of its proton, neutrons and electrons is called the mass defect of the atom. The energy equivalent of the mass defect is called the binding energy.

✓ The activity of a radioactive source is the number of decays per unit time.

✓ The decay constant λ is the ratio of the activity A to the number N of atoms present.

$$\lambda = A/N$$

✓ The decay equation can be written in terms of number N of atoms remaining undecayed or in terms of the activity A

$$N = N_0 e^{-\lambda t} \qquad A = A_0 e^{-\lambda t}$$

✓ The relationship between decay constant and half-life is

$$\lambda = \frac{0.693}{t_{\frac{1}{2}}}$$

Progress Check

31.1 The energy radiated by the Sun every second is 3.9×10^{26} J. Calculate the loss of mass of the Sun in one second.

31.2 Two deuterons, of mass 2.0141 u combine to form one helium atom of mass 4.0066 u in a fusion process. Calculate
  (a) the loss of mass in unified mass units,
  (b) the loss of mass in kilograms,
  (c) the energy released in the fusion process.

31.3 Radioactive nuclei very often decay into other radioactive nuclei, called daughter products. Consider radioactive element A decaying into radioactive daughter product B that decays into a stable nucleus C. Starting with N radioactive nuclei of element A and zero nuclei of elements B and C, sketch using the same axes for all three graphs, the shape of number of nuclei against time graphs for elements A, B and C.

Now answer these supplementary questions, and then check your sketches.
  (a) What is the total number of nuclei A, B and C at all times?
  (b) How do the graphs of the numbers of nuclei of A, B and C finish, after an infinitely long time?

31.4 Calculate the activity of a kilogram of uranium-238. The decay constant of uranium-238 is $4.88 \times 10^{-18}\,\text{s}^{-1}$.

31.5 A radioactive nuclide of cadmium, nucleon number 115 and proton number 48, decays by beta emission with a half life of 43 days.
  (a) Write a nuclear equation for this decay.
  (b) Calculate the decay constant λ of this nuclide.
  (c) Use the equation $N = N_0 \exp(-\lambda t)$ to determine the time it takes for the number of radioactive nuclei to fall to 1/2000 of its initial value.

Examination Questions XIII

1. Some data for the work function energy Φ and the threshold frequency f_0 of some metal surfaces are given in Figure 1.

metal	Φ / 10^{-19} J	f_0 / 10^{14} Hz
sodium	3.8	5.8
zinc	5.8	8.8
platinum	9.0	

Figure 1

  (a) (i) State what is meant by the *threshold frequency*. [2]
      (ii) Calculate the threshold frequency, in Hz, for platinum. [2]

  (b) Electromagnetic radiation having a continuous spectrum of wavelengths between 300 nm and 600 nm is incident, in turn, on each of the metals listed in Figure 1. Determine which metals, if any, will give rise to the emission of electrons. [2]

(c) When light of a particular intensity and frequency is incident on a metal surface, electrons are emitted. State and explain the effect, if any, on the rate of emission of electrons from this surface for light of the same intensity and higher frequency. [3]

(Cambridge International AS and A Level Physics 9702 Paper 41 Question 7 May/June 2013)

2. (a) (i) State what is meant by the *decay constant* of a radioactive isotope. [2]

(ii) Show that the decay constant λ and the half-life $t_{\frac{1}{2}}$ of an isotope are related by the expression

$$\lambda t_{\frac{1}{2}} = 0.693.$$ [3]

(b) In order to determine the half-life of a sample of a radioactive isotope, a student measures the count rate near to the sample, as illustrated in Figure 2.

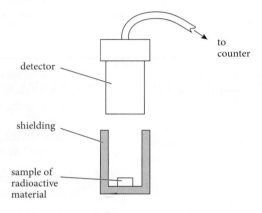

Figure 2

Initially, the measured count rate is 538 per minute. After a time of 8.0 hours, the measured count rate is 228 per minute.
Use these data to estimate the half-life of the isotope, in hours. [3]

(c) The accepted value of the half-life of the isotope in **(b)** is 5.8 hours.
The difference between this value for the half-life and that calculated in **(b)** cannot be explained by reference to faulty equipment.
Suggest two possible reasons for this difference. [2]

(Cambridge International AS and A Level Physics 9702 Paper 41 Question 9 May/June 2012)

3. Two deuterium $\left(^{2}_{1}\text{H}\right)$ nuclei are travelling directly towards one another. When their separation is large compared with their diameters, they each have speed v as illustrated in Figure 3.

Figure 3

The diameter of a deuterium nucleus is 1.1×10^{-14} m.

(a) Use energy considerations to show that the initial speed v of the deuterium nuclei must be approximately 2.5×10^{6} m s^{-1} in order that they may come into contact. Explain your working. [3]

(b) For a fusion reaction to occur, the deuterium nuclei must come into contact.
Assuming that deuterium behaves as an ideal gas, deduce a value for the temperature of the deuterium, in K, such that the nuclei have an r.m.s. speed equal to the speed calculated in **(a)**. [4]

(c) Comment on your answer to **(b)**. [1]

(Cambridge International AS and A Level Physics 9702 Paper 04 Question 5 October/November 2008)

4. (a) State what is meant by *nuclear binding energy*.   [2]

(b) The variation with nucleon number A of the binding energy per nucleon B_E is shown in Figure 4.

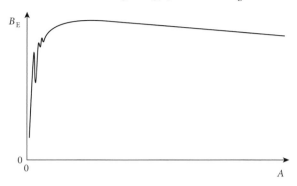

Figure 4

When uranium-235 ($^{235}_{92}$U) absorbs a slow-moving neutron, one possible nuclear reaction is

$$^{235}_{92}U + {}^{1}_{0}n \rightarrow {}^{95}_{42}Mo + {}^{139}_{57}La + 2{}^{1}_{0}n + 7{}^{0}_{-1}\beta + \text{energy}.$$

(i) State the name of this type of nuclear reaction.   [1]

(ii) On Figure 4, mark the position of

1. the uranium-235 nucleus (label this position U),   [1]
2. the molybdenum-95 ($^{95}_{42}$Mo) nucleus (label this position Mo),   [1]
3. the lanthanum-139 ($^{139}_{57}$La) nucleus (label this position La).   [1]

(iii) The masses of some particles and nuclei are given in Figure 5.

	mass / u
β-particle	5.5×10^{-4}
neutron	1.009
proton	1.007
uranium-235	235.123
molybdenum-95	94.945
lanthanum-139	138.955

Figure 5

Calculate, for this reaction,

1. the change, in u, of the rest mass,   [2]
2. the energy released, in MeV, to three significant figures.   [3]

(Cambridge International AS and A Level Physics 9702 Paper 42 Question 8 October/November 2013)

5. (a) State what is meant by a *photon*.   [2]

(b) It has been observed that, where photoelectric emission of electrons takes place, there is negligible time delay between illumination of the surface and emission of an electron.
State three other pieces of evidence provided by the photoelectric effect for the particulate nature of electromagnetic radiation.   [3]

(c) The work function of a metal surface is 3.5 eV. Light of wavelength 450 nm is incident on the surface.
Determine whether electrons will be emitted, by the photoelectric effect, from the surface.   [3]

(Cambridge International AS and A Level Physics 9702 Paper 42 Question 8 October/November 2012)

Appendix A

Aim: Appendix A provides you quick tips on how to prepare for an examination.

Basic Knowledge

There are some details that are the building blocks of any physics course. These facts must not just be remembered, they must be almost instinctive. So much so that the chance of you getting them wrong is almost inconceivable, however they are required. The following list is given in a definite order as later terms in the list depend on earlier ones. All of these quantities have a corresponding SI unit. The six base units you will need are:

Time	second (s)
Length	metre (m)
Mass	kilogram (kg)
Electric current	ampere (A)
Temperature	kelvin (K)
Amount of substance	mole (mol)

All the other quantities and units you will require are derived from these. The following lists provide a quick check.

Quantities	Corresponding unit
area = length × breadth	m^2
volume = length × breadth × depth	m^3
density = mass per unit volume	$kg\,m^{-3}$
frequency = oscillations per unit time	hertz Hz
velocity = distance per unit time with direction stated	$m\,s^{-1}$
acceleration = increase in velocity per unit time	$m\,s^{-2}$
momentum = mass × velocity	$kg\,m\,s^{-1}$ $(= N\,s)$
force = mass × acceleration = rate of change of momentum	newton N
work and energy = force × displacement	joule J $(= N\,m)$
power = work done per unit time	watt W
pressure = force per unit area	pascal Pa
charge = current × time	coulomb C
potential difference = energy per unit charge	volt V
resistance = potential difference per unit current	ohm Ω
capacitance = charge per unit potential difference	farad F
electric field strength = force per unit charge	$N\,C^{-1}$
magnetic flux density = force per unit current in wire of unit length	tesla T
magnetic flux = magnetic flux density × area	weber Wb
activity = radioactive decays per unit time	becquerel Bq

Powers of ten

Far too many marks are lost by students in tests and examinations as a result of using incorrect prefixes for powers of ten. The following list states the value of these prefixes. Note that capital letters usually apply to values greater than 1 and small letters for values less than 1. The k as in kg is an exception to this rule

				centi	c	0.01
				deci	d	0.1
kilo	k	1000		milli	m	0.001
mega	M	1 000 000	10^6	micro	μ	10^{-6}
giga	G	10^9		nano	n	10^{-9}
tera	T	10^{12}		pico	p	10^{-12}

Data and Formulae you are given

In tests and examinations, you might be given a list of numerical values which you will need to use in answering questions. You should use this data to the number of significant figures quoted. Note that g, the acceleration of free fall is usually given as $9.81\,\mathrm{m\,s^{-2}}$. In Appendix B you will find a list of useful equations. Make sure that you know what all the symbols stand for.

Examination Revision

This book covers the whole Cambridge International AS and A Level Physics Syllabus. Chapters 1 to 13 cover AS level topics and Chapters 14 to 31 cover the rest of the full A level. Since each chapter usually covers all the work in one section of the syllabus it makes sense to revise a chapter at a time. At the end of each chapter there are some straightforward questions. You should be able to read the chapter and answer the questions within an hour. There is usually no point in spending more time than this in one sitting as concentration will fall after this length of time. No doubt some of the chapters contain more familiar work to you than others. In that case you may well be able to cover two chapters of familiar material within an hour. In all periods of study the aim should be understanding and not memorising. Do not just read chapters. Have pen and paper to hand and work through theoretical parts and the questions.

In Tests and Examinations

Accuracy is crucially important here. The elimination of careless mistakes is essential. Powers of ten, calculator mistakes, algebra mistakes and sloppy writing often result in loss of marks. Many mistakes can be eliminated by three changes to your habits. These are –

1. Use more words in answering numerical questions. Words give more meaning to a problem; it becomes less mechanical.
2. Use one line for one idea. Do not string lots of different ideas altogether. Many students use the equals (=) sign as if it were " Now I know this I can go on to find something else". In this case it does not mean equals at all. The following shows an example of what NOT to do.

$$\text{``}F = 15 \times 9.8 = 147 = P = 147/3 = 49$$
$$area = 49 \times 0.0004 = 0.0196\text{''}$$

This would be much more meaningful and give less opportunity of making a mistake written as

$$force = m \times g = 15 \times 9.8 = 147\,\mathrm{N}$$
$$pressure = force/area = 147/3 = 49\,\mathrm{N\,m^{-2}}$$

This pressure on an area of $4\,\mathrm{cm^2}$ causes a force of $49\,\mathrm{N\,m^{-2}} \times 0.0004\,\mathrm{m^2} = 0.0196\,\mathrm{N}$

Keep one idea on one line and it is always worthwhile starting on the extreme left-hand edge of the space provided for the answer. If you do spot a mistake you will have space available for corrections.

3. Look critically at every answer you write. In the above example you might still suspect that something has gone wrong. A force of 147 N on a large area of 3 square metres seems unlikely, perhaps it said 3 square centimetres. Atmospheric pressure is 100 000 Pa! If an answer you have is not realistic then you must have made a mistake somewhere. Many powers of ten errors can be quickly eliminated if they are noticed. At one stage in writing this book I wrote in Question 17.3 that the

volume of a helium atom was $3 \times 10^{30}\,\mathrm{m^3}$. It was when I was working out the answer that the omission of a minus sign had resulted in a mistake of enormous magnitude. It was incorrect by a factor of 10^{60}! I quickly inserted the required minus sign but if I had not thought about the meaning behind the figures I might have left the mistake in the book. I hope there are not too many mistakes that I have not noticed. Everyone taking or teaching a physics course makes mistakes. The sensible people look out for mistakes and do not work through problems without thinking about the size of the numbers they are given by their calculators.

4. Too many students answer numerical problems by "proportion". Proportion has its place in answering but it has many pitfalls. For example If a car doubles its speed from $20\,\mathrm{m\,s^{-1}}$ to $40\,\mathrm{m\,s^{-1}}$, its kinetic energy is **NOT** doubled. Because the speed has to be squared, the kinetic energy becomes four times its original value. The momentum is doubled, but only if the direction has not changed, because momentum is a vector. Proportion cannot be used directly when considering square roots, exponentials and logarithms.

Conclusion

You must keep checking the remaining time when sitting any test or examination paper. If you get stuck just ignore the question – but do make certain you leave a blank space on the answer grid or paper too. If there is spare time at the end go back to any missing answers then. At this stage, if you are still stuck, just guess. However, do adjust your answer to the number of marks available. Do not answer a 6 mark question with one line of writing and do not answer a 1 mark question with 10 lines of writing.

You are not writing in an examination as you might in your own notebook. You must therefore write clearly. Sketch diagrams will always enhance your work. They do not need to be drawn with a ruler but they can show many details that are difficult to put into words. Understanding of the subject always shows through in your answers so that should always be your aim when revising. If you have a good understanding of the basics of the subject you can be sure of a good result if you eliminate careless mistakes and explain what you mean clearly.

Appendix B

Aim: Appendix B provides you the list of physical quantities, their symbols, definitions, and equations to find them.

Quantity	Symbol	Definition	Equation
Mass	M or m	These three quantities are base quantities on which the SI system is built.	
Length	l or d		
Time	t		
Area	A	For a rectangle, the length multiplied by the breadth	$A = l \times b$
Volume	V	For a regular shape the length multiplied by the breadth multiplied by the height	$V = l \times b \times h$
Density	ρ	The mass per unit volume	$\rho = m/V$
Speed	v	The distance travelled per unit time	$v = d/t$
Velocity	v	The distance travelled per unit time in a stated direction	$v = d/t$
Acceleration	a	The rate of change of velocity	$a = \Delta v/t$
Momentum	p	Mass multiplied by velocity	$p = m \times v$
Force	F	The rate of change of momentum, this equates in most cases to the mass multiplied by the acceleration	$F = \Delta mv/t$ $F = ma$
Work	W	The force multiplied by the distance moved in the direction of the force	$W = Fd$
Energy	W or E	The stored ability to do work	$W = Fd$
Power	P	The rate of doing work	$P = W$
Pressure	p	The force per unit area	$p = F/A$

Quantity	Symbol	Definition	Equation
		Terms required for AS level	
Current	I	This is another base quantity	
Charge	q or Q	For a constant current I the charge is the product of current and time	$Q = It$
Potential difference, p.d.	V	The energy transformed from electrical energy into other forms of energy per unit charge	$V = W/Q$
Electromotive force, e.m.f.	E	The energy transformed from other forms of energy into electrical energy per unit charge	$E = W/Q$
Resistance	R	The potential difference across a component per unit current	$R = V/I$
Resistivity	ρ	For a material the product of the resistance of the material and its area of cross section, divided by its length	$\rho = RA/l$
Electric field strength	E	The force acting per unit positive charge placed at the point in the field	$E = F/Q$
		Additional terms required for A level	
Potential at a point	V	The work done in bringing unit positive charge from infinity to the point	$V = Q/4\pi\varepsilon_0 r$
Potential gradient	E	The rate of change of potential with distance; it is equal numerically to the electric field	$E = -dV/dx$
Capacitance	C	The charge on a capacitor per unit potential difference	$C = Q/V$
Magnetic flux density	B	The force acting per unit current in a wire of unit length when at right angles to the field	$B = F/Il \sin\theta$
Magnetic flux	Φ	The product of the magnetic flux density and the area at right angles to the magnetic flux density	$\Phi = BA$
Magnetic flux linkage		The product of the magnetic flux and the number of turns of a coil through which the flux is passing	$n\Phi$
R.M.S. current	I_{rms}	The d.c. current that has the same heating effect as an a.c. current	$I_{rms} = I_{peak}/\sqrt{2}$
Transformer turns ratio		The number of turns in the secondary divided by the number of turns in the primary $= V_s/V_p$ for an ideal transformer	

Appendix

C

Aim: Appendix C provides you the list of SI units, their symbols, and definitions.

Unit	Symbol	Definition	In base units
kilogram	kg		kg
metre	m	These quantities (kg, m and s) are the quantities on which the system is based. You do not need to know their definitions.	m
second	s		s
metre squared	m^2		m^2
metre cubed	m^3		m^3
kilogram per cubic metre	$kg\,m^{-3}$		$kg\,m^{-3}$
metre per second	$m\,s^{-1}$		$m\,s^{-1}$
metre per second each second	$m\,s^{-2}$		$m\,s^{-2}$
newton second	$N\,s$		$kg\,m\,s^{-1}$
newton	N	Force required to give a mass of one kilogram an acceleration of one metre per second each second	$kg\,m\,s^{-2}$
joule	J	Work done when a force of one newton moves an object one metre in the direction of the force	$kg\,m^2\,s^{-2}$
watt	W	One joule per second	$kg\,m^2\,s^{-3}$
pascal	Pa	One newton per square metre	$kg\,m^{-1}\,s^{-2}$

Unit	Symbol	Definition	In base units
		Units required for AS level	
Ampere	A	The base definition depends on the force on a wire carrying the current in a magnetic field	A
Coulomb	C	One coulomb is the charge delivered when a current of one ampere exists for one second	A s
Volt	V	One volt is one joule per coulomb	$kg\,m^2\,A^{-1}\,s^{-3}$
Electromotive force	E		$kg\,m^2\,A^{-1}\,s^{-3}$
Ohm	Ω	One ohm is one volt per ampere	$kg\,m^2\,A^{-2}\,s^{-3}$
Ohm metre	Ω m		$kg\,m^3\,A^{-1}\,s^{-3}$
Newton per coulomb	$N\,C^{-1}$		$kg\,m\,s^{-3}\,A$
		Additional units required for A level	
Volt per metre	$V\,m^{-1}$	Equivalent to newton per coulomb	$kg\,m\,A^{-1}\,s^{-3}$
Farad	F	One farad is one coulomb per volt	$kg^{-1}\,m^{-2}\,A^2\,s^{-4}$
Tesla	T	One tesla is the flux density if the force on a wire carrying a current of one ampere is one newton	$kg\,A^{-1}\,s^{-2}$
Weber	Wb	One weber is the flux when a flux density of one tesla exists over an area of one square metre	$kg\,A^{-1}\,s^{-2}\,m^2$

Appendix D

Answers to Progress Check questions

Chapter 1

1.1 (a) 2860 g   (b) 54.3 g   (c) 0.048 kg
      (d) 13 680 s   (e) 75.2 days

1.2 (a) 10 000 cm^2 (b) 7.38×10^6 cm^3 (c) 6.58×10^{-6} m^3
      (d) 3450 kg m^{-3} (e) 30.6 m s^{-1}

1.3 (a) kg m^2 s^{-2} (b) kg m^{-1} s^{-2} (c) kg m^2 s^{-2}

1.4 All of these are possible, but not necessarily correct; dimensionless quantities cannot be taken into account.

1.5 (a) between 1000 J and 2000 J
      (b) around 8 m s^{-1}
      (c) between 1 W and 10 W depending on the size of the bird
      (d) around 5 m s^{-1}
      (e) between 5 and 10 m s^{-2}
      (f) close to 1000 kg m^{-3}
      (g) 10^7 Pa

1.6 (a) This is far too low. It is meant to be 2 kW.
      (b) This is faster than the speed of light, so is impossible.
      (c) At this temperature, the water would be tepid. To be hot, the temperature is more likely to be about 60 °C.
      (d) Atmospheric pressure is about 100 000 Pa, so the pressure in a balloon must be higher than that.
      (e) This figure can be used to determine the weight of a racing car, but not to determine the force the driving wheels exert to accelerate the car. For an emergency stop in an ordinary car, the deceleration needs to be greater than (−) g.

1.7 5.0 units at an angle of 39° to vector A

1.8 36 m s^{-1} at 33.7°

1.9 (a) 2.36×10^6 s   (b) $1.53 \times 10^{-4°}$ (c) 2.7×10^{-3} m s^{-1}

1.10 weight = 640 N, horizontal force = 447 N

1.11 (a) horizontal 2.9 N, vertical 5.6 N
       (b) lift = 10.4 N, wind force = 2.9 N

Chapter 2

2.1 Graph of R against $1/d^2$ gives gradient of $(2.21 \pm 0.04) \times 10^{-8}$ Ω m^2.
$\rho = \pi R d^2/4l$ = gradient $\times \pi/4l = (2.21 \times 10^{-8} \times \pi)/(4 \times 1 \text{ m})$
= 1.74 Ω m
uncertainty of 2% gives $\rho = (1.74 \pm 0.04) \times 10^{-8}$ Ω m

2.2 (a) $(1.93 \pm 0.4) \times 10^{-3}$ m^3
      (b) $(2.44 \pm 0.06) \times 10^3$ kg m^{-3}

2.3 The uncertainty should be given for the final figure. For (a), (b) and (c) this should be quoted as $g = 9.8 \pm 0.3$ and for (d) and (e) $g = 9.8 \pm 0.4$.

Chapter 3

3.1 606 km and south 38° west

3.2 20 006 km at 4.3° south of east

3.3 0.44 m s^{-2}

3.4 4.5×10^{-10} s

3.5 2.8 s

3.6 (a) 11.7 m s^{-1} (b) 8.8 m

3.7 (a) 39.2 m s^{-1} (b) 78.4 m

3.8 (a) 30 s   (b) 50 s
      (c) 900 m, 1500 m   (d) 160 s

3.9 (a) 21 s   (b) 615 m

3.10 (a) (i) $0.530 = (u \times 0.197\,46) + \frac{1}{2} \times g \times (0.197\,46)^2$

          (ii) $1.060 = (u \times 0.321\,80) + \frac{1}{2} \times g \times (0.321\,80)^2$

      (b) numerical value is 9.809 90 m s^{-2}, but with distances only accurate to 3 significant figures (sig figs) the value should be rounded down to 9.81 m s^{-2}

Chapter 4

4.1 (a) 36.5 N   (b) mass = 698 kg, weight on Earth = 6840 N

4.2 (a) Mass: it is the quantity of bread that matters.
      (b) Weight: lifting is providing a force in the opposite direction to the weight.
      (c) Mass: determines how difficult it is to accelerate the car.
      (d) Mass: prices are based on the value shown on a mass balance.
      (e) Mass: because the deceleration depends on the force applied and the car's mass.
      (f) Weight: the force towards the Earth is the important factor.
      (g) Weight: the rock climber is raising his/her centre of gravity against gravity.

4.3 10^{-5}

4.4 (a)

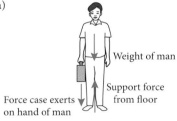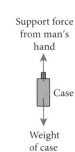

      (b)

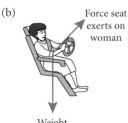

(c)

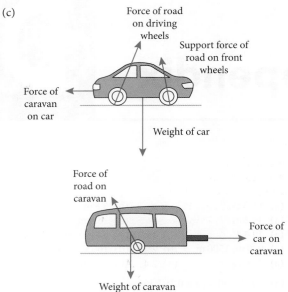

4.5 $5.9\,\mathrm{m\,s^{-1}}$

4.6 uranium nucleus: $0.0398 \times 10^6\,\mathrm{m\,s^{-1}}$ (forwards), neutron: $4.66 \times 10^6\,\mathrm{m\,s^{-1}}$ (backwards)

Chapter 5

5.1 (a) $1.6 \times 10^{-19}\,\mathrm{C}$ (b) $0.24\,\mathrm{A}$

5.2 (a) $\mathrm{N\,m^{-1}\,s}$ or $\mathrm{kg\,s^{-1}}$ (b) $1.6\,\mathrm{m\,s^{-1}}$

5.3 $M + T = W$ and $Mx = Ty$

5.4

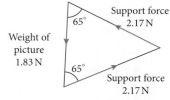

5.5 (a) $31.7\,\mathrm{cm}$ (b) $139\,\mathrm{N}$

5.6 $408\,\mathrm{N}$

5.7 $324\,\mathrm{N}$

5.8 (a) $100\,\mathrm{kN}$ (b) $140\,\mathrm{kN}$

5.9 $3000\,\mathrm{kg}$

5.10 $10.1\,\mathrm{g}$

5.11 $2.57 \times 10^{-10}\,\mathrm{m}$

5.12 (a) $50\,\mathrm{kg}$ (b) $720\,\mathrm{kg}$ (c) $610\,\mathrm{kg}$

5.13 $17.3\,\mathrm{kPa}$ / $11.5\,\mathrm{kPa}$

5.14 $7.7\,\mathrm{km}$. Atmospheric density is not constant; at 11 km altitude the density is about one-fifth of that at sea level.

5.15 (a) (i) $6170\,\mathrm{Pa}$ (ii) $9700\,\mathrm{Pa}$ (iii) $247\,\mathrm{N}$
     (iv) $388\,\mathrm{N}$ (v) $141\,\mathrm{N}$

(b) $141\,\mathrm{N}$

(c) the upthrust must be greater than the weight

Chapter 6

6.1 work = $1650\,\mathrm{J}$, power = $350\,\mathrm{W}$

6.2 (a) $80\,\mathrm{m}$ (b) $11.0\,\mathrm{m\,s^{-1}}$

6.3 (a) $165\,000\,\mathrm{J}$ (b) $165\,\mathrm{N}$

6.4 the force has to be applied over a distance 4.5 times greater

6.5 (a) $580\,\mathrm{N}$
    (b) seat, seat belt, floor of car i.e. any fixed object the person is touching

6.6 $3.24 \times 10^5\,\mathrm{J}$

6.7 (a) $33.7\,\mathrm{kW}$
    (b) the elevator is always balanced with a mass, equal to the mass of the elevator, that falls as the elevator rises

6.8 $34\,\mathrm{J}$ (this is the difference between its k.e. when thrown and its p.e. at height)

6.9

Device	Energy supplied	Energy wanted	Energy wasted
car	chemical	kinetic/potential	thermal
television	electrical	light/sound	thermal
electric motor	electrical	kinetic	**thermal**
loudspeaker	**electrical**	**sound**	**thermal**
microphone	**sound**	**electrical**	thermal
lift/elevator	**electrical**	potential	**thermal**
candle	**chemical**	**light**	thermal
dynamo/ generator	kinetic	electrical	**thermal and sound**
nuclear power station	nuclear	**electrical**	thermal
child at top of slide	potential	**kinetic**	thermal

(plus two further examples of devices you have chosen)

Chapter 7

7.1 (a) $1.96\,\mathrm{cm}$ (b) $2.30\,\mathrm{kg}$

7.2 stress = $4.20 \times 10^7\,\mathrm{N\,m^{-2}}$,   strain = 2.00×10^{-4} (no unit)
extension = $0.654\,\mathrm{mm}$

7.3 (a) Holding together a bundle of letters: a polymeric material such as rubber which gives a large extension with almost no plastic change
    (b) Making the sole of a shoe: a tough material that will not break even after a large amount of usage
    (c) Forming the bodywork of a car: a strong material such as high carbon steel, which will not break, but which can be moulded to shape during manufacture

(d) As a tow rope: a tough material that will not break easily even if a sudden very large force is applied to it (for example, nylon)

(e) As body armour: a tough material such as Kevlar®.

(f) As a building brick: fired clay, which has almost zero plastic behaviour but which is capable of remaining whole even when large forces are applied to it.

7.4 1700 J (to 2 sig figs)

Chapter 8

8.1 500 s

8.2 2.1×10^{22} m

8.3 1.25 MHz

8.4 7.4×10^{-9} W

8.5 (a) (i) $0.22\,\mathrm{J\,m^{-1}}$ (ii) $0.056\,\mathrm{J\,m^{-1}}$

(b) 2:1

8.6 (a)

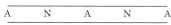

Length of pipe $= \frac{1}{2}\lambda$
Frequency = 70 Hz

A   N   A   N   A

For next arrangement, length of pipe $=\lambda$
Frequency now = 140 Hz
Other frequencies are 210 Hz, 280 Hz, etc.

(b) 35 Hz is lowest, 105 Hz, 175 Hz …

8.7 193 Hz

Chapter 9

9.1 Two suitable situations in which stationary waves are useful, for example:

(a) virtually all musical instruments set up stationary sound waves within the instrument

(b) in a laser, electromagnetic waves are reflected backwards and forwards, setting up a stationary electromagnetic wave; a small fraction of this wave is allowed to escape, producing the laser light beam

9.2 Interference occurs when two coherent light waves combine to give bright and dim regions. Diffraction occurs when waves spread out after travelling through a small opening, into what might be expected to be a region of shadow.

9.3 (a) green (b) 0.24 mm (c) $4\lambda = 2.12 \times 10^{-6}$ m

9.4 (a) red at 16.7°, 35.2°, 59.8°; blue at 11.1°, 22.6°, 35.2°, 50.2°, 73.8°

(b) red and blue overlap giving a magenta colour

9.5 radio, microwaves, infra-red, red light, violet light, ultra-violet, X-rays, γ-rays

Chapter 10

10.1 From the definition of a volt

1 volt = 1 joule per coulomb.

This gives

$$\text{volt} = \frac{\text{newton} \times \text{metre}}{\text{coulomb}}$$

so the unit volts per metre is identical to newtons per coulomb.

10.2 117 N

10.3 (a) (i) $16\,000\,\mathrm{N\,C^{-1}}$, (ii) 2.56×10^{-15} N, (iii) $2.8 \times 10^{15}\,\mathrm{m\,s^{-2}}$, (iv) $1.68 \times 10^{7}\,\mathrm{m\,s^{-1}}$, (v) 1.28×10^{-16} J

(b) (i), (ii) and (iii) are halved but (iv) and (v) remain unaltered

(c) use energy = p.d × charge = $800\,\mathrm{V} \times 1.6 \times 10^{-19}$ C

10.4 (a) 0.23 N repulsion (b) 1.1×10^{-7} N attraction

Chapter 11

11.1 Starting from the defining equations: $P = W/t$, $Q = It$, $V = W/Q$, $R = V/I$

(i) $P = W/t$ but $W = QV = ItV$
so $P = ItV/t = VI$

(ii) $V = IR$ so $P = VI = I^2R$

(iii) $I = V/R$ so $P = VI = V^2R/R^2 = V^2/R$

(iv) Then $W = Pt$ so $W = VIt = I^2Rt = V^2t/R$

11.2 (a) 12.5 A (b) 19.2 Ω (c) 2000 s

11.3 (a) 96 W (b) 2.4 MJ (c) 1.5 Ω

11.4 (a) 7.2 mC (b) 2.4 mA (c) 192 W

(d) 576 J (e) 3.3×10^{7} Ω

11.5 (a) 32 A (b) 960 MJ

11.6 (a) 440 Ω (b) 380 Ω

(c) 560 Ω this is not zero. 0/0 is indeterminate but a value can be obtained for very small currents as a result of using the gradient at 0,0.

11.7 (a) 30 V and 11.5 V (put a ruler across from the origin to point 30 V and 0.2 A)

(b) 100 Ω (your ruler will show maximum gradient, least resistance, on the knee of the graph, other values can be found the same way to obtain the sketch graph)

(c)

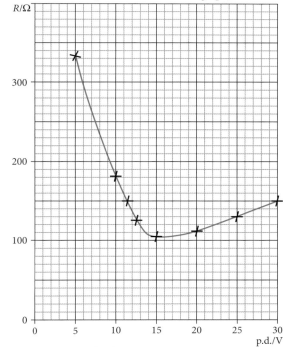

11.8 Resistivity (ρ) is given by the equation

$R = \rho l/A$ so $\rho = RA/l$

Unit of resistivity $= \Omega\,\mathrm{m^2/m} = \Omega\,\mathrm{m}$

11.9 133 m

11.10 164 Ω. The wire in the electromagnet has this resistance but additionally energy is required to generate the magnetic field. This will make the current lower than that which the resistance suggests.

Chapter 12

12.1 (a) 2360 kΩ (b) 40 Ω (c) 2.53 kΩ
(d) 8.0 kΩ (e) 10.9 kΩ (f) 25 kΩ

12.2 (a) 24 mA (b) 40 mA
(c) 37 mA (d) 40 mA

12.3 (a) equally, so all similar resistors have a current of 1 A
(b)

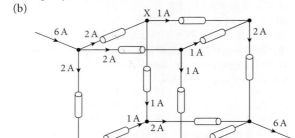

(c) 25 V = 2R + 1R + 2R, so R = 5 Ω

12.4 (a)

(b) This shows the e.m.f. of the cell together with its internal resistance.
The symbol

Is never used, even though it shows the internal resistance of the cell between the positive and the negative terminals.
(c) It is the total resistance of the whole circuit, 12 V/2.4 A = 5.0 Ω

12.5 (a)

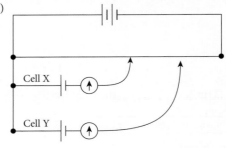

(b) 1.36 V
(c) This will increase the length required for balance, making it seem as though the e.m.f. being measured is larger. However if the reading for the standard cell and the required e.m.f are taken almost simultaneously, a correct e.m.f. will be obtained.

12.6 1.65 W when old, 10.3 W when new (assuming the resistance of bulb is unchanged)

	p.d. / V	current /A	resistance /Ω	charge /C	power /W	energy /J
battery	12	$\frac{480}{200} = 2.4$		480	12×2.4 = 28.8	12×480 = 5760
internal resistance R	$12 - 9.6$ = 2.4	2.4	$\frac{2.4}{2.4} = 1$	480	5.76	1152
resistance R_1	12×0.8 = 9.6	$2.4 - 1.6$ = 0.8	12	160	7.68	1536
resistance R_2	9.6	1.6	6	320	15.36	3072

12.7 (a) cable overheats and melts plastic insulation
(b) voltage drop across the resistance of the leads

Chapter 13

13.1 A

13.2 2.159×10^{-26} kg

13.3 8×10^{24}

13.4 (a) $^2_1H + ^2_1H \rightarrow ^1_0n + ^3_2He$
(b) $^4_2He + ^{14}_7N \rightarrow ^{16}_8O + ^1_1H$
(c) $^1_0n + ^{10}_5B \rightarrow ^7_3Li + ^4_2He$

Chapter 15

15.1 (a) $(\pi/2)$ rad (b) $(\pi/4)$ rad (c) $(\pi/180\,000)$ rad
(d) $(540/\pi)°$ (e) 180°

15.2 (a) 91.7 rad s^{-1} (b) 19.6 rad s^{-1}
(c) 2.66×10^{-6} rad s^{-1} (d) 0.465 rad s^{-1}

15.3 (a) 0.59 rad s^{-1} (b) 6.0 m (c) 8350 m s^{-1}

15.4 (a) 2.26 m s^{-2} (b) 122 m s^{-2} (c) 9.68 m s^{-2}

15.5 tension = 19.8 N, acceleration = 1.49 m s^{-2}, angular velocity = 2.49 rad s^{-1}

Chapter 16

16.1 (a)

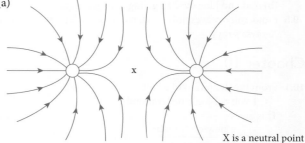

X is a neutral point

(b) If the mass of the left-hand star is greater, the field lines around it will be closer together indicating a stronger field, and the neutral point X will move closer to the right-hand star.

16.2 (a) $2.46\,\mathrm{m\,s^{-2}}$ (b) $8.46\,\mathrm{m\,s^{-2}}$
16.3 (a) $2.7 \times 10^{-3}\,\mathrm{m\,s^{-2}}$ (b) $2.650 \times 10^{-6}\,\mathrm{rad\,s^{-1}}$
  (c) $2.37 \times 10^{6}\,\mathrm{s}$
16.4 $24.9\,\mathrm{N\,kg^{-1}}$
16.5 Let x be the distance between the Earth and the Moon and m
  the mass of the satellite.
  Force of Moon on satellite $= GmM_m / (0.1x)^2$
  Force of Earth on satellite $= GmM_e / (0.9x)^2$
  Equating and cancelling gives
  $7.35 \times 10^{22}/ 0.1^2 = 5.98 \times 10^{24} /0.9^2$
  and $7.35 \times 10^{24} \simeq 7.38 \times 10^{24}$
16.6 $12.3\,\mathrm{km\,s^{-1}}$
16.7 $2.00 \times 10^{30}\,\mathrm{kg}$
16.8 (a) so that it moves in the direction of the Earth's rotation
  (b) so that the centre of its orbit is the centre of the Earth
  (c) its kinetic energy and its gravitational potential are not
    changing
16.9 period $= 5670\,\mathrm{s}$ and speed $= 7.6\,\mathrm{km\,s^{-1}}$

Chapter 17

17.1 Using $pV = nRT$ gives $R = PV/nT$
  P has unit of force / area $= \mathrm{N\,m^{-2}}$
  V has unit $\mathrm{m^3}$
  N has unit mol
  T has unit kelvin, K
  The unit for R is therefore
  $\mathrm{N\,m^3/m^2}$ mol K or N m/mol K. Since 1 N m = 1 joule, J, the unit
    of R can be written as $\mathrm{J\,K^{-1}\,mol^{-1}}$
17.2 (a) $6.44\,\mathrm{m^3}$ (b) $640\,\mathrm{min}$
17.3 (a) $0.0224\,\mathrm{m^3}$ (b) $1/12\,000$
17.4 (a) both have the same value, $6.07 \times 10^{-21}\,\mathrm{J}$ (b) $4:1$
17.5 $380\,\mathrm{K} = 107\,°\mathrm{C}$

Chapter 18

18.1 (a) $273\,\mathrm{K}$ (b) $310.6\,\mathrm{K}$ (c) $373\,\mathrm{K}$ (d) $713\,\mathrm{K}$
  (e) $193\,\mathrm{K}$ (f) $0\,\mathrm{K}$ (g) $5900\,\mathrm{K}$
18.2 (a) $-273.15\,°\mathrm{C}$ (b) $-53\,°\mathrm{C}$
  (c) $7\,°\mathrm{C}$ (d) $177\,°\mathrm{C}$
18.3 The percentage difference between $1\,000\,000\,°\mathrm{C}$ and
  $1\,000\,273\,\mathrm{K}$ is so small that it is unimportant. Even if accuracy is
  required, the variation in temperature across any star's surface
  will be much greater than $273\,\mathrm{K}$.
18.4 You ought not to be outside of these limits
  (a) $-60\,°\mathrm{C} \rightarrow -100\,°\mathrm{C}$ (Actually $-78\,°\mathrm{C}$)
  (b) $35\,°\mathrm{C} \rightarrow 38\,°\mathrm{C}$
  (c) $35\,°\mathrm{C} \rightarrow 45\,°\mathrm{C}$
  (d) $50\,°\mathrm{C} \rightarrow 70\,°\mathrm{C}$
  (e) $110\,°\mathrm{C} \rightarrow 130\,°\mathrm{C}$
  (f) $170\,°\mathrm{C} \rightarrow 220\,°\mathrm{C}$
  (g) $700\,°\mathrm{C} \rightarrow 1200\,°\mathrm{C}$
  (h) $1500\,°\mathrm{C} \rightarrow 3000\,°\mathrm{C}$

Chapter 19

19.1 (a) $31\,°\mathrm{C}$ (b) $360\,\mathrm{s}$
19.2 $32\,°\mathrm{C}$

19.3 Many thermometers used in automatic systems must give an
  electrical output. These thermometers are either thermocouple
  thermometers that produce an e.m.f or resistance thermometers,
  called thermistors, where an e.m.f. must be supplied.
  (a) The water temperature must not get too high. A thermistor
    thermometer is suitable.
  (b) The water temperature must be kept above $0\,°\mathrm{C}$. A
    thermistor thermometer is often used.
  (c) Even on the hottest day, the temperature must not rise above
    about $-12\,°\mathrm{C}$. A thermocouple thermometer can check this.
  (d) A thermistor can be used, so that it triggers an alarm at a
    temperature just above the hottest day imaginable.
  (e) It must switch off at $100\,°\mathrm{C}$. A thermocouple thermometer
    could trigger the switch to turn off.
  (f) As with a deep freeze.
  (g) A mercury-in-glass thermometer.
  (h) Too low a temperature, $12\,°\mathrm{C}$, causes a heater to come on.
  Too high a temperature causes windows to open. A thermistor
  can be used to control this.

Chapter 20

20.1 (a) $\pi/2$ rad (b) (i) $1.91\,\mathrm{rad\,s^{-1}}$ (ii) $8.6\,\mathrm{m\,s^{-1}}$
  (c) $84.6\,\mathrm{rad\,s^{-1}}$
20.2 $4.26\,\mathrm{Hz}$
20.3 (a) (i) $0.59\,\mathrm{s}$ (ii) $9.2\,\mathrm{m\,s^{-1}}$
20.4 (a) See black lines in graph.
  (b) The total energy is constant/conserved so there must be
    a third type of energy. This is the potential energy of the
    spring, and is shown as the purple line on the graph.

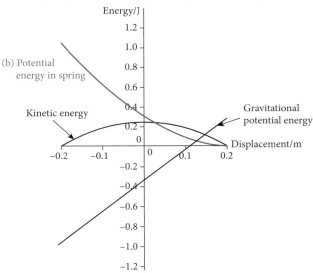

20.5 Destructive examples: Variable wind forces on the Tacoma
  Narrows bridge caused its collapse.
  Soldiers break step on small bridges to ensure that no resonance
  is set up.
  Constructive examples: Electromagnetic waves in a microwave
  oven.
  Sound waves in a trumpet.
  (Many other examples are possible.)

Chapter 21

21.1 (a) zero   (b) 0.36
21.2 0.277 W m^{-2}
21.3 4.9 cm

Chapter 22

22.1 (a) 192 kHz $\rightarrow$ 208 kHz   (b) 1580 kHz $\rightarrow$ 1620 kHz
     (c) 19.96 MHz $\rightarrow$ 20.04 MHz
22.2 1000
22.3 (a) 191 km   (b) 0.15 μW
22.4 (a) 9.6 × 10^{-12} W   (b) −135 dB
22.5 (a) 6.15 km   (b) 33

Chapter 23

23.1 One way is to put each stated unit into base units:
So F = C/V = A^2 s^2/J = A^2 s^2/N m = A^2 s^4/kg m^2
This gives F m^{-1} = A^2 s^4/kg m^3
And C^2 m^{-2} N^{-1} = A^2 s^2 m^{-2}/ kg m s^{-2} = A^2 s^4/kg m^3
23.2 (a) 80 000 V m^{-1} which is the same as 80 000 N C^{-1}
     (b)

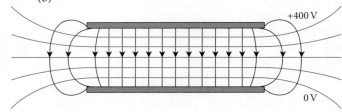

+400 V

0 V

23.3 (a)

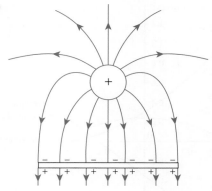

     (b)

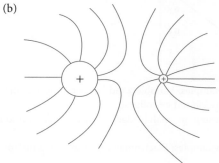

(c)

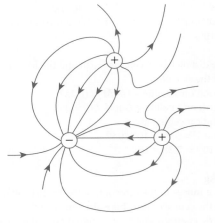

23.4 (a) 27.1 V   (b) 2.7 V

Chapter 24

24.1 (a) 5.0 μF   (b) 20 μF   (c) 5.9 μF   (d) 52 μF
24.2 parallel, series
24.3 1.0 C
24.4 5 in series and all in parallel with six others
24.5 77 V, 77 mC
24.6 28 μF

Chapter 25

25.1 0.0562 Ω
25.2 (a) If the density is unchanged then the volume must be
       unchanged also.
       The volume of the wire at the start is its
       length (*l*) × area of cross section (*A*).
       After stretching the volume is
       1.008 *l* × *A* /1.008 = *l* × *A*
     (b) 1.6%, that is the difference between 0.0553 and 0.0562 in
       question 31.1
25.3 (a) 0.52 V   (b) 9.7 V
25.4 (a) 3.4 V   (b) 8.6 V

Chapter 26

26.1 V_2 is at a potential of 8.000 V. The output V_o using a comparator
     circuit with an open loop gain is given by $V_o = A_{ol} (V_2 - V_1)$.
     When V_1 is at 7.999 V this gives
     $V_o = 10\,000 \times (8.000 - 7.999) = 10$ V
     As soon as V_1 becomes 8.001 V the equation becomes
     $V_o = 10\,000 \times (8.000 - 8.001) = -10$ V

26.2

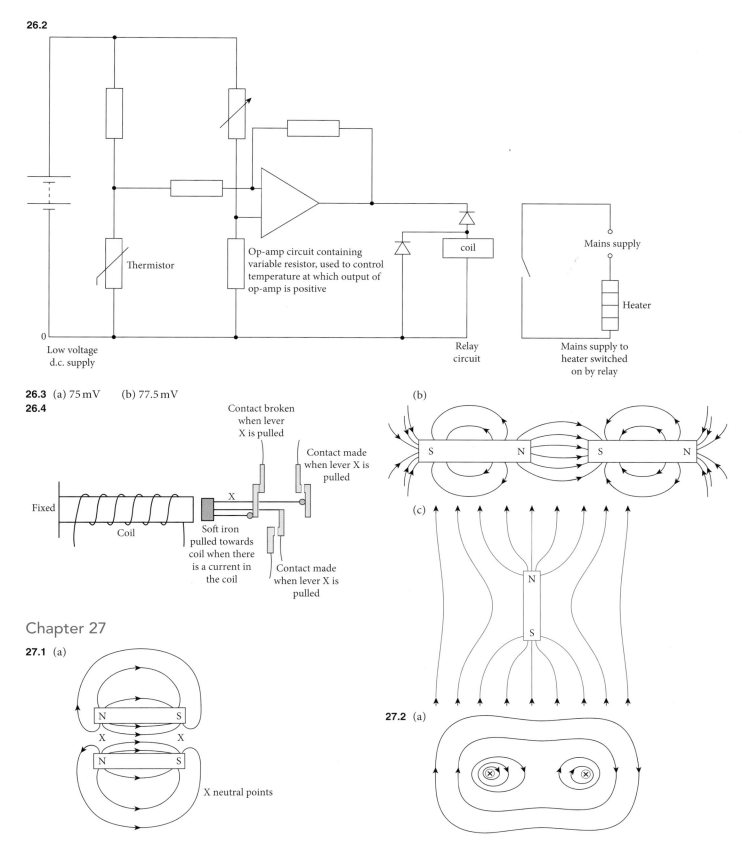

26.3 (a) 75 mV   (b) 77.5 mV

26.4

Chapter 27

27.1 (a)

X neutral points

27.2 (a)

(b)

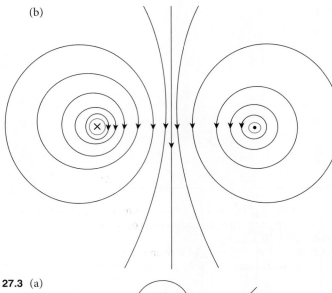

27.3 (a)

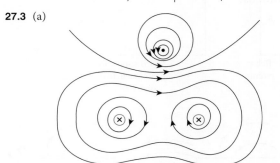

(b)

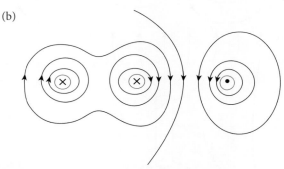

27.4 so that it attracts all the north poles of compasses

27.5

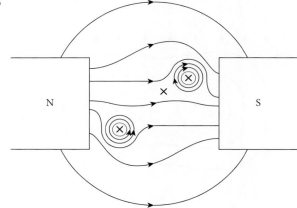

27.6 0.24 N

27.7 0.19 N m

27.8 7.9 mm

27.9 (a) 58.5 MHz   (b) 0.255 MHz

   (c) (i) Large actual changes in magnetic flux density arise from very small percentage changes in magnetic flux density.

   (ii) A small movement by the patient only causes a small percentage change in magnetic flux density, but this results in a large actual change in output.

Chapter 28

28.1 1.8×10^{-5} weber

28.2 0.26 V

28.3 (a) parallel to the magnetic field   (b) 1.19 Wb

   (c) 119 V   (d) 90 turns

Chapter 29

29.1 (a) 325 V   (b) 4000 W   (c) 2000 W   (d) 14.4 MJ

29.2 (a) voltage: sine wave pattern with maximum of 325 V and period 0.020 s

   current: sine wave pattern with maximum of 0.369 A and period 0.020 s

   power: sine wave pattern but always positive, with maximum of 120 W and period 0.010 s

   (b) changes are too fast for the eye to detect variation variations are small in any case since the temperature of the filament does not change very much in 0.01 s

29.3 (a) transformer, diode connected to one end of the secondary windings, capacitor in parallel with the output

   (b) 10.4 : 1

   (c) By using a large value capacitor, the change in the quantity of charge on the capacitor will be very small during the time it is charging or discharging. This implies that the input to the op-amp circuit will be almost constant.

   (d) 0.10 μF

29.4 (a) 31.3 Ω   (b) 7.62 A

   (c) 1910 W supplied, of which 1820 W goes to the heater

29.5 (a) (i) 400 A   (ii) 160 V   (iii) 410 V   (iv) 0.61 or 61%

   (b) (i) 10 A   (ii) 4 V   (iii) 10 004 V   (iv) 99.96%

   (c) use very thick cables, but this would be too ugly and too expensive

Chapter 30

30.1 (a) 3.62×10^{-19} J = 2.26 eV   (b) 3×10^{-19} s^{-1}

30.2 (a) The threshold frequency is that frequency for which the photons of radiation have enough energy to liberate electrons from the material of the illuminated electrode.

   (b) this frequency is higher than that for any visible light

   (c) The photon energy of ultra-violet radiation is higher than the photon energy of visible light.

   (d) 1.09×10^{6} m s^{-1}

30.3 (a) 6.6×10^{-34} J s

   (b) e.g. At $f = 16 \times 10^{14}$, stopping potential = 3.0 V
   At $f = 12 \times 10^{14}$, stopping potential = 1.3 V

   (c) 6.4×10^{-19} J = 4.0 eV

30.4 (a) 1.33×10^{8} m s^{-1} (b) 1.21×10^{-22} N s   (c) 5.49×10^{-12} m

30.5 Light from the Sun's surface has to pass through the Sun's atmosphere before it reaches the Earth. The atmosphere of the Sun is not as hot as its surface, so some of the radiation from the surface is absorbed by the atmosphere. For example, helium in the atmosphere of the Sun will absorb specific wavelengths of light, leaving a region on the Sun's spectrum less bright at certain wavelengths. (In fact, this was how helium was discovered. It is named after the Greek word for the Sun, 'helios'.)

30.6 $n = 2$: -3.40 eV

   $n = 3$: -1.51 eV

   $n = 4$: -0.85 eV

   $n = 5$: -0.54 eV

   (a) 0.97 eV   (b) 6.15×10^{14} Hz   (c) X-rays

30.7 (a) D   (b) C   (c) B   (d) A

Chapter 31

31.1 4.3 million tonnes per second!

31.2 (a) 0.0216 u   (b) 3.59×10^{-29} kg   (c) 3.23×10^{-12} J

31.3 (a) constant

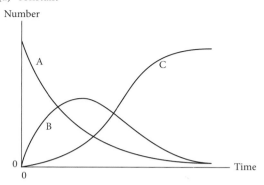

(b) the number of C nuclei is the same as the number of the original A nuclei; the numbers of A and B will be zero

31.4 1.24×10^7 s^{-1}

31.5 (a) $^{115}_{48}\text{Cd} \rightarrow {}^{0}_{-1}\text{e} + {}^{115}_{49}\text{In}$ + an anti−electron neutrino

   (b) 0.0161 day^{-1} (c) 472 day

Index

Note: Page numbers followed by f or t represent figures or tables respectively.

sound waves, 60, 60f
    frequency of, 60, 60f
    pressure variation in, 153f
    wavelength of, 60–61, 61f
specific acoustic impedance, 150
specific heat capacity, 126, 126t
specific latent heat of fusion, 128
spectra, 213–216
speed
    angular velocity and, 104
    defined, 14
    waves, 58
spring constant, 48
springs, 47–48, 47f
standard pressure, 33
state of gas, 129
stationary waves, 64–66, 64f, 65f
stopping voltage, 211, 211f
strain energy, 51–52, 51f, 52f
strain gauge, 175–176
strong nuclear force, 99
symbols, circuit diagrams, 82f
systematic uncertainty, 8

T

temperature, 121–125
    control, 122–124
    measurement of, 121–122
    scales, 124–125
    thermal equilibrium, 121
    variation of resistance with,
        215
tension, 47
terminal velocity, 18
thermal equilibrium, 121
thermal properties, materials,
    126–132
    change of state, 127–129, 127f
    specific heat capacity, 126, 126t
thermistor, 122, 123, 123f
thermocouple thermometer,
    122, 122f
thermometers, 121–122, 121f,
    122f. *see also* specific
    thermometers
Thomson, J.J., 93
threshold frequency, 212, 212f

torsion balance, 164, 164f
transformers, 200–203, 201f, 202f
transverse waves, 59–60, 59f

U

ultimate tensile stress, 50
ultrasound, 149–152
    defined, 149
    piezo-electric transducer,
        149, 149f
    scanning, 149–151, 150f
uncertainty, 8
    estimation of, 10
    measurement instrument, 9, 9f
    precision and accuracy, 8
    random, 8
    systematic, 8
underground supply cables,
    203–204
universal constant of
    gravitation, 110
upthrust, 28–29

V

valance band, 215
vectors, 3, 3t
    combining, 3–4, 4f
    resolution of, 4, 4f
velocity, 14
    angular, 104, 104f, 138, 138f
    escape, 112
    power in terms of, 40
    terminal, 18
velocity-time graphs, 15–16, 15f
Vernier calliper, 9, 9f
virtual earth, 179
viscous force, 29
volt, defined, 77
voltage, 77
voltmeter, 86

W

water
    density of, 117
water waves, 56, 57f
wavelength, 57

of sound waves, 60–61, 61f
in telecommunications,
    156, 156t
wave-particle duality, 213, 213f
waves, 56–63
    amplitude of, 57
    diffraction, 66, 66f
    Doppler effect, 62, 62f
    electromagnetic spectrum,
        61, 61t
    intensity of, 58–59
    interference, 66–67
    longitudinal, 59–60, 59f
    motion, 56, 56f, 57f
    phase difference, 57–58, 57f
    progressive, energy transfer
        by, 58
    sound, 60, 60f
    speed, 58
    stationary, 64–66, 64f, 65f
    terminology, 57–58
    transverse, 59–60, 59f
    water, 56, 57f
weber (Wb), 195
weight, 17
work
    defined, 37
    unit of, 37
work function, 212

X

X-rays, 216
    production of, 216, 217f
    use of, 217–218, 217–218f

Y

Young modulus
    defined, 48
    measurement of, 49–50, 49f,
        49t, 50t

Z

zero current, 88
zero output resistance, 178
zero resultant force, 21